# The
# John McPhee
# Reader

# The
# John McPhee
# Reader

EDITED BY

## William L. Howarth

Farrar, Straus and Giroux

NEW YORK

Library of Congress Cataloging in Publication Data

McPhee, John A.
The John McPhee reader.

A selection of writings which appeared
originally in the New Yorker.
Bibliography: p.
I. Howarth, William L. II. Title.
[AC8.M266 1976b]      081      76–46486
ISBN 0–374–17992–1

John McPhee's writings in this book were originally published in
*The New Yorker,* and were developed with the editorial counsel
of William Shawn, Robert Bingham, and C. P. Crow.

# Contents

# INTRODUCTION
# William L. Howarth

At his home in Princeton, New Jersey, John McPhee keeps a tidy collection of his books and magazine pieces. The volumes have a motley air, but they stand as one entity, the collected works of a single author. In his office on Nassau Street is a similar gathering, not as complete but still unified. Across the street is Firestone Library, the great research center of Princeton University, McPhee's alma mater. Firestone does not gather McPhee's books on a single shelf. Most are in the main stacks, in sections designated by call numbers for Recreation, Historical Science, Military Science, Education, and English Literature. Others are in special areas, such as the Sporting Books Room, and in satellite libraries across the campus, like the one for Urban and Environmental Studies.

Volumes so scattered might as well be in the collection of Locked Books, since their arrangement discourages readers from seeing them as the product of one mind and craft. Yet if McPhee were a novelist, poet, or playwright, his books would all be on the same shelf, in the English Literature section. Why has this happened? Because no one has a proper name for his brand of factual writing. He writes about real people and events, but not as an everyday "journalist" or reporter. He packs an impressive bag of narrative tricks, yet everyone calls his work "nonfiction." This label is frustrating, for it says not what a book is but what it is *not*. Since "fiction" is presumably made up, imaginative, clever, and resourceful, a book of "non-fiction" must *not* be any of those things, perhaps not even a work of art. If the point seems a mere quibble over terms, try reversing the tables: are Faulkner's books on Mississippi "non-history" just because they are novels?

Since 1964 McPhee has repeatedly jarred these assumptions with his books, which have stretched the artistic dimensions of reportage. His work has a large variety of backgrounds—sports, food, drink, art, science, history, geography, education—and a strong element of narrative control. He is not one of the so-called New Journalists, those celebrities who parade their neuroses or stump for public causes. McPhee never confesses, rarely preaches. He avoids publicity; other writers barter families and agents for a good notice. McPhee cherishes his family, has no agent, gives few interviews, poses for even fewer photos. His portrait has never appeared on a book jacket—and never will, if he has his way.

Why the modesty? In part, because McPhee is a shy man who treasures his privacy. His books depict similar "isolatoes," as Melville called them, like Bill Wasovwich in *The Pine Barrens.* Yet like Bill's friend, the ebullient Fred Brown, McPhee also has an ample gregarious streak. A good reporter, he moves through crowds easily, absorbing names, details, snatches of talk. He inspires confidence, since people rarely find someone who listens that carefully to them. Around Princeton, old neighbors and schoolmates remember him fondly, if not well. He cultivates a certain transparency in social relations, a habit derived from practicing his craft. To see and hear clearly, he keeps his eyes open and mouth shut.

Yet the writing speaks loudly enough, and it has consistently promoted his reputation since 1964. His steady production is a phenomenon in itself—one good book has followed another, regular as the seasons. By the early nineteen-seventies he was a bona fide literary success, touted by glowing reviews in major outlets, two National Book Award nominations, and full-page ads in *The New York Times.* Today his office phone is unlisted, but it rings constantly. His daily mail brings offers, queries, suggestions, pleas for support. Hollywood wants fictionalized screenplays of his factual books. Declined. A company in Massachusetts asks him to serve as its "writer in residence." Firmly declined. A travel agency, organizing hikers to pick litter at the base of Mount Everest, will pay round-trip expenses for him to record this ecological lark. Declined, but less firmly.

When Jimmy Carter, a cameo performer in McPhee's "Travels in Georgia," was asked to name his favorite writers, he gave a serious answer with his usual grin: Faulkner, Niebuhr, Thomas, Agee, and McPhee. That sort of compliment would make any writer flinch, yet most of McPhee's readers would agree on his merits. He has a knack for seeing subjects freshly, whether they are offbeat or already well known. His prose is taut or lyric, as the context demands. The stories are carefully organized, but not in normal time sequences. His writing has a distinct character, with traits familiar to devoted fans, yet each story differs from the last. If the path he travels is not clearly blazed, his stride still has persistent *class,* a word Americans use to mean the very best.

McPhee's own profile suggests some of the sources of his excellence. Born in Princeton in 1931, he has lived there almost continuously ever since. Princeton is the epicenter of his cartography, and its character defines most of his interests. Situated midway between New York and Philadelphia, the town is a cultural enclave in the suburban wilds. A haven for scholars and well-heeled commuters, Princeton also houses people of varied incomes and origins. During his childhood, McPhee's neighbors on Maple Street included a policeman, a doctor, a janitor, a newspaper editor, two football coaches, a butcher's cashier, and the Dean of the School of Engineering. A decade later, their house was occupied by a former Presidential candidate of the American Communist Party. While not a "typical" town, Princeton has been an adequate seedbed for McPhee, a place full of American custom and its infinite variety.

His great-grandparents emigrated from Scotland; his father, a physician, tended Princeton University athletes and several U.S. Olympic teams. Sports were an engrossing part of McPhee's youth, though not to the exclusion of scholarship. As a boy he attended Princeton scrimmages and games, often shagging punts or passes and returning them with his own precocious moves. He went to public schools in town, with notable achievements in English and basketball. His most influential teacher, Mrs. Olive McKee, assigned three compositions a week. With each paper he had to include a detailed outline of its beginning, middle, and end. Summers he spent at a canoe-tripping camp in Vermont, eventually becoming a counselor. After high school he went an extra year to Deerfield Academy before entering Princeton with the class of 1953. There he played basketball his first year and also took on an unusual outside activity. During his four collegiate years he appeared on "Twenty Questions," a weekly television and radio program originating from New York. The producers wanted one young person on the show's panel. Fond of games, he rapidly mastered the art of identifying mystery items —animal, vegetable, or mineral—with questions that could only be answered Yes or No. The training was probably useful for a future journalist; it taught him how to assemble facts and infer their hidden meanings.

At Princeton McPhee wrote and edited for *The Nassau Literary Magazine, The Princeton Tiger,* and other student publications. He did book and movie reviews for *The Daily Princetonian,* but instinctively avoided the grind of day-to-day, "scoop" journalism, where the work was swift and thin. As a senior he wrote "On the Campus," a page for *The Princeton Alumni Weekly.* The *PAW* circulates far and wide, and doing regular factual pieces for this large readership increased his desire to turn professional. His fondest dream was to write for *The New Yorker,* but it persistently rejected his early submissions. For Princeton's required senior thesis he lobbied successfully to write fiction instead of the usual research essay, ultimately submitting a sixty-five-thousand-word novel called *Skimmer Burns.* Like many first novels it was half autobiographical and half successful; but to McPhee went the rare distinction of setting an English Department precedent, and generations of would-be novelists have followed him on the "creative thesis" trail.

After college McPhee took a postgraduate year at Cambridge University, ostensibly to read literature and incidentally to play basketball. His team toured the British Isles and once played in the Tower of London, as he explains in an early essay, "Basketball and Beefeaters." Returning to Princeton, he tutored at a local school and then spent a few years at freelance work. The novel remained in early retirement, but he sold three television scripts to "Robert Montgomery Presents." He repeatedly tried to sell ideas or finished pieces to *The New Yorker,* with no success. By 1957 he had become a staff reporter at *Time* magazine, where he worked in "the back of the book," an area virtually unaffected by weekly news events. Mostly he wrote assigned material on films or stage shows, and some book reviews. As writer of the "Show Business" section, his cover stories on various stars ranged from Jackie Gleason to Richard Burton. The latter job he recalls with pleasure because it was his own idea. Burton was then at the peak of a serious acting career, about to abandon Shakespeare for his own Cleopatra. McPhee's story acclaimed the lofty realm Burton was leaving; it implicitly mourned his descent into gossip and vulgarity.

The work at *Time* was lucrative, exhausting, and ultimately deadening. *Time* had a hierarchical structure; younger writers mainly did what senior editors advised. Given an opportunity to join the "National Affairs" section, a sure route to the top, McPhee declined and continued to solicit *The New Yorker*'s attention. By then the magazine's early generation of editors and writers—Ross, Thurber, Parker, Benchley, Woollcott—had passed on, but redoubtable figures like Nash, Perelman, Wilson, and E. B. White were still there, under the editorship of William Shawn. Although they accepted "Basketball and Beefeaters" in 1963, the editors declined McPhee's subsequent proposal to write on Bill Bradley,

saying they had just run another basketball profile. McPhee looked it up
—the date was 1959. He wrote a long letter to the editors, five thousand
words describing his Bradley article, and they promised to read the
completed work, but nothing more. He delivered a seventeen-thousand-
word profile in December, 1964; it was accepted and printed the following month. Shortly thereafter he extracted an offer from Shawn to join
the magazine as a "staff writer."

He has held that post ever since, writing the dozen books featured
in *The John McPhee Reader*. While his work has matured over the years,
it has always arisen from a personal core. He has written on Scotland,
athletes, canoes, Deerfield, Princeton, Cambridge—and on all manner of
animals, vegetables, and minerals. While he has also developed subjects
from scratch, like pomology, aeronautics, and physics, he came to that
material by intuitive hunch, using a personal guidance system. His own
character, deliberately kept at the edge of a piece, still shapes the fabric
and texture of its center. Style *is* the man: wherever McPhee's prose is
short, compact, brisk, and edgy, there also is a facsimile of his own basal
metabolism. Yet the greatest of his virtues, *contra* the New Journalism,
is that readers need not know him to appreciate his writing.

One question they do ask is *how* does he work, and on that subject
McPhee freely converses. He often talks to writing classes in schools, and
since 1975 he has taught a seminar at Princeton as Ferris Professor of
Journalism. Although limited in enrollment, his course ("The Literature
of Fact") is popular because he devotes so much time and attention to
students. In teaching "the application of creative writing techniques to
journalism and other forms of non-fiction," as the catalogue statement
declares, McPhee often refers to his own books. Yet he also has the
students interview visitors, research set pieces, and submit ten compositions, which he discusses in private conferences. The course does not
prescribe his working procedures, since he does not believe one writer's
method should be a recipe for another.

*The New Yorker* encourages this tolerance, for as its staff writer
McPhee holds one of the most liberated jobs in modern journalism. At
the magazine there is an office he rarely uses, a cell flanked by those of
two staff writers he has never met. Staff writers are not required to be
in residence. They do not cover "story assignments" or write for "Special
Issues," since *The New Yorker* does not work those familiar beats. Any
staff writer may submit a brief sketch for "The Talk of the Town," the

regular opening feature, and certainly McPhee has contributed his share
of those breezy, unsigned reports. But mainly he works at his Princeton
office on longer projects, developed with the editorial counsel of Shawn
and others, chiefly Robert Bingham. *The New Yorker* has a first option
on all of McPhee's work. He is free to choose a subject and estimate its
length; the editors are equally free to criticize, accept, or reject his
proposal. If rejected, he may still write the piece and sell it elsewhere.
The magazine pays him quarterly advances, plus most expenses he incurs
for travel.

Travel occupies a large portion of McPhee's early work on a project.
Not overly fond of junketing, however, he has logged only whatever
mileage his stories have required. He prefers trains or cars over planes;
a car with canoe strapped on top is his ideal vehicle. In the car he often
takes along a tape player and several cassettes of his favorite Mozart or
Brahms. When he arrives at a wilderness site, his ears and spirit are well
massaged. Work has confined him largely to the eastern United States,
north and south, although books on David Brower and Ted Taylor
entailed journeys to the far West, as did "Ruidoso," a short piece on the
world's richest horse race, held annually in New Mexico. Across the
Atlantic he has concentrated on England and Scotland, but "Templex,"
a profile of the travel writer Temple Fielding, required a trip to Fielding's
home in the Balearic Islands east of Spain.

When McPhee conducts an interview he tries to be as blank as his
notebook pages, totally devoid of preconceptions, equipped with only the
most elementary knowledge. He has found that imagining he knows a
subject is a disadvantage, for that prejudice will limit his freedom to ask,
to learn, to be surprised by unfolding evidence. Since most stories are full
of unsuspected complexity, an interviewer hardly needs to *feign* igno-
rance; the stronger temptation is to bluff with a show of knowledge or
to trick the informant into providing simple, easily digestible answers.
Neither course is to McPhee's liking; he would rather risk seeming
ignorant to get a solid, knotty answer.

As a result, some of his interviewees have mistakenly believed he is
thick-witted. At times his speech slows, his brow knits, he asks the same
question over and over. When repeating answers, he so garbles them that
a new answer must be provided. Some informants find his manner relax-
ing, others are exasperated; in either case, they talk more freely and fully
to him than they normally would to a reporter. While McPhee insists
that his air of density is not a deliberate ruse, he does not deny its useful

results. Informants may be timid or hostile, unless they feel superior or equal to their interviewer. By repeating and even fumbling their answers, McPhee encourages people to embroider a topic until he has it entire. In an ideal interview he listens without interrupting, at liberty to take notes without framing repartee or otherwise entering the conversation.

McPhee's stories often develop from interviews with a principal informant, a strong personality who provides skeletal framing for the work. Finding this character may be an act of serendipity; in *The Pine Barrens* he accidentally met the indispensable Fred Brown, who knew all the people and nameless sandy roads of his region. Profiles built around a single character, like Frank Boyden or Thomas Hoving, are inevitably more planned from the outset; but in the cases of Ted Taylor and Henri Vaillancourt, McPhee was led to his central figure on the advice of informants, who play minor roles in the stories. He never uses tape recorders when interviewing, for they inhibit some people and are too subverbal for his purposes. The writing process must begin with *words*—a scrap of talk, bits of description, odd facts and inferences—and only a pencil and notebook will answer these needs with literacy and economy.

In some interviews he may play mental chess, anticipating answers or plotting questions, but usually he builds on what he has already seen and heard. Although he writes in a clear, left-handed script, the notes are unintelligible to anyone but himself. Yet they are not indiscriminate jottings; items entered in a notebook are likely to get into his final text as well. McPhee has a passion for details, for they convince readers that he deals in actualities. Added to his journalist's reverence for facts is a novelist's propensity for symbols. His task is to burnish objects until they become reflectors of character and theme. Instead of sermonizing on thrift or prodigality, he notes that Donald Gibbie's teapot is plugged with fourteen wood screws, or that the light in Lt. Arthur Ashe's closet at West Point is always burning.

By examining things as they are, he converts familiar objects into *synecdoches,* mere particles of experience that represent its totality. Oranges seem less ordinary when McPhee has recited their botany and history. In writing about basketball, he wanted to develop "a sense of the game itself" around Bill Bradley by learning and projecting the player's knowledge. He modestly credits Bradley with the book's power of articulation, yet creating a true replica of his informant's talk actually demanded great artistry, rather like a ventriloquist's. In *The Deltoid Pump-*

*kin Seed* McPhee more boldly pulls the narrative strings—his climax reports the inner thoughts of a test pilot in a tense situation—but always with an uncanny fidelity to outside facts like air speed, stability, angle of attack, and rate of climb.

When he starts to hear the same stories a third time, McPhee stops interviewing, returns to Princeton, and begins the tortuous process of composition. His working methods vary according to a project, but some steps are fairly constant. He first transcribes the notebooks, typing entries in order, occasionally adding other details or current thoughts as he goes. He likens this process to a magnet's attraction of iron filings; as the notes take shape, they draw from him new ideas about placement, phrasing, or possible analogies. When finished, he may have a hundred typed sheets of notes, enough to fill a large spring binder. He makes a photocopy of the original set and shelves it for later use. He then reads and rereads the binder set, looking for areas he needs to flesh out with research and reading at Firestone Library. The reading produces more notes, the notes more typed pages for his binder. Finally, he reads the binder and makes notes on possible structures, describing patterns the story might assume.

While its structure is forming, or when he senses how the story may end, McPhee often writes out a first draft of "the lead," a term journalists use to describe openings. In newspaper writing the lead is usually a single-sentence paragraph, designed to impart the classic who-what-where particulars of a story. In McPhee's work the lead is longer (fifteen hundred to two thousand words), more dramatic, yet rather more oblique. It establishes a mood, a setting, and perhaps some main characters or events, but not in order to put the story in a nutshell or even to hint at its full dimensions. One of his best leads is in "Travels in Georgia," where he manages to convey tone, style, characters, and theme in a few dramatic actions. Three people are riding in a Chevrolet across Georgia's back roads. They share some "gorp," exchange good-humored insults, and halt to eviscerate a turtle lying dead on the road. The action begins *in medias res* and continues without flashbacks or helpful exposition for several pages. When readers finally hit a backward loop, they already have a subliminal sense of who-what-where, and fulfilling this expectancy becomes McPhee's primary challenge in planning the rest of his story.

Having read the lead via telephone to an editor at *The New Yorker,* he goes back to the binder and begins to code it with structural notes, using titles like "Voyageurs," "Loons," or acronyms—"GLAT," "LASLE." These are his topics, the formal segments of narrative, which he next writes on a series of index cards. After assembling a stack, he fans them out and begins to play a sort of writer's solitaire, studying the possibilities of order. Decisions don't come easily; a story has many potential sequences, and each chain produces a calculus of desired and undesired effects, depending on factors like character and theme. When he has the cards in a satisfactory arrangement, he thumbtacks them to a large bulletin board. The shade of Mrs. Olive McKee, his high-school English teacher, smiles upon this array. McPhee defines the outline that finally emerges, in deference to her training, as "logical," but its logic is of no ordinary, abecedarian variety, A to Z or 1 to 10.

Cards on the board, committed to their structure, he next codes the duplicate set of notes and then scissors its sheets apart, cutting large blocks of paragraphs and two or three-line ribbons. In a few hours he has reduced the sheets to thousands of scraps, which he sorts into file folders, one folder for each topical index card on the bulletin board. These folders are pre-compositional skeletons of the narrative segments he will refine when writing a first draft. With the folders squared away in a vertical file, he is ready to write. A large steel dart on the bulletin board marks his progress. He stabs the dart under an index card, opens a folder, further sorts scraps and ribbons until this segment also has a "logical" structure. Then, without invoking the muse, he begins to type his first draft, picking up where the lead ends. When he finishes a folder, he moves the dart, gets the next folder, sorts it out, and continues to type.

Outlined in this fashion, McPhee's writing methods may seem excessively mechanical, almost programmatic in his sorting and retrieval of data bits. But the main purpose of this routine is at once practical and aesthetic: it runs a line of order through the chaos of his notes and files, leaving him free to write on a given parcel of work at a given time. The other sections cannot come crowding in to clutter his desk and mind; he is spared that confusion by the structure of his work, by an ordained plan that cannot come tumbling down. The strategy locks him in, gives him no easy exits from the materials at hand, which he must confront with that humorless partner, the typewriter.

Structural order is not just a means of self-discipline for McPhee the writer; it is the main ingredient in his work that attracts his reader. Order establishes where the writer and reader are going and when they will arrive at a final destination. As the reader begins a piece, he can be certain that McPhee always knew how it would end. He also knew where the center was, and how that middle would span its opposite structural members. At the center of *The Pine Barrens* stands a chapter on Chatsworth, "The Capital of the Pines," and Chatsworth itself stands but six miles from the region's geographical center. The dead-even spot of *Levels of the Game* is not at dead center, however, but twenty pages from the end. Ashe and Graebner have each won ninety-three points at that moment; McPhee rushes on to a swift denouement—"the next four points they play will decide it all." His closing chapters are usually antiphonal, setting poignant echoes from the past against ominous future rumbles. New Jersey's wild, legendary pines steadily shrink before the press of urban development. The fresh citrus market of old Florida wanes, a booming industry in concentrate rises. Atlantic City crumbles, but Monopoly goes on forever. One of his best endings is in *Encounters with the Archdruid,* where Brower and his opponent Dominy ride through the Colorado River's Lava Falls, their ceaseless quarrel silenced momentarily by the roar of pounding water.

McPhee is a craftsman; he understands that his work must always have inherent form. A potter knows that, and so do carpenters; it was Aristotle who said writers should have a similar goal. But writers have infinite options for order, and McPhee delights in playing any that do not violate his story's "logic." A book on tennis can imitate the game's back-and-forth, contrapuntal action; but it could also resemble a mountain climb, with an ascent, climax, and descent arranged in pyramidal form. The choice is McPhee's: either find an idea for order *in* the material or impose one *upon* it, selecting what Coleridge called the "organic" or "mechanic" principles of structure. McPhee has experimented with both: *Oranges* follows the life cycle of citrus fruit, while *Encounters with the Archdruid* was planned *a priori,* as a matrix into which he poured the molten confrontations of Brower and company. He has a certain preference for mechanic form, since it arises from human logic, but he trusts the organic principle enough not to condone formal manipulation for its own sake. Too much shuffling of those cards leads to fussy and baroque patterns, reflecting the self-indulgent mind of their maker. Yet he is also wary of simple organicism, where subject matter dictates a work's form. The story of a horse race need not run in an oval, nor must a canoe trip curve at its ends—those limited formal objectives are dull and pious, like the "shaped" verse of seventeenth-century poets.

McPhee wants to create a form that is logical but so unobtrusive that judgments of its content will seem to arise only in the reader's mind. And he also wants to stay loose himself, free to encounter surprises within the pattern he has formed. He is quite willing to manipulate contexts; in recounting Thomas Hoving's discovery of an ivory cross, McPhee cuts and reshapes time as though he, too, were a carver in ivory. In *The Deltoid Pumpkin Seed* he repeatedly digresses from the story's forward motion; his aim is to suggest an experiment in progress, lurching ahead ten yards and then around in circles. The pattern makes readers oscillate, too, between serious and satiric estimates of the experiment's probable fate. Despite his attraction to making these forms, he never trims evidence to fit a narrative pattern. When trouble begins on a canoe trip, "it comes from the inside, from fast-growing hatreds among the friends who started." That pattern an artist cannot control; McPhee accepts it with the "logic" of an athlete who respects the impartial rules of his game.

Writing a first draft is painful work for any writer, whether it moves like lightning or like glue. McPhee spends twelve-hour stints at his office, not writing constantly, but "concentrating" and distilling his research into prose. Some authors overwrite and later boil down; he culls before ever typing a phrase. He likens this method to the sport of curling, where great effort is spent sweeping the ice clean to advance each shot. With writing comes the need for endless decisions, mostly on what *not* to say, what to eliminate. The process is nerve-racking and lonely. His family sees less of him, he also cuts off most visitors and phone calls. Sometimes he talks to editors or friends about problems, but then generally follows his own counsel. Facing the typewriter for long stretches, he generates excess energy like a breeder reactor. A fly buzzing at sun-struck windows is not more manic, and often hard physical exercise is a welcome distraction. Tennis, squash, and basketball are favorite outlets; he professes to play at a level that "attracts ample company and no attention." In fact, he is capable of great intensity on the court, but he dislikes opponents who are arrogant or childish. Arthur Ashe plays in McPhee's preferred style, unpredictably full of contours and strata. Writing is the same sort of game: he has spent a long time learning to move *against* a habitual thought or phrase, which is always the easiest, oldest rut to follow.

The resulting prose style, rare in modern journalism, is fresh, strong, unaffected, and yet entirely idiosyncratic. His phrases and sentences come in many guises. A basic mode is simple declaration, arranged in strings of laconic grace: "Every motion developed in its simplest form. Every motion repeated itself precisely when he used it again." This description of Bill Bradley also describes McPhee's prose: taut, impersonal, yet carrying values like endurance, precision, solitude, success. He can write with eloquence, whether on his own or by hearing and reporting a character like Tom Hoving, who talks of his adolescence in a kind of poetry: "At noon we ate sandwiches and field tomatoes, and drank iced tea; then we slept off lunch in the cool earth of the corn furrows. The corn had a kind of mystery. You were out there and it was very high, all around you." On his students' papers at Princeton, McPhee often writes in the margins: "Busy." The terse comment defines that clarity and purity for which he constantly strives. Nothing could be less "busy" than his description of Havasu Canyon, a chain of deep, cold pools set amid baking desert scenery: "The pools were as much as fifteen feet deep, and the water in them was white where it plunged and foamed, then blue in a wide circle around the plunge point, and pale green in the outer peripheries." A good part of his style rests on knowing the professional "lingo" of a subject. He masters its vocabulary and syntax, even the jargon of atomic destruction—ploot, shake, jerk, kilojerk, megajerk. "A cross-section for neutron capture was expressed in terms of the extremely small area a neutron had to hit in order to enter a nucleus— say, one septillionth of a square centimetre—and this was known as a 'barn.' " But mostly the prose succeeds because its imagery is solid and expressive. The images do not just profess his values; they incarnate them. Here is a description of Clark Graebner's neighborhood: "The houses of Wimbledon Road appear to be in the fifty-to-seventy-thou-sand-dollar class and almost too big for the parcels of land allotted to them. They are faced with stratified rock, lightened with big windows, surrounded with shrubbery, and lined up in propinquous ranks like yachts at a pier."

Persistent good humor—of course the Graebners would live on "Wimbledon Road"—is another strong aspect of McPhee's style. He can paint a serio-comic scene, like the unforgettable Carranza Day ceremony in *The Pine Barrens,* replete with an Army band, beery Legionnaires, and a speaker who "had recently spent 'an unprecedented hour with the President of Mexico.' " The events are explicit yet improbable; their hilarity precipitates from a wicked trace of acid. Certain touches of *The New Yorker*'s elegance often grace his witty lines. Like the magazine, he uses trademark names—L. L. Bean, Adidas, The Glenlivet—but not to sell shoes or whiskey. Names specify a scene, sharpen the focus of his observation. This fascination with names produces a long monologue in *The Crofter and the Laird:* two full pages of Gaelic place names, each with an English translation, like "Sguid nam Ban Truagh (the Shelter of the Miserable Women)."

His best jokes are little asides that puncture a character's hyperbole. One chap, awestruck at having met David Brower in the desert, sparks McPhee's fire: "I wondered if the hiker was going to bend over and draw a picture of a fish in the sand." Later on, the name of Upset Rapid rests heavily on his companion rafters' tongues: "People say it as if they were being wheeled toward it on a hospital cart." "Travels in Georgia" has an unusual touch, an ironic motif established by the repeated acronym, "D.O.R." Carol Ruckdeschel, an environmental biologist, collects specimens of animals accidentally killed by autos and found Dead on the Road, or "D.O.R." Barely explained in the story's lead, McPhee gradually transfers "D.O.R." to other contexts, like a traffic jam around Newark Airport: "thousands and thousands of murmuring cars, moving nowhere, nowhere to move, shaking, vibrating, stinking, rotting, *Homo sapiens* D.O.R." By the end of his piece, the joke has become a powerful emblem of cultural decay: "D.O.R. gas station. It was abandoned, its old pumps rusting; beside the pumps, a twenty-year-old Dodge with four flat tires." In his moments of greatest hilarity, McPhee divines extreme analogies that provoke shock, laughter, and truth. One scene in *The Deltoid Pumpkin Seed* depicts John Kukon's frantic efforts to win a model airplane race. With time running out, he must find some means of gaining greater speed for a tiny aircraft. In his equipment box are four bottles of high-energy fuel, and one is the ultimate secret weapon: "Blend 4 had never been used. Kukon had never actually expected to use it. He had conceived of it as a fuel for a situation of extreme and unusual emergency. Its characteristics were that it would almost certainly destroy the engine that burned it, but meanwhile the engine would develop enough thrust to drive a sparrow to the moon."

Moving beyond a first draft, McPhee generally picks up speed. He makes few changes in his original structure, mostly just prunes sentences and polishes their style. The laborious planning and composing pay off here; his hardest stretches of work are over. A typist makes clean copies and off they go to *The New Yorker*. No official deadlines are set, but he usually meets self-imposed goals. Editors Shawn and Bingham read the final draft, rarely suggesting changes. McPhee has previously settled troublesome points with them; his copy gets its closest readings from three *New Yorker* institutions. The grammarian provides a meticulous parsing of every sentence and point of English usage. The legal office looks for potential libel. The "checkers" independently verify every assertion of fact. McPhee strives for total accuracy, hoping the checkers will not catch a flat-footed error. Few Ph.D. dissertations are read this carefully. The checkers retrace McPhee's steps, contact his informants, look up the books he read.

Exactly when his work appears in *The New Yorker* depends on many factors, including the magazine's current backlog and the seasonal aspects of the piece. "Firewood" cannot run well in July, for example, but is fine in early March. Like most writers, he endures the chore of proofreading with no visceral pleasure. His work is published in a single issue or in a series, depending on its length, usually under the rubrics "Profile" or "A Reporter at Large." Stories on white-water canoeing or enriched uranium have a nice incongruity in those glossy pages; the copy is bordered with ads for expensive gadgets and imported porcelain rabbits. *The New Yorker* copyrights everything, but transfers ownership to McPhee when he has arranged for book publication. To date, Farrar, Straus and Giroux have published all twelve of his volumes. The later texts are virtually unrevised; on a few occasions he has altered or added minor factual details. He also proofreads these works, even when caught up in the travel and interviewing for his next project.

A reviewer once suggested that some of McPhee's early books made too much of their "heroes," or main characters. The charge oversimplifies his idea of character; it also ignores some of his fundamental values. At the center of the misunderstanding are opposite ideals of heroic character, type and stereotype. If he really worshipped heroes, they would seem identical, a mere series of stereotypes. But McPhee has actually described many types of "heroes," and the types have grown more complex with each new book. Moreover, he always positions "heroic" figures against strong opponents, who shake them in tough confrontations. The central figures therefore represent different levels of heroic calibre, not a single ideal of excellence.

Bill Bradley has undeniably heroic dimensions: he is talented, disciplined, articulate, and rich. Yet he is also a paradoxical man, both self-conscious and self-effacing; able to analyze five parts of his hook shot, but also helplessly addicted to the narcosis of basketball: "It's getting dark. I have to go back for dinner. I'll shoot a couple more. Feels good. A couple more." McPhee contrasts Bradley's complete skills to the "aimless prestidigitation" of other stars who make brilliant shots but have no defensive or ball-handling skills. Yet he also catches Bradley in down cycles, hampered by injury or academic fatigue, and thus can show how the Princeton team of 1965 rallied to match its hero. In their final home game, Bradley is replaced by Kenny Shank, whom the crowd has made into a mock hero because he has so rarely played or scored all year. Yet Shank always played the best defense against Bradley in practice; he is the secret alter ego of an All-American scorer. When Shank rips off fourteen glorious points that night for a career high, Princeton's coach pays him the ultimate compliment: "He sent Bill Bradley into the game as Shank's substitute." The crowd vigorously cheers Shank's exit, "and the applause was now as genuine as it had ever been for Bradley himself." Shank's triumph tempers the heroic attributes of Bradley, established earlier in the profile. The hero and clod have briefly exchanged places, reversed their images in the mirror-like metaphor of basketball, which McPhee earlier calls a "multiradial way of looking at things."

In *Levels of the Game,* a reader instinctively wants to designate Ashe and Graebner as hero and villain, but the choice is not that simple. Ashe is the more admirable figure because he also has multiradial vision. Yet unlike Bradley, Ashe wins because he is inconsistent, disorderly, loose, and unpredictable. His background is more complex than Bradley's, his mind more striped and layered. Graebner is an exact *counterpart,* about as unlikable a character as McPhee has yet described: brutal, bigoted, and wholly predictable, doomed to lose because he is not flexible in a changing situation. By the story's end, he is more to be pitied than feared. Attempting one of Ashe's unorthodox shots, Graebner utterly fails to become another Kenny Shank: "An unbelievable shot for me to try—difficult in the first place, and under this pressure ridiculous. Stupid."

McPhee's heroes are people who remain in character but for whom character is always a shifting, spontaneous state. Frank Boyden runs an unprogrammed prep school, yet with plenty of strategic guile. If he has some touches of shallowness, Helen Boyden more than compensates with her learning and moral acuity: "When they are together, she makes light of him and he reacts in kind. She is the quicker of the two. He is funnier." Thomas Hoving seems an almost Renaissance ideal, a gutsy and pragmatic manager who is patient with the tedium of scholarship—and we learn why in catching a few glimpses of his father, a successful businessman who is lonely and one-dimensional in his off-hours life.

Other heroes in McPhee's canon have massive proportions, representing entire classes of people. The "pineys" are one of these groups, a people often characterized as vicious and inbred, who prove to be principled and well educated, by native standards. In the pines, outsiders are the real savages—big-city hoods build stills or dump bodies, arsonists start fires, poachers slaughter the deer, "developers" are bent on destroying a place that typifies American vitality. The crofters on Colonsay are made of similar stuff and face a parallel crisis: history has made them into thrifty recyclers who waste nothing, least of all the laird's sympathy for their anachronistic plight. The common enemy of these islanders is the outside world that has passed them by, ignoring their existence except on perfunctory ceremonial visits. In Georgia, McPhee discerns two broad classes of people, some who meander and some who straighten. Carol, Sam, and even the Governor are heroes with broad credentials, winners who endure because of their innate tolerance: "She had no exclusive specialty. She wanted to do everything. Any plant or creature, dead or alive, attracted her eye."

The broad base for this pyramid of heroes consists of assorted experts, people of talent or knowledge whom McPhee admires but hardly reveres. His experts rise above the simpler loyalties to culture and place; as technicians they respond only to the demands of their craft. The citrus scientists who support Florida's economy are from widely scattered places and care little about the financial effects of their work. Their motives are in sharp contrast to those native growers who graft with diseased stock or fail to inspect their fruit carefully. The disciples who build and fly Aereon 26 succeed at technology but fail at business, yet most readers are satisfied with the resulting balance sheet. Ted Taylor is a maverick expert, devoted to merging theoretical and applied physics, and just as committed to making science politically responsible. Perhaps the knottiest of McPhee's experts is Henri Vaillancourt, a builder of birch-bark canoes. Henri is all that a master artisan should be: patient, skillful, instinctive in his handling of tools and designs. He also seems a master woodsman, one who makes his own beef jerky. Yet on a canoe voyage the jerky moulders to a bright green, and he, too, proves "as green as his jerky," a maladroit canoeist, camper, and human companion.

McPhee does not venerate his heroes; he replicates them for our judgment as fully as he can. His principal aim is to maintain an artist's distance and catholicity, to bring alive all the possibilities of a story, not merely a few of its stronger points. He liked Bill Bradley for the totality of his play: "He did all kinds of things he didn't have to do simply because those were the dimensions of the game." The same devotion to *craft*, to a love of skilled enterprise itself, characterizes McPhee's approach to writing. Like Tom Hoving, he would gladly spend half his life learning to distinguish between a genuine work of art and an ingenious forgery. "A wise forger will make an error—an explainable error—because he knows that inconsistency can be a mark of genuineness, if the matrix of the inconsistency is right." By portraying his subjects with the same authenticity, he has raised them from the realms of food and games to the higher level of art.

McPhee sometimes comments on fellow artists as a way of defining the limits of his own craft. Seeing the actual river James Dickey described in *Deliverance*, McPhee complained at the conversion of that peaceful stream into "gothic nightmare." But a few hours later, hearing Johnny Cash on the car radio, he saw that hyperbole sometimes has its uses: "Cash's voice was deeper than ever. He sounded as if he were smoking a peace pipe through an oboe. Carol hugged herself." In his own work, McPhee strives for these balanced configurations of value. From a cast of assorted persons and events he builds complex narratives, alternating flattery and candor as they are deserved. John Olcott is one of the coolest aircraft test pilots going, but he often forgets to fill his car's gas tank—and then panics when the gauge reads "Empty." McPhee stands by his side, making notes, getting the facts, learning to see and say it all as he must, truthfully but with a consummate art.

Yet because he writes "non-fiction," libraries may continue to classify John McPhee's books under various headings instead of Literature, where they rightfully belong. *The John McPhee Reader* contains parts of all his books, and it will rest on a single shelf. It has no dedication, except perhaps to its trusted namesake, the John McPhee reader.

# The
# John McPhee
# Reader

# A Sense of
# Where You Are

McPhee first saw Bill Bradley on a basketball court in 1962, the winter of Bradley's freshman year at Princeton. McPhee knew a thing or two about basketball, having served on Princeton's freshman team himself, but watching Bradley play was a revelation: "Every motion developed in its simplest form. Every motion repeated itself precisely when he used it again. He was remarkably fast, but he ran easily. His passes were so good they were difficult to follow. Every so often, and not often enough, I thought, he stopped and went high into the air with the ball . . . and a long jump shot would go into the net."

The same estimate can apply to McPhee's story of Bradley, which developed two years later in a simple form, first as a long "Profile" for *The New Yorker,* then as a book-length narrative for Farrar, Straus and Giroux. This sequence, repeated with seeming precision and ease ever since, established the hallmarks of McPhee's brand of writing: exact details, shrewd observation, gifted phrasing, an orderly format. Less innovative than his later works, *A Sense of Where You Are* still has passes so good they are difficult to follow, and long jump shots that loft high in the air on their way to the net. The following extract is from McPhee's original "Profile." Other chapters in the book version record the triumphs of Bradley's senior year, when he became an Ivy League champion, N.C.A.A. semifinalist, Rhodes Scholar, and a lasting friend of his profiler.—*WLH*

Bradley is one of the few basketball players who have ever been appreciatively cheered by a disinterested away-from-home crowd while warming up. This curious event occurred last March, just before Princeton eliminated the Virginia Military Institute, the year's Southern Conference champion, from the N.C.A.A. championships. The game was played in Philadelphia and was the last of a tripleheader. The people there were worn out, because most of them were emotionally committed to either Villanova or Temple—two local teams that had just been involved in enervating battles with Providence and Connecticut, respectively, scrambling for a chance at the rest of the country. A group of Princeton boys shooting basketballs miscellaneously in preparation for still another game hardly promised to be a high point of the evening, but Bradley, whose routine in the warmup time is a gradual crescendo of activity, is more interesting to watch before a game than most players are in play. In Philadelphia that night, what he did was, for him, anything but unusual. As he does before all games, he began by shooting set shots close to the basket, gradually moving back until he was shooting long sets from twenty feet out, and nearly all of them dropped into the net with an almost mechanical rhythm of accuracy. Then he began a series of expandingly difficult jump shots, and one jumper after another went cleanly through the basket with so few exceptions that the crowd began to murmur. Then he started to perform whirling reverse moves before another cadence of almost steadily accurate jump shots, and the murmur increased. Then he began to sweep hook shots into the air. He moved in a semicircle around the court. First with his right hand, then with his left, he tried seven of these long, graceful shots—the most difficult ones in the orthodoxy of basketball—and ambidextrously made them all. The game had not even begun, but the presumably unimpressible Philadelphians were applauding like an audience at an opera.

Bradley has a few unorthodox shots, too. He dislikes flamboyance, and, unlike some of basketball's greatest stars, has apparently never made a move merely to attract attention. While some players are eccentric in their shooting, his shots, with only occasional exceptions, are straightforward and unexaggerated. Nonetheless, he does make something of a spectacle of himself when he moves in rapidly parallel to the baseline, glides through the air with his back to the basket, looks for a teammate he can pass to, and, finding none, tosses the ball into the basket over one shoulder, like a pinch of salt. Only when the ball is actually dropping through the net does he look around to see what has happened, on the chance that something might have gone wrong, in which case he would have to go for the rebound. That shot has the essential characteristics of a wild accident, which is what many people stubbornly think they have witnessed until they see him do it for the third time in a row. All shots in basketball are supposed to have names—the set, the hook, the lay-up, the jump shot, and so on—and one weekend last July, while Bradley was in Princeton working on his senior thesis and putting in some time in the Princeton gymnasium to keep himself in form for the Olympics, I asked him what he called his over-the-shoulder shot. He said that he had never heard a name for it, but that he had seen Oscar Robertson, of the Cincinnati Royals, and Jerry West, of the Los Angeles Lakers, do it, and had worked it out for himself. He went on to say that it is a much simpler shot than it appears to be, and, to illustrate, he tossed a ball over his shoulder and into the basket while he was talking and looking me in the eye. I retrieved the ball and handed it back to him. "When you have played basketball for a while, you don't need to look at the basket when you are in close like this," he said, throwing it over his shoulder again and right through the hoop. "You develop a sense of where you are."

Bradley is not an innovator. Actually, basketball has had only a few innovators in its history—players like Hank Luisetti, of Stanford, whose introduction in 1936 of the running one-hander did as much to open up the game for scoring as the forward pass did for football; and Joe Fulks, of the old Philadelphia Warriors, whose twisting two-handed heaves, made while he was leaping like a salmon, were the beginnings of the jump shot, which seems to be basketball's ultimate weapon. Most basketball players appropriate fragments of other players' styles, and thus develop their own. This is what Bradley has done, but one of the things that set him apart from nearly everyone else is that the process has been conscious rather than osmotic. His jump shot, for example, has had two principal influences. One is Jerry West, who has one of the best jumpers in basketball. At a summer basketball camp in Missouri some years ago, West told Bradley that he always gives an extra hard bounce to the last dribble before a jump shot, since this seems to catapult him to added height. Bradley has been doing that ever since. Terry Dischinger, of the Detroit Pistons, has told Bradley that he always slams his foot to the floor on the last step before a jump shot, because this stops his momentum and thus prevents drift. Drifting while aloft is the mark of a sloppy jump shot.

Bradley's graceful hook shot is a masterpiece of eclecticism. It consists of the high-lifted knee of the Los Angeles Lakers' Darrall Imhoff, the arms of Bill Russell, of the Boston Celtics, who extends his idle hand far under his shooting arm and thus magically stabilizes the shot, and the general corporeal form of Kentucky's Cotton Nash, a rookie this year with the Lakers. Bradley carries his analyses of shots further than merely identifying them with pieces of other people. "There are five parts to the hook shot," he explains to anyone who asks. As he continues, he picks up a ball and stands about eighteen feet from a basket. "Crouch," he says, crouching, and goes on to demonstrate the other moves. "Turn your head to look for the basket, step, kick, follow through with your arms." Once, as he was explaining this to me, the ball curled around the rim and failed to go in.

"What happened then?" I asked him.

"I didn't kick high enough," he said.

"Do you always know exactly why you've missed a shot?"

"Yes," he said, missing another one.

"What happened that time?"

"I was talking to you. I didn't concentrate. The secret of shooting is concentration."

His set shot is borrowed from Ed Macauley, who was a St. Louis University All-American in the late forties and was later a star member of the Boston Celtics and the St. Louis Hawks. Macauley runs the basketball camp Bradley first went to when he was fifteen. In describing the set shot, Bradley is probably quoting a Macauley lecture. "Crouch like Groucho Marx," he says. "Go off your feet a few inches. You shoot with your legs. Your arms merely guide the ball." Bradley says that he has more confidence in his set shot than in any other. However, he seldom uses it, because he seldom has to. A set shot is a long shot, usually a twenty-footer, and Bradley, with his speed and footwork, can almost always take some other kind of shot, closer to the basket. He will take set shots when they are given to him, though. Two seasons ago, Davidson lost to Princeton, using a compact zone defense that ignored the remoter areas of the court. In one brief sequence, Bradley sent up seven set shots, missing only one. The missed one happened to rebound in Bradley's direction, and he leaped up, caught it with one hand, and scored.

Even his lay-up shot has an ancestral form; he is full of admiration for "the way Cliff Hagan pops up anywhere within six feet of the basket," and he tries to do the same. Hagan is a former Kentucky star who now plays for the St. Louis Hawks. Because opposing teams always do everything they can to stop Bradley, he gets an unusual number of foul shots. When he was in high school, he used to imitate Bob Pettit, of the St. Louis Hawks, and Bill Sharman, of the Boston Celtics, but now his free throw is more or less his own. With his left foot back about eighteen inches—"wherever it feels comfortable," he says—he shoots with a deep-bending rhythm of knees and arms, one-handed, his left hand acting as a kind of gantry for the ball until the moment of release. What is most interesting, though, is that he concentrates his attention on one of the tiny steel eyelets that are welded under the rim of the basket to hold the net to the hoop—on the center eyelet, of course—before he lets fly. One night, he scored over twenty points on free throws alone; Cornell hacked at him so heavily that he was given twenty-one free throws, and he made all twenty-one, finishing the game with a total of thirty-seven points.

When Bradley, working out alone, practices his set shots, hook shots, and jump shots, he moves systematically from one place to another around the basket, his distance from it being appropriate to the shot, and he does not permit himself to move on until he has made at least ten shots out of thirteen from each location. He applies this standard to every kind of shot, with either hand, from any distance. Many basketball players, including reasonably good ones, could spend five years in a gym and not make ten out of thirteen left-handed hook shots, but that is part of Bradley's daily routine. He talks to himself while he is shooting, usually reminding himself to concentrate but sometimes talking to himself the way every high-school j.v. basketball player has done since the dim twenties—more or less imitating a radio announcer, and saying, as he gathers himself up for a shot, "It's pandemonium in Dillon Gymnasium. The clock is running out. He's up with a jumper. Swish!"

Last summer, the floor of the Princeton gym was being resurfaced, so Bradley had to put in several practice sessions at the Lawrenceville School. His first afternoon at Lawrenceville, he began by shooting fourteen-foot jump shots from the right side. He got off to a bad start, and he kept missing them. Six in a row hit the back rim of the basket and bounced out. He stopped, looking discomfited, and seemed to be making an adjustment in his mind. Then he went up for another jump shot from the same spot and hit it cleanly. Four more shots went in without a miss, and then he paused and said, "You want to know something? That basket is about an inch and a half low." Some weeks later, I went back to Lawrenceville with a steel tape, borrowed a stepladder, and measured the height of the basket. It was nine feet ten and seven-eighths inches above the floor, or one and one-eighth inches too low.

Being a deadly shot with either hand and knowing how to make the moves and fakes that clear away the defense are the primary skills of a basketball player, and any player who can do these things half as well as Bradley can has all the equipment he needs to make a college team. Many high-scoring basketball players, being able to make so obvious and glamorous a contribution to their team in the form of point totals, don't bother to develop the other skills of the game, and leave subordinate matters like defense and playmaking largely to their teammates. Hence, it is usually quite easy to parse a basketball team. Bringing the ball up the floor are playmaking backcourt men—selfless fellows who can usually dribble so adeptly that they can just about freeze the ball by themselves, and who can also throw passes through the eye of a needle and can always be counted on to feed the ball to a star at the right moment. A star is often a point-hungry gunner, whose first instinct when he gets the ball is to fire away, and whose playing creed might be condensed to "When in doubt, shoot." Another, with legs like automobile springs, is part of the group because of an unusual ability to go high for rebounds. Still another may not be especially brilliant on offense but has defensive equipment that could not be better if he were carrying a trident and a net.

The point-hungry gunner aside, Bradley is all these. He is a truly complete basketball player. He can play in any terrain; in the heavy infighting near the basket, he is master of all the gestures of the big men, and toward the edge of play he shows that he has all the fast-moving skills of the little men, too. With remarkable speed for six feet five, he can steal the ball and break into the clear with it on his own; as a dribbler, he can control the ball better with his left hand than most players can with their right; he can go down court in the middle of a fast break and fire passes to left and right, closing in on the basket, the timing of his passes too quick for the spectator's eye. He plays any position—up front, in the post, in the backcourt. And his playmaking is a basic characteristic of his style. His high-scoring totals are the result of his high percentage of accuracy, not of an impulse to shoot every time he gets the ball.

He passes as generously and as deftly as any player in the game. When he is dribbling, he can pass accurately without first catching the ball. He can also manage almost any pass without appearing to cock his arm, or even bring his hand back. He just seems to flick his fingers and the ball is gone. Other Princeton players aren't always quite expecting Bradley's passes when they arrive, for Bradley is usually thinking a little bit ahead of everyone else on the floor. When he was a freshman, he was forever hitting his teammates on the mouth, the temple, or the back of the head with passes as accurate as they were surprising. His teammates have since sharpened their own faculties, and these accidents seldom happen now. "It's rewarding to play with him," one of them says. "If you get open, you'll get the ball." And, with all the defenders in between, it sometimes seems as if the ball has passed like a ray through several walls.

Bradley's play has just one somewhat unsound aspect, and it is the result of his mania for throwing the ball to his teammates. He can't seem to resist throwing a certain number of passes that are based on nothing but theory and hope; in fact, they are referred to by the Princeton coaching staff as Bradley's hope passes. They happen, usually, when something has gone just a bit wrong. Bradley is recovering a loose ball, say, with his back turned to the other Princeton players. Before he turned it, he happened to notice a screen, or pick-off, being set by two of his teammates, its purpose being to cause one defensive man to collide with another player and thus free an offensive man to receive a pass and score. Computations whir in Bradley's head. He hasn't time to look, but the screen, as he saw it developing, seemed to be working, so a Princeton man should now be in the clear, running toward the basket with one arm up. He whips the ball over his shoulder to the spot where the man ought to be. Sometimes a hope pass goes flying into the crowd, but most of the time they hit the receiver right in the hand, and a gasp comes from several thousand people. Bradley is sensitive about such dazzling passes, because they look flashy, and an edge comes into his voice as he defends them. "When I was halfway down the court, I saw a man out of the corner of my eye who had on the same color shirt I did," he said recently, explaining how he happened to fire a scoring pass while he was falling out of bounds. "A little later, when I threw the pass, I threw it to the spot where that man should have been if he had kept going and done his job. He was there. Two points."

Since it appears that by nature Bradley is a passer first and a scorer second, he would probably have scored less at a school where he was surrounded by other outstanding players. When he went to Princeton, many coaches mourned his loss not just to themselves but to basketball, but as things have worked out, much of his national prominence has been precipitated by his playing for Princeton, where he has had to come through with points in order to keep his team from losing. He starts slowly, as a rule. During much of the game, if he has a clear shot, fourteen feet from the basket, say, and he sees a teammate with an equally clear shot ten feet from the basket, he sends the ball to the teammate. Bradley apparently does not stop to consider that even though the other fellow is closer to the basket he may be far more likely to miss the shot. This habit exasperates his coaches until they clutch their heads in despair. But Bradley is doing what few people ever have done—he is playing basketball according to the foundation pattern of the game. Therefore, the shot goes to the closer man. Nothing on earth can make him change until Princeton starts to lose. Then he will concentrate a little more on the basket.

Something like this happened in Tokyo last October, when the United States Olympic basketball team came close to being beaten by Yugoslavia. The Yugoslavian team was reasonably good—better than the Soviet team, which lost to the United States in the final—and it heated up during the second half. With two minutes to go, Yugoslavia cut the United States' lead to two points. Bradley was on the bench at the time, and Henry Iba, the Oklahoma State coach, who was coach of the Olympic team, sent him in. During much of the game, he had been threading passes to others, but at that point, he says, he felt that he had to try to do something about the score. Bang, bang, bang—he hit a running one-hander, a seventeen-foot jumper, and a lay-up on a fast break, and the United States won by eight points.

Actually, the United States basketball squad encountered no real competition at the Olympics, despite all sorts of rumbling cumulus beforehand to the effect that some of the other teams, notably Russia's, were made up of men who had been playing together for years and were now possibly good enough to defeat an American Olympic basketball team for the first time. But if the teams that the Americans faced were weaker than advertised, there were nonetheless individual performers of good calibre, and it is a further index to Bradley's completeness as a basketball player that Henry Iba, a defensive specialist as a coach, regularly assigned him to guard the stars of the other nations. "He didn't show too much tact at defense when he started, but he's a coach's basketball player, and he came along," Iba said after he had returned to Oklahoma. "And I gave him the toughest man in every game."

Yugoslavia's best man was a big forward who liked to play in the low post, under the basket. Bradley went into the middle with him, crashing shoulders under the basket, and held him to thirteen points while scoring eighteen himself. Russia's best man was Yuri Korneyev, whose specialty was driving; that is, he liked to get the ball somewhere out on the edge of the action and start for the basket with it like a fullback, blasting everything out of the way until he got close enough to ram in a point-blank shot. With six feet five inches and two hundred and forty pounds to drive, Korneyev was what Iba called "a real good driver." Bradley had lost ten pounds because of all the Olympics excitement, and Korneyev outweighed him by forty-five pounds. Korneyev kicked, pushed, shoved, bit, and scratched Bradley. "He was tough to stop," Bradley says. "After all, he was playing for his life." Korneyev got eight points.

Bradley was one of three players who had been picked unanimously for the twelve-man Olympic team. He was the youngest member of the squad and the only undergraduate. Since his trip to Tokyo kept him away from Princeton for the first six weeks of the fall term, he had to spend part of his time reading, and the course he worked on most was Russian History 323. Perhaps because of the perspective this gave him, his attitude toward the Russian basketball team was not what he had expected it to be. With the help of three Australian players who spoke Russian, Bradley got to know several members of the Russian team fairly well, and soon he was feeling terribly sorry for them. They had a leaden attitude almost from the beginning. "All we do is play basketball," one of them told him forlornly. "After we go home, we play in the Soviet championships. Then we play in the Satellite championships. Then we play in the European championships. I would give anything for five days off." Bradley says that the Russian players also told him they were paid eighty-five dollars a month, plus housing. Given the depressed approach of the Russians, Bradley recalls, it was hard to get excited before the Russian-American final. "It was tough to get chills," he says. "I had to imagine we were about to play Yale." The Russians lost, 73–59.

Bradley calls practically all men "Mister" whose age exceeds his own by more than a couple of years. This includes any N.B.A. players he happens to meet, Princeton trainers, and Mr. Willem Hendrik van Breda Kolff, his coach. Van Breda Kolff was a Princeton basketball star himself, some twenty years ago, and went on to play for the New York Knickerbockers. Before returning to Princeton in 1962, he coached at Lafayette and Hofstra. His teams at the three colleges have won two hundred and fifty-one games and lost ninety-six. Naturally, it was a virtually unparalleled stroke of good fortune for van Breda Kolff to walk into his current coaching job in the very year that Bradley became eligible to play for the varsity team, but if the coach was lucky to have the player, the player was also lucky to have the coach. Van Breda Kolff, a cheerful and uncomplicated man, has a sportsman's appreciation of the nuances of the game, and appears to feel that mere winning is far less important than winning with style. He is an Abstract Expressionist of basketball. Other coaches have difficulty scouting his teams, because he does not believe in a set offense. He likes his offense free-form.

Van Breda Kolff simply tells his boys to spread out and keep the ball moving. "Just go fast, stay out of one another's way, pass, move, come off guys, look for one-on-ones, two-on-ones, two-on-twos, three-on-threes. That's about the extent," he says. That is, in fact, about the substance of basketball, which is almost never played as a five-man game anymore but is, rather, a constant search, conducted semi-independently by five players, for smaller combinations that will produce a score. One-on-one is the basic situation of the game—one man, with the ball, trying to score against one defensive player, who is trying to stop him, with nobody else involved. Van Breda Kolff does not think that Bradley is a great one-on-one player. "A one-on-one player is a hungry player," he explains. "Bill is not hungry. At least ninety per cent of the time, when he gets the ball, he is looking for a pass." Van Breda Kolff has often tried to force Bradley into being more of a one-on-one player, through gentle persuasion in practice, through restrained pleas during timeouts, and even through open clamor. During one game last year, when Princeton was losing and Bradley was still flicking passes, van Breda Kolff stood up and shouted, *"Will . . . you . . . shoot . . . that . . . ball?"* Bradley, obeying at once, drew his man into the vortex of a reverse pivot, and left him standing six feet behind as he made a soft, short jumper from about ten feet out.

If Bradley were more interested in his own statistics, he could score sixty or seventy-five points, or maybe even a hundred, in some of his games. But this would merely be personal aggrandizement, done at the expense of the relative balance of his own team and causing unnecessary embarrassment to the opposition, for it would only happen against an opponent that was heavily outmatched anyway. Bradley's highest point totals are almost always made when the other team is strong and the situation demands his scoring ability. He has, in fact, all the mechanical faculties a great one-on-one player needs. As van Breda Kolff will point out, for example, Bradley has "a great reverse pivot," and this is an essential characteristic of a one-on-one specialist. A way of getting rid of a defensive man who is playing close, it is a spin of the body, vaguely similar to what a football halfback does when he spins away from a would-be tackler, and almost exactly what a lacrosse player does when he "turns his man." Say that Bradley is dribbling hard toward the basket and the defensive man is all over him. Bradley turns, in order to put his body between his opponent and the ball; he continues his dribbling but shifts the ball from one hand to the other; if his man is still crowding in on him, he keeps on turning until he has made one full revolution and is once more headed toward the basket. This is a reverse pivot. Bradley can execute one in less than a second. The odds are that when he has completed the spin the defensive player will be behind him, for it is the nature of basketball that the odds favor the man with the ball—if he knows how to play them.

Bradley doesn't need to complete the full revolution every time. If his man steps away from him in anticipation of a reverse pivot, Bradley can stop dead and make a jump shot. If the man stays close to him but not close enough to be turned, Bradley can send up a hook shot. If the man moves over so that he will be directly in Bradley's path when Bradley comes out of the turn, Bradley can scrap the reverse pivot before he begins it, merely suggesting it with his shoulders and then continuing his original dribble to the basket, making his man look like a pedestrian who has leaped to get out of the way of a speeding car.

The metaphor of basketball is to be found in these compounding alternatives. Every time a basketball player takes a step, an entire new geometry of action is created around him. In ten seconds, with or without the ball, a good player may see perhaps a hundred alternatives and, from them, make half a dozen choices as he goes along. A great player will see even more alternatives and will make more choices, and this multiradial way of looking at things can carry over into his life. At least, it carries over into Bradley's life. The very word "alternatives" bobs in and out of his speech with noticeable frequency. Before his Rhodes Scholarship came along and eased things, he appeared to be worrying about dozens of alternatives for next year. And he still fills his days with alternatives. He apparently always needs to have eight ways to jump, not because he is excessively prudent but because that is what makes the game interesting.

The reverse pivot, of course, is just one of numerous one-on-one moves that produce a complexity of possibilities. A rocker step, for example, in which a player puts one foot forward and rocks his shoulders forward and backward, can yield a set shot if the defensive man steps back, a successful drive to the basket if the defensive man comes in too close, a jump shot if he tries to compromise. A simple crossover—shifting a dribble from one hand to the other and changing direction—can force the defensive man to overcommit himself, as anyone knows who has ever watched Oscar Robertson use it to break free and score. Van Breda Kolff says that Bradley is "a great mover," and points out that the basis of all these maneuvers is footwork. Bradley has spent hundreds of hours merely rehearsing the choreography of the game—shifting his feet in the same patterns again and again, until they have worn into his motor subconscious. "The average basketball player only likes to play basketball," van Breda Kolff says. "When he's left to himself, all he wants to do is get a two-on-two or a three-on-three going. Bradley practices techniques, making himself learn and improve instead of merely having fun."

Because of Bradley's super-serious approach to basketball, his relationship to van Breda Kolff is in some respects a reversal of the usual relationship between a player and a coach. Writing to van Breda Kolff from Tokyo in his capacity as captain-elect, Bradley advised his coach that they should prepare themselves for "the stern challenge ahead." Van Breda Kolff doesn't vibrate to that sort of tune. "Basketball is a game," he says. "It is not an ordeal. I think Bradley's happiest whenever he can deny himself pleasure." Van Breda Kolff's handling of Bradley has been, in a way, a remarkable feat of coaching. One man cannot beat five men —at least not consistently—and Princeton loses basketball games. Until this season, moreover, the other material that van Breda Kolff has had at his disposal has been for the most part below even the usual Princeton standard, so the fact that his teams have won two consecutive championships is about as much to his credit as to his star's.

Van Breda Kolff says, "I try to play it just as if he were a normal player. I don't want to overlook him, but I don't want to over-look for him, either, if you see what I'm trying to say." Bradley's teammates sometimes depend on him too much, the coach explains, or, in a kind of psychological upheaval, get self-conscious about being on the court with a superstar and, perhaps to prove their independence, bring the ball up the court five or six times without passing it to him. When this happens, van Breda Kolff calls time out. "Hey, boys," he says. "What have we got an All-American for?" He refers to Bradley's stardom only when he has to, however. In the main, he takes Bradley with a calculated grain of salt. He is interested in Bradley's relative weaknesses rather than in his storied feats, and has helped him gain poise on the court, learn patience, improve his rebounding, and be more aggressive. He refuses on principle to say that Bradley is the best basketball player he has ever coached, and he is also careful not to echo the general feeling that Bradley is the most exemplary youth since Lochinvar, but he will go out of his way to tell about the reaction of referees to Bradley. "The refs watch Bradley like a hawk, but, because he never complains, they feel terrible if they make an error against him," he says. "They just love him because he is such a gentleman. They get upset if they call a bad one on him." I asked van Breda Kolff what he thought Bradley would be doing when he was forty. "I don't know," he said. "I guess he'll be the governor of Missouri."

Many coaches, on the reasonable supposition that Bradley cannot beat their teams alone, concentrate on choking off the four other Princeton players, but Bradley is good enough to rise to such occasions, as he did when he scored forty-six against Texas, making every known shot, including an eighteen-foot running hook. Some coaches, trying a standard method of restricting a star, set up four of their players in either a box-shaped or a diamond-shaped zone defensive formation and put their fifth player on Bradley, man-to-man. Wherever Bradley goes under these circumstances, he has at least two men guarding him, the man-to-man player and the fellow whose zone he happens to be passing through. This is a dangerous defense, however, because it concedes an imbalance of forces, and also because Bradley is so experienced at being guarded by two men at once that he can generally fake them both out with a single move; also, such overguarding often provides Bradley with enough free throws to give his team the margin of victory.

Most coaches have played Princeton straight, assigning their best defensive man to Bradley and letting it go at that. This is what St. Joseph's College did in the opening round of the N.C.A.A. Tournament in 1963. St. Joseph's had a strong, well-balanced team, which had lost only four games of a twenty-five-game schedule and was heavily favored to rout Princeton. The St. Joseph's player who was to guard Bradley promised his teammates that he would hold Bradley below twenty points. Bradley made twenty points in the first half.

He made another twenty points in the first sixteen minutes of the second half. In the group battles for rebounds, he won time after time. He made nearly sixty per cent of his shots, and he made sixteen out of sixteen from the foul line. The experienced St. Joseph's man could not handle him, and the whole team began to go after him in frenzied clusters. He would dribble through them, disappearing in the ruck and emerging a moment later, still dribbling, to float up toward the basket and score. If St. Joseph's forced him over toward the sideline, he would crouch, turn his head to look for the distant basket, step, kick his leg, and follow through with his arms, sending a long, high hook shot—all five parts intact—into the net. When he went up for a jump shot, St. Joseph's players would knock him off balance, but he would make the shot anyway, crash to the floor, get up, and sink the dividend foul shot, scoring three points instead of two on the play.

On defense, he guarded St. Joseph's highest-scoring player, Tom Wynne, and held him to nine points. The defense was expensive, though. An aggressive defensive player has to take the risk of committing five personal fouls, after which a player is obliged by the rules to leave the game. With just under four minutes to go, and Princeton comfortably ahead by five points, Bradley committed his fifth foul and left the court. For several minutes, the game was interrupted as the crowd stood and applauded him; the game was being played in Philadelphia, where hostility toward Princeton is ordinarily great but where the people know a folk hero when they see one. After the cheering ended, the blood drained slowly out of Princeton, whose other players could not hold the lead. Princeton lost by one point. Dr. Jack Ramsay, the St. Joseph's coach, says that Bradley's effort that night was the best game of basketball he has ever seen a college boy play.

Some people, hearing all the stories of Bradley's great moments, go to see him play and are disappointed when he does not do something memorable at least once a minute. Actually, basketball is a hunting game. It lasts for forty minutes, and there are ten men on the court, so the likelihood is that any one player, even a superstar, will actually have the ball in his hands for only four of those minutes, or perhaps a little more. The rest of the time, a player on offense either is standing around recovering his breath or is on the move, foxlike, looking for openings, sizing up chances, attempting to screen off a defensive man—by "coming off guys," as van Breda Kolff puts it—and thus upset the balance of power.

The depth of Bradley's game is most discernible when he doesn't have the ball. He goes in and swims around in the vicinity of the basket, back and forth, moving for motion's sake, making plans and abandoning them, and always watching the distant movement of the ball out of the corner of his eye. He stops and studies his man, who is full of alertness because of the sudden break in the rhythm. The man is trying to watch both Bradley and the ball. Bradley watches the man's head. If it turns too much to the right, he moves quickly to the left. If it turns too much to the left, he goes to the right. If, ignoring the ball, the man focusses his full attention on Bradley, Bradley stands still and looks at the floor. A high-lobbed pass floats in, and just before it arrives Bradley jumps high, takes the ball, turns, and scores.

If Princeton has an out-of-bounds play under the basket, Bradley takes a position just inside the baseline, almost touching the teammate who is going to throw the ball into play. The defensive man crowds in to try to stop whatever Bradley is planning. Bradley whirls around the defensive man, blocking him out with one leg, and takes a bounce pass and lays up the score. This works only against naïve opposition, but when it does work it is a marvel to watch.

To receive a pass from a backcourt man, Bradley moves away from the basket and toward one side of the court. He gets the ball, gives it up, goes into the center, and hovers there awhile. Nothing happens. He goes back to the corner. He starts toward the backcourt again to receive a pass like the first one. His man, who is eager and has been through this before, moves out toward the backcourt a step ahead of Bradley. This is a defensive error. Bradley isn't going that way; he was only faking. He heads straight for the basket, takes a bounce pass, and scores. This maneuver is known in basketball as going back door. Bradley is able to go back door successfully and often, because of his practiced footwork. Many players, once their man has made himself vulnerable, rely on surprise alone to complete a backdoor play, and that isn't always enough. Bradley's fake looks for all the world like the beginning of a trip to the outside; then, when he goes for the basket, he has all the freedom he needs. When he gets the ball after breaking free, other defensive players naturally leave their own men and try to stop him. In these three-on-two or two-on-one situations, the obvious move is to pass to a teammate who has moved into a position to score. Sometimes, however, no teammate has moved, and Bradley sees neither a pass nor a shot, so he veers around and goes back and picks up his own man. "I take him on into the corner for a one-on-one," he says, imagining what he might do. "I move toward the free-throw line on a dribble. If the man is overplaying me to my right, I reverse pivot and go in for a left-handed lay-up. If the man is playing even with me, but off me a few feet, I take a jump shot. If the man is playing me good defense—honest—and he's on me tight, I keep going. I give him a head-and-shoulder fake, keep going all the time, and drive to the basket, or I give him a head-and-shoulder fake and take a jump shot. Those are all the things you need—the fundamentals."

Bradley develops a relationship with his man that is something like the relationship between a yoyoist and his yoyo. "I'm on the side of the floor," he postulates, "and I want to play with my man a little bit, always knowing where the ball is but not immediately concerned with getting it. Basketball is a game of two or three men, and you have to know how to stay out of a play and not clutter it up. I cut to the baseline. My man will follow me. I'll cut up to the high-post position. He'll follow me. I'll cut to the low-post position. He'll follow me. I'll go back out to my side position. He'll follow. I'll fake to the center of the floor and go hard to the baseline, running my man into a pick set at the low-post position. I'm not running him into a pick in order to get free for a shot—I'm doing it simply to irritate him. I come up on the other side of the basket, looking to see if a teammate feels that I'm open. They can't get the ball to me at that instant. Now my man is back with me. I go out to the side. I set a screen for the guard. He sees the situation. He comes toward me. He dribbles hard past me, running his man into my back. I feel the contact. My man switches off me, leaving the pass lane open for a split second. I go hard to the basket and take a bounce pass for a shot. Two points."

Because Bradley's inclination to analyze every gesture in basketball is fairly uncommon, other players look at him as if they think him a little odd when he seeks them out after a game and asks them to show him what they did in making a move that he particularly admired. They tell him that they're not sure what he is talking about, and that even if they could remember, they couldn't possibly explain, so the best offer they can make is to go back to the court, try to set up the situation again, and see what it was that provoked his appreciation. Bradley told me about this almost apologetically, explaining that he had no choice but to be analytical in order to be in the game at all. "I don't have that much natural ability," he said, and went on to tell a doleful tale about how his legs lacked spring, how he was judged among the worst of the Olympic candidates in ability to get high off the floor, and so on, until he had nearly convinced me that he was a motor moron. In actuality, Bradley does have certain natural advantages. He has been six feet five since he was fifteen years old, so he had most of his high-school years in which to develop his coördination, and it is now exceptional for a tall man. His hand span, measuring only nine and a half inches, does not give him the wraparound control that basketball players like to have, but, despite relatively unimpressive shoulders and biceps, he is unusually strong, and he can successfully mix with almost anyone in the Greco-Roman battles under the backboards.

His most remarkable natural gift, however, is his vision. During a game, Bradley's eyes are always a glaze of panoptic attention, for a basketball player needs to look at everything, focussing on nothing, until the last moment of commitment. Beyond this, it is obviously helpful to a basketball player to be able to see a little more than the next man, and the remark is frequently made about basketball superstars that they have unusual peripheral vision. People used to say that Bob Cousy, the immortal backcourt man of the Boston Celtics, could look due east and enjoy a sunset. Ed Macauley once took a long auto trip with Cousy when they were teammates, and in the course of it Cousy happened to go to sleep sitting up. Macauley swears that Cousy's eyelids, lowered as far as they would go, failed to cover his coleopteran eyes.

Bradley's eyes close normally enough, but his astounding passes to teammates have given him, too, a reputation for being able to see out of the back of his head. To discover whether there was anything to all the claims for basketball players' peripheral vision, I asked Bradley to go with me to the office of Dr. Henry Abrams, a Princeton ophthalmologist, who had agreed to measure Bradley's total field. Bradley rested his chin in the middle of a device called a perimeter, and Dr. Abrams began asking when he could see a small white dot as it was slowly brought around from behind him, from above, from below, and from either side. To make sure that Bradley wasn't, in effect, throwing hope passes, Dr. Abrams checked each point three times before plotting it on a chart. There was a chart for each eye, and both charts had irregular circles printed on them, representing the field of vision that a typical perfect eye could be expected to have. Dr. Abrams explained as he worked that these printed circles were logical rather than experimentally established extremes, and that in his experience the circles he had plotted to represent the actual vision fields of his patients had without exception fallen inside the circles printed on the charts. When he finished plotting Bradley's circles, the one for each eye was larger than the printed model and, in fact, ran completely outside it.

With both eyes open and looking straight ahead, Bradley sees a hundred and ninety-five degrees on the horizontal and about seventy degrees straight down, or about fifteen and five degrees more, respectively, than what is officially considered perfection. Most surprising, however, is what he can see above him. Focussed horizontally, the typical perfect eye, according to the chart, can see about forty-seven degrees upward. Bradley can see seventy degrees upward. This no doubt explains why he can stare at the floor while he is waiting for lobbed passes to arrive from above. Dr. Abrams said that he doubted whether a person who tried to expand his peripheral vision through exercises could succeed, but he was fascinated to learn that when Bradley was a young boy he tried to do just that. As he walked down the main street of Crystal City, for example, he would keep his eyes focussed straight ahead and try to identify objects in the windows of stores he was passing. For all this, however, Bradley cannot see behind himself. Much of the court and, thus, a good deal of the action are often invisible to a basketball player, so he needs more than good eyesight. He needs to know how to function in the manner of a blind man as well. When, say, four players are massed in the middle of things behind Bradley, and it is inconvenient for him to look around, his hands reach back and his fingers move rapidly from shirt to shirt or hip to hip. He can read the defense as if he were reading Braille.

Bradley's optical endowments notwithstanding, Coach van Breda Kolff agrees with him that he is "not a great physical player," and goes on to say, "Others can run faster and jump higher. The difference between Bill and other basketball players is self-discipline." The two words that Bradley repeats most often when he talks about basketball are "discipline" and "concentration," and through the exercise of both he has made himself an infectious example to younger players. "Concentrate!" he keeps shouting to himself when he is practicing on his own. His capacity for self-discipline is so large that it is almost funny. For example, he was a bit shocked when the Olympic basketball staff advised the Olympic basketball players to put in one hour of practice a day during the summer, because he was already putting in two hours a day —often in ninety-five-degree temperatures, with his feet squishing in sneakers that had become so wet that he sometimes skidded and crashed to the floor. His creed, which he picked up from Ed Macauley, is "When you are not practicing, remember, someone somewhere is practicing, and when you meet him he will win."

He also believes that the conquest of pain is essential to any seriously sustained athletic endeavor. In 1963, he dressed for a game against Harvard although he had a painful foot injury. Then, during the pregame warmup, it bothered him so much that he decided to give up, and he started for the bench. He changed his mind on the way, recalling that a doctor had told him that his foot, hurt the night before at Dartmouth, was badly bruised but was not in danger of further damage. If he sat down, he says, he would have lowered his standards, for he believes that "there has never been a great athlete who did not know what pain is." So he played the game. His heavily taped foot went numb during the first ten minutes, but his other faculties seemed to sharpen in response to the handicap. His faking quickened to make up for his reduced speed, and he scored thirty-two points, missing only five shots during the entire evening.

# The Headmaster

After graduating from Princeton High School in 1948, McPhee spent a year at Deerfield Academy in Deerfield, Massachusetts. Athletes and marginal scholars often spend a "post-graduate" year in this fashion, since brushing up one's grades and stats may enhance a college-admissions file. McPhee's purpose was less promotional: he had skipped a year of school and, in the opinion of his parents, needed more growth before entering college. An ideal place to send a boy from New Jersey public high, Deerfield was relatively free of the snobbish pretenses commonly associated with Eastern prep schools. It derived this character from its founder and headmaster, Frank L. Boyden, "a small, grumpy Labrador" of a man, McPhee recalled, who ran the school for sixty-six years, 1902–68.

A practical autocrat, one whose talent for management embraced funding, pep talks, and infield grounders, Boyden seemed the model educator, stamped in a pragmatic American mold: "One researcher spent a few days at the academy and finally said, 'Well, there isn't any system here, but it works.' " For all its sentiment, McPhee's profile of Boyden, like the man and his school, is "drier than a covered bridge" —solid, spare, and built to last, regardless of the traffic that passes through. This portion of *The Headmaster* depicts Boyden's essential grit; the book imparts a larger view of his past, his habits, and his typically crowded working day.—*WLH*

People seeing the headmaster for the first time often find him different from what they expected. Those who stay in the Deerfield community for any length of time quickly become aware that they are living in a monarchy and that the small man in the golf cart is the king, but visitors who have heard of him and know what a great man he is seem to insist that he ought to be a tall, white-haired patriarch. People see him picking up papers and assume it is his job. Coming upon a group of

23

women outside one of his old houses a few years ago, he took them in and led them through its ancient rooms. On the way out, one lady gave him a quarter. People walk right by him sometimes without seeing him. Someone once stopped, turned around, and said, "I'm sorry, Mr. Boyden. I didn't notice you."

"That's all right," he said. "No one ever does."

He loves such stories, perhaps in part because they help to fake out the faculty and the boys. How else, after all, could an inconspicuous man like that hold an entire community in the palm of his hand? When the stories come back to him, he lights up with pleasure. He has one way of judging everything: If it's good for the academy, it's good. He was once walking with an impressive-looking Deerfield faculty member when someone, a stranger, said, "Who was that?"

"That was the headmaster."

"Yes, but who was the little man with him?"

Boyden looked old when he was four, older when he was in college, and older still in the nineteen-twenties, but now he doesn't look particularly old at all. His hair is not white but slate-gray, and his demeanor, which hasn't changed in forty years, still suggests a small, grumpy Labrador. He sometimes dresses in gray trousers, a dark-blue jacket, and brown cordovan shoes—choices that are somewhat collegiate and could be taken as a mild sign of age, because for decades he wore dark-blue worsted suits and maroon ties almost exclusively, winter and summer, hanging on to each successive suit until it fell off him in threads. One of his jacket pockets today has a four-inch rip that has been bound with black thread. He doesn't care. He is an absolutely unself-conscious man. Let one scuff mark appear on a stair riser in his academy and he will quickly find a janitor and report it, but this kind of concern is entirely projected onto the school. He once got up on a cool July morning and put on an old leather coat covered with cracks and lined with sheepskin that was coming loose; he went off to New York in it and obliviously wore it all day in the sweltering city. After eighty-six years, his only impairment is bad hearing. "My ears are gone," he will say, and then he will walk into a roomful of people and pretend that there isn't a syllable he can't catch. He indulges himself in nothing. He will eat anything, and he usually doesn't notice the components of his meals, unless they happen to be root beer and animal crackers, which he occasionally eats for breakfast. He has been given honorary degrees by Harvard, Yale, Princeton, and seventeen other colleges and universities, but he apparently has not even a trace of a desire to be called Dr. Boyden, and no one calls him that except eraser salesmen and strangers whose sons are applying to the school.

"Never make a decision just to get something done," he says, and no one has ever accused him of being impulsive. His Director of Studies has said, "He has an infinite wisdom, which is as aggravating as hell. But anyone knowing him well who is faced with an important decision would go to him." This is, of course, most true of his students. They call him up in the summertime; they call him up from college; in later life, they call him up to ask if they should run for office. In conversation, he has the ability to give his undivided attention, and the perception to understand the implications of practically anything that is said to him. In this way, he has made several thousand people believe that he especially cares about them, which he does. He rarely loses his temper, but his capacity for absorbing criticism is not large. He is not proud in a narrow, personal sense; his pride is in his school and in his belief that he knows what is best for it. He is lost in the school, and there is nothing of him but the school. On vacation in Florida, he goes around in his blue worsted suit looking for people with money to help keep Deerfield going. He never goes near the water. He was once seen sitting in the lobby of the Breakers in Palm Beach reading a Deerfield yearbook. He is famous for his simplicity, which he cultivates. He is, in the highest sense, a simple man, and he has spent his life building a school according to elemental ideals, but only a complicated man could bring off what he has done, and, on the practical plane, he is full of paradox and politics. Senior members of his faculty, in various conversations, have described him as "a great humanitarian," "ruthless," "loyal," "feudal," "benevolent," "grateful," "humble," "impatient," "restless," "thoughtful," "thoughtless," "selfish," "selfless," "stubborn," "discerning," "intuitive," and "inscrutable"—never once disagreeing with one another. The headmaster's own view of himself, according to one of his two sons, is that he is "indestructible and infallible."

Boyden has the gift of authority. He looks fragile, his voice is uncommanding, but people do what he says. Without this touch, he would have lost the school on the first day he worked there. Of the seven boys who were in the academy when he took over in that fall of 1902, at least four were regarded by the populace with fear, and for a couple of years it had been a habit of people of Deerfield to cross the street before passing the academy. Boyden's problem was complicated by one of the trustees, who was so eager to close the school that he had actually encouraged these boys to destroy the new headmaster as rapidly as they could. The boys were, on the average, a head taller and thirty pounds heavier than the headmaster. The first school day went by without a crisis. Then, as the students were getting ready to leave, Boyden said, "Now we're going to play football." Sports had not previously been a part of the program at the academy. Scrimmaging on the village common, the boys were amused at first, and interested in the novelty, but things suddenly deteriorated in a hail of four-letter words. With a sour look, the headmaster said, "Cut that out!" That was all he said, and—inexplicably—it was all he had to say.

A few days later, a boy asked him if he would like to go outside and have a catch with a baseball. The two of them went out onto the school lawn and stood about fifty feet apart. The boy wound up and threw a smokeball at him, apparently with intent to kill. Boyden caught the ball and fired it back as hard as he could throw it. A kind of match ensued, and the rest of the students collected to watch. The headmaster and the boy kept throwing the baseball at each other with everything they had. Finally, the boy quit. "Of course, I was wearing a glove and he wasn't," says the headmaster, who is a craftsman of the delayed, throwaway line.

He believed in athletics as, among other things, a way of controlling and blending his boys, and he required all of them to participate throughout the school year. This idea was an educational novelty in 1902. He arranged games with other schools, and because there were not enough boys in Deerfield Academy to fill out a football team or a baseball team, he jumped into the action himself. He was the first quarterback Deerfield ever had. He broke his nose and broke it again. Taking the ball in one game, he started around right end, but the other team's defensive halfback forced him toward the sideline, picked him up, and—this was years before the forward-motion rule—carried him all the way back to the Deerfield end zone and dumped him on the ground. He was a much better baseball player. Ignoring his height, he played first base. He was a good hitter, and Greenfield, Springfield, and Northampton newspapers of the time include items with headlines like "BOYDEN GOES 3 FOR 4 AS DEERFIELD ACADEMY BEATS ATHOL 2 TO 0." In sports, he captured and held his school, and it may be in sports that he developed the personal commitment that kept him there. His teammates were won over by him. Their earlier antagonism became support. He convinced them that the school would go under without their help, and they discovered that they wanted to keep it going as much as he did. In one game, at Arms Academy, he ran after a high pop foul, caught the ball two feet from a brick wall, crashed into it, and fell to the ground unconscious. The boys told him to go home and recover and not to worry—there would be no disciplinary problems at the school during his absence.

A teacher, Miss Minnie Hawks, was hired shortly after the headmaster was, and she taught German and geometry while he taught algebra and physical geography. He used to take a rock into class with him, set it on his desk, and tell his students to write down everything they knew about the rock. But he was more interested in implications than he was in facts. His mind drifted quickly from science to behavior. "You're not youngsters anymore," he would say. "You're going to be the ones who run this town." He read a bit of the Bible to them every morning. Gradually, he acquired more teachers and spent less time in the classroom himself. He assembled a sound faculty and gave its members freedom to teach as they pleased. His own mark was made in moral education rather than in the academic disciplines. His first-hand relationship with his boys has always been extraordinary, and Deerfield students for sixty years have been characterized by the high degree of ethical sensitivity that he has been able to awaken in them. This is the area within which his greatness lies. From the start, he assumed responsibility not only for their academic development but also for their social lives, their recreation, and their religious obligations. He held dances, supplied dance cards, and, just to be sure that no one lacked interest, filled in the cards himself. After the dances, he got on the Greenfield-Northampton trolley car with his boys and girls and rode with them, making sure that each got off at the correct address. If he happened to be on the trolley's last run, he walked home—a distance of six miles. He believed in wearing the boys out. They dug ditches; they also made beehives, incubators, and wheelbarrows; and, with axes and crosscut saws, they cut lumber for lockers for their athletic equipment. In his first year, he set up a card table beside a radiator just inside the front door of the school building. This was his office, not because there was no room for a headmaster's office anywhere else, but because he wanted nothing to go on in the school without his being in the middle of it. Years later, when the present main school building was built, the headmaster had the architect design a wide place in the first-floor central hallway—the spot with the heaviest traffic in the school—and that was where his desk was put and where it still is. While he dictates, telephones, or keeps his appointments, he watches the boys passing between classes. He has a remarkable eye for trouble. If the mood of the student body at large is poor, he will sense it, and when one boy is disturbed, he will see it in the boy's face, and he will think of some minor matter they need to talk over, so that he can find out what the difficulty is and try to do something about it. He has maintained his familial approach to education despite the spread of bureaucracy into institutions and industries and despite the increased size of his own school. In his early years, he found that he could handle twenty-eight students as easily as fourteen, then fifty-six as easily as twenty-eight, and so on, until, in the late nineteen-forties, he had something over five hundred. The enrollment has remained at that level. "I can handle five hundred," he says. "Another hundred and I'd lose it."

Most schools have detailed lists of printed rules, and boys who violate them either are given penalties or are thrown out. A reasonable percentage of expulsions is a norm of prep-school life. Deerfield has no printed rules and no set penalties, and the headmaster has fired only five boys in sixty-four years. "For one foolish mistake, a boy should not have a stamp put on him that will be with him for the rest of his life," he says. "I could show you a list of rules from one school that is thirty pages long. There is no flexibility in a system like that. I'm willing to try a little longer than some of the other people do, provided there is nothing immoral. You can't have a family of three children without having some problems, so you have problems if you have five hundred. If you make a lot of rules, they never hit the fellow you made them for. Two hours after making a rule, you may want to change it. We have rules here, unwritten ones, but we make exceptions to them more than we enforce them. I always remember what Robert E. Lee said when he was president of Washington College, which is now Washington and Lee. He said, 'A boy is more important than any rule.' Ninety per cent of any group of boys will never get out of line. You must have about ninety per cent as a central core. Then the question is: How many of the others can you absorb?"

To say that Deerfield has no set rules is not to say that it is a place where a boy can experiment at will with his impulses. The academy has been described, perhaps fairly, as a gilded cage. The essential underlying difference between Deerfield and schools like Exeter and Andover is that Exeter and Andover make a conscious effort to teach independence and self-reliance by establishing a set of regulations to live by and then setting the boys free to stand or fall accordingly. Exeter and Andover boys can cut classes, within established margins, and they are provided with time they can call their own. Deerfield boys have several free hours each Sunday, but most of their time is programmed for them, and attendance is constantly taken. The headmaster's respect and admiration for Exeter and Andover are considerable, and he likes to quote a conversation he once had with an Andover headmaster, who said, "Maybe you're right. Maybe we're right. There is a need for both schools." Andover and Exeter, looking ahead to the college years, try to prepare their students for the freedom they will have, so that they can enjoy it and not suffer from it. Boyden believes that the timing of a boy's life requires more discipline in the secondary-school years than later, and that there is no point in going to college before you get there. "Boys need a sense of security," he says. "Discipline without persecution adds to that sense of security. People sometimes don't realize this, but boys like a control somewhere. We try to give them what you might call controlled freedom. We're the last bulwark of the old discipline. We're interested in new things, but I'm not going to throw away the fundamentals."

A new boy at Deerfield cannot have been there very long before the idea is impressed upon him that he is a part of something that won't work unless he does his share. The headmaster is able to create this kind of feeling in his boys to a greater degree than most parents are. All boys are given an equal footing from which to develop their own positions. There are no special responsibilities for scholarship boys, such as waiting on table. Everyone does that. In fact, the headmaster insists that scholarship boys not be told that they have scholarships, since that might injure the sense of equality he tries to build. His school, which grew so phenomenally out of almost nothing, has frequently been visited by curious educational theorists. One researcher spent a few days at the academy and finally said, "Well, there isn't any system here, but it works." Such people perplex Frank Boyden almost as much as he perplexes them. "People come here thinking we have some marvellous method," he says. "We just treat the boys as if we expect something of them, and we keep them busy. So many of our things simply exist. They're not theory. They're just living life. I expect most of our boys want to do things the way we want them done. We drive with a light rein, but we can pull it up just like that, if we need to. We just handle the cases as they come up."

His art as a disciplinarian often enables him to prevent things before they happen. He listens to the noise level in a group of boys, and watches the degree of restlessness; he can read these things as if they were a printed page. This is one reason he believes in meetings that involve the entire school. "You must have your boys together as a unit at least once a day, just as you have your family together once a day," he says. Evening Meeting is a Deerfield custom. The boys sit on a vast carpet in the anteroom of the school auditorium and listen to announcements, perhaps an anecdotal story from the headmaster, and reports of athletic contests and other activities. "Junior B Football beat the Holyoke High School Junior Varsity six to nothing this afternoon," says the coach of Junior B Football. "Charlie Hiller scored the touchdown with two minutes left in the game." In the applause that follows, this one low-echelon athlete gains something, and so does the school. On Sunday evenings, there is a vesper service, or Sunday Night Sing, as it is called, in which the boys sing one hymn after another, with a pause for a short talk by a visiting clergyman or educator. The lustre, or lack of it, in their voices is the headmaster's gauge of the climate of the student body for the week to come, and he accordingly chides them or exhorts them or amuses them or blasts them at Evening Meetings on succeeding days, often shaping his remarks around one of several precepts—"keep it on a high level," "be mobile," "finish up strong"—which he uses so repeatedly and effectively that the words continue to ricochet through the minds of Deerfield graduates long after they leave the school. "He has the trick of the wrist with a whole community," one of his teachers has said.

All discipline ultimately becomes a private matter between each boy and the headmaster. Most of the boys feel guilty if they do something that offends his sensibilities. Unlike his great predecessor Arnold of Rugby, he does not believe that schoolboys are his natural enemies; on the contrary, he seems to convince them that although he is infallible, he badly needs their assistance. A local farmer who was in the class of 1919 says, "When you thought of doing something wrong, you would know that you would hurt him deeply, so you wouldn't do it. He had twenty-four-hour control." A 1928 alumnus says, "It didn't matter what you did as long as you told him the truth." And 1940: "Whatever it was, you didn't do it, because you might drop a little in his eyes." He will give a problem boy a second, third, fourth, fifth, and sixth chance, if necessary. The rest of the student body sometimes becomes cynical about the case, but the headmaster refuses to give up. "I would have kicked me out," says one alumnus who had a rather defiant senior year in the early nineteen-fifties. The headmaster had reason enough to expel him, and almost any other school would have dropped him without a thought, but Boyden graduated him, sent him to Princeton, and, today, does not even recall that the fellow was ever a cause of trouble. Boyden is incapable of bearing grudges. He wants to talk things out and forget them. He is sensitive to the potential effect of his forbearance, so he has sometimes taken the risk of calling the student body together and asking for its indulgence. A boy once drank the better part of a fifth of whiskey in a bus returning from another school, reeled in the aisle, fell on his face, and got sick. The headmaster called the school together and said that for the sake of discipline in the academy at large he would have to let the boy go unless they would guarantee him that no episode of the kind would happen again. The headmaster was beyond being thought of as weak, so he got away with it. People often wonder what on earth could make him actually drop a boy, and the five cases in which he has done so are therefore of particular interest. All have a common factor: the offender was unremorseful. One of them was guilty of nineteen different offenses, including arson. Nevertheless, if he had told the headmaster that he was wrong, he could have stayed in school.

A boy of considerable talent once told the headmaster that he could write his English papers only between midnight and dawn. His muse, the boy claimed, refused to appear at any other time of day. The difficulty was that after the boy's inspiration ran out he invariably fell asleep and missed his morning classes. Like all geniuses, this boy was likely to attract imitators. The headmaster addressed the student body. "Are you willing to let Mac Farrell stay up all night writing his English papers?" he said. "Mac Farrell alone?" The boys agreed.

The headmaster has often put himself in an uncomfortable corner for a boy who is different. He once had two students—artistic cousins of Mac Farrell—who liked to paint and particularly liked to go out at night and do nocturnes. They did the cemetery by moonlight and the old houses in the edge of the glow of street lamps. The headmaster knew that this was going on, but he overlooked it. His own favorites have always been responsible, uncomplicated, outstanding athletes, and he cares even less about art than he knows about it, but, in his way, he was just the right headmaster for these two boys. "With a person as unDeerfield as myself," remembers one of them, who is now Curator of Graphic Arts at Princeton University, "he was sympathetic and understanding. He was patient and—what can I say?—incredibly wise in the way that he handled me."

Certain boys at Deerfield in earlier years would commit long series of petty crimes and believe that all had gone undetected. Then, finally, the headmaster would stop such a boy, pull out a small notebook, and read off to him everything he had done wrong since the first day of school. For years, the headmaster roved the campus late at night, like a watchman. Until the late nineteen-thirties, he made rounds to every room in every dormitory during study hours every night. Since then, he has made spot visits. He never gives a boy bad news at night. He never threatens. He uses shame privately. He more often trades favors than gives them. If a boy asks something of him, he asks something in return. There is no student government, nor are there faculty committees, helping to run Deerfield. The headmaster holds himself distant from that sort of thing. Senior-class presidents are elected on the eve of Commencement. Students who are in the school now say they would not want student government anyway, because they feel that it is a mockery elsewhere.

Boyden's principle of athletics for all has remained one of the main elements of the school's program, and Deerfield is unmatched in this respect today. Where once he did not have enough boys for even one team, he now has teams for all five hundred. When a boy at Deerfield chooses a sport, he automatically makes a team that has a full schedule of games with other schools. For example, Deerfield usually has at least eight basketball teams, each with game uniforms, away games, and all the other incidentals of the sport on the varsity level. This is true in soccer, baseball, football, tennis, lacrosse, hockey, squash, swimming, skiing, track, and cross-country as well. With few exceptions, every boy at Deerfield is required to take part in three sports a year. There is no set number of teams in any sport. According to the boys' choices, there may be a few more football teams one year and a few more soccer teams the next. Deerfield has sent on a share of athletic stars—football players such as Mutt Ray to Dartmouth and Archie Roberts to Columbia, for instance—but Deerfield is not really an atmosphere in which a great athlete is likely to develop. The headmaster's belief in sport is exceeded by his belief that everything has its place and time. Deerfield athletes are given no time for extra practice, nor are they permitted to practice any sport out of season. In the fall and the spring, the basketball courts are locked, and baskets are actually removed from the backboards.

In the early days, having the headmaster as a player produced some disadvantages for Deerfield teams. Once, in a pick-off situation in baseball, when he caught the throw from the pitcher and put his glove down, the opposing player slid safely under him. "Out," said the umpire. Any other baseball player would have congratulated himself on his luck, but the headmaster had to tell the umpire that the fellow had in fact been safe. From the start, he had been preaching sportsmanship to his boys. People who remember those days say that he was the first person in that part of the country to stress courtesy in athletics. "We may wish they were interested in other things," he said at the time, "but we must meet existing conditions, and since they will have athletic sports anyway, let us control them and make them a moral force." No matter how able a Deerfield player was or how close a game had become, if he showed anger he was benched. If a basketball player said anything the least bit antagonistic to the man he was guarding—even something as mild as "Go ahead and shoot"—a substitute would go into the game. Athletics was one of the ways in which Deerfield became known, and from the beginning the headmaster wanted his teams to be smartly dressed and thoroughly equipped. In the early years, he often spent at least a third of his salary on athletic equipment, and when a woman of the town offered a contribution to the school, he asked if he might use it for baseball uniforms. "Something has lifted the spirit of this community," she said to him. "Go and buy the best uniforms you can find, but don't tell anyone I gave the money for it."

The headmaster played on Deerfield teams until he was about thirty-five, and he was head coach of football, basketball, and baseball until he was nearly eighty. "I can't go to a funeral anywhere from Athol to Northampton without an elderly man's coming up and reminding me of a baseball game we once played against one another," he says. His sense of football has always been vague but imaginative. His blocking assignments were not precise. During his years as player-coach, he put straps on the belts of his linemen so that the backs—himself included—could hang on and be pulled forward for short gains. In baseball, he followed a simple strategy. "If you can put your glove on a fast ball, there is no reason you can't put your bat on it," he has said for sixty-four years. "Anyone can learn to bunt." Deerfield teams use the squeeze play as if there were no alternative in the sport. He continued to hit fungoes to his baseball teams until he was seventy-five years old. It was a high point of any Deerfield baseball day to watch him hit precise grounders to his scrambling infield. Toward the end of his coaching years, the headmaster found that he could not hit the ball with quite as much snap as he liked to give it. He complained that the ground was getting softer. His main talent as a coach was that he always seemed to know what a boy could do and then expected no more of him. He knew, somehow, when a pitcher was almost through. If his assistant coaches happened to prevail on him to leave a pitcher in a game, disaster usually followed. What he did not know about football he made up through his knowledge of boys, and he could win a game with the right remark. He once did so—in the early nineteen-twenties—by taking his quarterback aside and saying to him, "You're just like a race horse. Sometimes you're too tense to do your job. Take it easy. You'll run faster."

Visitors today sometimes think that the headmaster is a little theatrical when he walks up and down the sidelines—eighty-six years old, and wearing a player's duffel coat that almost reaches the ground—and acts as if he were on the verge of jumping into the game. Something they may not be able to imagine is what it must mean to him to remember the games against small local schools when he himself was in the backfield and there were fifteen or twenty boys in the academy, and now, more than sixty years later, to be watching his team make one touchdown after another until the final score is Deerfield 28, Exeter 0. As a semi-retired coach, the headmaster still gives the same pre-game talks he has always given. In a way that is desperate, unyielding, and total, he wants to win, but he wants to win with grace. "The consequence of poor sportsmanship is that you lose, somewhere along the line," he says. "Remember, it's better to lose in a sportsmanlike way than to win and gloat over it." And he goes along in that vein for a while, until he has satisfied the requirements of his conscience. Then he says, "Now, boys, let's not let up on them for a minute. Let's win this one, if possible, by forty points."

# Oranges

---

Florida evokes coastal images for its tourists, who seldom stray from that long shoreline of beaches, marinas, and condominiums. McPhee was always more attracted to the interior, where vast commercial groves produce citrus fruit unrivalled in yield and quality. His early travels there made him a confirmed citrophile, a condition that has ripened in later years. He keeps an office refrigerator stocked with sweet Valencias, eschews the ubiquitous concentrate, and tends a mental map of all stands within fifty miles selling a glass of freshly squeezed orange juice.

*Oranges* testifies to this alimentary passion, but not like other food books (*My Life with Olives,* etc.), nor, in its account of orange growers, pickers, and processors, as an industrial documentary on "men and their work." Here is a quantum advance over McPhee's previous efforts: the canvas is broader, deeper, more crammed with fact, more composed in volumes of line and space. The legwork that carried him through orange country also bears the plot line of his report; and his prodigious homework on citrus botany and history is neatly subsumed by this structure. He had stretched well beyond the range of personal experiences or interests, creating a report that was larger and finer than its nominal subject. Even the publisher was impressed: a jacket blurb allowed that "Mr. McPhee's astonishing book has an almost narrative progression." This portion describes the "Indian River"; the full story is a gracefully contrived mosaic of fact and insight, following the instructive pattern of a citrus growth and harvest cycle.—*WLH*

---

In the seventeen-seventies Londoners developed a craving for Jesse Fish oranges. These had thin skins and were difficult to peel, but the English found them incredibly juicy and sweet, and Jesse Fish oranges were preferred before all others in the making of shrub, a drink that called for alcoholic spirits, sugar, and the juice of an acid fruit—an

ancestral whiskey sour. More than sixty-five thousand Jesse Fish oranges
and two casks of juice reached London in 1776, and sixteen hogsheads
of juice arrived in 1778. It hardly mattered to the English who Jesse Fish
was, and it didn't seem to matter to Jesse Fish who his customers were.
Fish was a Yankee, a native of New York and by sympathy a revolution-
ary. Decades before the Revolution, he had retreated to an island off St.
Augustine to get away from a miserable marriage, and he had become
Florida's first orange baron.

There would have been others before him if Florida had not been
Spanish for more than two hundred years. Andalusia and Valencia were
golden with oranges, so the Spaniards hardly needed to start commercial
groves on the far side of the ocean. They planted citrus fruit in remote
places only for medical reasons. Columbus, under orders, carried with
him the seeds of the first citrus trees to reach the New World, and he
spread them through the Antilles, where they grew and multiplied so
vigorously that within thirty years some Caribbean islands were covered
with them. In all likelihood, Ponce de León introduced oranges to the
North American mainland when he discovered Florida in 1513. (The
Florida Citrus Commission likes to promote him as a man who was
trying to find the Fountain of Youth but actually brought it with him.)
Hernando de Soto planted additional orange trees during his expedition
to Florida in 1539. On all Spanish ships bound for America, in fact, each
sailor was required by Spanish law to carry one hundred seeds with him,
and later, because seeds tended to dry out, Spanish ships were required
to carry young trees instead. Sir Francis Drake levelled the orange trees
of St. Augustine when he sacked the town in 1586, but the stumps put
out new shoots and eventually bore fruit again. Nearly all were Bitter
Oranges. Indians, carrying them away from the Spanish colony, inadvertently scattered seeds in the Florida wilderness, and Sour Oranges
began to grow wild. (The first oranges in California were planted around
1800 at a Spanish mission. The first commercial grove in California was
established by a trapper from Kentucky in 1841, on the present site of
the Southern Pacific railroad station in Los Angeles.)

England, which had acquired sovereignty over Florida in 1763, gave
it back to the Spanish toward the end of the American Revolution, and
the Florida citrus business did not increase significantly for nearly forty
years, through the period that is known in Florida history as the Second
Occupation. After the territory became a possession of the United States,
in 1821, orange groves expanded rapidly in the St. Augustine area and
along the St. Johns River south of Jacksonville. There was also some

planting, in a minor way, on the Indian River. In 1834, two and a half million oranges were shipped north from St. Augustine, but on February 8, 1835, the temperature dropped as low as eleven degrees, salt water froze in the bays, and fifty-six hours of unremitting freeze killed nearly every orange tree in Florida.

One grove remained undamaged. It had been planted in 1830 by Douglas Dummett, a young man in his twenties, whose father had moved to Florida from New Haven, Connecticut, to establish a plantation of sugar cane. The site young Dummett had picked for his orange grove was on Merritt Island, between Cape Canaveral and the mainland, with the warm tidal waters of the Indian River on one side and of the Banana River on the other. His ground was high, the soil was rich in shell marl, and he had used wild Sour Orange trees as rootstocks, budding them with sweet oranges from a grove about fifty miles to the north. After 1835, orange growing in Florida was revived with buds from Dummett's trees. From the Dummett grove came the oranges of the Indian River, whose reputation soon spread so far that czars of Russia sent ships to fetch them.

The Indian River is not actually a river but a tidal lagoon, about two miles wide in most places and one hundred and twenty miles long, running between the Florida mainland and the Atlantic barrier beaches. Merritt Island is close to the Indian River's northern end. Dummett used to go out to meet trading schooners in a thirty-foot sailing canoe, its gunwales riding near the waterline under a load of oranges packed in barrels between layers of dried Spanish moss. He had made the canoe from a single log of cypress with the help of another orange grower, Captain Mills Olcott Burnham, a Vermonter who had moved to Florida for his health. Burnham had regained his strength so dramatically that he could lift two fifty-pound kegs, one in each hand, and hold them wide apart. After Congress passed the Armed Occupation Act—giving a hundred and sixty acres of Florida land to anyone who could fight off the Seminoles and hold his ground for seven years—Burnham, in 1842, led an unlikely group on an expedition south from Merritt Island, opening up the Indian River and establishing a community near the present site of Fort Pierce.

Florida was the only wilderness in the world that attracted middle-aged pioneers. The young ones were already on their way west toward California. The subtropics may actually have been fiercer than the plains, in that both areas had hostile Indians but Florida alone had its stupendous reptiles. Florida, even then, appealed to aging doctors, retired brokers, and consumptives; examples of each of these categories went bravely down the Indian River with Captain Burnham. So did Cobbett the Cobbler, who is described in contemporary accounts as having had a chalky face and a bright-red nose, which acted as a kind of wet bulb for whiskey. Cobbett the Cobbler could smell the stuff a mile away, and if a bottle was open anywhere in the settlement he would charge through the woods in its direction, yelling so primitively that the others instinctively reached for their rifles. Crazy Ned, a sailor who had once fallen from the topmast to the deck of a ship, was a beardless and irritable man whose injuries unfortunately made him appear, with each step he took, to be attempting to dive into the ground. Ossian B. Hart, who later became governor of Florida, was a violinist. When he played in the evening for his fragile and patrician wife, a periphery of snouts would appear beyond the veranda of his cabin. Hart was Heifetz to the alligators of the Indian River, and the settlement was safe when he was playing. Old Phil and Young Phil Herman might have been twins, not only because their features were similar but because Young Phil looked old and Old Phil looked young. They were actually father and son, and they had a peculiar sense of hospitality. After inviting guests to dinner, Old Phil would scatter crumbs under the table. In the middle of the meal, he would tap his foot, and up through a hole in the floor boards would come one of his trained snakes. While the snake writhed in and out among the legs of the guests, getting all the corn bread it could hold, Old Phil and Young Phil writhed with laughter in their chairs. Near U.S. 1, at Ankona, Florida, there is a memorial tablet that was set up in 1926 by the citizens of St. Lucie County, where most Indian River oranges now come from. "This monument was erected to commemorate the first white settlement on Indian River," it says. "In toil and perils they laid the foundation for the safety we enjoy today."

The settlement might never have ended if Burnham had not been away on a trip when his family and all other families departed in terror of an Indian uprising. The Indians liked Burnham so much that they hung around his house and passed the time of day with him when he was there, helping him with his work and cooking their meals in his pots and pans, but Burnham was in Charleston selling turtles to English importers when the Seminoles killed the settlement storekeeper, who had been cheating them. Word spread that the Indians were massing for a general slaughter, and the settlers prepared to escape, by sea.

Indians were running up the beach as the escape boat pulled away.

Major Russell, one of the settlement's leaders, was standing up in the boat like Washington crossing the Delaware. The Indians hated Russell and always had. One of them fired at him and nicked him in the arm. Feeling pain that night, Russell went into the boat's cabin and groped in the dark for a bottle of salve. Picking up a bottle of black ink by mistake, he poured it over his arm. When the sun came up, he thought he had gangrene. The others knew that it was ink, but they thought even less of Russell than the Indians did, and they said nothing.

None of them could have imagined what would happen. After the group reached St. Augustine and dispersed, Russell went to a doctor and told him to cut off his arm. The doctor said that the arm would get better, but Russell kept insisting, until the doctor did it. Russell died in Orlando thirty-one years later, presumably unaware of the actual truth about his gangrene. Captain Burnham, who had missed the evacuation of the settlement, happened to encounter his family in St. Augustine on his way home from Charleston. He took them back to the Indian River, but only as far south as Merritt Island, where he developed his orange grove and also became, for the rest of his life, the keeper of the lighthouse at Cape Canaveral.

After the Civil War, the grove of Douglas Dummett became increasingly celebrated. Not only was it the oldest in the state, but it also continued to be the largest. In New York, Dummett oranges were worth one dollar more per box than oranges from any other grove. Dummett didn't work particularly hard to achieve this kingship. Most of the time he was fishing, or hunting wildcats on the mainland with his pack of dogs. He was the fastest canoeman on the Indian River, and in the Seminole Indian War he had led a company of the militia so courageously that he was remembered for it. For a number of years he was a member of the Florida House of Representatives. At home, he lived in a small log cabin, and his children and their mother lived in another cabin two hundred feet away. Dummett ate alone out in the grove or in the cabin. His wife had left him years earlier, and the woman who had mothered his son and three daughters was a Negro. The son, Charles, shot himself when he was sixteen. His death was called an accident, but some people on Merritt Island thought he had done it because of the shame he was made to feel for having Negro blood. Dummett himself died in 1873 and is buried in an unmarked grave in an Indian River grove called Fairyland.

New orange growers who arrived after the Civil War tended at first to settle north of the Indian River region along the St. Johns River. The Great Freeze of 1835 had been dismissed as a fluke. It was thought that the freeze had been caused by a mountainous iceberg lying somewhere off St. Augustine, and that another one was unlikely to come. The growers, for economic reasons, wanted to be near the port of Jacksonville. One of the newcomers was Harriet Beecher Stowe, who, with her husband, Professor Calvin Stowe, bought about thirty acres in the village of Mandarin, in 1868. Florida accepted her warmly, partly because she was quoted in the Northern press, soon after her arrival, as having said that people in Florida were "no more inclined to resist the laws or foster the spirit of rebellion" than people in a state like Vermont. An article in the St. Augustine *Examiner* expressed satisfaction "that Mrs. Stowe has done this little to repair the world of evil for which she is responsible in the production of *Uncle Tom's Cabin.*" She taught Sunday school for Negro children in Mandarin, and taught them to read as well, and for seventeen years she ran a successful orange grove—apparently with very little help from her husband. The Professor had a white, airy beard that started on the crown of his head, made an island of his face, and stuck out a foot from his chin. He wore a small skullcap of flaming crimson, and he spent nearly all of his time reading books on the veranda of the Stowe house overlooking the St. Johns. "His red skullcap served mariners as a sort of daytime lighthouse," Mrs. Stowe wrote in an article in the *Christian Union.* In Northern markets, there was considerable demand for fruit boxes stencilled with the words "ORANGES FROM HARRIET BEECHER STOWE—MANDARIN, FLA." Mandarin had been called San Antonio under the Spanish, but the Americans had, more appropriately, renamed it, for a citrus fruit. The word "mandarin" is thought by many people to be a synonym for "tangerine." But tangerines are actually only a variety of mandarin that happened to originate in Tangier. All mandarins—including the Satsuma, the Clementine, the Cleopatra, the Emperor, and the King, or King Mandarin, Orange—have the so-called zipper skin that grows around the segments of the fruit like a loose-fitting glove.

The plantation society of the St. Johns was fairly metropolitan in contrast to life on the Indian River. Families had settled all along the Indian River, but even twenty years after the Civil War they were few enough so that when they saw a sail miles away they could usually tell by the cut of it who was approaching. At night, a family would go out in a small boat, light a lantern, talk, drift, and in thirty minutes catch enough fish to feed them for a week. On trips for supplies in sailboats, they would sometimes see ahead of them a darkness formed on the water's surface by five hundred acres of ducks. As a boat approached, the ducks would rise with a sound of rolling thunder, leaving on the water five hundred acres of down. Everyone slept on down pillows and down mattresses. The river was full of oysters. The shores were full of cabbage palms, whose hearts, boiled, were delicious. Currency was almost unknown. The nearest bank was in Jacksonville. When families put up Northerners who came for part of the winter, payment was often made by check at the end of a visit. For months, these checks would go up and down the Indian River as currency, until they had so many endorsements on them that they looked like petitions. In Titusville, near Merritt Island at the north end of the river, there was a group called The Sons of Rest. Any member who was seen with perspiration on his face was fined twenty-five cents. At the end of each month the money was used to buy a pair of overalls for the member who had worked the least. A man named Cuddyback won four pairs of overalls in a row and the organization disbanded. There was one lawyer on the river. He raised oranges because his practice was so small.

In 1881, Hamilton Disston, a maker of saws from Philadelphia, bought four million acres from the State of Florida in tracts that went almost from coast to coast. He sold off two million acres to a British land company and smaller amounts to other land companies in the United States, keeping some to promote on his own. Tantalizing propaganda began to come out of the state. The early circulars that reached Northern cities and farms usually told the approximate truth, saying, for example, that "many men on the Indian River live entirely upon the returns of a few large trees, spending the whole year in hunting and fishing—doing no work." In the *Horticulturist,* there had been a straight-faced report that an expert named Al Fresco, who had eaten oranges from Europe, the Azores, the West Indies, Australia, and Melanesia, had found none to compare with the oranges of Florida. After the Disston purchase, new stories like that one came out of the state every day. Pamphlets said that if a person put about eighteen hundred dollars into a new grove, he could expect that it would soon be worth thirty thousand. New England farmers read these things and hurried to Florida to share the new paradise with farmers from Georgia and the Carolinas, against whom they had been fighting less than twenty years before. "There is nothing to prevent the establishment in Florida of a race of rich men who will rank with the plantation princes of the old South," the Atlanta *Constitution* decided. Land was ceded to railroads, and hundreds of miles of track were put down within a few years—reaching from Jacksonville south to Orlando and west to Gainesville, and continuing down the spine of Florida to open up the Ridge. "Orange growing," wrote a promoter-in-residence at the Silver Springs Land Company, "is no dead level of monotonous exertion, but one that affords scope for the development of an ingenious mind." Englishmen in particular found this sort of argument irresistible, and one of the curiosities of the orange fever of the eighteen-eighties is that a high proportion of the people it attracted were English. A writer named Iza Duffus Hardy noted that they were "bronzed, hearty, healthy-looking young fellows, high-booted, broad-hatted, with their cheery English voices and jovial laughs, who ride over—sometimes on half-broken Texan ponies—from their respective 'places,' many a mile away, to spend a social hour in town, and report their progress for the benefit and encouragement of those who have not yet 'settled.' This one a year or two ago was a doctor in London, this an artist, that a barrister."

The Dummett grove on Merritt Island became the setting for an absurd charade. Dummett had died in 1873, and in 1881 his place was bought by a fake Italian duke and a fake Italian duchess. He called himself the Duc di Castellucio, and he hurled himself into the orange business. His wife contributed prose to the Jacksonville *Union* and the Titusville *Florida Star.* "The Neapolitans say 'Naples is a bit of paradise fallen from above,' " wrote the Duchess. "If this saying is true, certainly a bit of the same paradise has fallen on Indian River." The Duke and Duchess built an octagonal wooden palace that is still standing. Nearly all the rooms were octagonal, too, but some of them became irregular hexagons after the Duke and Duchess quarrelled so bitterly that they had a partition built precisely through the middle of the house and never spoke to one another again. While they were fighting, their oranges were flourishing, and the Dummett grove remained the largest in the state. The origins of the Duke remain obscure, but the Duchess was Jenny Anheuser, daughter of the St. Louis brewer.

Out on the river, meanwhile, stern-wheelers called the Ina, the Ibis, and the Indian River had begun to operate on regular routes, carrying hundreds of tourists and more settlers on every trip. Rockledge, just south of Cocoa, was for a time the wealthiest winter resort in the United States, and the travel writer C. Vickerstaff Hine called the Indian River "this occidental Adriatic." More and bigger stern-wheelers began to

crowd its channels, until, in 1893, they suddenly became obsolete. Henry
M. Flagler's Florida East Coast Railway had reached the river, and soon
paralleled the length of it on the way to Miami.

To orange growers who had chosen reasonably good land, it appeared that almost anything any promoter had ever written was true. No
one worried much about freezes. For one thing, it was an era of scientific
advances in which triumph over nature seemed not only possible but
inevitable. A cannon had been fired in the streets of Jacksonville in 1888
in the belief that the concussion would kill all the yellow-fever microbes
in the air of the city. Then came the most destructive freeze of the
nineteenth century in Florida. The Great Freeze of 1895 actually happened in two stages—a crippling one in December, 1894, then a killing
one on February 8, 1895, that sent freezing temperatures all the way to
the Florida Keys. Tens of thousands of trees were killed to the bud union,
and thousands more were killed to the ground. More than a billion
oranges had been shipped out of Florida in 1894. The freeze reduced that
figure the following year by ninety-seven per cent.

Many immigrant growers went back to Europe, and American
citizens left the state. Some of those who stayed sold palmetto fronds to
European buyers for conversion into artificial palm trees. Others planted
vegetables in the middles in their groves while they waited for new scions
and new trees to grow. The state's orange crop regained its 1894 level
in 1910, after more groves had been planted on the Ridge. The northern
plantations of the nineteenth century, in the area of Jacksonville, were
permanently abandoned. The population of Orlando was ten thousand
in 1890 and two thousand in 1900. Not until the twenties did it reach
ten thousand again.

The Dummett grove survived the 1895 freeze. Most of its trees have
since been replaced or rebudded, but six of the original ones that were
set out by Douglas Dummett in 1830 are still alive. Each has the girth
of a middle linebacker on a professional football team. The reputation
Indian River oranges established in the nineteenth century has never
flagged. In the eighteen-nineties, *Blackwood's Edinburgh Magazine* said,
"The Indian River orange is not to be mentioned in the same breath with
ordinary oranges. It is a delicacy by itself, hitherto unknown in the
world, and which Spain need never attempt to rival." By the nineteen-
twenties, the term "Indian River" had taken on such a ring of unques-
tioned quality that cities seventy-five miles inland apparently decided
they were seaports. The Ridge, for a while, became the west bank of the

Indian River, and the words "Indian River" appeared on orange crates going out of all parts of Florida. This eventually led to a cease-and-desist order issued in 1930 by the Federal Trade Commission and to the formation, the following year, of the Indian River Citrus League, a growers' organization dedicated to keeping the fame of Indian River citrus unimpeachable and the name parochial. An official Indian River area was established in 1941. It begins about ten miles north of Daytona Beach and continues south through Titusville, Cocoa, Melbourne, Vero Beach, Fort Pierce, and Hobe Sound to Palm Beach. The western demarcation line runs along about fifteen miles inland, more in the south.

Over the past decade or so, the River has grown about one-tenth the number of oranges grown on the Ridge. Each Indian River orange shipped North carries the words "Indian River" on its skin, and this has helped to foster the mistaken belief that the words signify a distinct type of orange rather than the area from which it comes. The same varieties are grown on the River as elsewhere—about fifty per cent Valencias, thirty per cent Pineapples, the rest Hamlins, Parson Browns, and so on. But Indian River oranges have about twenty-five per cent more sugar in them than oranges grown on the Ridge, and they contain more juice as well.

For a long time, people believed that salt airs coming off the Gulf Stream were somehow responsible for the quality of the Indian River orange, and many older growers still feel and will express a mysterious debt to the sea. Pomologists say that the salt-air theory is nonsense. Indian River soil is "heavy," as Floridians put it. That means, as one grower said to me, that "if you let it run through your fingers you can actually get your hands a little dirty." There is no doubt that it is richer than the deep sand on the Ridge; it holds nutrients and moisture better, and it grows a better tree. But the main reason Indian River oranges can be so good is that, until recently at least, most of them have been grown on Sour Orange rootstock. Sour Orange does poorly in the deep sands of the Ridge, and the vigorously foraging Rough Lemon is used there. But Sour Orange does well in the soil near the river. Experiments in Indian River groves have shown that a tree on Sour Orange rootstock will not produce as much fruit as a tree next to it that has been planted on Rough Lemon, but the fruit it does produce will be sweeter and juicier.

To tell the truth, I think the interior oranges, as Ridge oranges are sometimes called, have a little more spirit than oranges of the Indian River. I remember the first Indian River orange I ate when I went over there for a few days after several weeks on the Ridge. It was so sweet that it seemed just to melt away. It reminded me of a description I had read when I was hunting around in a ten-pound tome called *Memoirs of the Faculty of Science and Agriculture, Taihoku Imperial University.* Part of this volume summarizes the first book ever written on citrus fruit. Its author was a northerner who had gone to the south of China and had later rhapsodized in his book about the celebrated Milk Orange of Wen-Chou. "When it is opened, a fragrant mist enchants the people," he wrote. "It is called the Ju Kan, or Milk Orange, because of its resemblance to the taste of cream."

Most tourists who go to Florida probably have no idea what or where the Indian River is, but when they stop to buy oranges they often ask for Indian River fruit. As a result, roadside stands all over the state have huge billboards on their roofs which say "INDIAN RIVER ORANGES." Nearly all of these stands are legitimate. They have trucked-in fruit of the Indian River to satisfy the tourist demand. I remember a stand on the Ridge with a billboard that said, "PULITZER GROVES— PRIZE INDIAN RIVER CITRUS."

The ubiquitous appearances of the term have sometimes misled even regular winter-residents, some of whom think that "Indian River" signifies a type of orange rather than an area from which oranges come. One day in a restaurant in a central Florida town, I got into a conversation with a man who said he had spent the last twelve winters in Naples. He told me that few oranges were grown down there, but they were as fine as any grown anywhere because they were Indian River oranges. Naples is two hundred miles from the Indian River.

Tourists who stop at roadside stands and order a shipment of Indian River oranges almost always get what they order. The stands are merely showcases, and much of the fruit they show is plastic. The order slips are mailed to a packinghouse on the Indian River. For that matter, if a tourist orders Ridge fruit from a stand on the Ridge, the slip is mailed to a packinghouse. Two packinghouses take care of most orders from roadside stands—and department stores—in the state. A couple of years ago, the Indian River Citrus League found a number of roadside stands selling oranges from the Ridge across the counter in bags labeled *"Indian River."* Not all these offenders were in remote parts of the state. One stand selling counterfeit Indian River oranges was on the east side of

U.S. 1. A car veering into this stand might have knocked it into the Indian River.

On Merritt Island, I met an orange grower named Robert Hill, who showed me a good many trees in his grove that had lived through the 1895 freeze. He said that they had been set out by his grandfather, and that other trees on his property had been set out by his father. Narrow roads wind through Merritt Island between high walls of orange trees, which are interspersed with numerous houses of growers. Their holdings can be as small as five acres. Robert Hill's groves cover about fifty acres, and his house, one of the oldest on the island, is on a kind of high bank, perhaps thirty feet above the Indian River. Merritt Island was once covered with pines that yielded such fine lumber that it was known as Merritt Island mahogany. The pines still fringe the island in places, and they rise eighty feet or so above Hill's house. Pine needles cover the ground from the house to the water, and the trunks of the pines are two and a half feet thick. Among them, on Hill's property, is a high Indian mound. Through the pines, the river looks more like an estuary in Maine than a tidal lagoon in Florida. On the day that I was there, a steady breeze was blowing through the trees, and it was not difficult to see what had brought Douglas Dummett, Captain Burnham, and Robert Hill's grandfather to the Indian River.

Hill and I had lunch that day in a place called Ramon's, in Cocoa Beach, and as we were driving there, he pointed out to me the gantries of Cape Canaveral across a few miles of open sand. Ramon's was the sort of place that the eyes take two or three minutes to adjust to. It was as cool as it was dark, despite the smoke and the crowd, which included a high proportion of unattached women. Several bartenders appeared to be tiring under the strain of their work, although it was a few minutes before noon. A number of men were wearing sports shirts, but most were in business suits. Hill, in work clothes, seemed a little incongruous to me in Ramon's. He is a short, colloquial, and thoroughly unself-conscious man, and while we were drinking our second round of bourbon-and-water, he told me that places like Ramon's were what Merritt Island had needed for a long time. "This is living," he said.

The National Aeronautics and Space Administration has acquired three thousand acres of Merritt Island citrus groves. The trees have been leased back to their former owners, but the growers are not permitted to live in the groves or even to store equipment there. Hill's grove is part of the six thousand acres of citrus that remain outside of the space reservation. Aerospace industries, residential housing, and places like Ramon's are taking over so rapidly that in a few years there will be no citrus trees on the island, with the exception of those owned by the National Aeronautics and Space Administration. Hill's son has built a new house next to his father's, and he will probably stay there even if the family grove is cut down. He works for R.C.A. No space-age Chekhov is going to write a play called *The Orange Grove* about the Hill family of Merritt Island.

With aerospace and realty interests preëmpting the northern shores of the Indian River, new plantings have been made in the south. Until 1959, all groves were within two or three miles of the ocean. They had to be, since most of the length of the river is paralleled, a couple of miles inland, by vast savannas, which are largely under water nine months of the year. Much of the west bank of the river is a kind of loaf of ground, described by Floridians as a "bluff" even when it rises only thirteen feet above sea level. But it is high ground indeed compared to what lies beyond it. The savannas reach out to the western horizon, low and flat, filled with saw grass and cat-o'-nine-tails, small cypress trees, and occasional hammocks covered with cabbage palms. Otter live in the savannas, and alligators, wildcat, quail, deer, rabbit, wild turkey, water moccasins, and rattlesnakes. In 1959, the Minute Maid Company went into the savannas with earth-moving machines and heaved up a great ten-foot wall of earth surrounding seven thousand acres of marsh. Then they pumped out the water, graded the sandy soil, and planted six hundred thousand orange trees. It was an impressive feat, and it emboldened many other companies and syndicates to do the same.

Minute Maid itself has since made an even larger reclamation, a mere part of which, not yet fully bearing, is the largest lemon grove in the world. Lemons are even more sensitive to cold than oranges, and the 1895 freeze killed all the lemon trees in Florida. The new Minute Maid grove, which appears to be far enough south to be safe, marks their return—in any appreciable quantity—to the state.

I went out into the savannas one day with Hugh Whelchel, the county agent of St. Lucie County, whose job is to be a kind of intelligence service, communicating to farmers and fruit growers information that derives from scientific and academic circles. Whelchel, a tall and bald man of about forty, was a citrus major in the Class of 1949 at Florida Southern College, and, like all Florida county agents, he is officially ranked as an associate professor of the University of Florida. Riding out into the marsh country with him, in his pickup truck, I asked him about the ten-inch laceless boots he was wearing, because I had noticed that nearly everyone who works in Florida orange groves wears them. "They keep the sand out," he said. "I like a loose-fitting boot like these better than a tight boot, because fangs can go through these and not get to your leg."

"How often do you see a rattlesnake?" I asked.

"Oh, hell, I guess I kill ten or fifteen a year."

"You keep a gun here in the truck?"

"No. I got a jack handle in the back there."

We drove up a hill of dirt, over a dike, and down into the Minute Maid reclamation, where young trees had just come into bearing for the first time. The perfect geometry of the groves on the Ridge, with straight middles stretching for hundreds of yards, had always seemed remarkable to me. Some of the middles in this grove ran on for five miles.

The ground had been engineered and sculpted so that rainwater would run into furrows in the middles, then through swales and ditches into a perimeter canal, running all the way around the grove, inside the dike. The water is pumped over the dike into state flood-control canals. Whelchel said that water management is the chief concern of all citrus growers of the Indian River area, whether in the new reclamation land or in the older groves. The water table is often less than three feet down, and that is as far as roots can go. Sometimes, in a single day, enough rain falls to saturate the soil, and growers have to be prepared to drain off the excess or they will lose their trees. In spring, however, it is so dry that they have to pump the water back into the groves or the trees will die for lack of it. To be fully prepared for the dry season, Minute Maid left one square mile of savanna, in the center of each of its vast groves, untouched. The square mile acts as a reservoir. Since a tree's branch structure is proportionate in size to its root structure, Indian River trees are set in raised beds, as they have been since the nineteenth century. In this way, more root structure can grow above the water table. Nonetheless, Indian River trees are smaller than trees of similar age on the Ridge.

Nearly all of the new orange plantings in the reclaimed savannas are on Rough Lemon rootstock. The trees grow faster, bear more fruit, and are less susceptible to virus diseases than they would be on Sour Orange rootstock. Each individual orange is not up to the usual standard of the Indian River, but that hardly matters, since most oranges are now grown for concentrate plants—for the frozen people, as the makers of concentrate are often called in Florida—and a grower's profits are determined more by volume than by quality. The Rough Lemon rootstocks of the savanna plantations are disturbing to Whelchel and to other county agents and to many growers in the area. They feel that the rise of concentrate may be causing the end, in a sense, of the Indian River. The savanna plantations are officially part of the Indian River, and their owners could take advantage of the name if prices were high enough for them to want to market fresh oranges. Nearly all Indian River trees used to be on Sour Orange, but fifty per cent of them are now on Rough Lemon. "Packinghouses can be expected to discriminate against Rough Lemon fruit," Whelchel said. "But there is no guarantee of this. We can lose the golden name of the Indian River if we start shipping fresh fruit grown on Rough Lemon rootstock. A smart fresh-fruit advertiser would plug oranges grown strictly on Sour Orange."

One day, I went into an Indian River packinghouse to watch the objects of all this concern being readied for market. Citrus packinghouses are much the same wherever they are. In a sense, they are more like beauty parlors than processing plants. To make their oranges marketably orange, packers can do two things, one of which is, loosely speaking, natural and the other wholly artificial. The first is a process that was once known as "gassing," but the unpleasant connotations of that word have caused it to be generally suppressed, and most people now say "degreening" instead. Green or partly green oranges are put into chambers where, for as much as four days, ethylene gas is circulated among them. The gas helps eliminate the chlorophyll in the flavedo, or outer skin, which is, in a sense, tiled with cells that contain both orange and green pigments. The orange ones are carotenoids, the green ones are chlorophylls, and the chlorophylls are so much more intense that, while they are there, the orange color will not show through. Both of these pigments are floating around in a clear, colorless enzyme called chlorophyllase, which will destroy chlorophyll on contact but has no effect on anything else. The chlorophyll is protected from the enzyme by a thin membrane called a tonoplast. In chilly weather, the tonoplast loses its strength and breaks down, and the enzyme gets at the chlorophyll and destroys it. The orange becomes orange. It would seem to be simple enough to pick a green orange and put it in a refrigerator until it turns orange, but, unfortunately, the membrane that protects the chlorophyll from the enzyme will no longer react in the same way once an orange is picked.

In the early years of this century, Californians noticed that oranges tended to become more orange in rooms where kerosene stoves were burning. Assuming that the heat was responsible, orange men on both coasts erected vast wooden ovens called "sweat rooms," installed banks of kerosene stoves, and turned out vividly colored petroleum-smoked oranges. The more enthusiastic they got, the more stoves they put in. The emerging oranges were half dehydrated. And, with alarming frequency, whole packinghouses would burst into flame. That era closed when it was discovered that the ethylene gas produced in the combustion of the kerosene was the actual agent that was affecting the color of the oranges. Ethylene appears to anesthetize, or at least to relax, the membrane that protects the chlorophyll. All fruits take in oxygen and give off carbon dioxide through their skins, and some fruits, interestingly enough, give off ethylene gas as well when they breathe. A pile of green oranges will turn color if stored in a room with enough bananas. One McIntosh apple, puffing hard, can turn out enough ethylene to de-green a dozen oranges in a day or two.

Oranges are gassed in both California and Florida, often merely to improve an already good color. A once-orange orange which has turned green again on the tree will not react to it. Neither will an orange that is not ripe.

The second method of affecting the color of oranges is more direct: they can be bathed, at times, in a dye whose chemical name is 1-(2, 5-dimethoxy-phenylazo)-2 napthol, popularly known as Citrus Red No. 2. This is the only dye permitted by federal law. The use of it is against California law, and the law of Florida, as a kind of safeguard against criticism, requires that dyed oranges be labeled as such and that they contain ten per cent more juice than the established minimum for undyed oranges. In practice, this regulation affects only the Ridge, because Indian River packinghouses are, almost without exception, too proud to dye their oranges. Citrus Red No. 2 is an aggressive and unnerving pink, but, applied to the green and yellow-green and yellow-orange surfaces of oranges, it produces an acceptable color. How acceptable seems to differ with individuals, and, in a more remarkable way, with geography. Judging by sales figures, people in New England instinctively reject oranges that have the purple letters "COLOR ADDED" stamped on their skins. In the Middle West, though, color-added oranges are in demand. Stores have even put advertisements in Chicago newspapers announcing when color-added oranges were available. Distributors there say they could sell many more oranges if the packinghouses would intensify the dye. In Florida, citrus men sometimes say of Midwesterners, "These people don't want oranges. They want tomatoes."

In an average year, the color-add season only lasts for several weeks in the autumn. There is no need for dye in the winter. In the late spring, high-season Valencias may turn partly green again; the dye has an unsatisfactory effect on them, however, and is seldom used. In the course of a Florida season, as one variety follows another, there is a general rise in the internal quality of oranges, and high-season Valencias are, on the average, the best oranges available at any time in the year. They are often mottled with green, though, and many people pass them by.

The oranges in the Indian River packinghouse I visited had been gassed and were being washed in warm soapy water, brushed with palmetto-fiber brushes, and dried by foam-rubber squeegees and jets of hot air. Brushed again with nylon bristles to bring out their natural shine, they were coated with Johnson's Wax until they glistened like cats' eyes. The wax, which is edible, replaces a natural wax that is lost when the oranges are cleaned. Apples, cherries, and the rest of the pip and stone fruits look much the same when they enter a packinghouse as when they leave, but when oranges arrive they are covered with various things, from sooty mold to dust smeared by heavy dews. They have to be washed, but without their surface wax they would breathe very rapidly and begin to shrivel within hours. The natural wax therefore has to be replaced. Packers replace it and then some—but if they apply too much wax, the orange will suffocate and its flavor will become, at best, insipid.

Oranges are graded after they are waxed. Eight ladies stood beside a conveyor of rolling oranges, taking out the ones whose skins were blemished by things like wind scars, oil blotches from petroleum sprays, hail damage, and excessive russeting on the blossom end. The oranges they eliminated would go to concentrate plants. Eliminations, as they are called, are something quite different from culls—split or rotting oranges that are taken out before the beautifying process begins. The ladies who do the grading wear gloves, because a light pass of a fingernail over the surface of an orange can rupture oil cells, causing peel oil to well out onto the surface and not only discolor the orange but also nurture fungi that destroy it.

Oranges do not bruise one another the way apples sometimes do, and an orange, in fact, can absorb a blow that would finish an apple. Oranges can actually be bounced like rubber balls without damage, except that when they are dropped more than a foot they will start to breathe too rapidly. Truck drivers who bring them into the packing-houses from the groves wade along through rivers of oranges while they are emptying their trucks, taking care to slide their feet along the bottoms of the chutes, like trout fishermen moving upstream. Government inspectors, who work every day all day in packinghouses and concentrate plants, squeeze a standard boxful—an average of about two hundred oranges—from each truckload, and they order the entire lot destroyed if the sample is not about ten per cent sugar and does not amount to at least four and a half gallons of juice.

Oranges that happen to be going to New York cross the Hudson River on barges and enter the city at Pier 28 at the western end of Canal Street. All fresh fruit of any kind that is shipped to New York City for auction is sold at Pier 28. The pier's interior is like the inside of an aircraft hangar and fruits from everywhere are stacked in lots in long, close rows—oranges and grapefruit from the Ridge, California oranges, apples, avocados, pears, plums, cherries, lemons, grapes, pomegranates, and so on. Over at one side, separated by a wide area from all the other crates and boxes, is the fruit of the Indian River. A man from the Indian River is always there to look after it, and he has no counterpart elsewhere on the pier. Buyers walk around making notes, then they go upstairs into a room that could have been built as the auditorium of a nineteenth-century high school. The walls are made of tongue-and-groove boards and the wooden seats are set on frameworks of cast iron, which are bolted to the floor. The room seems to contain about ninety men and ninety lighted cigars. In London in the eighteenth century, oranges were auctioned "by the candle." A pin was pushed through a candle not far from the top, and when the candle was lighted, the bidding began. When the pin dropped, the most recent bidder got the oranges. In New York in the present era, oranges appear to be auctioned by cigar. The air in the auction room gets so heavy with smoke that if anything as light as a pin were to drop, it would probably stop falling before it reached the floor. The auctioneer sits on a stage, usually alone. The man from Indian River sits next to him when he auctions the fruit of the Indian River.

# The Pine Barrens

For many readers, *The Pine Barrens* is their favorite McPhee book, the one they reread and give to friends. It makes a story out of rich and forgotten materials, imparting a sense of place and people as works of fiction or reportage rarely do. Perhaps it enjoys this status because it describes a legendary piece of terrain: the "pines" of south-central New Jersey, a great sandy tract of sparsely populated forest that lies between the state's coastal resorts and its industrial corridor of Interstate 95. Within a day's drive of several million people stands this encircled and threatened wilderness, the improbable heart of Eastern megalopolis, set equidistant from Richmond and Boston.

McPhee envisions the pines as a *locus classicus,* the place in America where cultural traditions of North and South meet, where pre-Revolutionary history is recorded and post-Bicentennial battles will be fought by developers and ecologists. The region is both an archetype and another country; a place so at variance with modern norms that it breeds perfect descendants of America's original stock, "pineys" like Jim Leek: "There ain't nobody bothers you here. You can be alone. I'm just a woods boy. I wouldn't want to live in a town." To McPhee's readers, up to their hips with the bothers of town, that phrase is both angelus and alarm, since city boys are always designing giant jetports and amusement centers for the pines. Yet he elicits these responses only by insinuation, and by weaving a subtle pattern of narrative, dialogue, and exposition. The following selections set his principal scene, introduce the main characters, and perhaps suggest how a place like the Pine Barrens echoes its fabled Air Tune, a melody that is "there, everywhere, just beyond hearing."—*WLH*

# The Woods from Hog Wallow

From the fire tower on Bear Swamp Hill, in Washington Township, Burlington County, New Jersey, the view usually extends about twelve miles. To the north, forest land reaches to the horizon. The trees are mainly oaks and pines, and the pines predominate. Occasionally, there are long, dark, serrated stands of Atlantic white cedars, so tall and so closely set that they seem to be spread against the sky on the ridges of hills, when in fact they grow along streams that flow through the forest. To the east, the view is similar, and few people who are not native to the region can discern essential differences from the high cabin of the fire tower, even though one difference is that huge areas out in this direction are covered with dwarf forests, where a man can stand among the trees and see for miles over their uppermost branches. To the south, the view is twice broken slightly—by a lake and by a cranberry bog—but otherwise it, too, goes to the horizon in forest. To the west, pines, oaks, and cedars continue all the way, and the western horizon includes the summit of another hill—Apple Pie Hill—and the outline of another fire tower, from which the view three hundred and sixty degrees around is virtually the same as the view from Bear Swamp Hill, where, in a moment's sweeping glance, a person can see hundreds of square miles of wilderness. The picture of New Jersey that most people hold in their minds is so different from this one that, considered beside it, the Pine Barrens, as they are called, become as incongruous as they are beautiful. West and north of the Pine Barrens is New Jersey's central transportation corridor, where traffic of freight and people is more concentrated than it is anywhere else in the world. The corridor is one great compression of industrial shapes, industrial sounds, industrial air, and thousands and thousands of houses webbing over the spaces between the factories. Railroads and magnificent highways traverse this crowded scene, and by 1985 New Jersey hopes to have added so many additional high-speed roads that the present New Jersey Turnpike will be quite closely neighbored by the equivalent of at least six other turnpikes, all going in the same direction. In and around the New Jersey corridor, towns indistinguishably abut one another. Of the great unbroken city that will one day reach at least from Boston to Richmond, this section is already built. New Jersey has nearly a thousand people per square mile—the greatest population density of any state in the Union. In parts of northern New Jersey, there are as many as forty thousand people per square mile. In the central area of the Pine Barrens—the forest land that is still so undeveloped that it can be called wilderness—there are only fifteen people per square mile. This area, which includes about six hundred and fifty thousand acres, is nearly as large as Yosemite National Park. It is almost identical in size with Grand Canyon National Park, and it is much larger than Sequoia National Park, Great Smoky Mountains National Park, or, for that matter, most of the national parks in the United States. The people who live in the Pine Barrens are concentrated mainly in small forest towns, so the region's uninhabited sections are quite large—twenty thousand acres here, thirty thousand acres there—and in one section of well over a hundred thousand acres there are only twenty-one people. The Pine Barrens are so close to New York that on a very clear night a bright light in the pines would be visible from the Empire State Building. A line ruled on a map from Boston to Richmond goes straight through the middle of the Pine Barrens. The halfway point between Boston and Richmond —the geographical epicenter of the developing megalopolis—is in the northern part of the woods, about twenty miles from Bear Swamp Hill.

Technically, the Pine Barrens are much larger than the thousand or so square miles of them that remain wild, and their original outline is formed by the boundaries of a thick layer of sand soils that covers much of central and southern New Jersey—down the coast from the outskirts of Asbury Park to the Cape May Peninsula, and inland more than halfway across the state. Settlers in the seventeenth and eighteenth centuries found these soils unpromising for farms, left the land uncleared, and began to refer to the region as the Pine Barrens. People in New Jersey still use the term, with variants such as "the pine belt," "the pinelands," and, most frequently, "the pines." Gradually, development of one kind or another has moved in over the edges of the forest, reducing the circumference of the wild land and creating a man-made boundary in place of the natural one. This transition line is often so abrupt that in many places on the periphery of the pines it is possible to be at one moment in farmland, or even in a residential development or an industrial zone, and in the next moment to be in the silence of a bewildering green country, where a journey of forty or fifty miles is necessary to get to the farms and factories on the other side. I don't know where the exact center of the pines may be, but in recent years I have spent considerable time there and have made outlines of the integral woodland on topographic maps and road maps, and from them I would judge that the heart of the pine country is in or near a place called Hog Wallow. There are twenty-five people in Hog Wallow. Some of them describe it, without any apparent intention to be clever, as a suburb of Jenkins, a town three miles away, which has forty-five people. One resident of Hog Wallow is Frederick Chambers Brown. I met him one summer morning when I stopped at his house to ask for water.

Fred Brown's house is on an unpaved road that curves along the edge of a wide cranberry bog. What attracted me to it was the pump that stands in his yard. It was something of a wonder that I noticed the pump, because there were, among other things, eight automobiles in the yard, two of them on their sides and one of them upside down, all ten years old or older. Around the cars were old refrigerators, vacuum cleaners, partly dismantled radios, cathode-ray tubes, a short wooden ski, a large wooden mallet, dozens of cranberry picker's boxes, many tires, an orange crate dated 1946, a cord or so of firewood, mandolins, engine heads, and maybe a thousand other things. The house itself, two stories high, was covered with tarpaper that was peeling away in some places, revealing its original shingles, made of Atlantic white cedar from the stream courses of the surrounding forest. I called out to ask if anyone was home, and a voice inside called back, "Come in. Come in. Come on the hell in."

I walked through a vestibule that had a dirt floor, stepped up into a kitchen, and went on into another room that had several overstuffed chairs in it and a porcelain-topped table, where Fred Brown was seated, eating a pork chop. He was dressed in a white sleeveless shirt, ankle-top shoes, and undershorts. He gave me a cheerful greeting and, without asking why I had come or what I wanted, picked up a pair of khaki trousers that had been tossed onto one of the overstuffed chairs and asked me to sit down. He set the trousers on another chair, and he apologized for being in the middle of his breakfast, explaining that he seldom drank much but the night before he had had a few drinks and this had caused his day to start slowly. "I don't know what's the matter with me, but there's got to be something the matter with me, because drink don't agree with me anymore," he said. He had a raw onion in one hand, and while he talked he shaved slices from the onion and ate them between bites of the chop. He was a muscular and well-built man, with short, bristly white hair, and he had bright, fast-moving eyes in a wide-open face. His legs were trim and strong, with large muscles in the calves. I guessed that he was about sixty, and for a man of sixty he seemed to be in remarkably good shape. He was actually seventy-nine. "My rule is: Never eat except when you're hungry," he said, and he ate another slice of the onion.

In a straight-backed chair near the doorway to the kitchen sat a young man with long black hair, who wore a visored red leather cap that had darkened with age. His shirt was coarse-woven and had eyelets down a V neck that was laced with a thong. His trousers were made of canvas, and he was wearing gum boots. His arms were folded, his legs were stretched out, he had one ankle over the other, and as he sat there he appeared to be sighting carefully past his feet, as if his toes were the outer frame of a gunsight and he could see some sort of target in the floor. When I had entered, I had said hello to him, and he had nodded without looking up. He had a long, straight nose and high cheekbones, in a deeply tanned face that was, somehow, gaunt. I had no idea whether he was shy or hostile. Eventually, when I came to know him, I found him to be as shy a person as I have ever had a chance to know. His name is Bill Wasovwich, and he lives alone in a cabin about half a mile from Fred. First his father, then his mother left him when he was a young boy, and he grew up depending on the help of various people in the pines. One of them, a cranberry grower, employs him and has given him some acreage, in which Bill is building a small cranberry bog of his own, "turfing it out" by hand. When he is not working in the bogs, he goes roaming, as he puts it, setting out cross-country on long, looping journeys, hiking about thirty miles in a typical day, in search of what he calls "events"—surprising a buck, or a gray fox, or perhaps a poacher or a man with a still. Almost no one who is not native to the pines could do this, for the woods have an undulating sameness, and the understory—huckleberries, sheep laurel, sweet fern, high-bush blueberry—is often so dense that a wanderer can walk in a fairly tight circle and think that he is moving in a straight line. State forest rangers spend a good part of their time finding hikers and hunters, some of whom have vanished for days. In his long, pathless journeys, Bill always emerges from the woods near his cabin—and about when he plans to. In the fall, when thousands of hunters come into the pines, he sometimes works as a guide. In the evenings, or in the daytime when he is not working or roaming, he goes to Fred Brown's house and sits there for hours. The old man is a widower whose seven children are long since gone from Hog Wallow, and he is as expansively talkative and worldly as the young one is withdrawn and wild. Although there are fifty-three years between their ages, it is obviously fortunate for each of them to be the other's neighbor.

That first morning, while Bill went on looking at his outstretched toes, Fred got up from the table, put on his pants, and said he was going to cook me a pork chop, because I looked hungry and ought to eat something. It was about noon, and I was even hungrier than I may have looked, so I gratefully accepted his offer, which was a considerable one. There are two or three small general stores in the pines, but for anything as fragile as a fresh pork chop it is necessary to make a round trip from Fred's place of about fifty miles. Fred went into the kitchen and dropped a chop into a frying pan that was crackling with hot grease. He has a fairly new four-burner stove that uses bottled gas. He keeps water in a large bowl on a table in the kitchen and ladles some when he wants it. While he cooked the meat, he looked out a window through a stand of pitch pines and into the cranberry bog. "I saw a big buck out here last night with velvet on his horns," he said. "Them horns is soft when they're in velvet." On a nail high on one wall of the room that Bill and I were sitting in was a large meat cleaver. Next to it was a billy club. The wall itself was papered in a flower pattern, and the wallpaper continued out across the ceiling and down the three other walls, lending the room something of the appearance of the inside of a gift box. In some parts of the ceiling, the paper had come loose. "I didn't paper this year," Fred said. "For the last couple months, I've had sinus." The floor was covered with old rugs. They had been put down in random pieces, and in some places as many as six layers were stacked up. In winter, when the temperature approaches zero, the worst cold comes through the floor. The only source of heat in the house is a wood-burning stove in the main room. There were seven calendars on the walls, all current and none with pictures of nudes. Fading into pastel on one wall was a rotogravure photograph of President and Mrs. Eisenhower. A framed poem read:

> God hath not promised
> Sun without rain
> Joy without sorrow
> Peace without pain.

Noticing my interest in all this, Fred reached into a drawer and showed me what appeared to be a postcard. On it was a photograph of a woman, and Fred said with a straight face that she was his present girl, adding that he meets her regularly under a juniper tree on a road farther south in the pines. The woman, whose appearance suggested strongly that she had never been within a great many miles of the Pine Barrens, was wearing nothing at all.

I asked Fred what all those cars were doing in his yard, and he said that one of them was in running condition and the rest were its predecessors. The working vehicle was a 1956 Mercury. Each of the seven others had at one time or another been his best car, and each, in turn, had lain down like a sick animal and had died right there in the yard, unless it had been towed home after a mishap elsewhere in the pines. Fred recited, with affection, the history of each car. Of one old Ford, for example, he said, "I upset that up to Speedwell in the creek." And of an even older car, a station wagon, he said, "I busted that one up in the snow. I met a car on a little hill, and hit the brake, and hit a tree." One of the cars had met its end at a narrow bridge about four miles from Hog Wallow, where Fred had hit a state trooper, head on.

The pork was delicious and almost crisp. Fred gave me a potato with it, and a pitcher of melted grease from the frying pan to pour over the potato. He also handed me a loaf of bread and a dish of margarine, saying, "Here's your bread. You can have one piece or two. Whatever you want."

Fred apologized for not having a phone, after I asked where I would have to go to make a call, later on. He said, "I don't have no phone because I don't have no electric. If I had electric, I would have had a phone in here a long time ago." He uses a kerosene lamp, a propane lamp, and two flashlights.

He asked where I was going, and I said that I had no particular destination, explaining that I was in the pines because I found it hard to believe that so much unbroken forest could still exist so near the big Eastern cities, and I wanted to see it while it was still there. "Is that so?" he said, three times. Like many people in the pines, he often says things three times. "Is that so? Is *that* so?"

I asked him what he thought of a plan that has been developed by Burlington and Ocean Counties to create a supersonic jetport in the pines, connected by a spur of the Garden State Parkway to a new city of two hundred and fifty thousand people, also in the pines.

"They've been talking about that for three years, and they've never give up," Fred said.

"It'd be the end of these woods," Bill said. This was the first time I heard Bill speak. I had been there for an hour, and he had not said a word. Without looking up, he said again, "It'd be the end of these woods, I can tell you that."

Fred said, "They could build ten jetports around me. I wouldn't give a damn."

"You ain't going to be around very long," Bill said to him. "It would be the end of these woods."

Fred took that as a fact, and not as an insult. "Yes, it would be the end of these woods," he said. "But there'd be people here you could do business with."

Bill said, "There ain't no place like this left in the country, I don't believe—and I travelled around a little bit, too."

Eventually, I made the request I had intended to make when I walked in the door. "Could I have some water?" I said to Fred. "I have a jerry can and I'd like to fill it at the pump."

"Hell, yes," he said. "That isn't my water. That's God's water. That's God's water. That right, Bill?"

"I *guess* so," Bill said, without looking up. "It's good water, I can tell you that."

"That's God's water," Fred said again. "Take all you want."

Outside, on the pump housing, was a bright-blue coffee tin full of priming water. I primed the pump and, before filling the jerry can, cupped my hands and drank. The water of the Pine Barrens is soft and pure, and there is so much of it that, like the forest above it, it is an incongruity in place and time. In the sand under the pines is a natural reservoir of pure water that, in volume, is the equivalent of a lake seventy-five feet deep with a surface of a thousand square miles. If all the impounding reservoirs, storage reservoirs, and distribution reservoirs in the New York City water system were filled to capacity—from Neversink and Schoharie to the Croton basin and Central Park—the Pine Barrens aquifer would still contain thirty times as much water. So little of this water is used that it can be said to be untapped. Its constant temperature is fifty-four degrees, and, in the language of a hydrological report on the Pine Barrens prepared in 1966 for the United States Geological Survey, "it can be expected to be bacterially sterile, odorless, clear; its chemical purity approaches that of uncontaminated rain-water or melted glacier ice."

In the United States as a whole, only about thirty per cent of the rainfall gets into the ground; the rest is lost to surface runoff or to evaporation, transpiration from leaves, and similar interceptors. In the Pine Barrens, fully half of all precipitation makes its way into the great aquifer, for, as the government report put it, "the loose, sandy soil can imbibe as much as six inches of water per hour." The Pine Barrens rank as one of the greatest natural recharging areas in the world. Thus, the City of New York, say, could take all its daily water requirements out of the pines without fear of diminishing the basic supply. New Jersey could sell the Pine Barrens' "annual ground-water discharge"—the part that at the moment is running off into the Atlantic Ocean—for about two hundred million dollars a year. However, New Jersey does not sell a drop, in part because the state has its own future needs to consider. In the eighteen-seventies, Joseph Wharton, the Philadelphia mineralogist and financier for whom the Wharton School of Finance and Commerce of the University of Pennsylvania is named, recognized the enormous potentiality of the Pine Barrens as a source of water for Philadelphia, and between 1876 and 1890 he gradually acquired nearly a hundred thousand contiguous acres of Pine Barrens land. Wharton's plan called for thirty-three shallow reservoirs in the pines, connected by a network of canals to one stupendous reservoir in Camden, from which an aqueduct would go under the Delaware River and into Philadelphia, where the pure waters of New Jersey would emerge from every tap, replacing a water supply that has been described as "dirty, bacterial soup." Wharton's plan was never executed, mainly because the New Jersey legislature drew itself together and passed prohibiting legislation. Wharton died in 1909. The Wharton Tract, as his immense New Jersey landholding was called, has remained undeveloped. It was considered as a site for the United States Air Force Academy. The state was slow in acquiring it in the public interest, but at last did so in 1955, and the whole of it is now Wharton State Forest.

All the major river systems in the United States are polluted, and so are most of the minor ones, but all the small rivers and streams in the Pine Barrens are potable. The pinelands have their own divide. The Pine Barrens rivers rise in the pines. Some flow west to the Delaware; most flow southeast directly into the sea. There are no through-flowing streams in the pines—no waters coming in from cities and towns on higher ground, as is the case almost everywhere else on the Atlantic coastal plain. I have spent many weekends on canoe trips in the Pine Barrens—on the Wading River, the Oswego, the Batsto, the Mullica. There is no white water in any of these rivers, but they move along fairly rapidly; they are so tortuous that every hundred yards or so brings a new scene—often one that is reminiscent of canoeing country in the northern states and in Canada. Even on bright days, the rivers can be dark and almost sunless under stands of white cedar, and then, all in a moment, they run into brilliant sunshine where the banks rise higher and the forest of oak and pine is less dense. One indication of the size of the water resource below the Pine Barrens is that the streams keep flowing without great declines in volume even in prolonged times of drought. When streams in other parts of New Jersey were reduced to near or total dryness in recent years, the rivers in the pines were virtually unaffected. The characteristic color of the water in the streams is the color of tea —a phenomenon, often called "cedar water," that is familiar in the Adirondacks, as in many other places where tannins and other organic waste from riparian cedar trees combine with iron from the ground water to give the rivers a deep color. In summer, the cedar water is ordinarily so dark that the riverbeds are obscured, and while drifting along one has a feeling of being afloat on a river of fast-moving potable ink. For a few days after a long rain, however, the water is almost colorless. At these times, one can look down into it from a canoe and see the white sand bottom, ten or twelve feet below, and it is as clear as an image in the lens of a camera, with sunken timbers now and again coming into view and receding rapidly, at the speed of the river. Every strand of subsurface grass and every contour of the bottom sand is so sharply defined that the deep water above it seems, and is, irresistibly pure. Sea captains once took the cedar water of the Pine Barrens rivers with them on voyages, because cedar water would remain sweet and potable longer than any other water they could find.

According to the government report, "The Pine Barrens have no equal in the northeastern United States not only for magnitude of water in storage and availability of recharge, but also for the ease and economy with which a large volume of water could be withdrawn." Typically, a pipe less than two inches in diameter driven thirty feet into the ground will produce fifty-five gallons a minute, and a twelve-inch pipe could bring up a million gallons a day. But, with all this, the vulnerability of the Pine Barrens aquifer is disturbing to contemplate. The water table is shallow in the pines, and the aquifer is extremely sensitive to contamination. The sand soil, which is so superior as a catcher of rain, is not good at filtering out or immobilizing wastes. Pollutants, if they happen to get into the water, can travel long distances. Industry or even extensive residential development in the central pinelands could spread contaminants widely through the underground reservoir.

When I had finished filling the jerry can from Fred Brown's pump, I took another drink, and I said to him, "You're lucky to live over such good water."

"You're telling me," he said. "You can put this water in a jug and put it away for a year and it will still be the same. Water from outside of these woods would stink. Outside of these woods, some water stinks when you pump it out of the ground. The people that has dug deep around here claims that there are streams of water under this earth that runs all the time."

In the weeks that followed, I stopped in many times to see Fred, and saw nearly as much of Bill. They rode with me through the woods, in my car, for five and six hours at a time. In the evenings, we returned to Fred's place with food from some peripheral town. It is possible to cross the pines on half a dozen state or federal roads, but very little of interest is visible from them. Several county roads—old crown roads with uneven macadam surfaces—connect the pine communities, but it is necessary to get off the paved roads altogether in order to see much of the forest. The areas are spacious—fifty, sixty, and seventy-five thousand acres—through which run no paved roads of any kind. There are many hundreds of miles of unpaved roads through the pines—two tracks in the sand, with underbrush growing up between them. Hunters use them, and foresters, firefighters, and woodcutters. A number of these sand roads have been there, and have remained unchanged, since before the American Revolution. They developed, for the most part, as Colonial stage routes, trails to charcoal pits, pulpwood-and-lumber roads, and connecting roads between communities that have disappeared from the world. In a place called Washington, five of these roads converge in the forest, as if from star points, and they suggest the former importance of Washington, but all that is left of the town is a single fragment of a stone structure. The sand roads are marked on topographic maps with parallel dotted lines, and driving on them can be something of a sport. It is possible to drive all day on the sand roads, and more than halfway across the state, but most people need to stop fairly often to study the topographic maps, for the roads sometimes come together in fantastic ganglia, and even when they are straight and apparently uncomplicated they constantly fork, presenting unclear choices between the main chance and culs-de-sac, of which there are many hundreds. No matter where we were—far up near Mt. Misery, in the northern part of the pines, or over in the western extremities of the Wharton Tract, or down in the southeast, near the Bass River—Fred kept calling out directions. He always knew exactly where he was going. Fred was nearly forty when the first paved roads were built in the pines. Once, not far from the Godfrey Bridge on the Wading River, he said, "Look at these big pines. You would never think that I was as old as these big pines, would you? I seen all of these big pines grow. I remember this when it was all cut down for charcoal." A short distance away, he pointed into a high stand of pitch pines and scarlet oaks, and he said, "That's the old Joe Holloway field. Holloway had a water-powered sawmill." In another part of the woods, we passed a small bald area, and he said, "That's the Dan Dillett field, where Dan made charcoal." As the car kept moving, bouncing in the undulations of the sand and scraping against blueberry bushes and scrub-oak boughs, Fred kept narrating, picking fragments of the past out of the forest, in moments separated by miles: "Right here in this piece of woods is more rattlesnakes than anyplace else in the State of New Jersey. They had a sawmill in there. They used to kill three or four rattlesnakes when they was watering their horses at noon. Rattlesnakes like water. . . . See that fire tower over there? The man in that tower— you take him fifty yards away from that tower and he's lost. He don't know the woods. He don't know the woods. He don't know the woods. He don't know nothing. He can't even fry a hamburger. . . . I've gunned this part of the woods since I was ten years old. I know every foot of it here. . . . Apple Pie Hill is a thunderstriking high hill. You don't realize how high until you get up here. It's the long slope of a hill that makes a high one. . . . See that open spot in there? A group of girls used to keep a house in there. It was called Noah's Ark. . . . I worked this piece of cedar off here. . . . I worked this bog for Joe Wharton once. My father used to work for Joe Wharton, too. He used to come and stay with my father. Joe Wharton was the nicest man you ever seen. That is, if you didn't lie to him. He was quiet. He didn't smile very often. I don't know as I ever heard him laugh out loud. . . . These are the Hocken Lowlands." The Hocken Lowlands surround the headwaters of Tulpehocken Creek, about five miles northwest of Hog Wallow, and are not identified on maps, not even on the large-scale topographic maps. As we moved along, Fred had a name for almost every rise and dip in the land. "This is Sandy Ridge," he said. "That road once went into a bog. Houses were there. Now there's nothing there. . . . This is Bony's Hole. A man named Bony used to water his horse here." Every so often, Fred would reach into his pocket and touch up his day with a minimal sip from a half pint of whiskey. He merely touched the bottle to his lips, then put it away. He did this at irregular intervals, and one day, when he had a new half pint, he took more than five hours to reduce the level of the whiskey from the neck to the shoulders of the bottle. At an intersection of two sand roads in the Wharton Tract, he pointed to a depression in the ground and said, "That hole in the ground was the cellar of an old jug tavern. That cellar was where they kept the jugs. There was a town here called Mount. That tavern is where my grandpop got drunk the last time he got drunk in his life. Grandmother went up to get him. When she came in, he said, 'Mary, what are you doing here?' He was so ashamed to see her there—and his daughter with her. He left a jug of whiskey right on the table, and his wife took one of his hands and his daughter the other and they led him out of there and past Washington Field and home to Jenkins Neck. He lived fifty years. He lived fifty years, and growed cranberries. He lived fifty years more, and he was never drunk again."

One evening, when it was almost dark and we were about five miles from Fred's place, he told me to stop, and he said, "See that upland red cedar? I helped set that out." Red cedar is not native in the Pine Barrens, and this one stood alone among the taller oaks and pines, in a part of the forest that seemed particularly remote. "I went to school there, by that red cedar," Fred said. "There was twenty-five of us in the school. We all walked. We wore leather boots in the winter that got soaked through and your feet froze. When you got home, you had to pull off your boots on a bootjack. In the summer, when I was a boy, if you wanted to go anywhere you rolled up your pantlegs, put your shoes on your shoulder, and you walked wherever you was going. The pigs and cows was everywhere. There was wild bulls, wild cows, wild boars. That's how Hog Wallow got its name. They call them the good old days. What do you think of that, Bill?"

"I wish I was back there, I can tell you that," Bill said.

# The Separate World

In 1859, when the population of the central Pine Barrens was about as large as it has ever been, the area had nonetheless remained wild enough for the *Atlantic* to report, "It is a region aboriginal in savagery, grand in the aspects of untrammelled Nature; where forests extend in uninterrupted lines over scores of miles; where we may wander a good day's journey without meeting half-a-dozen human faces; where stately deer will bound across our path, and bears dispute our passage through the cedar-brakes; where, in a word, we may enjoy the undiluted essence, the perfect wildness, of woodland life." The magazine feared, however, that accelerated development would soon clear this wild country. "It is scarcely too much to anticipate that, within five years, thousands of acres, now dense with pines and cedars of a hundred rings, will be laid out in blooming market-gardens and in fields of generous corn," the article concluded. "Five years hence, bears and deer will be a tradition, panthers and raccoons a myth, partridges and quails a vain and melancholy recollection, in what shall then be known as what was once the pines." The trend the *Atlantic* anticipated was the reverse of the one that actually took place. As the last of the iron furnaces gradually blew out and the substitute industries failed, people either left the pines or began to lead self-sufficient backwoods lives, and while the rest of the State of New Jersey developed toward its twentieth-century aspect, the Pine Barrens all but returned to their pre-Colonial desolation, becoming, as they have remained, a distinct and separate world. The people of the pines came to be known as pineys—a term that is as current today as it was at the turn of the century. After a generation or two had lived in isolation, the pineys began to fear people from the outside, and travellers often reported that when they approached a cabin in the pines the people scattered and hid behind trees. This was interpreted, by some, as a mark of lunacy. It was simply fear of the unknown.

The pineys had little fear of their surroundings, from which they drew an adequate living. A yearly cycle evolved that is still practiced, but by no means universally, as it once was. With the first warmth of spring, pineys took their drags—devices with tines, something like hand cultivators—and went into the lowland forests to gather sphagnum moss. This extraordinary material has such a capacity for absorbing water that one can squeeze it and twist it and wring it a dozen times and water will still come pouring out. Since the water is acidulous and somewhat antiseptic, sphagnum moss was used by soldiers during the Revolution when they lacked ordinary bandages. Florists provided a large part of the market for the pineys' moss. Boxes of cut flowers sent out by florists' shops all over the East used to contain—under and around the flowers—protective beds of sphagnum from the pines. Plastic moss has largely replaced sphagnum moss in the floral trade, but a market remains for it, and some people still gather it.

In June and July, when the wild blueberries of the Pine Barrens ripened on the bush, the pineys hung large homemade baskets around their necks, bent the blueberry bushes over the baskets, and beat the stems with short clubs. The berries, if just ripe enough, rained into the baskets. Fred Brown told me one day that he had knocked off his share of "huckleberries" in his time, and that many people still go out after them every summer. In the vernacular of the pines, huckleberries are blueberries, wild or cultivated. Huckleberries are also huckleberries, and this confuses outsiders but not pineys. Fred explained to me, when I pressed him, that "hog huckleberries" are huckleberries and "sugar huckleberries" are blueberries. He said, "Ain't nothing for a man to go out and knock off two hundred pounds in less than a day." In 1967, the average price for wild blueberries was fourteen cents a pound. People who gather wild blueberries now use No. 2 galvanized tubs instead of baskets. They beat the bushes with lengths of rubber hose. "Wild berries got a better taste than cultivated berries," Fred said. "Mrs. Wagner's Pies won't make pies with just cultivated berries." Millions of blueberry bushes grow wild in the pines, but when a forester who was doing field work for a doctoral thesis recently asked a piney assistant to cut one down, the piney refused.

Cranberries followed blueberries in the cycle of the pines. Cranberries grow wild along the streams and are white in the summer and red in the fall. In the eighteen-sixties and eighteen-seventies, people began to transplant them to the cleared and excavated bogs where ore raisers had removed bog iron, and that was the beginning of commercial cranberry growing in the Pine Barrens, where about a third of the United States total is now grown. Cranberry bogs are shallow basins, dammed on all sides, so that streams can fill them in late autumn and keep cold winter winds from drying out the vines. The older bogs were turfed out by hand, and the dams were built from the turf. In the fall, the berries were harvested by hand, with many-tined wooden scoops that went through the vines like large claws. Cranberry scoops are so primitive in appearance that they are sold as antiques in shops on Third Avenue and in Bucks County. In a few bogs in the Pine Barrens, scoops are still used, and only five years ago all bogs used them.

In winter, the cycle moved on to cordwood and charcoal. Woodcutters, in the seventeenth century, were among the first people in the pines.

They were needed in the iron era, they remained when it was over, and they are still there. They are getting a good price for their pulpwood—seven dollars a cord. With a chain saw, a man can cut a cord of pine in less than an hour. "Oak isn't worth nothing, but the pine is way up," Fred Brown said one day. Charcoal burning also continued beyond the iron era and was actually a major occupation in the Pine Barrens until the Second World War. In the eighteen-fifties, fifty schooners made regular runs with charcoal from the Pine Barrens to New York. Countless four-mule teams hauled charcoal over the sand roads to Philadelphia in covered wagons. Eight-mule teams hauled larger wagons, full of the best grade, to the Philadelphia mint. Almost any piney knew how to make charcoal, and the woods were full of little clearings, which is one reason that so many culs-de-sac branch from the sand roads. Full-time colliers specialized in charcoal to the exclusion of most of the other occupations in the yearly cycle. They frequently made their pits with someone else's wood. They moved around a lot, nomadically, living in shacks that had no floors, or in tepee-shaped structures made of cedar poles and turf. They stored their supplies—mainly salt pork and apple whiskey—in turf-covered dugouts, in which they hid and sometimes died when wildfires overcame the forest. Charcoal pits were actually above-ground. They had the shape of beehives and were twenty feet high. To make them, colliers stacked cordwood in vertical tiers and covered the wood with chunks of sandy turf, known as floats. The colliers dropped burning kindling into a hole in the top and then sealed it over. They poked holes in the sides with a stick called a fagan, and kept watch over the pit day and night. If blue smoke came out, too much oxygen was involved in the combustion, and the colliers plugged a few holes. If white steam came out, the wood inside was charring perfectly. This went on for about ten days. The late George Crummel, the Indian collier of Jenkins Neck, had a dog that could watch a pit and would awaken him if the ventilating holes needed attention. With Crummel gone, there are only two or three colliers left in the Pine Barrens. The last important market was for bagged charcoal for back-yard cooking, but the modern briquette has all but eliminated that. Most "charcoal" briquettes are made in gasoline refineries as a petroleum by-product. On this subject, Fred Brown said one day, "These here charcoal brick-a-bats, or whatever you call them, that they sell—look at them, all you have to do is *look* at them. You *know* they didn't come from no tree."

Venison, of course, was available the year round to pineys, who have always felt detached about game laws. The sphagnum-blueberry-cran-berry-wood-and-charcoal cycle was supplemented in other ways as well —most notably in December, when shiploads of holly, laurel, mistletoe, ground pine, greenbriar, inkberry, plume grass, and boughs of pitch pine were sent to New York for sale as Christmas decorations. Small birch trees were cut in short lengths and turned into candleholders. People who specialized in pine cones became known as pineballers, and the term is still used. The Christmas business continues to be an important source of income in the pines. Modern pineballers pick about three thousand cones in a day. They like to get them from the dwarf forests—the Plains, as they are called—because the trees there are shorter than men, and can be picked clean. At the moment, pineballing is not as remunerative as huckleberrying. Pineballers are getting only three dollars and seventy-five cents per thousand cones, or about eleven dollars for a day's work. Pineys once sold rosin, turpentine, pitch tar, and shoemaker's wax. They cut laurel stems to sell to makers of pipes. They dug the roots of wild indigo for medicinal use (wild indigo is, among other things, a stimu-lant), and they cut the bark of wild cherry (a tonic) and collected pipsis-sewa leaves (an astringent). They sold laurel, ilex, and rhododendron to landscape gardeners. They sent wild flowers into the cities—trailing arbutus, swamp pinks, wild magnolias, lupine, azaleas, Pine Barrens gentians. They made birdhouses out of cedar slabs, and they still do. They sold box turtles by the gross to people in Philadelphia, who used the turtles to keep cellars free of snails—a market that has declined.

While isolation in the woods was bringing out self-reliance, it was also contributing to other developments that eventually attracted more attention. After the pine towns lost touch, to a large extent, with the outside world, some of the people slid into illiteracy, and a number slid further than that. Marriages were pretty casual in the pines late in the nineteenth century and early in the twentieth. For lawful weddings, people had to travel beyond the woods, to a place like Mt. Holly. Many went to native "squires," who performed weddings for a fee of one dollar. No questions were asked, even if the squires recognized the brides and the grooms as people they had married to other people a week or a month before. Given the small population of the pines, the extreme rarity of new people coming in, and the long span of time that most families had been there, some relationships were extraordinarily complicated and a few were simply incestuous. To varying degrees, there was a relatively high incidence in the pines of what in the terms of the era was called degeneracy, feeblemindedness, or mental deficiency.

In 1913, startling publicity was given to the most unfortunate stratum of the pine society, and the effects have not yet faded. In that year, Elizabeth Kite, a psychological researcher, published a report called "The Pineys," which had resulted from two years of visits to cabins in the pines. Miss Kite worked for the Vineland Training School, on the southern edge of the Pine Barrens, where important early work was being done with people of subnormal intelligence, and she was a fearless young woman who wore spotless white dresses as she rode in a horse-drawn wagon through the woods. Her concern for the people there became obvious to the people themselves, who grew fond of her, and even dependent upon her, and a colony for the care of the "feebleminded" was founded in the northern part of the Pine Barrens as a result of her work. Her report told of children who shared their bedrooms with pigs, of men who could not count beyond three, of a mother who walked nine miles with her children almost every day to get whiskey, of a couple who took a wheelbarrow with them when they went out drinking, so that one could wheel the other home. "In the heart of the region, scattered in widely separated huts over miles of territory, exists today a group of human beings as distinct in morals and manners as to excite curiosity and wonder in the mind of any outsider brought into contact with them," Miss Kite wrote. "They are recognized as a distinct people by the normal communities living on the borders of their forests." The report included some extremely gnarled family trees, such as one headed by Sam Bender, who conceived a child with his daughter, Mollie Bender Brooks, whose husband, Billie Brooks, sometimes said the child had been fathered by his wife's brother rather than her father, both possibilities being strong ones. When a district nurse was sent around to help clean up Mollie's house, chickens and a pig were found in the kitchen, and the first implement used in cleaning the house was a hoe. Mollie, according to Miss Kite, was "good-looking and sprightly, which fact, coupled with an utter lack of sense of decency, made her attractive even to men of otherwise normal intelligence." When Billie and all of their children were killed in a fire, Mollie said cheerfully, "Well, they was all insured. I'm still young and can easy start another family." Miss Kite reported some relationships that are almost impossible to follow. Of the occupants of another cabin, she wrote, "That May should call John 'Uncle' could be accounted for on the basis of a childish acceptance of 'no-matter-what' conditions, for the connection was that her mother was married to the brother of John's other woman's second man, and her mother's sister had had children by John. This bond of kinship did not, however, keep the families long together." Miss Kite also told of a woman who came to ask for food at a state almshouse on a bitter winter day. The people at the almshouse gave her a large burlap sack containing a basket of potatoes, a basket of turnips, three cabbages, four pounds of pork, five pounds of rye flour, two pounds of sugar, and some tea. The woman shouldered the sack and walked home cross-country through snow. Thirty minutes after she reached her home, she had a baby. No one helped her deliver it, nor had anyone helped her with the delivery of her nine other children.

Miss Kite's report was made public. Newspapers printed excerpts from it. All over the state, people became alarmed about conditions in the Pine Barrens—a region most of them had never heard of. James T. Fielder, the governor of New Jersey, travelled to the pines, returned to Trenton, and sought to increase his political momentum by recommending to the legislature that the Pine Barrens be somehow segregated from the rest of New Jersey in the interest of the health and safety of the people of the state at large. "I have been shocked at the conditions I have found," he said. "Evidently these people are a serious menace to the State of New Jersey because they produce so many persons that inevitably become public charges. They have inbred, and led lawless and scandalous lives, till they have become a race of imbeciles, criminals, and defectives." Meanwhile, H. H. Goddard, director of the research laboratory at the Vineland Training School and Miss Kite's immediate superior, had taken the genealogical charts that Miss Kite had painstakingly assembled, pondered them, extrapolated a bit, and published what became a celebrated treatise on a family called Kallikak—a name that Goddard said he had invented to avoid doing harm to real people. According to the theory set forth in the treatise, nearly all pineys were descended from one man. This man, Martin Kallikak, conceived an illegitimate son with an imbecile barmaid. Martin's bastard was said to be the forebear of generations of imbeciles, prostitutes, epileptics, and drunks. Martin himself, however, married a normal girl, and among their progeny were generations of normal and intelligent people, including doctors, lawyers, politicians, and a president of Princeton University. Goddard coined the name Kallikak from the Greek *kalós* and *kakós*— "good" and "bad." Goddard's work has been discredited, but its impact, like that of Governor Fielder's proposal to segregate the Pine Barrens, was powerful in its time. Even Miss Kite seemed to believe that there was some common flaw in the blood of all the people of the pines. Of one pinelands woman, Miss Kite wrote, "Strangely enough, this woman belonged originally to good stock. No piney blood flowed in her veins."

The result of all this was a stigma that has never worn off. A surprising number of people in New Jersey today seem to think that the Pine Barrens are dark backlands inhabited by hostile and semi-literate people who would as soon shoot an outsider as look at him. A policeman in Trenton who had never been to the pines—"only driven through on the way downa shore," as people usually say—once told me, in an anxious tone, that if I intended to spend a lot of time in the Pine Barrens I was asking for trouble. Some of the gentlest of people—botanists, canoemen, campers—spend a great deal of time in the pines, but their influence has not been sufficient to correct an impression, vivid in some parts of the state for fifty years, that the pineys are weird and sometimes dangerous barefoot people who live in caves, marry their sisters, and eat snakes. Pineys are, for the most part, mild and shy, but their resentment is deep, and they will readily and forcefully express it. The unfortunate people that Miss Kite described in her report were a minor fraction of the total population of the Pine Barrens, and the larger number suffered from it, and are still suffering from it. This appalled Elizabeth Kite, who said to an interviewer in 1940, some years before her death, "Nothing would give me greater pleasure than to correct the idea that has unfortunately been given by the newspapers regarding the pines. Anybody who lived in the pines was a piney. I think it a most terrible calamity that the newspapers publicly took the term and gave it the degenerate sting. Those families who were not potential state cases did not interest me as far as my study was concerned. I have no language in which I can express my admiration for the pines and the people who live there."

The people of the Pine Barrens turn cold when they hear the word "piney" spoken by anyone who is not a native. Over the years since 1913, in many places outside the pines, the stigma of degeneracy has been concentrated in that word. A part of what hurts them is that they themselves are fond of the word. They refer to one another freely, and frequently, as pineys. They have a strong regional pride, and, in a way that is not at all unflattering to them, they *are* different from the run of the people of the state. A visitor who stays awhile in the Pine Barrens soon feels that he is in another country, where attitudes and ambitions are at variance with the American norm. People who drive around in the pines and see houses like Fred Brown's, with tarpaper peeling from the walls, and automobiles overturned in the front yard, often decide, as they drive on, that they have just looked destitution in the face. I wouldn't call it that. I have yet to meet anyone living in the Pine Barrens who has in any way indicated envy of people who live elsewhere. One reason there are so many unpainted houses in the Pine Barrens is that the pineys believe, correctly, that their real-estate assessments would be higher if their houses were painted. Some pineys who make good money in blueberries or cranberries or in jobs on the outside would never think of painting their houses. People from other parts of New Jersey will say of Pine Barrens people, "They don't like to work. They can't seem to hold jobs." This, too, is a judgment based on outside values. What the piney usually says is "I hate to be tied down long to any one job." That remark is made so often in the pines that it is almost a local slogan. It expresses an attitude born of the old pines cycle—sphagnum in the spring, berries in the summer, coaling when the weather is cold. With the plenitude of the woodland around them—and, historically, behind them—pineys are bored with the idea of doing the same thing all year long, in every weather. Many of them have to, of course. Many work at regular jobs outside the woods. But many try that and give it up, preferring part-time labor—always at rest in the knowledge that no one who knows the woods and is willing to do a little work on his own is ever going to go hungry. The people have no difficulty articulating what it is that gives them a special feeling about the landscape they live in; they know that their environment is unusual and they know why they value it. Some, of course, put it with more finesse than others do. "I'm just a woods boy," a fellow named Jim Leek said to me one day. "There ain't nobody bothers you here. You can be alone. I'm just a woods boy. I wouldn't want to live in a town." When he said "town," he meant one of the small communities in the pines; he preferred living in the woods to living in a Pine Barrens town. When pineys talk about going to "the city," they usually mean Mt. Holly or the Moorestown Mall or the Two Guys from Harrison store on Route 206. When Jim Leek said "nobody bothers you" and "you can be alone," he was sounding two primary themes of the pines. Bill Wasovwich said one day, "The woods just look nice and it's more quieter. It's quiet anywhere in the pines. That's why I like it here." Another man, Scorchy Jones, who works for the state Fish and Game Division, said this to an interviewer from a small New Jersey radio station: "A sense of security is high among us. We were from pioneers.

We know how to survive in the woods. Here in these woods areas, you have a reputation. A dishonest person can't survive in the community. You have to maintain your reputation, or you would have to jump from place to place. A man lives by his reputation and by his honesty and by his ambition to work. If he doesn't have it, he would be an outcast. These people have the reputations of their parents and grandparents ahead of them—and they are proud of them, and they want to maintain that same standard. They don't worship gold. All they want is necessities. They would rather live than make a lot of money. They live by this code. They're the best citizens in this country." Later in the interview, Jones said, "Unless these wild areas are preserved, we're going to get to the point where dense population is going to work on the nervous systems of the people, and the more that takes place, the poorer neighbors they become. Eventually, like birds or animals confined to too small an area, they will fight among themselves. Man is an animal as well." People known in the pines as "the old-time pineys"—those who lived wholly by the cycle, and seldom, if ever, saw an outsider—are gone now. When the United States Army built Camp Dix on the northwestern edge of the Pine Barrens during the First World War, civilian jobs were created, and many people of the pines first got to know what money was and how to use it. Paved roads first crossed the pines in the nineteen-twenties. Electrical lines, the Second World War, and television successively brought an end to the utter isolation of the pineys. But so far all this has not materially changed their attitudes. They are apparently a tolerant people, with an attractive spirit of live and let live. They seem to like hard work, if not steady work, and they like to brag about working hard. When they say they will do something, they do it. They seem shy, like the people who went before them, but when they get to know an outsider they are not shy and will generously share their tables, which often include new-potato stews and cranberry potpies. I have met Pine Barrens people who have, at one time or another, moved to other parts of the country. Most of them tried other lives for a while, only to return unreluctantly to the pines. One of them explained to me, "It's a privilege to live in these woods."

# The Air Tune

One day, Fred Brown told Bill and me that when he was eighteen he liked his women in the age range of fifteen to sixty-two. He also told us a story about a fight he once had over a woman. He said he had been "jumped by three guys" one night when he walked into the Peacock Inn, in Chatsworth, a pine town about six miles north of Hog Wallow. "The girl—they wanted her, she wouldn't have them," he said. "They couldn't go with her. I could. They had all tried me singlehanded and they knowed they couldn't handle me one at a time. Ander Bozarth got his jaw broke. I throwed him across the pool table and his head hit the pocket that was iron. Bill Green—I throwed him over the bar and he went right into the big barrel full of bottled beer and ice. Bill Ford was next. Howard Sooy, who was watching—he was a friend of mine—he couldn't stand to see three on one. He grabbed Bill Ford and knocked him out. I was eighteen. I would say the girl was around forty." Fred brags winningly. One reason he is so good at it is that bragging is an honored craft where he lives, an element in the general art of storytelling, which was once of enough importance in the Pine Barrens to give rise to a class of local Homers, some of whom did nothing at all but travel through the woods telling tales. Big Bill Estell, who died in 1882, told stories for a living, and explained to people that he was too heavy for light work and too light for heavy work. Cracky Wainwright—whose name, in the pines, is pronounced Wineright—went around telling stories and stopped off at his own house once a year. Ander Bozarth, the fellow whose jaw Fred Brown disassembled in Chatsworth, was a male Scheherazade, known for his ability to tell a different story every night for months. Stories were told beside burning charcoal, and beside bonfires that used to blaze at night in cranberry-harvest time, when, before the automobile, pineys slept in the woods near the bogs they were working in. Most stories at least began with truth, but some never gave it a nod.

In the late nineteen-thirties and early nineteen-forties, a graduate student from the English Department of Indiana University went around the Pine Barrens collecting stories. He was motivated in part by the somewhat melancholy knowledge that the development of broadcasting was going to wash away much of this part of regional American life. The student, Herbert N. Halpert, is now a professor of English at Memorial University, in Newfoundland. His doctoral dissertation was called "Folktales and Legends from the New Jersey Pines." He dated each story he heard. On June 19, 1941, a piney named Charles Grant told Halpert, "I heard old Cracky Wainwright say he seen two black snakes come together, and they was both mad. He seen they was going to fight, so he stood and watched them. The one got ahold of the other one's tail and began to swallow it. And the other one got ahold of the other one's tail and began to swallow *him*. He said they kept on fighting and swallowing one another until both snakes was swallowed. There wasn't *any* snake left there at all." Grant also told Halpert a story about a piney who went around for a long time claiming that he had a pair of horns in his shack seventeen feet from tip to tip. People liked this brief story and kept asking the man to tell it. Eventually, as Grant remembered it, "He said no, that was one lie he had told so much he believed it himself. He said he had told about putting the horns up in the middle of his shack so much he believed they was there. So he said the last time he was there he made up his mind he would crawl up there and see if there was anything there. He said he went up there and there they was—seventeen foot from tip to tip." On June 26, 1941, a piney named George White told Halpert, "I heard of this old fellow travelling, and he had a jug of liquor with him. Come by this pond and he was taking a drink. And the frogs hollered, 'Jug-and-all, jug-and-all.' And he threw the jug and all in, because he thought the frogs wanted jug and all." On September 1, 1942, Stacy Bozarth, a collier, told Halpert about a man who had killed a deer. "He hit him with one shot and hit him in the hind foot and hit him in the ear," Bozarth said. "Now how could he do it? Can you tell me? Well, I can tell you. Well, the deer had his hind foot up scratching his ear."

After reading these stories, I repeated them to Fred Brown, who blew air through his teeth and said he had heard them all. He said *he* could tell me a *true* story. He asked if I had heard about a couple named Will and El Nichols. "Will and El Nichols dreamed three times—this ain't second-handed, this is first-handed—they dreamed three nights straight that there was an iron-handled drawer buried up to Tulpehocken, on the road that goes from the Joe Holloway Field and comes out to the High Crossing. They dreamed that there was a box there—with an iron drawer in it—near an old-fashioned walnut tree right along the road. Neither one told the other that they had dreamed anything.

One morning, they got up and Will said to El, 'I'm going up to Tul-pehocken.' 'So am I,' said El. They went up, and dug, and found a box full of buckskin bags full of gold coins. I've seen the hole where they dug that out. They would never tell how much gold they got, but they had nothing before and they had money the rest of their lives, and they had it when they died. They lived down here to Bulltown." Fred had an afterthought. "People used to put gold coins in buckskin bags and bury them all over these woods," he said.

The Pine Barrens have had two Paul Bunyans and one Merlin. Jesse Johnson is a local legendary figure who is said to have been seven feet tall and to have been capable of carrying two horseloads of stone. The other strongman hero was a woodchopper, and he is said to have been capable of cutting ten cords of wood in a day. His name was Salt Caesar. The wizard of the pines was Jerry Munyhon. He could make a cat's paw come through a keyhole. He could cause axes to chop wood by them-selves. He could cause money to multiply. He was bulletproof. And he once caught a bullet that was fired at him and handed it to the man who had done the shooting. From some distance away, Munyhon could cause a man to stop in his tracks. Munyhon's cane was superior to Toulouse-Lautrec's. Munyhon's cane, on its own, could *go and get* whiskey. Muny-hon is said to have lived in one of the iron towns, and to have died in the eighteen-sixties. Once, he asked for work at an iron furnace and was turned down. He stopped the furnace by causing it to fill with black and white crows. He got the job, and the crows flew away. Munyhon once came upon a six-mule team that was trying, unsuccessfully, to pull a wagon with a huge boiler on it up a hill. He had a Leghorn rooster under his arm, and he tied it to the tongue of the wagon and said, "Shoo!" The rooster pulled the load up and over the hill. Of all his powers, Munyhon's most widely celebrated one was a remarkable ability to create in the minds of women the illusion that they were walking in thigh-deep water when in fact they were walking on dry land. Up went their skirts.

Munyhon's water trick has parallels that go back as far as King Solomon, who pulled a similar trick on the Queen of Sheba. His horse-powered rooster has antecedents in the lore of several European nations. European sources can be found for many of the legends of the pines. In America, the Pine Barrens have been a kind of cultural middle ground, where regional traditions overlap. Halpert wrote in his dissertation, for example, "This region is the meeting place for the Northern and South-ern folk-song traditions. Certain songs and ballads are found in New

England and other Northern states. Others are encountered only in the Southern states. In South Jersey, the various tides of immigration met, and here one often finds a husband and wife, one singing the Northern variances and the other the Southern, each of course insisting that his or her version is the true one." Men who sing have always been particularly respected in the Pine Barrens, where the test of a singer's repertory is: Can he sing from morning until evening without repeating himself? Pineys once made violins out of red maple from the swamps. Sam Giberson (1808–84), known throughout the pines as Fiddler Sammy Buck, one night told a group of people that he thought he could beat any competitor both as a fiddler and as a dancer—"and," he went on, "I think I can beat the Devil." On his way home, Giberson met the Devil himself at a bridge. The Devil told him to play his violin, and while Giberson played the Devil danced. Then the Devil played the violin while Giberson danced. Giberson was the kind of dancer of whom people said things like "I seen him put a looking glass on the floor and dance on it—he was that light when he danced." But the Devil danced even more lightly and beautifully than Giberson, and the Devil played the violin more sweetly. Giberson conceded defeat. The Devil then said that he was going to take Giberson to Hell unless he could play a tune that the Devil had never heard. Out of the air, by Giberson's account, a tune came to him—a beautiful theme that neither Giberson nor the Devil had ever heard. The Devil let him go. That is what Giberson told people on the following day and for the rest of his life. The tune is known in the Pine Barrens as Sammy Giberson's Air Tune. No one, of course, knows how it goes, but the Air Tune is there, everywhere, just beyond hearing. Giberson drank a lot, like many of the fiddlers of his time.

Fred Brown said he might have competed with a man like Giberson once, but not at the age of seventy-nine. "I can't jig no more like I used to," he told me. "My legs won't twist around like they would. Wherever there was music, I used to jig. For years, we had a dance every Friday night to Chatsworth, in the hall. Now they go to a bar somewhere, and get half drunk, and go home. The younger people, they don't never waltz or two-step or time-and-a-half."

The Pine Barrens once had their own particular witch. Pineys put salt over their doors to discourage visits from the Witch of the Pines, Peggy Clevenger. It was known that she could turn herself into a rabbit, for a dog was once seen chasing a rabbit and the rabbit jumped through the window of a house, and there—in the same instant, in the window

—stood Peggy Clevenger. On another occasion, a man saw a lizard and tried to kill it by crushing it with a large rock. When the rock hit the lizard, the lizard disappeared and Peggy Clevenger materialized on the spot and smacked the man in the face. Clevenger is a Hessian name. Peggy lived in Pasadena, another of the now-vanished towns, about five miles east of Mt. Misery. It was said that she had a stocking full of gold. Her remains were found one morning in the smoking ruins of her cabin, but there was no trace of the gold.

The Pine Barrens also have their own monster. This creature has been feared in the woods—on a somewhat diminishing scale—from the seventeen-thirties to the present. It is known as Leeds' Devil, or the Jersey Devil, and a year or so ago the Trenton *Times* ran an article, with a Pine Barrens dateline, that said, "State Police from the Tuckerton Barracks today are searching for a wild beast. . . . Trooper Alfred Potter reported finding a footprint that was so large a man's hand could not cover it. . . . Many remember the legend of the Jersey Devil." From "a farm in a woodland swamp," the beast had carried away two large dogs, three geese, four cats, and thirty-one ducks. Remains of these animals were found, but that was all that was ever found. If the perpetrator was Leeds' Devil, the haul was modest, for Leeds' Devil had in the past been said to have devoured small children and to have mutilated strong young men. Over the years, the physical appearance and the personal history of the monster have been variously described. There are two main versions of its birth, which occurred early in the eighteenth century—one that a woman named Leeds so scornfully treated a preacher who was trying to convert her that the preacher told Mrs. Leeds her next child would be the offspring of Satan, and the other that Mrs. Leeds had so large a family that she cursed all unborn children and said she hoped she would give birth to the Devil, which she did. The Devil child's appearance was said to combine the features of a bat and a kangaroo. It was described in Cornelius Weygandt's book *Down Jersey* as "a leather-winged, steel-springed jumper of goat size that could clear a cranberry bog at a bound." (A variant was that it had a horse's head, the wings of a bat, and a serpent's tail.) It tore at its mother's flesh while it nursed. At the age of four, it killed its mother and its father and began its terrible wanderings, cutting the throats of hogs, horses, cattle, sheep, children, women, and men, and leaving cloven tracks. People used to hang up lanterns to scare the Jersey Devil away. Most people in the Pine Barrens now look upon the Jersey Devil as pure legend, but there are many who do not. Unexplained and sinister events will still cause its name to be spoken in serious voices.

Bill Wasovwich, for his part, is not certain whether he believes or disbelieves. "I was out in a swamp once on a moonlight night," he told me. "A mist came up, laying out in there like a blanket. You've seen those nights. Fog was rising up like a thing coming through water. Something screamed. My hat flew off my head. I ran home, through briars. My arms was all cut up when I got home."

Fred Brown believes. "The Jersey Devil is real," he told me. "That is no fake story. A woman named Leeds had twelve living children. She said if she ever had another one she hoped it would be the Devil. She had her thirteenth child, and it growed, and one day it flew away. It's haunted the earth ever since. It's took pigs right out of pens. And little lambs. I believe it took a baby once, right down in Mathis town. The Leeds' Devil is a crooked-faced thing, with wings. Believe what you want, I'm telling you the truth."

# A Roomful of Hovings
## and Other Profiles

This essay on Thomas Hoving is the first of McPhee's formal experiments with biographical "profiles." In it he drops the usual time line of history and leapfrogs about, sporting with destiny as his subject did. The form is a good match for Hoving, whose life has been a series of eclectic roles: the prodigal youth who became director of a great museum, a scion of Fifth Avenue who built playgrounds in New York's most blighted neighborhoods. He has had many pasts, not one; not one personality or mood, but a dozen. Studying him was like taking a stroll through one of his galleries; the eye steadily slipped from one picture to the next, seeing contrasts but not always a sequence of display.

As its title suggests, "A Roomful of Hovings" solves this problem by creating a gallery, a roomful of eleven portraits, each titled according to its dominant theme or setting. Then McPhee arranges the portraits so readers can supply a chronology of their own—much as a curator traces the provenance of a work of art, sorting bits of scattered evidence into an intelligible whole. In the climactic episode, Hoving does just that with the Cross of Bury St. Edmunds, thus allowing McPhee to comment on his own methods for determining order and value. All the prior episodes are pendulum swings for Hoving, as he sways between greater and lesser moments, from sophomoric binges to shrewd bargains with international art dealers. McPhee and Hoving were exact contemporaries at Princeton, but hardly similar in temperament or ambition. Walking this gallery, one glimpses how alike they are below the surface, and regrets only slightly that the director had a better biographer than did most of his favorite artists.—*WLH*

# A Roomful of Hovings

## FIFTH AVENUE

Each day, nearly all day, Thomas P. F. Hoving stood somewhere near the Short Portly rack in the John David clothing store at 608 Fifth Avenue. He wore a double-breasted sharkskin suit, with a fresh flower in his lapel. On his face was a prepared smile. He was a floorwalker. This was the summer of 1950, and he was nineteen years old.

"May I help you, sir?" Hoving would say to almost anyone who came through the door.

"I'd like to see Mr. Gard."

"Gard! See-You!" Hoving called out, and Mr. Gard, a master salesman, sprang forward.

See-Yous were people who asked for specific clerks. Otherwise, customers were taken in rotation. It was not unknown in that era for clothing salesmen to slip substantial honoraria to floorwalkers to get them in the habit of turning non-See-Yous into See-Yous. But Hoving was unbribable. He had learned that every salesman recurrently dreams of a rich Brazilian who—when it happens to be the dreamer's turn to wait on him—will walk into the store and order fifty-five suits. Hoving would do nothing that might spoil this dream. The door opens again, and a tall, slim, wilted-looking man enters the store and dispiritedly examines a display of ties; then he crosses to the rack of 42 Regulars and begins to finger the sleeves of the suits. This man is a Cooler. His constitution has just been defeated by the incredible heat outside, and he has come into the store to recover. Hoving is merciless. He says, "May I help you, sir?"

"Just looking," the Cooler says.

"Sir, you don't belong in this section," Hoving says. "You are a 39 Extra-Long."

To show Coolers what they were up against, Hoving would lead them directly to the area of the Hickey-Freeman suits—the best in the store, one hundred and twenty-five dollars and up. Hoving's idea of a summer place was Edgartown, on Martha's Vineyard. He hated this job —or, more precisely, he hated the idea of it—but it was apparently designed by his father as a part of a program of training, for his father, Walter Hoving, who was then president of Bonwit Teller and is now chairman of Tiffany & Co., happened to own, as well, the John David chain of stores. Young Hoving learned a lot there. He could fold a suit and wrap it in ten seconds; he also noticed that prostitutes who came into the store generally hunted for contacts along the suit racks, while homosexuals used the shoe department. Every lunchtime, all summer long, he went to the Forty-second Street Horn & Hardart and ate the same meal —hamburger, mashed potatoes, and a ball of chocolate ice cream.

When Hoving, after a brilliant year as City Parks Commissioner, had just become (at the age of thirty-six) Director of the Metropolitan Museum of Art, he reflected, one day, on the John David summer. "Mr. Gard and Mr. Mintz were important influences on my life as a floorwalker," he said. "They told me, 'Don't buckle in. Do it honest. Only schnookers will ask to be brought out of rotation. The rich Brazilian will come to every man in his lifetime.' " Hoving said that he had not believed in the rich Brazilian until a day when one came in. "He bought twenty Hickey-Freeman suits," Hoving recalled. "The young salesman who had him was going bo-bo. Around the first of August, that summer, I began to get the ague from standing on my feet all the time. The man we all worked for was called Colonel Ladue. He had owned the chain before my father did, and had been retained to run it. You had to call him 'Colonel' or he'd get disturbed. You *know* what kind of a guy that is. He had an adder's glance—without a nod, without a smile, without a crinkle of the eye. That summer killed me on the mercantile business."

EDGARTOWN

Hoving in Edgartown, in the summers of his adolescence, was a part of what he describes as "a wild bicycle set, semi-richies, cultured Hell's Angels of that period." They had names like Grant McCargo, Dikey Duncan, and David Erdman, and they numbered up to fifteen or twenty, with girls included. Hoving was not the leader; he could apparently take or leave everybody. Nonetheless, he was thought of by some of his friends' mothers, though they seldom had anything really gross or specific to cite, as the sort of boy who was probably a corrupting influence on their children. He went out with a scalloper's daughter. His family didn't give him much money—never more than two dollars a week—so he washed cars, worked in a bicycle-repair shop, painted sailboats, caddied for golfers, and set pins in a bowling alley. Sailing races were the main preoccupation of the pack, and Hoving was always a crewman, never a skipper—in part, he says, because he never had a skipper's feel for the wind and the sea, and in part because he never owned a boat. All the boys wore blue or white button-down shirts. Hoving had both kinds, too, but he also appeared in patterned sports shirts, which were an emblem of immeasurable outness. He didn't care. Everybody wore a stopwatch around his neck, for the racing. One day, when the boys were fifteen, they discovered another use for the stopwatches. Grant McCargo bought a case of ale—"local poison, eighteen cents a can"—and, as Hoving continues it, "we all went into the graveyard and sat on friendly stones; we had shot glasses, and every thirty seconds everybody drank a shot of the ale until we were completely zonked." He played tennis barefoot, and his idea of real action was a long, cool ride in the breakers. "Great! Great!" he would say when he felt an impulse for the surf. "Let's go out to Barnhouse Beach and get boiled in the rollers." When he went to the beach, he took books along, in his bicycle basket, and he read them while he was lying in the sun recovering from the rollers. Robert Goldman, who later roomed with Hoving at Princeton and is now a writer of musical plays, was an occasional visitor to Edgartown in the years when Hoving was there. "He had a precocity typical of New York kids," Goldman remembers. "You know, you leap right from childhood into being twenty-one. Tommy was always hip, always absorbed with upper bohemia. He made newspapery references. He was the first person I ever heard use the word 'great' in that special sense. Everything was 'great.' I went to Edgartown uninvited once, and I was pretty much on the outside of things, and a situation came up one day when Hoving said, about me, 'Hey, let him play.' I've never forgotten it. He was an unaffected city kid, with spirit to him. He never made me feel like an intruder. Some of the others did." Hoving clowned and joked a lot, and he haunted an empty house once with Dikey Duncan (using sheets, chains, and foghorns) until the police put a stop to it, but he was actually quite shy, and he felt sure that he was not at all popular. One index of popularity in Edgartown, however, was the number of bicycles that could be found stacked outside one's house, and wherever Hoving was living was where the biggest stack of bicycles was. To be sure, this was in part because of the warm personality, unfailing generosity, and utter permissiveness of his mother, who was apparently neither as staid nor as consciously social as most of the other parents in Edgartown, and whose house (always a rented one) was a sanctuary for young people from discipline of any kind. She had been divorced from Tom's father when Tom was five years old. Her name was—she died in 1954—Mary Osgood Field Hoving, her nickname was Peter, and she was a descendant of Samuel Osgood, the first Postmaster General of the United States. Her father, Tom's grandfather, was such a fastidious man that he kept a diary of the clothes he wore. His wife left him, and from the age of two Tom's mother was brought up by an aunt. She married Walter Hoving when she was a débutante, pretty and blond, a cutout exemplar of the girl of the nineteen-twenties. Although she never married again, men were always attracted to her in clusters, and—according to Nancy Hoving, Tom Hoving's wife—"old half successes with moon in their eyes still ask about her." Some of her friends would act, on occasion, as surrogate fathers to Tom and his older sister, Petrea, or Petie, turning up at child functions where parents are supposed to appear. Both Tom and his mother had strong tempers, and the two of them would sometimes have conflagrationary fights. Friends once came upon them sitting in a doorway in Edgartown together, weeping. Tom eventually learned not to participate —to act, when something unpleasant came up, as if it weren't there. (This is a faculty he is said to have kept.) His mother's emotions sometimes overflowed in the opposite direction as well, and the more demonstrative she was toward him, apparently, the more he pulled away, developing a general aloofness that characterized him for some years— until he was ready to take part in things on his own terms. Remembering himself at Edgartown, he once said, "I'm sure the other mothers thought, Poor Peter, with a son like that! I was pretty scrawny, uncoördinated, and slovenly." He fought constantly with his sister (he once pushed her out on a roof and locked the window), but he was unusually close to her—they were two years apart in age—and he has named his only daughter Petrea for her. His particular friend was Dikey Duncan, whose family held the Lea & Perrin's Worcestershire Sauce franchise in the United States. Hoving and Duncan had the same attitude, according to Hoving's description: "Cool. We cooled it, you know. The same thoughts came to us. Dikey was bland, thin, and wiry, and he had a delightful irresponsible touch. We all used to go out to South Beach and play capture-the-flag, then sit around a great fire and get zonked. Dikey, who liked whiskey, would suck away at this bottle of Black Death.

Everybody else drank Seabreezes. There were periods of forty days when we were never not drunk in the evening. One night, Dikey shambled down to the yacht club and insulted many parents, and our introduction to booze came to a grinding halt." Grant McCargo had a car (something Hoving never had), and the others would monitor McCargo's speed with their stopwatches, having determined beforehand the distances between various landmarks on the island. McCargo, as Hoving remembers him, was a silent young man who was very much worth listening to when he spoke, and his favorite object was a Wright & Ditson tennis-ball can, from which he drank his Seabreezes. ("He was always getting fuzz in his mouth, and the drinks tasted of rubber.") With the tennis-ball can in one hand and the steering wheel in the other, McCargo used to drive all the way across Martha's Vineyard at night with the headlights turned off, while Hoving, Duncan, and additional passengers assessed his progress with their stopwatches. Hoving's Edgartown era came to an end after a beach party. The pack turned over a large sand-moving machine and set its fuel tank ablaze. Hoving caught the next ferry for the mainland, and he has never been back to Edgartown. With a mixture of shame and dramaturgy, he has always claimed that he can never go back, because the rap for the sand-moving machine is on him still. He is a lover of intrigue, secrecy, and mystery, and he sometimes finds shadows more interesting than the objects that cast them. He could, of course, go back to Edgartown, but not as a boy, and that is probably what he actually means. David Erdman, the skipper whom Hoving served as crewman summer after summer, cannot remember that Hoving in Edgartown gave even the faintest of hints of the future that awaited him. "He showed no artistic inclinations at all," Erdman said recently. "If I had been told that he would eventually be the Director of the Metropolitan Museum, I would have laughed and laughed and said, 'You've got to be kidding.' "

R O R I M E R

In the spring of 1959, when Hoving was a graduate student in art history at Princeton, he gave a lecture at an annual symposium at the Frick Collection, in New York, on certain antique sources of the Annibale Carracci frescoes in the Farnese Gallery, in Rome. The symposium was known among graduate students as "the meat market"—a place where the young are examined by experienced eyes from museums, galleries, and universities, and where futures can be made or ruined. Hoving's palms had been damp for weeks. He feared, among other things, the presence of Erica Tietze-Conrat, an art scholar who attended the symposium unfailingly and had been known to stand up in the middle of a young man's reading and shout, in a martial Wagnerian accent, "You! Are! Wrong!" Hoving, acting on a reasonable guess, had found unmistakable similarities between ancient sculptures in the National Museum in Naples and figures in the Carracci frescoes in the Farnese. He had learned that the sculptures now in Naples were actually housed in the Farnese Palace when Carracci was doing his work there, and this was the gist of what he presented at the symposium, in a twenty-minute talk illustrated with slides. Erica Tietze-Conrat did not interrupt him, and when he had finished she applauded strongly. "A few moments later," as Hoving continues, "a man, 39 Short Portly, whom I didn't know, came up to me and asked if, in my work on the Farnese Gallery, I had encountered records of a large sixteenth-century marble table inlaid with semiprecious stones that had once been in the center of the gallery. I said I did not remember seeing anything about such a table, and he asked if I had time to have a look at it, since he happened to have it. I said sure. I had no idea who the man was, and I guess he assumed that I knew. He had deep, deep, penetrating, steady brown eyes that didn't blink. He led me out onto Fifth Avenue and a number of blocks north, up to the Metropolitan Museum. We went in at the Eighty-first Street entrance and up the stairs to the office of the Director, and by then I had figured out that he must *be* the Director, but, to tell you the truth, I had no idea who the Director of the Metropolitan Museum *was*. So I kept sidling around his desk while he talked—trying to get a look into his 'in' box, you know—and finally I saw his name, James J. Rorimer."

After they had looked over the marble table, which is now in the center of a room full of Italian Renaissance paintings, Rorimer asked Hoving what he was going to do when he left graduate school. Hoving said that he thought he might work in a gallery and that he had already been interviewed by George Wildenstein and a man at Knoedler's. "Really?" Rorimer said. "I'm surprised. Go to a dealer and you'll never work at any museum in the United States. Go to a museum and you can later work, if you like, at any dealer's shop in the world."

Rorimer invited Hoving to come into the city and have lunch with him each Wednesday for a while, and Hoving did. Later that year,

Hoving went to work for the Museum, at an annual salary of five thousand and five dollars. He soon became a curatorial assistant in the Museum's Medieval Department and at The Cloisters, and one of his first assignments was to write a letter of declination to a New York dealer who had offered for sale, in a letter with a photograph, a twenty-four-by-twenty-six-inch marble Romanesque relief that was then somewhere in Italy. In a margin of the dealer's letter Rorimer had written, "Not for us." The photograph looked so interesting to Hoving that he asked his superiors in the Medieval Department if he could study the relief for a while before writing to the dealer. He was told, with fatherly understanding, to go ahead and do that, and for a week he went through book after book and hundreds of pictures, but he found nothing that could help him to trace the source of the relief and discover whether there was any substance to his feeling that it was of uncommon interest. So he wrote the letter ("We regret to say that we do not feel that this piece will fit into our collection . . .") and sent it off, but the matter continued to preoccupy him and he kept looking. Two days later, in a book on twelfth-century Tuscan sculptures, he found a picture of a Romanesque marble pulpit that had once stood in the Basilica of San Piero Scheraggio, in Florence—a church that became completely entombed in Cosimo de' Medici's administrative offices, the Uffizi, when they were constructed in the sixteenth century. Hoving eventually learned that Dante had spoken from this pulpit, and so had St. Antoninus and Savonarola. In 1782, the pulpit had been dismantled and moved just across the Arno from Florence to a church in Arcetri, where it is today—three-sided, and standing against a wall. The pulpit is decorated with six reliefs, carved in fine yellow-white Maremma marble, which have been called the masterwork of Florentine Romanesque sculpture. As Hoving studied photographs of these scenes, all from the story of Christ, he was struck by the thought that the piece he had turned down in his letter to the dealer belonged among them, but he couldn't see how it would fit in. He sought out publications about the pulpit, one of which had appeared as recently as 1947 and one as early as 1755. A Florentine scholar named Giuseppe Carraresi had written in 1897 that he believed the pulpit had once been a freestanding structure (not set against a wall, as it is today) and had originally been decorated with seven reliefs, the eighth space being left open as an entryway. The trail was getting extremely warm. The scene in the photograph submitted by the dealer was of the Annunciation. There was no Annunciation scene among the reliefs still on the pulpit, although an Annunciation would logically belong among them. Finally, Hoving noticed something odd about an inscription that ran along a marble slab under one of the reliefs. The inscription said, *"Angeli penden- tem deponunt cuncta regentem"*—"The angels let down the hanging King of Kings." But angels were not lowering Christ from the Cross in the scene above; He was being let down by Joseph and Nicodemus. Between the word *"Angeli"* and the word *"pendentem"* was a vertical break in the marble, directly below the left-hand edge of the Deposition relief. The *"i"* in *"Angeli"* was slightly curved and was formed in a different way from any other *"i"* in the pulpit inscriptions. The *"i"* was, in fact, demonstrably a fragment of a *"u,"* the rest having been broken away, and the original word could not have been the plural *"angeli"* but must have been the singular *"angelus,"* just right for the beginning of an inscription under a relief—the missing seventh relief—showing Mary being visited by an angel of the Lord. Rorimer, with surprise and consid- erable pleasure, told Hoving to write a second letter to the dealer, putting the Annunciation relief on reserve for the Metropolitan Museum.

Earlier, when Rorimer assigned Hoving to The Cloisters, he told him that in certain ways he envied him. Rorimer, himself a medievalist, had worked for the Museum since his graduation from Harvard, and he had developed The Cloisters, in its present location, from the beginning, after a Rockefeller gift in 1934 established the site and the building. As curator of The Cloisters, Rorimer liked to spend many hours carefully going over medieval sculptures with ultraviolet light. He loved the disci- plines of scholarship and the pleasures of exploratory trips to Europe. And, as Director of the Museum—which he became in 1955—he missed these things. Hoving had been at The Cloisters only a few months when Rorimer took him on a long trip, mainly through France, Spain, and Italy—wives and, in Rorimer's case, children included: eighty-five hun- dred miles in a green 1953 Chevrolet station wagon with license plates from Ohio, where Rorimer had a farm. He wanted to show Hoving all his sources—dealers, private collections, friends, university people. The trip was the most important single influence on Hoving's development in the Museum. He got the feel of Europe as Rorimer knew it, saw the architecture through Rorimer's eyes, and, along the way, formed a deep friendship with Rorimer himself.

In the Loire Valley, Rorimer climbed out through a window of a château in order to escape from a boring guided tour, with all the other Rorimers and the Hovings following. Everywhere they went—in every church, museum, or other monument—Rorimer said, "Pick out the three best things. What would you like to have? Why?" Then he would incite what Hoving describes as "great fierce mock arguments." One of these concerned the portal carving at the Cathedral of Angers and whether or not it had been restored. The Hovings and the Rorimers stayed overnight in Angers, and in the morning Hoving got up at six o'clock and went to have another look at the portal. As he rounded a corner of the cathedral, he met Rorimer, coming the other way. On the third day of the trip—after a lazy, wine lunch—Rorimer went to sleep at the wheel. Hoving did almost all the driving for the rest of the trip. Rorimer always had a pocketful of cigars, and he filled the car with smoke and laughter. When guidebooks were available, he and Hoving looked at them only after they had visited the places and objects described, the better to practice their eyes. On an altar in the old cathedral in Salamanca, they saw a seated copper-gilt, Limoges-enamel Madonna that was, as Hoving remembers it, "resplendent, with almond, stunning eyes." The piece was so resplendent, in fact, that they began to argue over whether it had more likely been made in the twelfth century or in, say, 1959. Rorimer posted his children in key places to look out for guards; then he and Hoving took off their shoes, climbed the altar, and studied the enamel surface through a pocket glass. "It's glorious," Rorimer said as he peered through the glass. "This proves to both of us that you've got to get right to a thing. You can't do it from a distance. You've got to touch it." Rorimer had a passion for professional anonymity and secrecy. Ordinarily, he had about him an air of cloaked movements and quiet transactions, of undisclosable sources and whispered information —a necessity, surely, in the museum world, and something that Rorimer had refined beyond the dreams of espionage. Accordingly, when he and Hoving turned up, by arrangement, at a certain garage in Genoa, Rorimer carried a French newspaper and instructed Hoving to speak only in French while they went inside and viewed, for the first time, the Annunciation relief from the pulpit in Arcetri. Afterward, Rorimer coolly covered his tracks by leaving the French newspaper in the garage. Then they drove to Arcetri, to look at the pulpit itself. Leading away from the front of the church in which the pulpit stands is an extremely narrow street called Costa di San Giorgio, and many museum people from various countries have houses and apartments there—for example, John Pope-Hennessy, who is, inevitably, known as John the Pope and is now Director of the Victoria and Albert Museum, in London.

Rorimer, of course, wanted to visit the church without attracting any attention at all, but the green Chevrolet station wagon became wedged between facing buildings on the Costa di San Giorgio, and Italians poured out of doorways and surrounded the car. Soon museum types were swarming all over Rorimer: "How long have you been here?" "Where are you staying?" "Why didn't you let us know you were coming?"

Some months after Rorimer and Hoving returned to New York, Erich Steingräber, Director General of the Germanic National Museum, in Nuremberg, came to the Metropolitan, at Rorimer's invitation, and spent more than half a year studying the collection. Hoving attached himself to Steingräber, and for days and days they went around the Museum, opening cases, handling things, and talking about them. Hoving says, "He taught me everything in the book—how to look at a work of art, how to judge its style, the tricks of forgers. There was a difference between Rorimer and Steingräber as connoisseurs. Jim liked big things —masses, big spaces, façades, tapestries. He was not interested in iconography; he was interested in the large scale. Steingräber loved enamels, carvings, reliquary caskets, small sculpture, jewelry. I like them all, but I don't have Jim's gift for the massive things."

In November, 1965, when the Mayor-elect offered Hoving the job of Commissioner of Parks for the city, Hoving went into Rorimer's office and said, "Jim, he's offered me the big marbles. What shall I do?"

Rorimer said, "No matter what I told you, you'd resent it."

"I'm going to think about it tonight," Hoving said.

Rorimer slapped his desk, and Hoving thought he could see in Rorimer's face both anger and disappointment. Rorimer said, "All I can say is, I know what I would do if I were your age." Hoving has never been completely sure that he understood what Rorimer meant.

"I hope that someday I will be allowed to come back," Hoving said a week later.

"You will," Rorimer said. "Absolutely."

Hoving went to the May, 1966, board meeting at the Museum as a trustee ex officio, a position he held automatically as Parks Commissioner. Rorimer also had him sit in that day on an impromptu meeting of the purchasing committee, which considers works of art, looks at slides, and makes decisions. Hoving remarked of one piece that the Museum ought to pass it up, because it was very similar to something they already had. Rorimer said, "Just because you're our landlord, you don't have to tell us what to do." Hoving remembers that Rorimer was in great form that day, full of vivacity and jokes, sitting on the edge of his desk and swinging his legs. He died that night, while he slept.

## SCHOOLBOY

Hoving sometimes refers to private schools as zoos. He went to four. The first one, Buckley, phased him out, as Hoving puts it, in the fourth grade. The school's explanation was smooth with use. Perhaps Tommy needed more individual attention, a smaller school? Eaglebrook, a pre-prep school in western Massachusetts, was chosen. He was there for five years, and they were the best years of his youth. Items from the school's records show that although Hoving came from "an unstable back-ground," he eventually made an "excellent social adjustment" and was a "friendly, outgoing, engaging, fun-loving, irrepressible, happy-go-lucky, impulsive, irresponsible, but industrious" boy, who got into "a good healthy amount of trouble." He was extremely thin, but he played football, baseball, and hockey, and he became (and still is) an expert skier. He played the piccolo and the flute. He spent a great amount of time reading. The I.Q. that had been reported from Buckley was not particularly high, but he earned excellent grades. C. Thurston Chase, the retired headmaster of Eaglebrook, remembers him as "a likable scamp, a good guy, not a future Met director," and Chase goes on to say, "He had a very dominating father—handsome, driving, cocky, and lonely—whose charm wore thin when he visited Eaglebrook. He wanted the boy to be vigorous, hard-studying, and successful. Tom was easygoing, and not overly ambitious. He was interested in creative and artistic things, but not overly energetic about it. He reacted unfavorably to his dad's pushing. His mother was quite different. She was loving, soft, and lonely." In 1942 and 1943, when Hoving was eleven and twelve, he spent the summer at Eaglebrook. A work camp had been established there, so that students from various schools could help relieve the wartime labor shortage on local farms. Today, when he reflects upon his childhood, it is this experience on the farms of the Pioneer Valley that seems to come most readily and fondly to mind. "I liked hoeing best," he says. "Walk-ing. Moving. Competing with the guy in the next furrow. We hoed corn, hoed potatoes, hoed tobacco. It was hot and humid under the gauze of the tobacco tents. We clipped onions and thinned out apple blossoms, and we grew our own food in gardens around Eaglebrook. There were three hundred of us altogether. We'd go out early in the morning and start in on a mile of corn. We drank too much water at first, and fainted. Then we learned the rhythm of that kind of work from Polish farm ladies. We made twenty-five cents an hour. At noon, we ate sandwiches and field tomatoes, and drank iced tea; then we slept off lunch in the cool earth of the corn furrows. The corn had a kind of mystery. You were out there and it was very high, all around you. I learned to chew tobacco. When you were working, chewing gave you something to do and kept you from getting thirsty. After a while, I became a foreman—thirty cents an hour, wow!—and I blew a whistle to get people back into the furrows. At night, we had dinner out on the grass around the school. We talked, and sang. Someone had a guitar. And we had interminable puppy-love affairs. On Saturday nights, we would go off in a truck to Greenfield or some other hot frontier town and buy bubble gum and cinnamon rings, go to two movies, and drink incredible amounts of Moxie." During the school year, Hoving frequently took his turn as a dish rinser in the school kitchen ("It was thrilling to work in the deep sink; it isolated you into manhood"), and one of his early heroes was Dick Davis, the school cook, who remembers him as a fairly tall and very neat boy who always had his hair combed and who "had a little chip on his shoulder about his father but still was proud of his father." Eaglebrook considered Hoving so outstanding that his name was carved in six-inch block letters in a traditional place of honor above a fireplace, where it appears today. He moved on, in 1946, to Exeter, where he lasted six months. He was thrown out for general insubordination. In the moment that precipitated his dismissal, he slugged a six-foot-five-inch Latin teacher, who had given him an A-$^2$, signifying that his work was excellent but his attitude poor. "The place was too big for me," Hoving says now. "It was a junior college. There was no discipline there. I drove people out of their skulls. Getting tossed out changed me. It took my confidence down. My father was furious and wouldn't speak to me for a while. Exeter said I was immature, sloppy, and slovenly, and had bad attitudes. This got to me." Curiously, he established a remarkable number of enduring friendships in his short time there, and although he finished prep school at Hotchkiss, it was with Exeter friends that he roomed at college. At Exeter, he was given the nickname Loper—for his long, loping gait on the athletic fields—and his Exeter friends call him Loper today. As a goalie in intramural hockey, he mimicked the gestures and language of the pros. "He was like a George Plimpton fantast," one of his teammates remembers. "He was always hitting the sides of the cage with his stick—you know, playing a role, in the best sense—and shouting, 'On the right! On the right!' He was about twenty per cent too much. He knew all the words. I wouldn't exactly say he knew the music. Oh, and he had this squint, like a large, lean Chinese who has tasted something bad, ducking that almond of a head into his shoulders." When Hoving arrived at Hotchkiss, he had already entered what some of his friends and relatives have described as the introverted era of his life. He frequently got up at five-thirty in the morning and went to the library, alone. He paid a cleaning woman for the use of a key to a large closet, so that he could go in there and read after 10 P.M., when the lights went out. He made high grades, but he apparently passed through the school like a shadow. His favorite teacher, confronted recently with Hoving's name, thought a moment and then said, "He did not blaze a trail across my memory." Another teacher remembered Hoving as "an aloof and standoffish boy, colorless, reticent, self-contained, quite beyond criticism, but not caught up in a warm way with the class," and added, "Altogether, one would not have a feeling that he would become the public figure he is." Hoving was known among his Hotchkiss classmates as Schmo. "Most of them thought I was a real jerk," he said recently. "I was very, very withdrawn and introspective. They were a pretty sophisticated bunch of cats, and pretty dull. The student council tried to stop me from smoking. I don't buy when my contemporaries tell me they don't like my attitude. I didn't go to the football or basketball games. I was a loner. I was on the outs. I was totally uninterested in school spirit. I had gone to boarding school since the fourth grade, and I had seen enough rah-rah. I lived for vacations. The thought of being locked up there for weeks and weeks—I used to sweat with the horror of it. If you see your life in terms of weather, Hotchkiss was overcast and threatening. Trees were green there in my last year, because it was my last year." That year, 1949, he was elected to the Cum Laude Society, the preparatory-school equivalent of Phi Beta Kappa. On January 30, 1967, he received a telegram from the Hotchkiss student council: "IN RECOGNITION OF YOUR SUCCESS, A HOLIDAY HAS BEEN GIVEN IN YOUR HONOR."

ART AND FORGERY

   When Hoving was twenty, he had a summer job with a large interi-
or-decorating company that had been hired by Walter Hoving to beautify
a branch store in Ohio. His own account of this job is as follows: "So
there I was, with the boys clawing and scratching. The firm needed
someone who was straight—a 'non-creative type,' as they put it—to
catalogue the materials they were going to use and to see to it that the
stuff got to Ohio." Paintings were among the materials that the decorator
was using, and one of Hoving's responsibilities was to collect certain
works—"turgid nineteenth-century landscapes, third-rate Barbizon
School"—at a restorer's shop in the East Fifties. While he was there one
day, he noticed a couple of Utrillos in a bin, and a Boudin, and a Renoir.
Then he saw a half-finished Utrillo and, in a bin next to it, an Utrillo that
had only just been begun and was little more than a sketch on canvas.
Noting Hoving's absorption, the owner of the shop offhandedly informed
him that a good Utrillo took about thirty minutes to do, that a Boudin
came out best if it was done almost all at once, but that a Renoir took
at least a day. Since then, Hoving has never looked at a Boudin or an
Utrillo without deep suspicion. He believes that he can tell Renoirs. The
owner of the shop also said to him, "Who the hell knows the difference?"
—a question that would, of course, become a major one in Hoving's life.
At the time of the Hungarian uprising, when he was twenty-five and had
completed one year of his course of graduate study, he went into a
dealer's shop in Vienna, where he saw a painting that he recognized as
Goya's "Man at the Grindstone." His first thought was "It's a fake." But
he knew that this particular Goya belonged in the Budapest Museum of
Fine Arts, and it was rumored that any number of Hungarian art treasures were being taken out of Hungary. He left the shop and returned with
books on Goya. He studied the painting, and when other people came
into the shop the dealer deftly made sure that the Goya was hidden. The
dealer managed to suggest that the canvas was too hot to bring much of
a price. Hoving finally bought it for two hundred dollars. He paid and
he learned. "Trust your first impression," he says. "Always trust your
immediate kinetic reaction. Don't think of how it could be possible. That
guy did a great con job on me. During the Hungarian revolution, every

forger in Vienna was busy forging private and public Hungarian treasures." In 1964, as an assistant curator at the Metropolitan, aged thirty-three, he was considering for purchase a bronze-and-enamel pax, a votive object meant to be kissed. Something about it bothered him. He used a microscope and saw clearly that it could not have been kissed over a long period of time. Real paxes show unbelievably soft wear. Under the microscope, this pax showed minute scratches. It had been kissed artificially. "When you consider a work of art, what do you do?" Hoving asks. "The process is basically intuitive, but it is good to have a guideline. Write down that absolutely immediate first impression, that split second. Write anything. 'Warm.' 'Cool.' 'Scared.' 'Strong.' In six years of studying hundreds of items for the Museum, I never ended up feeling warm about something I had written 'Cool' about, or the reverse. Then ask yourself: Does it have a use? A purpose? If it's a late-fourteenth-century casket, say, has it been used? Look where it has been worn. Is the wear haphazard? Forgers cannot possibly reproduce that. Many forgeries fall down because things have not been used. In the Middle Ages, nothing was made just to be observed. Everything had a purpose, either as an icon or as something else. Once, with Erich Steingräber, I studied a finger reliquary that was in a storeroom at The Cloisters. The piece had a ring on it that could not be removed. Rings were usually later gifts, placed on finger reliquaries as a kind of homage. Steingräber was very suspicious. On the ring was a fine emerald. Gems on reliquaries were usually not of top quality. The reliquary was riveted together, and there was no way to get into it. Reliquaries were not tombs. There were times when their liturgical use required that the actual relic inside be handled directly. All these items built up, and the thing began to disintegrate. We removed the rivets and found that the interior could not have held a finger. We eventually discovered that the thing had been made in a workshop in Paris for a man with a gem collection who loved reliquaries. You peel a work of art like an onion. Shred every layer from it. Is it in the style of the time? How many styles exist within it? Study the iconography and the manner in which it is handled. What does it intend to say? Parallels, parallels, always seek parallels. Use scientific means—ultraviolet light, X-rays, and so forth—but always in context with your eye. Scientific analyses can be used for or against a work, like statistics. Your eye is king. Get in touch with other scholars—everybody you think is expert. The idea that there is fierce competition among museums in this respect is laughable. Everyone helps everyone. Learn the history of the piece—where it is from, what collections it has belonged to, all the information surrounding its discovery. Then get the work of art with you and live with it as long as you possibly can. You have to watch it. Watch it. Come across it by accident. I used to have the staff at The Cloisters put things where I would come across them by accident. A work of art will grow the more it is with you. It will grow in stature, and fascinate you more and more. If it is a fake, it will eventually fall apart before your eyes, like a piece of plaster. . . . Max Friedländer, the great art historian, once said, 'It may be an error to buy a work of art and discover that it is a fake, but it is a sin to call a fake something that is genuine.' Nothing in art history is more glorious than bringing something back from the shadow of being thought fake. The only way to know art history is to be saturated. If you are going to buy early-Christian glass, you *know* all the known early-Christian glass. You *know* what forgers do. They put on a piece something that will draw most of your attention, such as a simulated-antique repair. They usually do it so the repair looks kind of rinky-dink. We once discovered that we had a forgery in which the forger had taken old wood and old canvas, painted it, rolled it, created beautiful craquelure, damaged the whole thing, and restored it in three different styles. It was beautiful, and well it might have been. The forger was the father of one of the greatest painters of the twentieth century. Steingräber taught me that wormholes made by real worms are L-shaped. The test is, you pluck out a hair and push it into a wormhole and see if it bends. Punched holes don't bend. However, I once came upon a piece that was supposed to be fifteenth-century German wood sculpture, and I learned that the maker had used actual worms to eat the thing. A wise forger will make an error—an explainable error—because he knows that inconsistency can be a mark of genuineness, if the matrix of the inconsistency is right. We have two beautiful fifteenth-century silver censers. One is authentic, and the other is an unbelievably beautiful copy. The forger *put his toolmarks on the old piece.* I love forgeries! I love the forger's mentality! Once, with two carvers and two other art historians, I tried to make an ivory forgery myself, so I would have the experience. Why ivory? For one thing, no scientific test will show you a damn thing about ivory. We picked an epoch from which there are two known dated pieces, vastly different from each other. One is classical, one is hieratic, and they were both made in Rome around A.D. 400. We decided to do a classical one. Old senatorial families in Rome in that era ordered classical ivories, because they were trying to look ancient—like members of the Racquet

Club trying to recapture imperial days. There are ways to age modern ivory. You put it on a roof for a while and let the elements do it, or you bake it in a tin box with pine needles, or you skin a rabbit and bury the ivory in the skin. We did it with the pine needles. To get a smooth patina, I rubbed the ivory on the inside of my thigh for hours and hours. We removed dust from the interstices of an old ivory and applied it to the new one. Then we showed it to five experts. Four thought it was real. Later, we destroyed it. . . . There is a standing dictum about forgery: It will never last beyond one generation. The style of the maker is permeated by his generation. No matter how he tries, his own time will eventually show in what he does. There is a lot of forged Coptic on the market today. Coptic is strong, overstyled, overstated. Our day is like this. Primitive art is collected for its strength and its brutality. Our age appreciates this and seeks it out. Therefore, Coptic art is being forged today. We are too close to it to see the forger's style. People a generation hence may howl with laughter and wonder how we could have been fooled. In 1880, in the time of the salons and so forth, Viollet-le-Duc did some restorations in Notre-Dame de Paris, Amiens, and other cathedrals. He tried to bring back the High Gothic of the fourteenth century, but it isn't honest Gothic in our eyes; it's too smooth and elegant and 1880. . . . What limits a forger is that he has to be cautious. He can't be free in his creation. The simplest kind of forgery is the direct copy. You walk into a shop and see something, and you know the original is in the Vatican, and that's that. Another kind is the pastiche—something copied from parts of many things and put together in a way that repeats nothing over all. Then, there is the thing that is not a copy and not a pastiche but totally inventive and completely within the feeling of a time. This is the toughest, the one that gets you. The Etruscan Warriors that were once here in the Museum were not copies, and they were of the time. The forger, Alfredo Fioravanti, had sat down and thought it through. Han van Meegeren studied Vermeer and decided that he must have had an earlier style that was different. Then van Meegeren forged an early phase of Vermeer. The wildest forgery that I have ever dealt with personally was an over-life-size Virgin and Child in limestone that was offered for sale to the Museum. The dealer claimed that it was 1380 to 1400—the very beginning of the super-elegant and aristocratic International Style. Call it German—I can't tell you where it actually was. The photographs he sent were stunning. Rorimer and I went to see it. The guy had put it on a pedestal in one of the most beautiful churches in Europe. His cousin was the sacristan. Rorimer thought it was French and didn't belong there. We were cautious, but we almost bought it. Then word came from a colleague in New York that he had found it in an old sale catalogue, and had learned that a gallery had sold it for fifteen hundred dollars to the dealer who was now trying to sell it to us for three hundred and fifty thousand. He was selling a real piece forged to look older than it was. The piece was early sixteenth century, and he had substituted on forged stone the graceful trumpet folds of the International Style for the hard zigzag of the later period. This dealer and I are the same age, and he is a friend of mine and a hunting companion. I confronted him with the entire story, supported by photographs, but he has never admitted what he did. Last week, he sent me pictures of another object that he wants to sell, and it appears to have been worked on by the same 'restorer.' This dealer is an imp of a man with a constant smile, and he always says to me, 'Tomás, do not worry. I would never do anything to *you.*' "


FATHER AND SON

It is said on Fifth Avenue that the fashion image of Bonwit Teller is the image of Walter Hoving, and that while he was its president there was not a store on the Avenue that was not terrified of Bonwit's. Walter Hoving, a truly visionary merchant, believes that the customer is not always right, and the twin plinths of his philosophy are good taste and quality merchandise. Before going to Bonwit Teller, he built the modern Lord & Taylor, giving the store the stylish veneer it enjoys today. He began as a recruit in the training squad at Macy's, and—something unheard of in the department-store milieu—he skipped the buying phase completely and straightaway became a merchandise manager. Moving on to Montgomery Ward, in Chicago, he completely did over the mail-order catalogue to give it a contemporary feeling. The rising curve of his later experience on Fifth Avenue made a curious loop in 1959, when maneuvers that he himself had initiated backfired and he was pushed out of Bonwit Teller. Tiffany & Co. was his consolation prize. Very much a man of the city as well as of the Avenue, Walter Hoving was once elected mayor in the *Daily News* straw vote. Several times, he was actually asked to run for mayor, but he always declined, explaining privately that he was not interested because he had been born in Sweden and could never be President. He said also that he thought it an impossibility to be mayor and not to be corrupt. In the great sales-tax fight of 1943, Mayor Fiorello LaGuardia called Hoving "that floorwalker." Hoving said, "Yes, and he is the little flower in my buttonhole." Hoving started the U.S.O., and he was assistant manager of Thomas E. Dewey's first Presidential campaign. (Curiously, a speech writer and key figure in the same campaign was Elliott Bell, the editor of *Business Week,* who is now Tom Hoving's father-in-law.) Walter Hoving has been known among his employees as a man of little or no humor but of considerable warmth, energetic leadership, and generosity in his attention to the ideas of others, always giving full credit where due. Except in the first respect —for humor pours out of Tom Hoving like wine out of a bottle—the description is one that also has been made by colleagues of Walter Hoving's son. Johannes Hoving, the father and grandfather of the two more recent Hovings, was a Swedish heart surgeon who emigrated to avoid political heat in Stockholm. His wife, Helga Theodora Petrea, was a Danish opera star and had once been a favorite of the King of Denmark. They lived on 114th Street, in what is now Spanish Harlem. At the age of forty, Johannes Hoving retired and returned to Sweden, where he spent most of the rest of his life writing a five-volume history of the Hoving family, a project that was underwritten by generous support from his two sons in America, Walter and Walter's brother, Hannes, who is now a dentist in Ossining. Thomas Pearsall Field Hoving was born in New York, on January 15, 1931. His early childhood was spent in Lake Forest, Illinois. He was a fat, blond little boy. He remembers his father's dressing up as a spook, in a flowing sheet, and calling himself Diplodocus. He remembers real candles on a Christmas tree and putting them out with pieces of wet cotton on the tips of long bamboo rods. He remembers a ferocious police dog his father had, named Pansy. And he remembers living with his sister and a nanny in a place called the Deerpath Inn while his mother and father were getting their divorce. One frightening night, the inn burned down. From the age of five, Tom lived in New York apartments with his mother and sister, and as the years passed he emptied countless water-filled wastebaskets out of apartment windows. He decorated a long hallway in one apartment as an Egyptian tomb, the result of a temporary fascination with Egyptology that he had developed at the Metropolitan Museum. "I'd just go right in—ssah!—right into the Egyptian wing," he says of his boyhood visits to the Museum. "The Egyptian wing—none of the other trash. I remember the shawabti figures very well. I didn't care much for the mummies. I examined the reliefs and the cartouches, and I looked deeply into the lips of King Akhenaten—because all we have is the lips." An even greater influence on Hoving's young mind was Loew's Seventy-second Street Theatre, which was, in a sense, his fifth prep school, and the colorful and colloquial language he uses today often seems to be coming from a sound track. On Friday evenings, Petie and Tom would go over to the River House to have dinner with Walter Hoving and their stepmother, Pauline van der Voort Steese Dresser Rogers Hoving, who had been the widow of Colonel Henry H. Rogers, the son of one of the founders of the Standard Oil Company. When Tom, aged eight, met her for the first time, he crawled under a desk and stayed there. Later, he took one of her rings and buried it in the Park. For some time, Petie and Tom visited their father and stepmother every Friday night. On these occasions, Walter Hoving had them bow and curtsy to empty chairs; he took assessments of their fingernails; and he taught them table manners, which they lacked. Sometimes the children visited their father and stepmother on a three-thousand-acre estate in Southampton that had once belonged to Colonel Rogers. The children were left pretty much alone to wander among its terraces, gardens, and colonnades. The great house was more or less in the neo-baronial style of William Randolph Hearst —a kind of San Simeon East—and across a large pond was a smaller house, built in the form of the stern of a Spanish galleon. Colonel Rogers had used a sixty-five-foot boat to ferry guests across the pond. There was a sheep meadow that could be used to park eight hundred automobiles. Under the main house, an elaborate system of tunnels led to a steam bath, a wine cellar, a ship-model museum. Tom and Petie spelunked among these tunnels and roamed the vast property outside. When he was ten and she was twelve, they were given a pickup truck to go around in. They took Errol Flynn out for a drive once and didn't know who he was. There was an apple tree that overlooked the pond, and Tom used to sit in its branches for hours. "I would just sit there and look at the pond and think," he remembers. "When they saw me in my tree, they left me alone."

In 1949, Walter Hoving, who was then a trustee of Brown University, said to his son, "You can go to any college in the country, but I'll only pay your way to Princeton." Tom now conjectures that his father may have been mindful that a number of Tom's Edgartown friends were

going to Brown. On the day of Tom's graduation from Princeton, his
father gave him a thousand dollars and said, perhaps to spur him on,
"There. That's all you'll ever get from me." Tom's wife, Nancy, says that
by the time they were married, later that year, they had nothing in the
bank. In 1955, just after Tom was discharged from the Marine Corps,
he called his father from California to say that he had given a great deal
of thought to what he wanted to do, and had decided to go to graduate
school. To Tom's considerable surprise, his father seemed quite pleased.
"In my time, graduate school wasn't really necessary, but now I believe
it is," Walter Hoving said on the phone. "I think you're doing the right
thing." Unfortunately, he had misunderstood. He thought that Tom was
referring to the Harvard Business School, when in fact Tom's intention
was to take a Ph.D. program in art history at Princeton. When this
bubble reached the surface and popped, Walter Hoving said "Art history?" and went on to make it clear that he considered the subject
nonsense and would not underwrite such a plan. Tom applied for and
got a scholarship at Princeton for graduate study.

During Tom's undergraduate years, Walter Hoving had signed up
both of his children for a series of Johnson O'Connor career-aptitude
tests, to help gauge their futures. Petie, who, like Nancy, went to Vassar,
remembers that "Tommy was brilliant in damned near everything, so
Daddy decided that the Johnson O'Connor tests were no good." Petie's
own career, unlike Tom's, followed their father's. She has worked for
Lord & Taylor for the past four years, and before that she was at Bonwit
Teller for fourteen years. She is married to a real-estate man and has
three sons, but in the office she is Miss Hoving, buyer for the department
that handles misses' dresses in the thirty-to-a-hundred-and-twenty-five-
dollar range. She says that some of the older employees at Lord & Taylor
occasionally shake her hand and say glowing things about her father,
who is still a kind of presence there, and is regarded as the great figure
in the store's history. "People really worship him there, and at Bonwit's,
too," Petie says. "Yet I don't think he has a personal friend in the world.
There are many parallels between Daddy and Tom. Both are outgoing,
warm, full of action, and adored by the people who work for them. Both
are strong in their opinions. But their opinions differ, of course. Tom is
very liberal, very up to date, angry, and wanting to do things about it.
Daddy is for Barry Goldwater, and so on. The opinions Daddy has were
not wrong twenty years ago."

Twenty years ago, when Walter Hoving was still being mentioned as a candidate for mayor, Tom was at Hotchkiss. Now Tom is the Hoving in town. He is sensitive to the implications of this, and seems at times—with never a word spoken—to be attempting to protect his father, and he goes out of his way to suggest that his rapport with his father is close. When Tom was sworn in as Commissioner of Parks, on December 1, 1965, in the Central Park boathouse, a reporter looked blankly at Walter Hoving, who was standing with other members of the family, and said, "Hey, are you Mr. Hoving's father?" A few weeks later, several hundred engraved invitations went into the mails. "I'd like you to meet my son Tom, the new Parks Commissioner," the invitations said. "So come if you can and have a drink with us at the Racquet Club on Wednesday, January 5th, between 5 and 7—Walter Hoving." Petie has kept a large scrapbook on her brother and his time in office. She pasted her father's invitation into it and wrote across a corner of the card, "Tom's *Bar mizvah!!* 1966."

PARKS

One winter evening, Mayor Lindsay sat down in his living room and, for an hour, considered the loss of his Parks Commissioner. "I caught hell for appointing him," he said first. "People said to me, 'Who's he? A minor curator from The Cloisters.' But Tom has a natural, unstudied political talent. There's nothing he can't do. . . . He is a thoroughly civilized man. He understands the dynamics of institutional life. In the Museum, he'll make the mummies dance. I knew that if the trustees came to him, I would lose him. He said to me, 'It's impossible not to accept,' and, of course, that's true. It's like a call to a judgeship. It's impossible not to accept." After a pause, apparently for reflection on what he had just said, the Mayor continued, "It's like cutting off my arms and legs to see Tom leave. He's going into an important city institution, bear that in mind. He's been the best company in the administration. In this business, you have so little time to yourself that when you do have it you get choosy about your company. If I went to the movies or the opera, Tom is one of the few people I would always want to have come along. I think he has a complicated future. There's a limit to how long a young man can run a great institution. This is the sadness, sometimes,

of university presidents who are there too young. Incidentally, and in
passing, he would be a great candidate for mayor."

Lindsay first met Hoving in a hallway of an apartment building in
1960. They were both passing out pamphlets having to do with Lindsay's
1960 congressional campaign. "God damn it, how did we get two people
working the same building?" Hoving said. Then he saw who the other
man was. In 1965, Hoving wrote a white paper for Lindsay's mayoral
campaign, detailing what was improvable about the city parks system,
and the white paper reflected the principles on which Hoving acted
throughout his tenure as commissioner. In graduate school, he had
studied the planning of ancient cities, and as an undergraduate he had
developed an enduring admiration for the man who created the great
parks of New York, Frederick Law Olmsted. Hoving approached his job
with a historical and conceptual bias in relation to the nature of open
areas in an urban milieu. He thought that they should be something more
than a scattering of topographical interruptions in the infrastructure of
the city, and should be designed and used so that they would have the
same effect as works of art—"to teach, to enrich, to relax, and to in-
spire." When Hoving actually began his work as commissioner, he
proved, to the astonishment of almost everyone who had ever known
him, that he could generate more froth per day than all the breakers on
the beaches of Queens. His assistants filled fifty-two scrapbooks with
newspaper clippings having to do with the city's parks during his first
year in office. His so-called Happenings drew thousands of people into
the parks to, say, fly kites (five thousand kites), paint masterpieces on a
hundred and five yards of canvas (three thousand painters), build castles
of plastic foam, or see meteor showers (clouded out). People began to
gather around him in multitudes at these affairs. Girls ran up and threw
their arms around him. He was Hans Christian Hoving. When the
Goldman Band opened its summer season in Central Park in 1965, five
hundred people were there. In 1966, Hoving arranged a Gay Nineties
party for the band's opening and thirty-five thousand were there. They
gave him a twenty-minute standing ovation. But Happenings happen and
are over. Basic principles, and construction, linger. Hoving's work had
a great deal of depth as well as reach and verve. When he took over, he
said he wanted to change the Parks Department's basic approach to
design. Highway engineers had been creating structures and parkscapes
for the city, working with maps and charts, away from the sites. No one
in the rest of the world would ever have thought of asking New York

for help in the planning of parks. Hoving said, "I want to make the Parks Department's work the absolute highest quality in the United States." And he did. He brought a full-time architect into the department for the first time ever, and he himself raised the money privately for the architect's salary, to get around the drag of Civil Service. As consultants, he tried to get some of the best-known architects in the world. They were cool until he had been in office about three months, and then they began to respond—Philip Johnson, Marcel Breuer, Edward Larrabee Barnes, John Carl Warnecke, and Kenzo Tange, who did the National Gymnasium for the Olympics in Tokyo. Some of these consultants have taken on work for the department. Tange and Breuer (with the landscape architect Lawrence Halprin) are designing a sports park that will occupy the World's Fair Grounds and will include facilities for almost every sport that can be played in a city—football, badminton, drag racing, archery, basketball, swimming, tennis, baseball, softball. Breuer, Johnson, and Barnes developed competing designs for the new three-hundred-stall public and police stables that will be built beside the Eighty-sixth Street Transverse in Central Park. They all lost to the firm of Kelly & Gruzen, who shrewdly put the stables underground, preserving the Park above. Hoving said early in 1966 that he wanted to open up a bicycle and walking trail on the old Croton right-of-way in the Bronx. Felix Candela, the Mexican architect who is celebrated for thin-shell concrete construction, is expected to design a bridge that will eliminate the one major break left in the trail. Any kind of bridge would have done the job functionally, but Hoving reached out for one of the greatest structural engineers in the world. Confronted with the need to choose a designer for a new community swimming pool in the Bedford-Stuyvesant section of Brooklyn, Hoving and the Director of Park Design, Arthur Rosenblatt, decided that to choose a great architect would not be good enough. They chose, with inspiration, Morris Lapidus, out of whose pen ran the Fontainebleau, the Eden Roc, and half the other hotels in Miami Beach, and the Summit and the Americana in New York. A twenty-nine-year-old architect designed a Central Park playground just north of the Tavern on the Green. A center for old people will be going up in Tomkins Park, in Brooklyn. A recreation center for young people, with a swimming pool, clubrooms, and jukeboxes, will be built on West Twenty-fifth Street, in Manhattan, and will have an illuminated theatre marquee with blinking lights telling what is going on inside. Among the hundreds of ideas that Hoving has left behind, one is that park facilities should be thought of as if they were profit-making ventures, because the purpose is to bring people into them.

Hoving said at the outset that he wanted to create vest-pocket parks in small spaces throughout the city and portable parks (that is, parks with equipment that could be taken up and used again) in lots that were temporarily empty. He established a dozen vest pockets, and the portables, it was hoped, would follow. He said that he wanted to close the roads of Central Park to motor vehicles on Sundays, in favor of bicyclists, and he said that he wanted to establish parks on piers, to bring the people closer to the city's beautiful harbor. He made the first moves toward opening the piers and succeeded in opening the roads. After one year, he left more than events behind, and, long before his time ended, other cities here and in Europe were asking for his advice—San Francisco, London, the District of Columbia, Boston, Cleveland, Akron, Yonkers. "The most significant thing we accomplished is the entire change of direction in design," Hoving says. "We are now the innovators in the country."

That winter evening, soon after Hoving had resigned as Parks Commissioner, the Mayor said, "Running a huge department is a big political office. Tom rose to it like a bird. He stumbled occasionally, and he walked in with his jaw now and then, but each time he got stronger and better. His antenna is good. There's no disguising anything with Tom. If I ran again for this office—or, indeed, for any other office, which is most unlikely; in fact, zero chance—I would turn again to Tom." Even before Hoving went into the Parks Department in 1965, he had decided to leave the Metropolitan Museum. He was going to accept the directorship of the Wadsworth Atheneum, in Hartford. He made this decision because he felt that the general experience of the Hartford position— running a large museum and collecting in all fields of art history ("You know, Chinese porcelain, Renaissance bronzes")—would improve his chances of one day becoming the Director of the Metropolitan Museum, which was his ambition, he has disclosed, almost from the moment he started to work there. Rorimer had been curator of The Cloisters before becoming Director of the Metropolitan, and Hoving feared that the trustees would want to vary the pattern. He says that he is sure he would never have been chosen had it not been for his time in government, and that the commissionership prepared him for the job in the Museum as the Wadsworth Atheneum never could have.

CURATOR

In the Fuentidueña Chapel at The Cloisters, there is a Romanesque
doorway from the Church of San Leonardo al Frigido, in Massa-Carrara,
Tuscany. It is a beautiful thing, carved in Carrara marble, and its architrave depicts, in some twenty figures, the entry of Christ into Jerusalem.
Close inspection shows that the head of an apostle in the center of the
architrave has a yellowish color, quite different in tone from the rest of
the apostle's body and from all the other figures. In 1893, a Countess
Benkendorff-Schouvaloff wrote from Nice to Italian archivists in Milan
to tell them that the doorway, which had been taken from the Massa-
Carrara church when it fell into ruin some years earlier, was installed
in her villa in Nice. Hoving learned all this in 1960, as an ancillary result
of his research on the Annunciation relief from the Romanesque pulpit
in Arcetri. He wrote to a friend in Nice asking him to go see the present
Count Benkendorff-Schouvaloff and have a look at the doorway. The
friend wrote back and said, as Hoving paraphrases the letter, that "the
Count had split long ago" and there was now a high-rise housing project
where the Benkendorff-Schouvaloff villa had once stood. Hoving reasoned that Romanesque doorways don't just disappear. This one had to
be somewhere. He wrote and asked his friend to keep looking. Soon the
friend wrote and said that the doorway was lying in pieces behind the
housing project. A local dealer in Nice was sent to have a look and he
cabled, "CONDITION TERRIBLE, NOT MARBLE." A year later, happening
to be in Nice, Hoving went to the housing project and searched around
in the weeds out back, just for his curiosity's sake. In high grass among
old apple trees he found the blocks of stone. They were marble, all right,
and they were in excellent condition. "It was easy to get the doorway out
of France," he says. "The French couldn't have cared less, because it was
an Italian doorway. When the Benkendorff-Schouvaloffs moved it to
Nice, Nice was a part of Italy. So the doorway never left Italy. Italy left
*it.*" The heads of two apostles were missing from the architrave. One is
still missing, but Hoving found the other—the piece with the yellowish
cast—in a beauty parlor in the center of Nice.

Much as the pulpit relief led Hoving to the San Leonardo doorway,
the doorway led him to a holy-water font, also from Tuscany, that had

been carved at about the same time. Hoving found the font at 125 East Fifty-seventh Street, in the shop of the dealer Leopold Blumka. He just happened to see it there while he was out for a Saturday-morning walk, and he was struck by the close stylistic similarity between the figures on the font and the figures on the Massa-Carrara doorway. (In another shop on East Fifty-seventh Street, he later found, and bought for the Museum, a pendant that proved to be one of two known reliquaries of St. Thomas à Becket.) The holy-water font now stands beside the doorway in the Fuentidueña Chapel at The Cloisters. In the St. Guilhem Cloister, which is adjacent to the Fuentidueña Chapel, is the Annunciation relief from Arcetri. As Hoving moves from room to room in The Cloisters and looks at one object after another, including his own acquisitions, he says, "Ooh!" and "Ah!" and "Great!" and "Unbelievable!" In the Treasury, he stops before a wood carving of Sts. Christopher, Eustace, and Erasmus that was done by Tilmann Riemenschneider, of Würzburg, in 1494. "Look how that crackles with energy," he says. "It's linden wood, but see how dark it is. It was probably stained in the nineteenth century. The thing is incredible, isn't it? Look at those faces. I bought it here, in New York. It cost like hell, but nobody remembers how much now—and who cares? We *have* it." He moves on to a reliquary shrine that once belonged to Queen Elizabeth of Hungary (acquired by him in 1962), a reliquary bust of St. Juliana (1961), and a Rhenish Crucifixion carved by an unknown master (1961), of which he says, "This is one of the most beautiful Calvaries ever made. It was in an auction and sold for a sum so low that I could have bought it out of my paycheck."

As a curator, Hoving went to Europe six or seven times a year on acquisitional ventures, staying in cheap hotels in Paris near the Boul' Mich ("Ratty hotels, always ratty—I like to be *anonyme*"), stuffing himself on Bélon oysters ("Hepatitis? Who cares? You might as well go big"), and trying to get to bed by 1:30 A.M. in order to be in reasonable shape to see dealers the next day ("whose names, of course, I cannot divulge"). He ranged from London to Istanbul, but the most important acquisition of his career he made in Zurich. He had heard, from a friend in a museum in Boston, that a man named Ante Topic-Mimara—a Yugoslav by birth, an Austrian by citizenship, and a resident of Tangier—possessed an ivory cross of uncertain origin, which he kept in a bank vault in Zurich. The general suspicion, Hoving learned, was that Topic-Mimara's cross was a fake—in part because of inconsistencies in its iconography and in its inscriptions. For example, where ordinary liturgical phraseology would read *"Iesus Nazarenus Rex Iudeorum,"* an inscription on Topic-Mimara's cross read *"Iesus Nazarenus Rex Confessorum."* Hoving had written his doctoral dissertation on medieval ivories. He wrote to Topic-Mimara asking for photographs of the cross. Topic-Mimara replied that he was making no photographs available but that if Hoving would meet him in Zurich he would show him the cross itself, and that Hoving would find it "something unique in the world." All this had such a melodramatic resonance that it did seem to add up to forgery, but Hoving still had not had that "first impression," that "immediate kinetic reaction," and he went to Zurich to have it. He found Topic-Mimara to be "heavyset, 46 Short Portly, with a stubble, slightly hunched shoulders, a rapid walk, slightly turned-in feet, darkish hair, and a face like a crowd." Topic-Mimara spoke Serbo-Croatian, German, and Italian. In Italian, he said to Hoving, "I am a simple, humble man. A humble artist. I live in Tangier." The bank vault was subterranean, and there Topic-Mimara had cabinets full of objects—goblets, ancient glass, stained glass, pieces of tapestry. Withholding the cross, he showed the other things to Hoving, piece by piece. In time, Hoving learned that Topic-Mimara had acquired most of these things just after the Second World War, when he moved from city to city and country to country buying art treasures that were available and relatively cheap because of the disasters of war. With the complicity of an American colonel, he had filled two boxcars in Berlin with uncounted treasures and removed them to Tangier. Now, in 1961, in Zurich, after running through his current repertory, he finally brought out the cross, wrapped in a large black cloth. When Topic-Mimara removed the cloth, Hoving looked at the cross for a moment, and then wrote, on a piece of paper in his hand, "No doubt." Re-creating the moment, he said recently, "It was staggering. A truly great, great thing. Just exactly where it fitted into history I didn't know, and at that point I didn't give a damn. It didn't seem to have the nervous, fluttering quality of the eleventh century, so I guessed the twelfth." Hoving asked for photographs to take back to New York, but Topic-Mimara still refused. Each day, for three days, Hoving went to the vault and spent eight hours looking at the cross. Topic-Mimara sat near him and read newspapers. At noon, they ate sandwiches. Each day, as they entered the room, Hoving set his Rolleiflex on a table in front of Topic-Mimara and again appealed for pictures. He was always turned down. Topic-Mimara left him alone in the vault only once, and as he went out he picked up the Rolleiflex and slung its strap over his shoulder. "I'll be back in ten minutes. Take all the pictures you care to," he said. "I will," Hoving said. As the door closed behind Topic-Mimara, Hoving reached into his shirt, where he had a Minox. Quickly adjusting the tiny camera, he took eight pictures of the cross. Then he continued his study. Carved in walrus ivory, the two-foot cross had sixty-three cryptically abbreviated inscriptions in Greek and Latin and a hundred and eight carved figures, which were sharply detailed and extraordinarily alive in their gestures and expressions—in Hoving's words, "a great crowd of deeply undercut figures, distributed over the surface in a lacy network, carved with breathtaking skill." He decided that, among other qualities leading him to the same conclusion, the cross had so many irregularities that no forger could possibly have made it. He also decided that given the long, beautifully postured figures, the damp-fold elegance of the draperies, and the complicated carving, it had to be English. Topic-Mimara, for his part, never said where or how he had obtained it. Hoving took the Minox film to Munich and had it developed with supreme care in the Minox laboratories there. He then went to Erich Steingräber and showed him the pictures. Steingräber said that the cross could not be other than authentic. When Hoving returned to the United States, the pictures of course sparked the interest of Rorimer, and, in turn, of Kurt Weitzmann, a professor of art and archeology at Princeton and the foremost voice in the world on Carolingian and Romanesque ivories. When Weitzmann saw the pictures of the cross, he said, "I must go to see it." On separate occasions during the year that followed, Rorimer and Weitzmann both visited the vault in Zurich, and came away with positive reports. Weitzmann said that the cross was unparalleled. Meanwhile, word reached Rorimer that Rupert L. S. Bruce-Mitford, of the British Museum, was coming to conclusions about the cross himself. "There is a sense of timing in this sort of thing," Hoving says. "A museum man has to sense when to wait things out, when to bluff, and when to move fast. The trustees did not want to meet Topic-Mimara's full price, and we were trying to wait him out. Then, one day, Rorimer's sources told him that the British Museum was really on the move, and Rorimer said to me, 'You go tomorrow.' " Hoving, following a plan that he and Rorimer worked out, went to Zurich with ski boots under his arm, so that he would appear to be just passing through on his way to the snowfields. He ran into Topic-Mimara in a hotel lobby, and Topic-Mimara, who was wearing a fez, said to him, "You shouldn't have come.

The English are coming tomorrow. I have given them a complete option."

Bruce-Mitford soon arrived with Peter Lasko, a colleague. "Ah, here is Hoving, just passing through on a ski trip," Lasko said.

Bruce-Mitford said, "Well, Mr. Hoving, I imagine you feel something like Paul Revere."

Hoving felt more like a skier who had just fallen into a ravine. In the end, however, Topic-Mimara limited the option to three weeks, and Bruce-Mitford was unable to meet the deadline—apparently because the Exchequer would not approve of a sterling drain as heavy as Topic-Mimara's price, which was well over two hundred thousand pounds. In the morning of the twenty-second day, Hoving and Topic-Mimara went back to the vault. "You are also buying the rest of my collection, of course," Topic-Mimara said. Hoving said no, he was not. Then, in Hoving's words, "Topic-Mimara handed me the cross and I handed him the money, and a bank vice-president was standing there watching this, losing his mind." Hoving wrapped up the cross and sent it home air freight. Then he went to Paris for a few days to relax. The piece he had just acquired has been said to be more valuable than the entire Guelph Treasure.

Continuing his research, Hoving attempted to find where and when the cross was made. It had no recorded history. Nothing whatever was known about it except that it had been in the collection of Ante Topic-Mimara. In New York and in Princeton, Hoving went through hundreds of photographs of Romanesque English art, looking at every kind of work—stone carvings, illustrated manuscripts, metalwork, cathedral façades, ivory. When he had looked at everything, he found that he had set aside seven photographs in which were figures that had struck him as having stylistic similarities to the figures on the cross. Two of the photographs were of objects of unestablished origin. The five others were all of things that had been made in or near the Suffolk village of Bury St. Edmunds. Hoving deciphered the sixty-three Greek and Latin inscriptions on the cross. Sixty-three seemed to him to be an inordinate number for anyone to put on a two-foot piece—a very literary and English thing to do. Although the inscriptions were arranged in flowingly graceful patterns, written communication was obviously an even more important element in the intent of the maker. So Hoving put all the inscriptions together and read them as a literary whole. The message that emerged was powerfully anti-Semitic, condemning the Jews for killing the Saviour whose existence their own prophets had foreseen and proclaimed. Hoving then searched through the Patrologia Latina—which includes two hundred and eighty-two volumes—for anti-Jewish writings and disputations, particularly in medieval England. In a typical disputation, a Christian would speak and then a Jew would answer. "I found that these disputations were learned and friendly until the middle of the twelfth century, but after that the Christian had all the lines," Hoving says. "The Jew would answer back with stupidities. This was fraudulence, McCarthyism, on the part of the writers. A wave of anti-Semitism had obviously arisen at that time. Of the inscriptions on the cross, with all their linguistic irregularities, I found twenty-two in the Patrologia Latina." Hoving then went to England and worked in the Courtauld Institute of the University of London. The evidence he assembled, both stylistic and historical, continued to point to Bury St. Edmunds. He learned that on June 10, 1181, a young boy of Bury St. Edmunds was murdered, supposedly by crucifixion, and that the death was blamed on Jews. He learned that a monk named Samson was elected abbot of the Benedictine monastery of Bury St. Edmunds in 1182, that Samson was a particularly vehement leader of anti-Semitic campaigns, and that fifty-seven Jews were killed in a riot, of unexplained origin, in 1190, in Bury St. Edmunds. Hoving went to Bury St. Edmunds, where almost nothing is left of the abbey, and stood on Samson's grave. At Cambridge University, nearby, he went to Pembroke College, whose library houses many volumes of twelfth-century Bury St. Edmunds manuscripts, bound in deerskin. At random, he removed a volume marked M-72 from its shelf. It was the Gospel of St. Mark, and it had been copied in the decade 1140–50. At some later date, another hand had written an annotation below the words *"Rex Iudeorum." "Rex Confessorum,"* the annotation said, with a further note that this change in language was occasioned by "the perfidiousness of the Jews." Reflecting on that moment, Hoving says, "I had a long way to go, but the matter was essentially solved with this discovery." From then on, evidence accrued more rapidly, and in the Bury Bible, made in Bury St. Edmunds in the twelfth century, he found populated initials whose figures looked almost exactly like those on the cross—the same sharp outlines, precise gestures, pointed beards, and damp-fold garments. He was able to date the cross (1181–90) and to conclude that it had been made for, and under the direction of, Abbot Samson. "The cross is a virtual seminar in the style of the late twelfth century," he wrote in a paper that he plans soon to expand to book length. "In the figures, one can detect the inexorable and fascinating change from a Romanesque to a decidedly early-Gothic point of view implicit in the development of increasing attenuation and a dramatic movement away from the confining surface. The literary content voiced in the proliferating scrolls or cut into the flesh of the ivory is, like the figural carvings, the Passion and Resurrection. But it goes a step further, for it also rails against those who did not believe in Christ as Saviour and Messiah—namely, the Jews. It is against this poor, alien people and their synagogue, harried and persecuted throughout centuries, that the text of the cross directs itself with wrath. The cross may not be the only medieval monument that carries on a polemic against the Jews, but it is not matched in vehemence. The passage of time makes the contents of these writings no less harsh. But it must be remembered that this is the accepted attitude of the church militant of the late twelfth century. Today there may appear to be an incongruity between such superb artistic form and the vehemence of a number of the inscriptions, but in Romanesque times religious tolerance did not exist. The cross is intellectual, yet pedantic; clever, yet forced. It is English, above all—imaginative, dramatic, literary, independent of rules, far too rich, yet poetic and adventurous in its attempt to be encyclopedic. It even reaches beyond its insular character and expresses what was in the wind throughout the entire Christian world during the late twelfth century, for the cross is symbolic of the crusading spirit, both good and evil. It is one of those rarest of works of art that are both the strength and weakness of its era—the mark and the explanation of an entire epoch." It stands in an illuminated glass enclosure on a pedestal in the center of the Fuentidueña Chapel at The Cloisters, where people can see it from a distance of inches and can walk around it and examine all of its sides. "Look at it," Hoving says, standing before it. "Isn't it beautiful? Look at the work that went into it. Can you *imagine* someone thinking that was a fake?" The 1966 Annual Report of the Metropolitan Museum, which was published some months before Hoving was appointed director, listed four great acquisitions that marked the eleven years of the directorship of the late James Rorimer: Rembrandt's "Aristotle Contemplating the Bust of Homer"; the Merode Altarpiece, which is Robert Campin's Flemish triptych showing the Annunciation; the Antioch Chalice, once thought by scholars to be the Holy Grail; and—as the fourth of these treasures has come to be called—the Cross of Bury St. Edmunds.

PRINCETON

On Friday, January 12, 1951, Hoving and his Princeton roommates decided that the time had come to pull themselves together, that their general and flagrant neglect of the university curriculum was approaching a critical intensity, and that the weekend then beginning should be spent in solid intellectual endeavor by all, since the term's final examinations would begin on Monday. The principal architect of this plan was Thomas S. Godolphin, a brilliant young man who, like Hoving's other roommates, had known Hoving at Exeter. Godolphin further reasoned that what the group needed most was a long and untroubled night's sleep, and that they should all go to a movie that night, turn in early, and address themselves to their work first thing in the morning. Between the movie house, in Palmer Square, and their room, in Holder Hall, was a delicatessen. Walking back toward the campus after the film, the roommates passed the delicatessen, and one of them suggested that they assure themselves of a perfect night's sleep by having a glass or two of milk punch before sacking out. So they bought a gallon of milk. Milk punch had become a favorite among them, and they had a large assortment of sweets and spices that they liked to put in it to complement the basics—milk and whiskey. Their favorite drink the year before, when they were freshmen, had been Seabreezes. The freshman year had not been an inspired one for this group. "We were just doing prep school all over again," Hoving says now. "And that carried us through. I had an appalling cut record. I went to classes in the first week of each term and didn't go again until finals. I went a lot to New York, and haunted the Orpheum Dance Palace, in Times Square. An extremely temporary charge account was established for me at a night club called La Rue, in order to get me out of the Orph and also out of the Automat Bar on Eighty-sixth Street, a favorite place of mine, where you put a quarter in a slot and got a Martini—you know, pretty pestiferous. Dikey Duncan, who was at Brown, came down frequently to the city, and we once ran up a five-hundred-dollar bill at the night club, setting up everybody in sight. Dikey tried to pass himself off as the youngest-ever president of Lea & Perrins. We wore white ties and tails every night. We'd hit a few debbie parties and sink back into the Rue." In Princeton, meanwhile,

Hoving watched his classmates from an aloof perspective, made sarcastic, cynical, and funny remarks about everything he noticed, and showed no interest at all in extracurricular activities, with one brief exception. He tried hard to get into the Press Club, a semi-professional organization through which undergraduates serve as paid stringers for newspapers and the wire services. He had worked during the summer of 1949 as a copyboy at the *Daily Mirror,* where—as he describes it—his job was to "fold carbon sandwiches, go out for heroes, and place bets." He continues, "The *Mirror* was a bookie joint, as far as I could see. The teletype room was enclosed in glass, and every time the race results came in from some track the crush of people almost broke the glass. The writer I liked best had a drawerful of comic books. I myself wrote letters-to-the-editor. Two kinds—singers and howlers. We used to write howlers by pounding our fists on a table for a while to warm up." In the university Press Club competition, he extended himself to interview a man who was pushing a wheelbarrow all the way across the American continent and happened to be passing near Princeton, but, even with that scoop to his credit, he lost out to Tom Godolphin. Godolphin was a superior poker player, and he and Hoving used to play regularly in the afternoons. Robert Goldman, the playwright, who was another of the roommates, recalls these games vividly. "Afternoon cards in college is serious cards," he says. "I remember Loper with the green eyeshade doing the Cincinnati Kid. If anybody had had the sleeve guards, he would have put them on." Things continued in this pattern through the autumn and early winter of the sophomore year, and on the Friday night in 1951 before the first-term examinations the roommates drank their milk punch and then collected supplies for another batch. There was a fireplace in their room, and they built a memorable fire. They started up a player piano they had, and when they ran out of liquor they borrowed more from neighboring rooms and invited the occupants to join them. At about 2 A.M., they drew their curtains and established a proctor watch, and when university proctors entered the Holder courtyard the milk-punch party observed a period of silence. Soon they began to feed the fire with T-shirts, shoes, phonograph records, and minor pieces of furniture. In the early morning, they got a ten-gallon can of milk from the Walker-Gordon dairy, which is two miles from Princeton, and by late afternoon they were putting Drambuie, vodka, curaçao, crème de menthe, gin—everything they could find—into the punch. The party went on through Saturday evening, and in the early hours of Sunday morning the fireplace fire was still going. They had put chairs and pillows into it, and several worsted suits. They had, in fact, burned up almost everything in the room except the player piano. Some-one went out and came back with an axe. The piano played on while it was being hacked to pieces, and all the pieces were given in tandem to the flames. Princeton's grading system goes from a high of 1 to a low of 7, and at the end of the senior year a student's final departmental grade must be better than a 4 or he gets no degree. Hoving's average at the end of that first term in his sophomore year was 4.46. "I have been to several serious, artistic Happenings where, in a highly creative and avant-garde way, pianos have been smashed," he said recently. "I watch this with a ghostly smile."

In the second term of his sophomore year, Hoving went to a precep-torial in Art 301, a course he had signed up for that dealt with sculpture from the Renaissance to the present. Princeton students, in most courses in the humanities, go to two lectures and one preceptorial each week. In preceptorials—or precepts, as they are called—five or six students sit around a table with a professor and exchange ideas on the assigned reading and related material. This system was initiated by Woodrow Wilson when he was president of Princeton, and since Wilson's time a student's performance in precepts has always been an important part of his final grade. This particular art precept was attended by two seniors, three juniors, two graduate students (sitting in), and one sophomore, Hoving. The professor, Frederick Stohlman, set on the table a graceful piece of metalwork that had several flaring curves and was mounted on a base of polished hardwood. Stohlman asked each student, in turn, to say whatever came into his head about the object. Hoving heard the others using terms like "crosscurrents of influence," "definitions of space," "abstract approaches to form," "latent vitality," and "mellifluous harmonies." He felt unconvinced, unimpressed, unprepared, utterly nervous, and unsure in the presence of older and more knowledgeable students. A warm flush came over the back of his neck—something that still happens when he finds himself in an uncomfortable position. Finally, Stohlman and the others looked at him, and waited for his contribution. "I don't think it is sculpture," he blurted out. "It's beautifully tooled, but it's not sculpture. It's too mechanical and functional." Stohlman, an authority on Limoges enamels, was an inspiring teacher, and it was he who, some weeks later, first put into Hoving's hands a work of art of importance—a piece of Roman glass. Now, in the precept, he looked at the other students and warned them of the dangers of getting caught in their own lecture notes, and went on to say that anything should be looked at first as an object in itself, and not in the light of secondary reading or artistic theory. Finally, he pointed out that the sophomore was right—that the thing on the table was an obstetrical speculum. "From that moment on, I had fantastic confidence," Hoving says. "I was never again afraid to say, 'I don't believe that.' Three weeks later, if that hadn't happened, I might have been talking about elegant *sfumato* and sweeping diagonals, but, fortunately, I have never looked at a work of art through a cloud of catchwords. In the technical language of the history of art, you can draw a cocoon around anything, whether it is a Campbell Soup can or an obstetrical speculum. That's what those cats in the precept did. A work of art should be looked at as a humanistic experience, an object on its own. It betrays what it is immediately." Hoving got a 1 in that course. He decided to major in art and archeology, and for the next two years he made regular trips to New York for drawing courses at the Art Students League. In Princeton, he retreated from nearly all non-academic activity of any kind, roomed alone during his last two years, and was seldom seen even by his friends. He audited undergraduate art courses that he was not enrolled in, and he sat in on graduate seminars. He wrote his senior thesis on "The Origin and Development of the Early Christian Basilica." His final departmental grade was a straight 1, and he was graduated from the university with highest honors.

SEVENTY-THIRD STREET

On a bamboo easel in one corner of the living room of Hoving's apartment, at 150 East Seventy-third Street, stands a work by Dan Basen in which a hundred and eight finishing nails have been inserted in canvas like pins in cloth, all in regimented patterns of "X"s and palisades; the whole of it, nails and canvas, is painted white. The room itself appears to have been last painted in the early nineteen-thirties, and, its contents aside, suggests a room in an old hotel in, say, Scranton, Pennsylvania. On one wall is a Ruth Abrams abstract called "Woman Sleeping," and across the room is another Abrams—this one representational, of a woman brooding. Five hooks-and-eyes of graduated sizes, mounted on a plaque, are labelled "Sex," sculptor anonymous. Framed and under

glass is a large sketched composition by Knud Nielsen that consists of
fragments of Hoving: several aspects of his head, and a study of his hands
—tapered, talon fingers holding the head of a griffin. On a freestanding
set of shelves is a Basen head of Hoving, made from blocks and chips
of wood that Basen nailed together, partly wrapped in strips of canvas,
and daubed with paint. The likeness is remarkable. Across the room is
a Basen fetish—two mobile boxes within a third box, which has been
screwed to the wall; on top of the exterior box is a full-size model, made
of wood with photographs glued to it, of the Cross of Bury St. Edmunds.
On a two-foot-long table near the door is a sixteenth-century French
marble sculpture of the Virgin and nursing Child. In a glass-front cabinet
are a fourteenth-century French ivory (half of a diptych); a fifth-century
Syrian drinking glass that was found with the Antioch Chalice and was
eventually given by the King of Sweden to Hoving's grandfather; an
Etruscan terra-cotta head; a Günther Uecker icon, consisting of a board
with a nail in it; and a fifteenth-century Russian icon given to Hoving
by Ante Topic-Mimara. By the cabinet is a cloud box by Adrian Guillery
and Dick Hogle, who also did a six-foot cylindrical "Column of Light"
that stands in another corner of the room, and, elsewhere in the apartment, a four-foot mechanical man whose head lights up in various colors
when it watches a television set. The mechanical man, according to
Hoving, "mixes his own bulbs." Resting on another living-room table
one evening not long ago were an original sketch by Charles Dana
Gibson, several sketches by Mario Avati, and a sketch of a woman with
open skirts by Egon Schiele. On the floor behind a chair was a small,
portable hi-fi, and in it a Judy Collins record was turning. She was
singing Bob Dylan's "Just like Tom Thumb's Blues":

> "Don't put on any airs
> When you're down on Rue Morgue Avenue
> They got some hungry women there
> And they'll really make a mess outta you."

Hoving said, "I think it's the saddest song I've ever heard, and I'm
not even sure I know what it's about. I'm hung up on Judy Collins." The
hour was six-thirty. He had a pitcher of Martinis in one hand, and he
sat down in a chair and began to open the day's mail. "Swine!" he cried
out, and tossed a letter aside. He glanced at another letter and wrote
"Hire him" across the top of it. A third letter invited Hoving to join a

club. "I hate memberships," he said. "I once had a summer membership in the Racquet Club and I couldn't stand it—the snobs running and screaming." The phone rang. "No, it's O.K., it's all right," he said. "I think we ought to go for that; the ring is beautiful. The whole *Schmier* . . . See if you can haggle them down. We'll try to use curator's funds. The time has to be critical, and it's getting very hairy." He snapped his fingers. His life, after a year in the Parks Department, seemed to have become a series of snaps—snap decisions, snapped fingers. Moreover, he was then working at two jobs. He was still Commissioner of Parks and, *de facto,* he was Director of the Museum. "I've been too damned busy to be thoughtful," he said. "But I was taking stock of myself last night, and I'm terribly dissatisfied. At times like that, I see myself as a failure —going into things, having all the fun, and getting out without taking care of the details." His daughter, Trea—a pretty, blond nine-year-old who goes to the Spence School—was sitting beside him, trying to learn how to play a recorder. Hoving wondered aloud if she couldn't learn somewhere else. She stayed where she was. He looked cross-eyed and shrugged. His wife, Nancy, arrived home from work and made herself a drink. She works downtown, in the office of the city's Coördinator of Addiction Programs. Both she and Hoving have their own Hondas. After a while, that evening, they got into an argument. It was political, not personal, having something to do with Bed-Sty, which is how both Hovings refer to the Bedford-Stuyvesant section of Brooklyn. Mrs. Hoving is at least as fast on her feet as Hoving. When, during their Bed-Sty argument, he responded to a question with a circumlocution, she said, "Don't give me a public answer." Hoving clapped his lips up and down, like hands. Hoving is not only a verbal wit but a facial comedian as well. His face moves all the time while he talks. He winces, wags his eyebrows, and smiles the smile of a cozy wolverine. A few minutes later, he was describing, in words and sounds, a sailboat luffing and flapping through a narrow inlet. The talk had changed to his summer plans—five short cruises, spaced out from June to September, as a member of the foredeck gang of a friend's fifty-foot racing sloop called Blixtar. He has raced to Bermuda five times on Blixtar. Three years ago, Blixtar was nearly run down by a freighter in a black fog. "You felt this clammy, crawling fear," Hoving said. He whistled, wailed, and made foghorn sounds. He went on, "Then we heard the slap of the screws—thwa thwa thwa—and the thing went by us a hundred feet away." The talk centered for a while on dangerous situations, and soon Hoving was demonstrating how Sicilians, as they leave their houses in the morning, automatically swivel their heads to check on the mood of Mount Etna. While Hoving was a graduate student, he lived in Italy for a year, studying in Italian museums and working for several months at an archeological dig in Sicily. During that year, he also painted, sketched, wrote short stories, and began to keep a personal journal that, within two years, exceeded two hundred thousand words. It contains compact but incredibly thorough descriptions of every building and every object of artistic interest he visited, and it also includes essays on subjects as disparate as cybernetics and Italian rock 'n' roll, and an eloquent chronicle of the infancy of his daughter. Most notably, though, it is a record of the self-questioning of a man in his middle twenties who seemed to want more than anything else to know the extent of his potentialities as a painter and a fiction writer, and who wondered if, alternatively, he would ever be able to find himself in the scholarly discipline of art history. All that, however, was now on the shelves of cabinets in the living room, and he was describing what it felt like to lie down on the black earth in the crater of Etna. "You could hear the lava bubbling—blump blump blump—and all these zonked bees walked all over you," he said. "Millions of bees are attracted to the sulphur, which does something to them. They're all up there taking trips. Every step you take, you crunch generations of bees. Fow! Shall we go?" He meant to dinner. During his time as Parks Commissioner, a secretary typed out a schedule for him every day, and he sometimes made as many as three speeches in eight hours, and seldom spent an evening at home. That night, he and his wife had accepted an invitation to The Four Seasons.

An enormous Picasso hangs there, eighteen feet high. Hoving said, looking up at the painting, "I would pay seventy-five thousand dollars for that. It's just beautiful."

His wife said, "Do you know how much the restaurant paid?"

"A hundred thousand," Hoving said, and his eyebrows bounced up and down.

## EIGHTY-SECOND AND FIFTH

Hoving, wearing a turtleneck jersey and a sports coat, stood just inside the main entrance of the Metropolitan Museum. "Come in. Come in. Don't touch! Don't touch!" he said, and he turned and walked through the Great Hall, with his hands clasped behind his back. This was a Sunday morning in March, and the place was empty. His eyes swept the high, vaulted, train-station ceiling and ran down the grimy walls. He said, "Note the great space, the classical reminiscences, in 1911 style. We're going to sandblast. Shall we go to the Gyppies?" As he would have done twenty-five years ago, he went first to the halls of Egyptian art. His eye was caught by a stone relief of sailors in action. "People say that Egyptian art is pattern-repetitive," he said. "It isn't. Look at that rope disappear and reappear beyond the sail. This was utter realism to them. . . . Look here. . . ." The god Amun, from the Temple of Amun, at Karnak—pure gold, seven inches high. "That's one of the best pieces in the joint. How would you like to own *him?*" Hoving walked on through a roomful of Egyptian gold until a jewel casket that belonged, in 1900 B.C., to the Princess Sit Hat-Hor Yunet arrested his attention. He said, "Talk about Art Nouveau, Mies van der Rohe, or anything at all, this is just as beautiful as any piece of furniture made throughout history." In the Chapel of Ra-em-Kui, he stopped before a wall decorated with beasts. "Look at those horn shapes," he said. "That couldn't have been done by a people who had any written language but the hieroglyphic. If any other museum in this country had this chapel alone, it would consider itself to have an Egyptian collection." The government of the United Arab Republic has given the United States a temple from Dendur, below the Aswan Dam, in gratitude for the American money that helped save Abu Simbel. American museums were competing for the temple at that time, and Hoving wanted it very much. The stone of the temple is porous, and vulnerable to erosion in a humid climate. Hoving had had a new two-million-dollar wing designed (and approved by the Museum's trustees) just to hold the temple. As conceived by Hoving, the walls of the new wing would be sheer glass, so that the temple would be visible—most dramatically when illuminated at night—from Fifth Avenue and from the surrounding acreage of Central Park. Meanwhile, the Smithsonian Institution, in Washington, his chief competitor, wanted to put the temple outdoors, on the bank of the Potomac. "They think they're going to dip it in something," Hoving said. "In our vast, glass case, it would glow like a work of art, which it is. That temple makes me so nervous I can't sleep." (It has since been awarded to the Metropolitan Museum.)

Hoving wandered on through the Museum without pattern or plan, and kept quoting Rorimer: "What are the three things you like best? Pick three." Picking his own in the Ancient Near Eastern collection, he stopped by a sculpture in heavy black diorite. It had been carved from a cube, and very little of the cube had been removed in order to reproduce the likeness of Gudea, ruler of Lagash. "Look at that little black atom bomb," Hoving said. "That is one of the few pieces here I would take off and go lumping down the track with. This entire Ancient Near Eastern collection has been built up since the mid-nineteen-fifties. Look at that Syrian bull. How would you like to have *that* and touch it every day? When you consider that these Sassanian pieces weren't here ten years ago, you can see the sort of thing that can be done. People think this Museum is loaded, but I don't think we have enough. We should develop the pre-Columbian collection. Do you know how many great Nabataean bronzes we have? None. There may be stuff we have no idea of the existence of. The notion that we're supposed to collect only master-pieces is a little bit false. Concepts of masterpieces change. We're collect-ing for five hundred years from now. We're after the top quality, but since the Museum is a great encyclopedia of man's achievement, we also collect backup material—footnotes and appendices to great chapters in art history. Every great treasure needs a supporting cast. Come on upstairs. I'll show you what I mean." A minute later, Hoving stood in a roomful of Rembrandts. The Museum has so many Rembrandts that they go around a corner and out into an antechamber as well. Hoving's attention settled on "Aristotle Contemplating the Bust of Homer," which Rorimer bought for two million three hundred thousand dollars, and in which Aristotle wears over his shoulder a blue-gold and almost iridescent chain of honor, presumably given to him by Alexander the Great. "We have thirty-two Rembrandts," Hoving said. "The collection was outstanding before the 'Aristotle' arrived. But reaching out for it was important, because the 'Aristotle' became the preëminent Rembrandt in the collection. Look at that chain. That alone is worth two million three. We hate to put that figure down anywhere, but all you can say is—it was worth it. Look at the thought, the loneliness, in that human, moving face. When I learned the other day that the National Gallery had bought that Leonardo—the 'Ginevra de' Benci'—for six million dollars, I couldn't sleep all night. We should have reached for it. The reputation of the Metropolitan has always been based on its power to acquire things without reserve. A museum can lose that sort of knife-edge. It's a matter of attitude. If you lose that *one* day of going for the great thing, you can lose a decade. Any trustee should be able to write a check for at least three million dollars and not even feel it. We are a collecting institution, and mobility is the only thing that wins in this game of collecting—making a decision and moving out. If I live to the year 2000, before I die there will be a painting sold for twenty-five million—well, a work of art, not necessarily a painting." He stopped for a moment before two other Rembrandts—"Man with a Magnifying Glass" and "Lady with a Pink"—and said that in his opinion they were "on a level" with the "Aristotle." Close by was a painting called "Old Woman Cutting Her Nails." "That's not a Rembrandt," Hoving said. "It's probably Nicolaes Maes. The label says, 'Signed and dated Rembrandt, 1648.' There are subtleties in the museum business, let me tell you. Do you want to know what quality is? Come look at this." He took off as if he were a floor-walker on his way to the Hickey-Freeman suits. Finally, he stopped before a van Eyck, showing, in two panels, the Last Judgment and the Crucifixion, with green country, behind the cross, reaching away to snow-covered mountains. "In my opinion, this is A No. 1 in the Flemish collection," he said. "Why? Just look at it. The color. The drama. Possibly it is not van Eyck. The Alps bother me. Whatever it is, it is a great painting. Do you want to see my favorite picture in the Museum? This way. You know, people say art is long and life is fleeting. In my opinion, it is the other way around. Mummius bought all the great treasures of Lysippus and Praxiteles. Nothing remains. We don't have *a single thing* from the workshop of Praxiteles. Nothing is preserved from the vaunted collections of Rome. Private collections disappear quickest of all. You have to band together to last, and this is one of the arguments for a big museum. There it is—the Havemeyer Degas. Isn't that something?" He was standing in a roomful of French Impressionists, and his gaze was fixed on Degas's "Woman with Chrysanthemums," his own subjective choice as the treasure of treasures in the Museum. "There is something about it—I can't explain it, I don't know how to describe it," he said. "Keep looking at it. You have to stand here and hang into it. Absorb its nature. Forget the label. Ask yourself questions. Look at the thought in the woman's face. What is she thinking? What is she about to say? Everything clicks in this painting. It has classical assurance. Just as a flower piece, it is staggering. It's, for me, got everything." He then walked away quickly, and, on his way out of the room, paused a moment in front of the full-lipped woman in Renoir's "By the Seashore." He said, "Look at the difference between this Renoir and that turgid portrait over there—when he began to sell out." He waved a thumb at Renoir's "Mme. Tilla Durieux." Then he went around a couple of corners and stopped at Cézanne's "Man with a Straw Hat" and, near it, Monet's "La Grenouillère" and "The Green Wave." All three were identified as having come from the Havemeyer Collection. "What an eye Mrs. Havemeyer had!" Hoving said. "She picked the best of the best. Wow! What an eye! All the ones that make you thump forward. Come look at this Goya." He moved like a ray through several walls until he stood before "A City on a Rock," in which a city stands on a butte above a battle scene of terrible bloodshed and burning flesh. "That's a stunning picture," Hoving said. "I don't know what it's all about. It made a great impression on me when I was fifteen years old. Some people think that it isn't a Goya, that it's too loose, but since it's a Havemeyer, I'd give it the benefit of the doubt. How many incorrectly attributed pieces there are in the Museum depends on who you talk to. With a million and a half things in the house, there have to be some errors. Look at these drawings." He was now walking through a temporary show of Goya drawings. "Our collection of Goya drawings is just sickeningly great," he went on. "About ninety per cent of all our prints and drawings are kept in storage, but don't let that mislead you. One of the great myths about the Museum is that lurking below the main floor are fabulous treasures. You bring most of them up and show them and—ickkk." He doubled back on himself and was soon standing before three enormous battle scenes— each on about a hundred and seventy-five square feet of canvas—by Giovanni Battista Tiepolo. He said that he had bought them for the Museum in 1965, he was not sure where. His eyebrows moved up and down like brushes, somehow carrying the implication that he had walked out of Italy on stilts, with these great canvases rolled around his legs. "The Museum has never done anything slightly illegal," he said. "And you had better believe that. We are no more illegal in anything we have done than Napoleon was when he brought all the treasures to the Louvre. Our scope is excellent, but if I were to tell you what we want most, prices would go up—keep that in mind. Our collecting is done in secrecy. In the world of art, drop a spoon in Cleveland and ten seconds later they hear about it in Munich. Are you beginning to feel why I like coming back to the Museum? In The Cloisters, I was surrounded by objects—things, rather than people. I needed to get away from it for a while. After Jim Rorimer died, the six youngest trustees of the Museum became a committee to choose a new director. As a trustee ex officio, I advised them not to get someone young, because a young man probably couldn't stay with it for thirty years. They brought this up again when they hired me, and all I could say to them was that it is one of the onuses of the board of trustees to decide when to get rid of a director. I don't really know what I'm going to do. Flamboyant promises come out during political campaigns, but, hell, the Museum has a fine structure and its intentions have been clear since it was chartered in 1870. We collect, preserve, exhibit, and educate. My job is to make the Museum sensitive to its time and to people living in that time. When I see an area where I want to collect—maybe because I see a gap, maybe because a great piece has come on the market—my only standard will have to be overall quality. I'll have to think very deeply about what the work of art does, not only in its aesthetic nature but in its historical and humanistic nature —how it sums up its time, how it expresses its creator. You build with an eye to having as few gaps as possible, and you try to fill some of your own gaps as well. God knows, I have plenty of them—prints, Oriental art, American painting, American sculpture. My expertise is medieval, but I hope that I know quality. Jim Rorimer was a medievalist, but that didn't stop him. From collecting Rembrandts, for example. There's another kind of gap I'd like to bridge, too—the one that exists between museums and universities. The relationship is now one of some suspicion on both sides. Museum people think of professors as too theoretical, dull, chained to an iconographical point of view, immersed in photographs, lacking in connoisseurship. University people think of museum people as dilettantes, not well trained and bent toward social activity. In Europe, the museum man is more on the level of the professor. We have good people and we need more. We should have endowed chairs here, and a scholarly journal. We need a firmer foundation of scholarship. The Museum has a great scholarly contribution to make. On the popular side, we have to find a better way to educate the people who come in here— thirty-six thousand on a Sunday afternoon alone. We need some kind of storefront, a place near the door where they can go and, through modern media, be prepared for the task of looking, and for the scope of what we have. In the age of television, the contemplative attitude that people once took before paintings has left us. You don't have to be Marshall McLuhan to figure that out. The way to get people to *see* the paintings now is to tell them what they're looking at. I'm not a great fan of our tape-recorded guides. They don't go far enough. I'd like to put in a system of jacks under each painting, each work of art, of major importance. There could be a jack for religious symbolism, a jack for quick biography of the artist, a jack for general history, another for technique. You plug yourself into the jacks and learn as much as you want to. To set up something like that throughout the Museum might cost several hundred thousand dollars, but that's nothing. In the decorative arts, the hyper-ideal is to show things to people as if they had them in their hands. That's all I can say. Now I have to go do it. Gene Moore, who does windows at Tiffany, is coming here to do a display of Greek gold, silver, and jewels. I'd like to do that sort of thing throughout the place—use industrial designers, interior decorators. As a general thing, we should be unobtrusive, but in the past we have been so unobtrusive that objects have suffered for it. Also, we've been criticized for not having enough shows, and that's right. We're about to do one called 'In the Presence of Kings.' We have twenty-two hundred objects, from all over the Met, that are known to have been intimately associated with rulers. About six hundred of them will be in the exhibition. We have Marie Antoinette's dog kennel. I'm going to do the tape for the 'King' show myself. I'll improvise it." He stopped and looked up at Salvador Dali's "Crucifixion," and an expression of distaste came over his face. "A remarkable example of modern Spanish painting," he said, blinking three times, rapidly.

The empty rooms were suddenly filled with the sound of footsteps, and a group of men and women walked past with an assistant to Hoving whose name is Harry Parker. "Actors," Hoving explained. "They're rehearsing fragments of plays that they will do in front of paintings: Pirandello in front of Pollock, *Phèdre* among the Greek amphorae—that sort of thing. People will just come upon them unexpectedly; nothing will be scheduled. It's Harry's idea. I don't know the point of it, but I know it will work. Come look at this Bingham. . . ." The canvas, by George Caleb Bingham (1811–79), shows two men in a canoe on a smooth river, with a dark lupine animal in the bow, and is called "Fur Traders Descending the Missouri." "This will stack up to any painting done in Europe in that period," Hoving continued. "People have been over-Europeanized. The expatriate influence is still on us. Americans, dissatisfied with American life, went to Europe, and praised what they saw. They had no eye for what had gone on here. Two hundred years from now, people will look all this over and reëvaluate it for what it is. It will all reshuffle itself." He drifted on into the first of several rooms full of modern American paintings, stopped to adjust a cushion on a Mies van der Rohe chair, and looked for a moment out of a window that faced Central Park. Two bicyclists, riding side by side, moved north up the Park drive. "What three things do you like best?" he said, and he turned to face Larry Poons' "Tristan da Cunha," a particularly effective piece of optical art—many pink eggs on a bright-orange field—which cannot be closely observed without a certain optical pain. "Most Op Art is mechanical and not subtle," Hoving said. "This one captures you and draws you within it. Take any still-life painter from the Dutch to Cézanne. They're just putting *things* onto canvas. There's no reason it can't be done this way." He crossed the room to Jackson Pollock's "Autumn Rhythm," which to an unsympathetic eye could appear to be a drop cloth over which a ceiling was painted black, brown, and gold by a man with a shaking hand. "This is a great painting," Hoving said. "It takes a long time to figure out why. You know, the Japanese once did ceramics that they deliberately broke. They would make a crack in a perfect pot. It fascinated them—one haphazard imperfection in something otherwise perfectly formed. This Pollock has some of that element. It seems haphazard, but the forms are there. Look at that series of ellipses hunched in the center. When I look at it, I don't think. I just look at all the shapes. It's big. Limitless." Then he walked on, past twenty or thirty canvases, and stopped before Charles Demuth's "I Saw the Figure 5 in Gold," which possibly contains as much action as any work that could be done on canvas. The figure 5, repeated twice, emerges out of what appears to be a pattern of architectural fragments, an urban vortex, centered on a bright-red metallic engine that is hurtling who knows where. "In collecting modern paintings, we try to decide what are the best pieces that a man has done," Hoving said. "Then we try to get the absolute best one —the best, without any question, that he has ever done. That's what it's all about." He went over to another window and stood there looking out for a moment before continuing. "I once had a secret wish to become director of the Museum of Modern Art, but I really couldn't be happy in any museum but this one," he said. "I couldn't stand being categorized into one era."

# Levels of the Game

By most standards, the semifinal match in men's singles played at Forest Hills on September 8, 1968, was not climactic. Arthur Ashe beat his Davis Cup teammate, Clark Graebner, in four sets, with scores of 4–6, 8–6, 7–5, 6–2. The finals looked more promising, for Ashe had a chance to become the first American to win the men's singles since 1955. The next day he was victorious, becoming also the first black male ever to win the finals. Lots of room for copy here, as sports stories go, but not in the semifinal contest.

Watching that earlier match, McPhee was intrigued by its Byzantine levels of competition. Ashe and Graebner were the same age and rank among world-class players, yet the net dividing them sharply dramatized their differences of race, culture, training, and style. One could portray them as opposites *and* equivalents, caught in the existential conflict of serve and volley, but with room for lobs or spins into the past. McPhee obtained a videotape of the match, studied it closely, and later asked each player to watch as well. As spectators they talked constantly, re-creating their thoughts and emotions with uncanny precision. At this level of their game, the opportunities for insight were almost inexhaustible.

In formal terms, *Levels of the Game* is an elaborate work, comprised of sharp, contrapuntal rallies that display McPhee's large repertoire of narrative strokes. The following extract gives a sample of his skills, set against the doubled story of Ashe and Graebner's early training. Even this fragment suggests the outcome, where only one player can win.— *WLH*

"People say that Arthur lacks the killer instinct." (Ronald Charity is commenting.) "And that is a lot of baloney. Arthur is quietly aggressive—more aggressive than people give him credit for being. You don't get to be that good without a will to win. He'll let you win the first two sets, then he'll blast you off the court." Ronald Charity, who taught Arthur Ashe to play tennis, was himself taught by no one. "I was my own protégé," he says. Charity is approaching forty and is the head of an advertising and public-relations firm in Danville, Virginia. Trim, lithe, in excellent condition, he is still nationally ranked as one of the top ten players in the A.T.A. In 1946, when he began to play tennis, as a seventeen-year-old in Richmond, there were—male and female, all ages —about twenty Negroes in the city who played the game, and none of them played it well. Charity, as a college freshman, thought tennis looked interesting, and when, in a bookstore, he saw Lloyd Budge's *Tennis Made Easy* he bought a copy and began to teach himself to play. When he had absorbed what Budge had to say, he bought Alice Marble's *The Road to Wimbledon,* and, finally, William T. Tilden's *How to Play Better Tennis.* "It just happened that I could pull off a page and project into my imagination how it should be done," he says. Blacks in Richmond could play tennis at the Negro Y.W.C.A., where Charity developed his game, and, a little later, four hard-surface courts were built at Brook Field, a Negro playground about two miles from the heart of the city. Arthur Ashe, a Special Police Officer in charge of discipline at several Negro playgrounds, lived in a frame house in the middle of Brook Field. When Arthur Ashe, Jr., was six years old, he spent a great deal of time watching Ronald Charity play tennis, and would never forget what he felt as he watched him: "I thought he was the best in the world. He had long, fluid, graceful strokes. I could see no kinks in his game."

"I guess by that time I was about the best in Richmond—you know, black tennis player," Charity continues. "One day, Arthur asked me if I would show him how to play. He had had no tennis experience. I put the racquet in his hand. I taught him the Continental grip. That's what I was playing with. At first, I would stand six feet away from him, on the same side of the net, and throw balls to him while he learned a stroke. The little guy caught on so quickly. When the stroke had been taught, I would cross the net and hit it with him. We practiced crosscourt forehands, forehands down the line, crosscourt backhands. We played every summer evening. There was a little backboard there. All day long, he would practice. We had a club—the Richmond Racquet Club, all grown men—and we let him join it. His game improved. One day, when he was playing someone his own age, he kept looking around after he hit good shots, to see who might have been watching. I bawled him out for it. I told him if he continued to do anything like that I wasn't going to be bothered with him anymore. He never did that anymore. He was a quiet child, observant. He took in everything, and read a lot. He was very disciplined. The level of his game kept going up. Finally, I called Dr. Johnson at Lynchburg. In fact, I carried Arthur up there. It was on a Sunday. He was ten years old."

Dr. Johnson's house, two stories, frame, painted brown and white, is about twice the size of any other house in the neighborhood. It has four upstairs bedrooms, one of which Arthur shared with another boy. The basement playroom appears to be a copy of a small night club on a busy highway. The columns that support the floor above are encased in blue mirrors. Red leatherette couches and lounge chairs are set about in groups. Glass doors, which are generally locked, close off a bar that is commercial in grandeur and is fully appointed and equipped. Tennis trophies shine from every shelf. There is a ping-pong table, for hand-eye coördination. Off the lounge is a shower room. A basement door and stairwell lead to a formal garden, and across the garden is the tennis court, surrounded by a rusting fence and high telephone poles that support floodlights. The tennis court abuts the sidewalk that runs in front of the doctor's house, and is several feet above the sidewalk level, held there by a retaining wall of poured concrete. People walking by have a sneaker's-eye view of the action. On the other side of Pierce Street is a small general store, and next to the store are two narrow, vacant houses that have no doors and few windowpanes. Boards nailed on a slant across the doors carry boldly lettered but apparently ineffectual warnings against vandalism and trespass. Behind Dr. Johnson's house is a combined garage and tool shed that contains a curious device. From a bracket on the floor to a beam above runs a vertical elastic cord, drawn fairly taut. About two feet off the floor, the cord passes through the center of a tennis ball. The height of the ball is adjustable. The developing tennis players hit this ball with pieces of broom handle cut twenty-six inches long, the exact length of a tennis racquet. The device, known as the Tom Stow Stroke Developer, was invented by the teacher of Sarah Palfrey, Helen Jacobs, Margaret Osborne, and J. Donald Budge. Dr. Johnson has almost every teaching device known to the game. On the court are two Ball-Boy machines, a rebounding net, and a service stand, which holds a ball in perfect position overhead for practicing serves. Players who are new to the Junior Development Team swing broom handles at the Tom Stow Stroke Developer until they can connect consistently with the ball and not the cord. Then they take their broom handles to the court and use them instead of racquets. Dr. Johnson calls this "learning how to *see* the ball." When they can play proficiently with the broom handles, actually rallying, they are advanced to the use of strung frames. The Junior Development Team has generally had eight or ten members. In recent summers, white boys have applied for admission, and Dr. Johnson has let some in. Dr. Johnson's effect on his neighborhood has been analogous to his effect on the outside world. In the living room of his next-door neighbor's house, a small, one-story place on the far side of the tennis court, is a table on which are twenty-nine tennis trophies. Near the table is a television set. Two teen-age boys, the winners of the trophies, are watching Ashe and Graebner, at Forest Hills, on television. Graebner hits a serve that splits the court, landing on the line between the service boxes and almost instantly thereafter smashing into the stadium wall. Ashe does not even lift his racquet. He is not bothered by an ace that is perfect. "If the ball goes right on the line in the center, there is nothing you can do," he will say. "There is something in your mind that says you can't get there." The score is fifteen-all, second game, second set. One of the boys watching television sighs audibly through his teeth: "Shhhhh . . ."

When Arthur first saw Dr. Johnson's place, it looked much as it does now. The houses across the street were occupied then. The fence around the court was less rusty. There was no night lighting. But the training gadgets were there, and a group of high-school boys were intently learning not only how to play but, more important, how to win. "My ambition was to develop somebody who could win the U.S.L.T.A. Interscholastic Championship—that was it, pure and simple," Dr. Johnson says. "I had so many players right on the verge. Then they would fall off." When Arthur had been there less than three days, Dr. Johnson decided he was unteachable, and told him he was going to send him home. Arthur's trouble was that he responded to the Johnson method by telling Dr. Johnson—and Dr. Johnson's son Robert, who did a lot of the teaching—how Ronald Charity would have done things, with the implication that Ronald Charity knew more than they did. Dr. Johnson called Arthur Ashe, in Richmond, and suggested that he come and get his son. Among the talents of Arthur Senior, the discipline of children was not the least. Once, at Brook Field, when Arthur Junior threw his racquet in exasperation, he heard the screen door of his house slam before the racquet hit the ground. His father was on the tennis court three seconds later, and Arthur Ashe, Jr., has not to this day flung a racquet in anger again. Now Arthur Senior drove straightaway to Lynchburg, stepped onto Dr. Johnson's tennis court, and asked his son if he wanted to stay with Dr. Johnson. When Arthur Junior said he did, his father said, "Then you do everything he says, no matter what he tells you." Assuring Dr. Johnson that the problem no longer existed, Arthur Senior left Lynchburg. Dr. Johnson would always thereafter praise Arthur Ashe as the most unquestioningly obedient tennis player he had ever coached. If Dr. Johnson told Arthur to hit to an opponent's backhand and nowhere else, Arthur would hit to the backhand even if the other player edged over so far that ninety per cent of the court was on his forehand side. "Whatever strategy you gave him to play, he wouldn't change to save his life," Dr. Johnson says. "He did what you told him, even if he lost at it."

Training time was divided among the players, and Arthur, lowest in age and seniority, had to spend a lot of time standing around watching the older boys play, much as Rodney Laver, a few years earlier, had spent a lot of time standing around the tennis court on his family's farm in tropical Australia waiting for his older brothers to finish playing. The boys in Lynchburg would take turns hitting against a Ball-Boy until they missed, or until they had hit a hundred times—always concentrating on one stroke until they had it under control. They rarely played points. "I believe in practice," Dr. Johnson told them. "You can learn more." There was one boy there near Arthur's age level. His name was Horace Cunningham. He lived just across the street from Dr. Johnson, and, as the Doctor continues the story, "He could beat Arthur's socks off. Arthur was the worst player. He was always the last one to leave the court—that was one thing in his favor. But everybody could beat him."

In Arthur's eyes, the Doctor was an imperial figure—"an immensely rich Negro, with his tennis court and his Buick, and his seemingly endless supply of money. At ten and eleven years old, I was always rather awed by the guy. The world is very small then. To tell you the truth, I hated everything about Dr. Johnson's at that time, except playing tennis. I hated weeding the gardens, cleaning the doghouse. I was the youngest, and I had to clean the doghouse every day."

Dr. Johnson to this day takes visitors out back, shows them the concrete-floored pen where he keeps his hunting dogs, and demonstrates how easy the enclosure is to clean. "All he had to do was use a water hose," he says. "Some kids are lazy. The least they can do is to weed the garden, roll the court, clean the doghouse—when I am paying for their room and board. Arthur's trying to have some fun, griping about that." Standing there with the hose in his hand, Dr. Johnson looks away toward the tennis court and forgets all about the dog pen. "Even when Arthur started going off to play in the tournaments, Horace could beat him—on this court. But Horace could *not* beat Arthur in the tournaments. That was a different situation." They travelled in the Buick—Baltimore, Washington, Durham—and when Arthur was a little older and began to go to some tournaments on his own, Dr. Johnson called him, wherever he might be, to talk over his matches. Arthur was based in Lynchburg every summer until he was eighteen, the fixed element in a squad whose personnel changed frequently, as Dr. Johnson did his own kind of weeding. The Junior Development Team functioned in part on contributions from interested people in the A.T.A., but Dr. Johnson put thousands of dollars of his own specifically into Arthur's career. Three white businessmen in Richmond—an insurance broker, a department-store executive, and a legitimate-theatre executive—contributed significant amounts, and Arthur's father gave more than he could afford. Arthur once overheard him saying that he was a little sorry his son had chosen a sport as expensive as tennis. The cost of equipment alone was more than a thousand dollars a year.

When Arthur was fifteen, Dr. Johnson tried to enter him in the junior tournament of the Middle Atlantic Lawn Tennis Association, which was held at the Country Club of Virginia, in Richmond. The Middle Atlantic L.T.A., a semi-autonomous subdivision of the U.S.L.T.A., refused to process the application. So Arthur could earn no ranking among boys in his home section of the country, although by now he was ranked fifth among boys in the United States. The following summer, 1959, the Middle Atlantic Championships were held at the Congressional Country Club in Bethesda, Maryland, and Arthur's application arrived "too late." In 1960, Arthur won the junior championship of the A.T.A. *and* the A.T.A. men's-singles championship. He was seventeen. He has sometimes been compared, in his sport, to Jackie Robinson in baseball, but the analogy is weak and foreshortens the story. Jackie Robinson was part of a pool of many hundreds of first-rate baseball players, and was chosen from among them to cross the color line. Arthur, at the age of seventeen, had beaten and far outdistanced all the Ronald Charitys there were. Already he stood, as he has remained, alone. Even at that time there was not one Negro in the United States who could effectively play tennis with him, and there is none now. In June, 1961, he went to Charlottesville in the Buick with Dr. Johnson, and he won the U.S.L.T.A. national Interscholastic Championship without losing a set. He remembers what he thought at that moment in his life:

"I saw that it was conceivable that I might win someday at Forest Hills."

In 1962, the Interscholastic Championships, which had been held in Charlottesville for sixteen consecutive years, were moved to Williamstown, Massachusetts.

Ashe wants to level things. He is uncomfortable looking uphill at Graebner, who hits another serve of almost unplayable force but just close enough to be reached. Ashe dives for it and stops it with his racquet. His return floats across the net and drops near the sideline. Graebner has difficulty believing that the ball has come back. He is not reacting. "Unbelievable," he says to himself. "Too tough." After this momentary lapse, he sprints for the ball, and is completely off the court when he gets to it. Despite Graebner's hesitation, and despite the inconvenient location of Ashe's shot, Graebner has reached the ball in time not only to hit it but to drive it. Many players think Graebner is slow, for somehow, to an athlete's eye, he looks slow, and they will say something like "From the waist up, Graebner is the fastest in the world, but his feet are in his way." Ashe does not wholly agree. "Graebner is mechanically fast," he will say. "He's not that agile. He can't reverse directions well, but once he gets rolling in one direction he is fast. You've got to finesse Graebner. He's as strong as an ox. Get the ball anywhere within a two-step radius of his body and you're dead. You can't go through him. You've got to go around him or over him." Graebner says, "I don't look fast, but I get to the ball."

Graebner's drive is deep to Ashe's backhand corner, and Ashe intercepts it with a beautiful, fluid crosscourt stroke. In the followthrough, he is up on his toes, arms flaring. Ashe's backhand is one of the touchstones of modern tennis. Graebner is disturbed. He is thinking. "There it is. There Arthur goes, swinging freely." Arthur swinging freely is something that scares players of all nations. When he is behind, or otherwise in trouble, he reacts by hitting all the harder, going for a winner on every ball. Graebner moves to cover the shot. Graebner may not be technically agile, but he is moving like a cat right now. Ashe is a little surprised, and thinks, "Good God! Clark is covering that net like a blanket." Graebner gets the ball with a lunging backhand volley, his shoes slip on the grass, and he breaks his fall with his left arm. The volley is deep. Ashe detonates another splendid backhand, down the line. But Graebner recovers his balance and stops the ball at the net, dinking a shot that Ashe, sprinting, cannot reach. "What a greasy shot!" Ashe says to himself. "Gee, that pisses me off. He just greased it. I hit two great shots, then he greased one. It barely got over the net, and it died in the grass."

Now, for the first time in the match, Graebner double-faults. He scowls angrily toward the Marquee, the sheltered stands at the eastern end of the stadium, where his wife, Carole, is sitting with Ashe's father and Robert J. Kelleher, president of the U.S.L.T.A. Carole is the trim in Graebner's racquet—the extra bit of nylon stringing that determines rough or smooth. Graebner's angry look seems to say that he believes it was Carole who served the double fault. She absorbs this, by grace and by agreement. "I tell him to look over at me when he gets mad, because I would rather have him get mad at me than at anyone else—or at himself," she explains. For one reason or another—not always anger—Graebner looks at Carole about a hundred times a match. "I try to give him an opportunity to meet my eyes after each point, if he wants to," she goes on. "If he needs a little pick-me-up, I am there." If she is not there, he may fall apart. Once, in Australia, in a tight moment, he looked for Carole and she had gone off momentarily for refreshments. "Where's Carole? Where's Carole?" he said, and he ran around behind the grandstand looking for her. Now, at Forest Hills, she raises one hand and makes a patting motion, as if she were soothing an invisible horse. This signal means "Calm down." If she raises two clenched fists, it means "Come on, now. Get your second wind. This is a big point." If she puts one hand on top of her head and shakes her head, it means "Unbelievable!"—or, in translation, "Good shot." Graebner responds to these messages in part because his wife, whose maiden name was Carole Caldwell, is a world-class tennis player. She is ranked sixth among women players in the United States. She plays very little now, but she has been ranked as high as fourth in the world, and might be there still if she did not have two children under two years of age. "I think these are the only times that Clark publicly acknowledges me as a knowing player," she says. "Off the court, he does not acknowledge that I know much about the game. I live my tennis through Clark now, so I don't miss it so much. During matches, I'm perfectly frank with him. If he's not playing well, I'll let him know. I think he could be the best there is. Up to now, I don't think he has really worked at it. He is a natural player, not a made player. I think he sometimes thinks, 'Oh, what the hell. If God didn't give it to me, why go after it?' He sometimes loses faith in himself. As soon as he starts to lose, or get depressed, his shoulders drop. I don't think Clark would admit this, but in some respects I am his self-confidence. He will not admit that he is the biggest baby in the world, and he is by far. You wouldn't exactly call him docile. If he makes a great point, I clap hard. He'll turn and smile sometimes." At Forest Hills in 1965, Carole and Clark won the national husband-and-wife doubles championship, and she says she will never enter it again, because they fought constantly and Clark complained that she wouldn't do what he told her to do. "I've won a lot of tournaments. Let me play my own game," she said to him. A few minutes later, Clark told her to lob, so she hit the ball down the line. Even recreationally, they almost never play together now, except when Clark has not played for a long time and wants to regroove. Men frequently hit with women to regroove their strokes. Carole is a good-looking blue-eyed brunette, attractively selfless, gifted with discipline, constantly starving herself to control the figure that gave her the big tennis game that made her fourth in the world. She grew up in Santa Monica. She has girlish animation, and, blushing through it, she discloses that she was named "for Carole Lombard, who was married to Clark Gable."

Ashe is thinking, "Graebner just looked at his wife." And behind Arthur's impassive face—behind the enigmatic glasses, the lifted chin, the first-mate-on-the-bridge look—there seems to be a smile. Progress against Graebner in any given match, many players believe, can be measured directly by the number of times Graebner has looked at his wife.

Ashe tries to pass Graebner, and hits the ball into the net a foot and a half below the tape. Graebner has him forty-thirty. Ashe looks within himself angrily, thinking, "You choked on that one, boy."

As Graebner gets ready to serve for the game, Ashe tells himself, "You . . . better . . . be . . . tough . . . now."

Crunch. Ashe flails and misses. "Fault!" cries Frank Hammond, who is the service linesman on the side of the court where Ashe is at the moment playing. There are thirteen officials around the court, and Ashe and Graebner know them all. Frank Hammond's job is particularly sensitive—watching the service line in a match between two players whose styles revolve around their ballistic serves. Both Ashe and Graebner specifically asked for Hammond today, in part because they like him, and in part because they consider him the best service linesman at Forest Hills. Unconsciously, they may also feel drawn to Hammond because he is—literally—Santa Claus on a grand scale. He is a large, jolly man of national reputation, who, purely for his own amusement, is an itinerant Santa Claus, appearing in a different city each Christmas season. This year, he plans to be at Lord & Taylor, in New York. Ashe mumbles, "Good call, Frank." Ashe is still alive in this game, thanks to Santa Claus's photoelectric eyes. The serve was a half inch long.

Graebner's second serve curves in. Ashe meets it with a graceful, underspinning backhand. Graebner leans forward to volley from his shoetops. The ball is floating before Ashe now. Graebner is at the net, astride the center line, perfectly balanced and ready, but he has given Ashe too much time. Ashe hits another backhand—a hard, rolling, top-spin backhand, with unimprovable placement. It slants past Graebner so fast he can take only one step in its direction, and it skips through the chalk of the sideline—a duster, as players call a shot that stirs the chalk. For the first time in the match, Ashe has forced Graebner, serving, to deuce. "Oh, God! His play will pick up from here," thinks Graebner, who has read this sort of tea leaf before. Ashe's great shot does not necessarily mean that others will immediately follow, but it reminds Graebner of what can emerge, suddenly, from beneath the general surface of play. Moments later, Graebner, moving with extraordinary antic- ipation, picks off a forehand drive and, with an adroit, slicing drop shot off his steel racquet, puts the ball away. "I actually have more touch with the steel than anyone else," Graebner will say. "Graebner grips the racquet so tight he can *feel* the ball," Ashe observes. "He must get writer's cramp."

Advantage Graebner. Crunch. The serve is too much—unplayable. Game to Graebner. Games are one-all, second set.

The match, for a time, becomes a simple exhibition of the service stroke. Ashe may not have quite Graebner's power, but his serves—in the vernacular of the game—move better than Graebner's do. They follow less predictable patterns, and they come off the grass in less expectable ways. "I can feel my serve from my toes to my fingertips," he will say. "I don't have to look. It just flows." In two games against Ashe's service, the only point Graebner wins is given to him in the form of a double fault. This, to Arthur Ashe, Sr., is a sign of impatience on the part of his son. He says, "When Arthur Junior rushes himself, he gets into trouble." Mr. Ashe is an axiomatic man. When he says things like that, he does not seem to be making a comment so much as he seems to be promulgating a law of the universe. Somewhat darker than Arthur Junior, he is just under six feet tall and has a small mustache and a full, round face. He wears bifocal glasses with black metal rims. He is a disciplinarian by profession, and he has a kind of stern, forthright self-assurance that is not put on for the job. In several ways, he differs notably from his son. Arthur Junior is particularly articulate, and Mr. Ashe is not particularly articulate. His education stopped when he was eleven years old. Arthur Junior's personality is contained, controlled, withheld. In Arthur Senior there is no studied cool. His smile is quick. He jokes a lot. He is easy to know.

For some years now, he has lived in the country near Gum Spring, thirty-five miles northwest of Richmond. He gets up at five-thirty in the morning. ("If I stay in bed after five-thirty, I get mischievous.") He drives into Richmond in a white Ford pickup that has an aluminum enclosure behind the cab and contains a chain saw and dozens of other tools, which equip him for his three jobs and his various categories of responsibility. He wears, typically, a red shirt, gray cotton trousers, a gray cap. A bunch of keys hangs from one hip. He has his own landscaping business and his own janitorial business, and he seems to specialize in medical centers, banks, and office buildings in the new industrial parks of Richmond's west end. "You've got to scramble," he says. "You've got to give from one hand to gain on the other." He has eight employees. Some of them irritate him by following customs that run counter to his axioms—for example, when he gives them eighty dollars' pay on a Friday and they borrow two dollars from him on Monday. From 2 P.M. until 10 P.M. each day, he works for the city. In the Department of Recreation and Parks, he is not only a Special Police Officer but also a pool engineer and the supervisor of tennis courts. He carries a nightstick, handcuffs, and a gun, but he wears no uniform. His primary duty is to maintain order, and he doesn't seem to mind that his work has made him from time to time unpopular. Humor spills out of him wherever he goes. He goes into a hardware store during the hunting season and asks for a three-gun rack for his car. The salesman says, "Why do you need a *three*-gun rack, Arthur?" and the answer is "You always need a third gun so you can shoot your wife."

Mr. Ashe has five houses—four in Richmond and the one in Gum Spring—and he says that he maintains all these dwellings less for the rents than as a form of self-protection. "I'm like a groundhog. Shoot at him and he has another home to scurry off to." He built his house in Gum Spring with his own hands, using materials that he salvaged from houses and other buildings that were razed when Interstate 95 cleaved

Richmond some years ago. His property is isolated among cornfields and woods of oak and pine on a narrow asphalt road. The house is one-story, thirty-six by forty-six feet, with walls of cement block painted aquamarine. Mr. Ashe is an adept carpenter, plumber, electrician, and mason, and for a number of years he regularly took Arthur Junior to Gum Spring to work on the new house.

"Arthur Junior toted boards, mixed mortar, pulled nails, helped set the block. He did any damned thing I told him to do."

"Daddy is a Jack-of-all-trades, but that's not my bag. I hated it, but I never let him know. We went out every weekend. I had no choice."

"You give from one hand to gain on the other."

The living room at Gum Spring is full of tennis plaques and trophies, won by Arthur and his brother John, who is five years younger. On one wall hang a copy of the Twenty-third Psalm stamped in brass and a portrait of Christ painted on a china plate. Above the psalm and the plate is the head of an eight-point stag. "The first time Arthur Junior went deer hunting was in King William County." (His father gets inordinate pleasure from telling this story.) "He was just a boy. I put him on a stump and told him to wait for deer. He was nervous, just like his mother. He's got over it now, but he was nervous. And *seven* deer came toward him, and he shouted, 'Daddy! Daddy! Daddy!' I shouted, 'Shoot that damn gun.' He killed two." The house is heated with wood fires, and the stove in the kitchen is also fuelled with wood. In every room is the scent of burning oak. As Mr. Ashe drives around the countryside near Gum Spring, he turns into a fanatic for neatness and tidiness, and gets visibly angry at the sight of houses surrounded by automobile parts, miscellaneous cordwood, old oil drums, piles of scrap lumber. He says that people have no right to mess up the landscape that way. Then he drives into his own property, which is bestrewn with automobile parts, miscellaneous cordwood, oil drums, scrap lumber, and gravel, and he explains that things are different here, because he knows exactly what and where everything is and the use to which he intends to put it.

There are six in the family. Arthur Junior and John have a stepsister, Loretta, and a stepbrother, Robert. Soon after John was born, his mother (and Arthur's) died. Several years later, Mr. Ashe married Lorraine Kimbrugh, a practical, witty, conversational woman, who frequently keeps Arthur up until two or three in the morning talking about his travels and the worlds he plays in. Robert and Loretta are in high school. John is a Marine sergeant, recently home from Vietnam. More solid in build than his older brother, he is an excellent general athlete, but not a specialist. In high school in Richmond, he won letters in football, basketball, baseball, track, and tennis. Nonetheless, in finding his own way he is inevitably encountering the inconvenience of being so closely related to Arthur Ashe. A football scholarship is open to him at Duke, but he is thinking of staying in the Marine Corps.

Some people have criticized Mr. Ashe for "hustling" lumber to build the Gum Spring house. "It's against their pride," he explains. "But they have notes on their houses, and I don't." He still makes regular calls at the Richmond city dump to look for scrap lumber and other materials. He has built a large combined garage and tool shed using heavy-gauge tin highway signs—"Fredericksburg 25," "Williamsburg 99"—as siding. In this building is a twenty-one-foot aluminum-hulled power boat with a 100-horsepower engine. With his family, he cruises and fishes the rivers and tidewaters of Virginia. Arthur Junior is never reluctant to go on these trips, for fishing is his bag, too.

Graebner serves the fourth game of the second set, and in the entire game there are eight shots. Two are misfired serves. Two are aces. Ashe gets his racquet on the ball only twice. Dr. Graebner, on the edge of his chair, is pleased. "He's taking his time. He's reading Arthur nicely. He's hitting well." As it happens, Dr. Graebner is not at Forest Hills but at his home, on Wimbledon Road, in Beachwood, Ohio, where, with Clark's mother, he is watching the match on a television screen that seems almost as large as the huge picture window behind it. Through the window is an awning-shaded terrace, and beyond that a compact lawn. "I just wish he'd learn to smile on the court, because he looks so grim, and he just isn't," Mrs. Graebner says. When Clark moves with correct anticipation to cover a shot, Dr. Graebner says, "He read that well." The houses of Wimbledon Road appear to be in the fifty-to-seventy-thou-sand-dollar class and almost too big for the parcels of land allotted to them. They are faced with stratified rock, lightened with big windows, surrounded with shrubbery, and lined up in propinquous ranks like yachts at a pier. Arthur Ashe has visited the Graebners' house several times, and he remembers it in blueprint detail. "You walk in the front door. You face steps. The dining room is on the left-hand side. The living room is on the right, and beyond it a den. Beyond the dining room, the kitchen. Big back yard. Four bedrooms." The Graebners' living-room shelves are filled with tennis trophies, in place of books. The room has big furniture—big couches, big easy chairs, big lamps, big coffee tables.

Mrs. Graebner is a large woman with a strikingly attractive face, curiously like Carole's, and she, too, is a dieter of fearful discipline. Dr. Graebner is extremely dental. He has bright-white, flawless teeth—a kind of self-portrait—in an open face that smiles readily. He speaks quickly and nervously, often in an engaging monologue. Tennis players who visit his home uniformly like him, and find him amusing because he asks them questions ("How are you? How was your trip? How is your game?") and, not waiting for replies, answers all the questions himself ("It's nice to see you so well. There's nothing like a good, smooth flight. You're having your best year"). Attentively, he worries over his guests. "That's all right. We'll get a towel. It will be O.K. All right. There will be no difficulty," he says, and he all but concludes by saying, "Relax, now. It won't hurt a bit." After thirty years of close contact with temporarily muted people, he has mastered the histrionisms of his craft. He winks, interviews himself, speaks always reassuringly, and couples his skeins of language with "but"'s and "and"'s, never stopping. Crunch. Ace. Right down the middle. "He's taking his time. He's hitting well." Dr. Graebner is almost completely absorbed in Clark—in everything from the mechanical functioning of his game to the general politics of tennis, which can take on cinquecento overtones when powers meet to set up a tournament draw—and many of Dr. Graebner's long-standing, old-Clevelander patients have learned that the last thing they want to say as they sit down in the chair is "How's Clark?"

Dr. Graebner's hair, crew cut, is speckled salt-and-pepper gray, but he looks so much like Clark that the two could be mistaken for brothers. He is just over six feet tall. Like Clark, Dr. Graebner has a quick, hot temper. "My father and I are very similar. He is tight, keyed up, a perfectionist, a hard worker. He does orthodonture—everything but surgery. He's a nervous person, I guess. So am I. We keep a lot inside ourselves. He doesn't drink, smoke, or swear. I don't do anything to an extreme, but I am not a puritanical soul."

"My father can barely read and write. In his own simple way, though, he is very broadminded. He is receptive to new ideas. He shows little concern for social conventions. He is a benevolent man. He gives money and clothes to the poor. He was always strict, but fair. He doesn't drink. So far as I know, he has never bought a bottle of liquor. We do have home-made wine—peach wine, blackberry wine. If my father had a million dollars, he wouldn't change. He is not by any means a social climber. I'm convinced of that." Mr. Ashe was born on a farm in South

Hill, Virginia. He had eight brothers and sisters. His father, Pink Ashe, was a carpenter-bricklayer-farmer who grew tobacco and corn. When Arthur Senior was twelve, he went to Richmond to make his living, but he had been working part time almost all his life—cleaning yards, carrying wood, cleaning chicken houses. In Richmond, he became a butler-chauffeur. He was thirteen when he got his driver's license. For five years, he worked for Mr. and Mrs. Charles Gregory, of 2 River Road, driving them around the city, or answering the door as butler or waiting at table in a white coat. He describes Gregory as "a wealthy dude." Mrs. Gregory paid him two dollars and fifty cents a week, of which he unfailingly sent all but the fifty cents to his mother in South Hill. He was still in his teens when he went to work for the city.

At a program one evening at the Westwood Baptist Church, Arthur Senior met a tall, good-looking girl with long, soft hair and a face that was gentle and thin. Her name was Mattie Cunningham. People called her Baby. He soon married her. "She was just like Arthur Junior. She never argued. She was quiet, easygoing, kindhearted. She had a very strict mother, too, brother. She worked at Miller & Rhoads' department store." Asked if she sold things behind a counter, he asks back, "Are you kidding? In those days, that was impossible. . . . She read a lot. She was serious—a very serious-minded person, especially with that boy when he was first born." Arthur Junior carries his birth certificate in his wallet —July 10, 1943, "born alive at 12:55 P.M." All he remembers of his mother is an image of her standing by a door of the house in Brook Field, in a blue corduroy bathrobe, on a day when she was taken to a hospital. His father tells a story surrounding the events that followed: "In one of the oak trees outside the house, there was a bluejay bird singing up a storm. I carried Arthur Junior's mother to the hospital that morning. The bird sang for a week. I threw rocks at it. I shot at it with a .38, but not to kill it. The bird sang for a week and would not stop. A call came at five-twenty one morning from the hospital, and the bird stopped singing." His wife had been twenty-seven.

Becoming a lone parent seemed to increase in Arthur's father his already rigorous sense of discipline. When Arthur entered first grade, at the Baker Street School, near Brook Field, Mr. Ashe walked with him at the boy's pace and timed the journey. Arthur had exactly that many minutes to get home from school each day or he was in trouble. If he was late, his father took it for granted that something was wrong. In time, when Arthur wanted to work a paper route, his father would not let him do it. He thought it was too dangerous. "I kept the children home pretty close," he says. "My children never roamed the streets. A regular schedule was very important. A parent has got to hurt his own child, discipline him, hold him back from things you know aren't good for him. I don't believe in arguing and fussing. I can't stand it and never could. I don't believe in speaking two or three times, neither." He set maxims before his son like stepping stones. "You don't get nowhere by making enemies," he said. "You gain by helping others." And "Things that you need come first. Foolishness is last." "I told Arthur these things for his future, for his own good," Mr. Ashe goes on. "I told him I wanted him to get an education and get himself qualified so people could respect him as a human being. I wanted him to be a gentleman that everybody could recognize, and that's what he is right now."

It was a five-minute walk from the house in Brook Field to the house of the nearest neighbor, and to see his boyhood friends Arthur Junior would walk around the tennis courts, around the pool, through the parking yards of the Manhattan For Hire Car Company, and into the neighborhood beyond. Brook Field was encircled with light industry—the Bottled Gas Corporation of Virginia, the Valentine Meat Juice Company. "I didn't live in a so-called ghetto situation. I never saw rat-infested houses, never hung out on corners, never saw anyone knifed. I wasn't made aware of it all until I went to college. We were never poor. Not even close. Things weren't that tough for me. I've never had a job in my life. In a way, I envy people who have had. The field behind my house was like a huge back yard. I thought it was mine. Brook Field was just an athletic paradise, a dream world for a kid who likes to play sports. Tennis, baseball, horseshoes, basketball, football, swimming—you name it. The pool was so full of kids in the summer you couldn't see the water. I had no problems at all. There was really no reason in the world for me to leave the place. Everybody came to me. The athletic equipment was kept in a box in my house." Mr. Ashe spent half his time encouraging athletic games and the other half breaking up crap games. Brook Field, which has since been bulldozed and turned into the site of Richmond's new general post office, was lined and interspersed with oak trees, and Arthur, lying in bed at night during summer thunderstorms, kept waiting for lightning to shiver the big limbs, but it never did. And there was some latent fear, which surfaced now and again in remarks of Arthur Senior's, that the bottled-gas company might blow up, and that if it did the family would go with it. One night, something leaked at the gas company and two-hundred-foot flames raced into the sky. The big tanks, however, did not explode. "And that might have been the best thing that ever didn't happen to me."

Arthur's mother had taught him to read when he was four. He was an A student all through school. He never read detective stories, Westerns, or comic books. "I didn't want to waste a dime on comic books. Ridiculous. The dime would be gone in five minutes." For the most part, he read biographies and general factual writing, and he went through the World Book Encyclopedia. He read books beside the tennis courts when he wasn't playing, and he would continue this habit during tournaments in later years. In high school, he played the trumpet in a combo called the Royal Knights, but he actually mixed very little with his classmates, for his tennis increasingly took him out of their milieu. He was a good pitcher and a good second baseman, but his high-school principal, impressed by his development in tennis under Dr. Johnson, kept him from playing on the high-school baseball team. Black high schools in Richmond, in his era, had no tennis teams. Before long, and because of him, they would all have tennis teams.

Mr. Ashe's curfew during those years was 11 P.M. "Arthur, when Daddy says eleven o'clock, I mean *in* the house at eleven o'clock. See that car out that window? You're going to be driving that soon. You're going to wreck it trying to get home by eleven. You had better show me what you can do on foot before I let you drive that car." Arthur's father pondered all invitations that came Arthur's way, and screened out most of them. ("If I let him go to all the parties he was invited to, he wouldn't be where he is today.") Once, Arthur was invited to a party by a young lady whose father was a school principal and whose mother was a teacher. Arthur Senior approved of that one, and Arthur went. He was not home by eleven. His father went after him. When Mr. Ashe appeared in the doorway, the girl called out, "Hey, Art. Here is your antique father." Mr. Ashe tells this story without a smile.

Every Sunday, Arthur had to go to the Westwood Baptist Church. He refers to the experience as "a chore." "It's very tough to tell a young black kid that the Christian religion is for him," he says. "He just doesn't believe it. When you start going to church and you look up at this picture of Christ with blond hair and blue eyes, you wonder if he's on your side. When I got to college, I quit going to church. I go every once in a while now, out of curiosity." The ceramic Christ on the wall at Gum Spring has blond hair and brown eyes.

Dr. and Mrs. Graebner go to services every Sunday and to prayer meeting every Wednesday at the Cedar Hill Baptist Church, and they think that Clark is not as religious as he should be. They try to do whatever they can to bring Clark closer to God, and they always have tried to. He was a malleable child—in his mother's words, "a real nice boy, not difficult to handle, active but not mischievous." He fished for crawdads in the Rocky River, and he roller-skated around and around the blocks of Lakewood with a little neighbor named Nancy Gallo. There were no boys for him to play with, but he didn't seem to mind. He would always be more at ease with women than with men. In his teens, he began to dress with what he took to be suavity; he affected a camel's-hair coat and looked like a mannequin from Rogers Peet. He and his doubles partner Warren Danne chased girls together, and Warren was as impressed with Clark in this form as he was with Clark the tennis player. "Girls really liked him. He was *very much* at home with them," Warren says. When Clark was sixteen and going steady with a girl called Bubbles Keyes, he had "total use" of the family Imperial—in effect, his own car. When he needed money, he just asked for it, and if the purpose was reasonable he got it. "I was probably spoiled to some degree, as are most only children. Now that I have mine, I can see how easy it is to spoil a child. You love them so much." Clark's intense concentration on tennis worried his mother a little. She felt that he should have another outlet, and the one she chose to encourage was figure skating. Clark was trained at the Cleveland Skating Club by the best available professionals, and, with his natural sense of rhythm and his gyroscopic balance, he became an outstanding performer. But he could leave skating alone. He eventually had enough of "judges dumping all over you if you were off by one-tenth of a second—I couldn't stand that."

The Cleveland Skating Club had four cement indoor tennis courts and ten *en-tout-cas* outdoor courts, so Clark spent a high proportion of his formative years there, making the trip every afternoon on "the rapid," and going home, after office hours, with his father. (The tennis facilities are now called the Cavalry Tennis Club and are a separate, integrated organization, because "a citizen do-gooder," as Mrs. Graebner describes him, noted some years ago that the courts were on public land rented from the city, and therefore membership should be open to all. The solution was to create the Cavalry Club. Skating Club members could join Cavalry or not, as they chose, and the Graebners immediately signed up.) In his early teens, Clark became good enough to play with his father and his father's friends—"people I would consider hackers now"—and Dr. Graebner and Clark became a doubles team, competing in father-and-son tournaments. In the Western Championships, in Cleveland, they played several times against Dr. Robert Walter Johnson, of Lynchburg, and his son Robert. Clark was so young the first time that the Johnsons felt sorry for him, according to Dr. Johnson, so they eased up and gave him one game. That gave Clark the lift he needed, and the Graebners beat the Johnsons. Meeting in the same tournament in another year, the Johnsons beat the Graebners. Twice, the Graebners were national finalists in the U.S.L.T.A. father-and-son tournament. Tennis players remember how solicitous Dr. Graebner was toward Clark, and how he tried artfully to coax Clark along when he made an error. "Don't worry, honey. Don't worry, honey," Dr. Graebner would say. "Forget it. Concentrate on the next one." In later seasons, when Clark had become much the stronger player of the two, it was he who carried his father in these tournaments, and other tennis players remember that Clark used to get irked and impatient when his father missed shots, and he would grit his teeth and say to his father, "Just get me *one* point, will you?"

Clark's companion on the rest of the circuit was his mother, for Dr. Graebner had his practice and generally had to stay home. In a Chrysler New Yorker and, later, Imperials, singing along on snow tires all summer, because she felt they were safer in rain, she drove Clark and Warren Danne from Cleveland to St. Louis to Springfield to Louisville to Champaign—the cities of the tennis big-little league, where boy tennis players of the highest levels compete with one another as the season advances toward Kalamazoo. In the mind of a new American tennis player, Kalamazoo is Wimbledon. The national championships for the very young are held in August in Kalamazoo. Clark, when he was twelve, met Arthur Ashe at Kalamazoo, but, in the patterns of the draw, did not play against him. "I thought I was pretty good at twelve," Clark says. "Then I went to Kalamazoo and lost love and love in the first round. Actually, I played well. All the games went to deuce. I just didn't win them. Ray Senkowski, a six-footer who was shaving—a big Polack guy, you know —he just annihilated me, score-wise."

Clark won at Kalamazoo two years later, but meanwhile something of tangential but considerable importance would happen to him there, and to Arthur as well. Kalamazoo is often the scene of what in the career of a young tennis player is the equivalent of the day of the *alternativa* in the life of a young bull-fighter—the day of his doctorate, his confirmation, his *bar mitzvah.* If a boy tennis player is good enough to show the slightest signs of world-class potential, a man inevitably approaches him at some moment at Kalamazoo and says, "Son, I'm from the Wilson Sporting Goods Company, and I'd like to give you a couple of racquets."

It could be Dunlop, Bancroft, Spalding. They're all there. It was Wilson that knighted Arthur Ashe. He was fifteen when Wilson gave him, in his words, "two racquets and a couple of covers that first time, no shoes, no strings." Since then, he has never used another kind of racquet. When he is in Chicago, he goes to the Wilson factory and picks out several dozen frames, which are put aside and sent to him, usually in lots of four, as he requests them. His Tony Trabert model used to be the Barry MacKay model, and before that the Alex Olmedo, and before that the Don Budge. It has always been the same racquet, and Ashe has used it in its various incarnations because he thinks it is the stiffest racquet that Wilson makes. "I'm a flippy player anyway. Any racquet that gives me more flip gives me trouble." He picks them out at the factory because he wants the stiffest of the stiff. He seldom breaks one, but after he has used one for a while the head gets floppy—the racquet becomes something like a riding whip—and he throws it away. He has his racquets strung at sixty pounds of tension, but no two stringing jobs are alike, so he hits with several racquets and picks out favorites. When he comes onto the court for a match, he brings two incumbent favorites, spins them, and picks one, mystically. He plays through the match with one racquet. So does Graebner. Both Ashe and Graebner say that only Pancho Gonzales and a few others change racquets frequently during a match, and they both say that Pancho is "psycho" about it. Both Ashe and Graebner use four-and-five-eighths-inch handles. Ashe is not sure what his racquet weighs. "I don't know. I don't care. Some players worry about their racquets to the quarter ounce. And they have to be strung just so. Christ, in my opinion if you worry about that crap you go out there and you can't play. You'll seldom find me with more than four racquets. I run through them, and that's it."

Graebner was anointed by Wilson, too. He was only thirteen when, at Kalamazoo, the Wilson man hit a few balls with him, then gave him two racquets and two covers. The following year, he reached the five-racquet category, and after that he went into the unlimited class. Graebner, too, has been loyal to Wilson, but Dunlop once nearly achieved him. He tried the Dunlop Maxply Fort, the racquet Rod Laver uses, and its touch impressed him. He told Wilson all about it and suggested that Wilson custom-make for him a racquet exactly like the Dunlop and paint "WILSON" on it. Wilson craftsmen built mock Dunlops for Graebner for years—until he changed to steel. This happened when Graebner, pounding away with his wooden racquet in the 1967 National Clay Court Championships, in Milwaukee, had such a bad case of tennis elbow that his elbow at the time included everything from his wrist to his shoulder. His arm felt as if it were about to fall off. He lost in singles, but he had a particular desire to hang on in the doubles, because he and his partner, Marty Riessen, had won the National Clay Court doubles twice before and could keep the trophy permanently if they won again. Graebner called Wilson in Chicago and had steel racquets rushed to Milwaukee. The steel racquet, invented by René Lacoste, was something new and unproved, but it was easy to swing, less resistant to air. It was as if a scalpel had been designed to replace a hunting knife. For Graebner, though, it was more like the sword in the stone. He and Riessen won in Milwaukee and retired the trophy; then Graebner's arm stopped hurting, and Graebner, totally committed to steel, went on to be a finalist that season at Merion, Orange, and Forest Hills—his best year ever. The tennis circuit began to glitter with steel racquets. Billie Jean King gave up wood, and to Pancho Gonzales the new racquet meant that his playing life might be extended by a couple of hundred years. The steel racquet bends like a whip when it hits, and that was just the complement Graebner needed for his firm, wrist-locked strokes. "It made me serve harder. The ball comes off the racquet so much more quickly. The stringing is different. The gut is suspended inside the frame, like a trampoline. It is a little harder to control a volley, but I shortened my backswing, because the ball climbs off the racquet so much more quickly, and now I seldom miss a return of serve. The steel racquet is the greatest thing since candy." Multitudes of hacks are now hacking with steel, but the boom that Graebner prominently helped to begin has not reached everywhere. Steel seems to have been used therapeutically where therapy was needed, but Laver still hits with his Dunlop, Ken Rosewall uses wood, and so does Arthur Ashe, who says, "Most people don't know what they're talking about when they talk about steel racquets. I'm doing fine with the wood racquet. Why should I change?"

Kalamazoo was also the probable place for initial contact between young players and the haberdashers of tennis. Ashe has been styled in free Fred Perry shirts and shorts since he was a schoolboy, and for at

# 150   JOHN McPHEE

least as many years Graebner's *couturier* has been the versatile René
Lacoste. Mrs. Graebner observed all this, and everything else at Kalamazoo, with some detachment. It occurred to her that there might be
reasons that eleven- and twelve-year-olds ought not to be assembled to
play for national championships. She noticed that many of the young
players wept when they lost. "I thought they were a terribly intense, very
emotional bunch of little boys. Arthur never showed it. He had been
trained not to. But the others complained about everything. They complained about what courts they were assigned to play on. I wondered if
Kalamazoo was good for them, and I still wonder. Now that I look at
Clark, I think the weighing was in his favor. But if he had not got this
far, I wonder if he would have been hurt." Meanwhile, she made many
friends among the tennis mothers and, from sheer exposure, learned a
lot about the game. She did not play it then, but she began to coach Clark
with some effectiveness, because she could watch him play and tell him
accurately what he was doing wrong. "You're not tossing the ball high
enough. You're breaking your wrist on your forehand. On your backhand, you're swinging late."

Clark was sixteen when, at Kalamazoo, he suddenly felt such pain
in his back that he could hardly hit the ball. He refused to default, and
he lost, hitting a kind of crippled half stroke. His mother drove him
home, and when they arrived his difficulty was so severe that he had
trouble getting out of the car. He had osteochondrosis. Two of his lower
vertebrae were not calcifying rapidly enough and had become, in Mrs.
Graebner's words, squashed flat. Osteochondrosis characteristically attacks the upper vertebrae of prodigious young piano players, whose
spinal columns bend like canes toward the keyboard. In Clark's case, the
vertebrae in the small of his back were affected. Reaching high for serves
had probably made the situation acute. For nearly two weeks, he had to
lie flat on his back while a device was made that would surround his body
like a steel birdcage from armpits to hips, held in place by a tight
leather-and-canvas corset. The physician said that in the brace Clark
could do anything, but when he did not wear it he would have to lie still,
in bed. The day the brace came, Clark put it on and played tennis, but
he could make only pathetic moves. The next day, he lost, love and love,
to one of the worst players at his club. For some time after that, he played
against women, and the fatigue produced by the strain of fighting the
brace put circles under his eyes. Time and again he crashed to the
ground, but he kept playing, and five weeks after he acquired the brace

he played a match against a fairly good male opponent and—despite numerous falls—won. "That's it. I can do anything," he said to his mother. When he eventually returned to the circuit, she massaged him regularly with salve or alcohol. Other tennis players rather unsympathetically began to classify him as a "mama's boy." He wore the brace every day for fourteen months. In it, on a debilitatingly hot day—105° —in Midland, Texas, he won the National Jaycee junior-singles championship. Because he was an adolescent just coming into his full growth, the brace would influence his bearing for the rest of his life. It forced and fixed his posture. In it, he could not bend at the waist. He still doesn't. When he brushes his teeth in the morning, he places his feet apart and leans like an A-frame against the mirror. He is capable of bending at the waist, but he is out of the habit. He rarely bends to volley. He walked in the brace, as he still does, like an Etruscan warrior—his spine in absolute plumb, his chin tucked in, his implied plume flying. Graebner's walk, famous in tennis, has been almost universally interpreted as a strut.

"Look at him. He thinks he's Superman."

"Look at the way he walks."

"*Look* at the cocky bastard."

Certain aspects of Graebner's personality that occasionally surface tend to support these views, but his physical silhouette, the distinctive figure he cuts, is more relevant mechanically than psychologically. It is the signature of the osteochondrosis.

Arthur Ashe, who seems to like Graebner well enough but would not ordinarily put himself out to defend him, rises quickly when he hears unfair remarks to the effect that Graebner's success has gone to his head and then into his imperial bearing. "He appears to strut," Ashe will point out, "but he can't walk any other way."

"People have their jealousy streaks in them," Arthur's father will say. The effects upon him of his son's fame have been considerable. He says that a number of people in Richmond have become cold toward him. They never mention Arthur's success; in fact, they seem to resent it. "Some whites don't recognize Arthur Junior, and the colored are still worser. It's getting tougher and tougher all the time, in a way of speaking. I think I've lost a lot of friends. But I think I've gained some. About fifty-fifty. Some people think Arthur Junior is getting his daddy a lot of money. They say, 'That tennis player you got has really set you up, hasn't he?' " Mr. Ashe regards this as jokeworthy. His summation of the whole of Arthur's development as a tennis player is "It hung me for some money." His present landscaping and janitorial businesses grew out of odd jobs he took to help pay for Arthur's tennis. He cut grass, scrubbed floors, washed windows, and when he still didn't have enough he borrowed from the Southern Bank & Trust Co., whose branch banks he now keeps clean. Asked why he bothered to do all that, he gives an uncomplicated answer: "*Why?* Because Arthur was out there doing good." He told Arthur, "Do what you want to do, as long as you do it right. But the day you slack up is the day Daddy is going to slack up with his money."

"Arthur's Daddy promised he'd buy anything for him." (Dr. Johnson is reminiscing.) "His Daddy is a great talker, but he doesn't do everything he talks about. . . . His Daddy once had a reputation for being strictly Uncle Tom. He's moving out a bit now." Mr. Ashe says what he thinks, and he shouts when he talks about human relationships. "You respect everybody whether they respect you or not!" he bellows. "Never carry a grudge! I've seen Negroes wreck their lives through hatred of whites!" He believes out loud in law and order. "There's a certain class of people—there's a certain class of people you've got to handle by judge." For tennis tournaments in Richmond involving Arthur Junior and other high-level players, Mr. Ashe, as supervisor of tennis courts for the Department of Parks and Recreation, has set up the nets. Certain Negroes—by no means a small number—have offered him all sorts of abuse for that. They say that he is a V.I.P. and should be prominently displayed in a box seat, and should not degrade himself by working as a flunky. Driving through northside Richmond in his pickup truck past solid-looking brick houses close together on compact lots, he says that this is where the "hank-to-do," or upper-class, Negroes live, and he says that he himself is a "crooked-knees" Negro, which he defines as someone who has no class at all. "I don't have any picks and pets," he will say. "I make everybody come by me, rich or poor. If you school it out and then think back on it, you can figure that out. I respect you the same way I respect the President of the United States. If he came to my house, I'd give him the same bed you slept in. If he didn't like it, he could get the hell out. I just want people to treat me as a human being. I'm sure my son is the same."

Ashe returns serve with a solid forehand, down the line. Graebner, lunging, picks it up with a backhand half volley. The ball floats back to Ashe. He takes a three-hundred-degree roundhouse swing and drives the ball crosscourt so fast that Graebner, who is within close reach of it, cannot react quickly enough to get his racquet on it. Hopefully, Graebner whips his head around to see where the ball lands. It lands on the line—a liner, in the language of the game. "There's Ashe getting lucky again."

Ashe does a deep knee bend to remind himself to stay low. Graebner hits a big serve wide, and a second serve that ticks the cord and skips away. Double fault. Carole pats the air. Calm down, Clark. Graebner can consider himself half broken. The score is love-thirty. Ashe thinks, "You're in trouble, Clark. Deep trouble."

"I'll bet a hundred to one I pull out of it," Graebner tells himself. Crunch. His serve is blocked back, and he punches a volley to Ashe's backhand. Ashe now has two principal alternatives: to return the ball conservatively and safely, adding to the pressure that is already heavy on Graebner, or to cut loose the one-in-ten shot, going for the overwhelming advantage of a love-forty score by the method of the fast kill. Ashe seems to have no difficulty making the choice. He blasts. He misses. Fifteen-thirty.

Graebner serves, attacks the net, volleys, rises high for an overhead —he goes up like a basketball player for a rebound—and smashes the ball away. Thirty-all.

Now the thought crosses Graebner's mind that Ashe has not missed a service return in this game. The thought unnerves him a little. He hits a big one four feet too deep, then bloops his second serve with terrible placement right into the center of the service court. He now becomes the mouse, Ashe the cat. With soft, perfectly placed shots, Ashe jerks him around the forecourt, then closes off the point with a shot to remember. It is a forehand, with top spin, sent crosscourt so lightly that the ball appears to be flung rather than hit. Its angle to the net is less than ten degrees—a difficult, brilliant stroke, and Ashe hit it with such nonchalance that he appeared to be thinking of something else. Graebner feels the implications of this. Ashe is now obviously loose. Loose equals dangerous. When a player is loose, he serves and volleys at his best level. His general shotmaking ability is optimum. He will try anything. "Look at the way he hit that ball, gave it the casual play," Graebner says to himself. "Instead of trying a silly shot and missing it, he tries a silly shot and makes it." If Ashe wins the next point, he will have broken Graebner, and the match will be, in effect, even.

Again Graebner misses his first serve. Ashe, waiting for the second, says to himself, "Come on. Move in. Move in. I should get it now." When

Ashe really feels he has a chance for a break, the index of his desire is that he moves in a couple of steps on second serves. He takes his usual position, about a foot behind the baseline, until Graebner lifts the ball. Then he moves quickly about a yard forward and stops, motionless, as if he were participating in a game of kick-the-can and Graebner were It. Graebner's second serve spins in, and bounces high to Ashe's backhand. Ashe strokes it with underspin. Graebner hits a deep approach shot to Ashe's backhand. Ashe hits a deft, appropriate lob. Graebner wants this point just as much as Ashe does. Scrambling backward, he reaches up and behind him and picks out of the sun an overhead that becomes an almost perfect drop shot, surprising Ashe and drawing him toward the net. At a dead run, Ashe reaches for the ball and more or less shovels it over the net. Graebner has been moving forward, too, and he has stopped for half a second, legs apart, poised, to see what will happen. The ball moves toward his backhand. He moves to the ball and drives it past Ashe, down the line. Graebner is still unbroken. But the game is at deuce. It is only the second time Ashe has extended him that far.

After this game, new balls will be coming in—all the more reason for Ashe to try to break Graebner now. Tennis balls are used for nine games (warm-up counts for two), and over that span they get fluffier and fluffier. When they are new and the nap is flat, wind resistance is minimal and they come through fast and heavy. Newies, or freshies, as the tennis players call them, are a considerable advantage to the server—something like a supply of bullets. Graebner meanwhile serves wide to Ashe's forehand, and Ashe hits the return with at least equal velocity. Graebner is caught on his heels, and hits a defensive backhand down the middle. It bounces in no man's land. Ashe, taking it on his backhand, has plenty of time. His racquet is far back and ready. Graebner makes a blind rush for the net, preferring to be caught in motion than helpless on the baseline. But Ashe's shot is too hard, too fast, too tough, too accurate, skidding off the turf in the last square foot of Graebner's forehand corner. Advantage Ashe.

"Look at that shot. That's ridiculous," Graebner tells himself. He glances at Carole, who has both fists in the air. Pull yourself together, Clark. This is a big point. Graebner takes off his glasses and wipes them on his dental towel. "Stalling," Ashe mumbles. While he is waiting, he raises his left index finger and slowly pushes his glasses into place across the bridge of his nose. "Just one point, Arthur." Graebner misses his first serve again. Ashe moves in. He hits sharply crosscourt. Graebner dives for it, catches it with a volley, then springs up, ready, at the net. Ashe lobs into the sun, thinking, "That was a good get on that volley. I didn't think he'd get that." Graebner reaches for the overhead and smashes it directly at Ashe. Ashe, swinging desperately, belts it right back at him. Graebner punches the ball away with a forehand volley. Deuce. Ashe is rattling the gates, but Graebner will not let him in. Carole has her hand on the top of her head. Unbelievable.

Graebner serves, moves up, and volleys. Ashe, running, smacks an all-or-nothing backhand that hums past Graebner and lands a few inches inside the line. Graebner says to himself, "He's hitting the lines, the lucky bastard. The odds are ten to one against him and he makes the shot. That bugs me." Advantage Ashe.

Jack Kramer, broadcasting the match, says that this is the best game not only of this match but of the entire tournament so far. Again Ashe needs just one point and he will be leading four games to two. Graebner serves. Ashe returns. Graebner half-volleys. Ashe throws a lob into the sun. Graebner nearly loses it there. He can only hit it weakly—a kind of overhead tap that drops softly at Ashe's feet. This is it. Ashe swings —a big backhand—for the kill. The ball lands two feet out. Graebner inhales about seven quarts of air, and slowly releases six. It is deuce again.

Donald Dell, the captain of the Davis Cup Team, is sitting in the Marquee. He says, "Arthur has hit five winners and he hasn't won the game. He looks perturbed." Dell knows Ashe so well that he can often tell by the way Ashe walks or stands what is going on behind the noncommittal face. But Ashe is under control. He is telling himself, "If you tend to your knitting, you will get the job done." Graebner's first serve, which has misfired seven times in this game, does not misfire now. Ashe reacts, swings, hits it hard—a hundredth of a second too late. The shot, off his backhand, fails by a few inches to come in to the sideline. Advantage Graebner.

Carole's fists are up. Clark adjusts his glasses, wipes off his right hand, and bounces the ball. He serves hard to Ashe's forehand. The ball, blasted, comes back. Disappointment races through Graebner's mind. "I'm serving to his forehand. His forehand is his weakest shot. If the guy returns his weakest shot all the time, he's just too good." Graebner tries a drop shot, then goes to his right on the sheer gamble that Ashe's response will take that direction. It does. Graebner, with full power, drives an apparent putaway down the line. But Ashe gets to it and blocks the ball, effecting what under the circumstances is a remarkably good lob. Graebner leaps, whips his racquet overhead, and connects. The ball hits the turf on Ashe's backhand and bounces wide. Ashe plunges for it, swings with both feet off the ground, and hits the ball so hard down the line that Graebner cannot get near it. Graebner can be pardoned if he cannot believe it. For the fourth time, the game is at deuce.

"Arthur is just seeing the ball better, or something," Graebner tells himself. But Graebner sees the ball, too, and he hits a big-crunch unplayable serve. Advantage Graebner.

Serve, return, volley—Ashe hits a forehand into the tape. Ashe has not been able to get out from under. Games are three–all, second set.

# The Crofter
# and the Laird

Like many Scots, McPhee is fond of his cultural traits: he admires tartan neckties and insists that unblended malt whisky is a civil drink. In 1967 he happily spent an entire spring in Scotland, living with wife and bairns on Colonsay—an island crag in the Inner Hebrides, off the mainland's western coast. At Colonsay the last chief of clan Mhic a' Phi (thus in Gaelic) was killed, and by the late eighteenth century many of the other Highland clans were also broken, victims of civil strife or English misrule from the south. Scottish culture further waned in the nineteenth century, as immigrants left for America and other lands. McPhee's return to the home of his ancestors was perhaps both sentimental and ritual, a final effort to reclaim his clan.

This book celebrates the shape of community life, with its constant ebb of boast and gossip, daydreams and legends. Colonsay is a microcosmic place, "less like a small town than like a large lifeboat," manned by a crew whose stations bear the archaic titles of crofter (tenant), laird (owner), and factor (overseer). Bound in tangled lines of loyalty and distrust, the islanders sail toward an unpromising future, one McPhee suggests may be as gloomy as his old chieftain's fate.

In a story that is both personal and archetypal, McPhee had to become less a neutral observer and more fully portrayed as a character. His anecdotes are funnier, more frequent, less obliquely thrust forward; his learning and tastes, especially for food and language, are abundantly evident. And the reciprocal affection of Colonsay also comes through, as the islanders open themselves to his discovery of the place where they live, but never quite own.—*WLH*

As a boy, Donald Gibbie—as he has always been called, because the name identifies him as Donald son of Gilbert—went to the common grazing each morning as soon as he got up, to locate and bring in the cows. Sometimes he was told to fetch a horse as well. First he found and then he followed the tracks of the animals, which he recognized individually, in the dew. The search and the return took as much as two hours, for the common grazing, which the McNeills shared with seven other crofters, was a little more than six hundred acres, and to find the animals Donald Gibbie often had to go to very high ground, near the summits of A' Bheinn Bhreac (the Speckled Peak) and Binnean Riabhach (the Brindled Pinnacle). These hills are only about four hundred feet high, but they are considerable hills nonetheless, since they rise almost straight from the ocean. Every day, also, Donald Gibbie took two pails and walked four hundred yards to a well for water. The language of the house was Gaelic and Gaelic only. He learned English in school, from a teacher who taught all levels from age five to fourteen, as the Colonsay teacher still does. He also learned to step to the side of the road, take off his cap, and bow his head when the laird went by in a gig driven by a coachman in a bowler hat. (Automobiles were not introduced to the island until 1947.) The house, with its stone walls and its slate roof, was of a design repeated on crofts throughout the Highlands. Covered by blankets woven from Colonsay wool, Donald and his younger brother slept on corn-chaff mattresses in the room loft, under the steeply peaked slate roof, and his mother and father slept in the other upstairs room, the kitchen loft. Below the room loft was "the room," which took up half the house on the ground floor and was twelve feet by twelve. It was set apart for visitors, for first-footings, for wedding receptions, and for little else. The entire house had something like six hundred square feet of living space (less than the size of one floor of a New York brownstone), yet twenty-five per cent of it was set apart from daily use. Even today, Donald and his family do not really use "the room," and it serves them as little more than an enormous storage closet. "The room" was separated from the kitchen by a thick stone partition that contained a fireplace on each side. The kitchen was literally and completely the living room. It had a drop-leaf table, a long wooden seat near the fire, various chairs, settees. In the fireplace were a cast-iron cooking surface and a cast-iron oven. That is how the kitchen still looks. When Donald was twelve, he took over the milking of the cows. His mother used to make seventeen pounds of butter a week, in a plunger churn. It was also when he was twelve that he saw the mainland for the first time. His mother took him there for a tonsillectomy. When he was fourteen, he had to give up his education, because then, as now, a Colonsay child who wanted an education beyond the limits of the Colonsay school had to go to the mainland, finding room and board there in a hostel or with a mainland family, and since that cost more money than a crofter could afford, the only way to go was to take competitive examinations and qualify for a bursary from the Scottish Education Department. Donald Gibbie took the examinations but didn't qualify. The Second World War began, and, still scarcely in his teens, he was drafted into the coal mines of Fife and Kent. By the time he came home, he probably looked pretty much the way he does now—of middle height, with long, dark hair, dark eyes, high and prominent cheekbones, lips that seem to be permanently pursed and pensive, and a strong and tense frame.

He worked on one of the island farms for a while, and he became, as well, a lobsterman. He has long since given up being a lobsterman commercially, but he still knows the name and address of every Colonsay lobster. One day, after I had been telling him what I thought to be the truth—that there was no lobster on earth that was remotely similar or qualitatively comparable to the lobster of Maine—Donald Gibbie put on a pair of knee-length rubber boots, and, while the tide dropped, we walked the three miles from the croft to the outer shoals of the Ardskenish Peninsula, where the best lobsters are. The Ardskenish Peninsula juts a couple of thousand yards into the Atlantic in a southwesterly direction, and its low, fairly even ground is so unprotected that people who have been caught out there by strong northeasterly winter gales have sometimes had to crawl back against the wind, or they have simply stayed there lying flat, for hours if necessary, waiting for the wind to drop. A farmhouse, two stories high, standing empty, projects upward incongruously from the middle of the peninsula. The sun was shining that day, the wind was gentle, and along the periphery of Ardskenish the low tide left clear pools among the skerries. Brown Atlantic seals and one gray seal dived from rocks as we splashed along through the tidal pools. The seals swam around offshore, heads up, watching us with what had at first been alarm and now seemed to be interest and irritation. Donald Gibbie obviously knew exactly where he was going. With light, athletic motions, he moved as fast as he could, impatiently, over great pompadours of seaweed and through rock basins filled with still water. Now and then he went in deeper than the tops of his boots, but he had cut holes over the toes to let the water spurt out. He had with him a piece of heavy wire, about a quarter inch in diameter and five feet long. It was bent somewhat like a shepherd's crook at one end. Finally, in one of the tidal pools, he stopped at a place where, under the water, a small cavern, perhaps a foot high, went far back under an overhanging ledge of rock. Donald took the wire and reached with it into the cavern, his body assuming something of the stance of a fencer. Slowly he moved the wire from side to side, working it around as much of the cavern interior as he could probe. After two minutes or so, he said, "He's not there now." We moved on, as before, in and out of water, over seaweed beds, until Donald Gibbie stopped at another cavern. That lobster was not there, either. Donald Gibbie remarked that perhaps the tide was not low enough for him to get into some of the best places, and he was sorry about it, because he had thought the tide would be several feet lower that day. The walk home was beginning to look like a long one. Then, after bending over in front of the third lobster house and working the wire back and forth, he said, "I've got one." For three or four minutes he slowly turned and agitated the wire. He wasn't trying to hook the lobster, he explained, he was just trying to anger it. Very slowly, he began to draw out the wire, meanwhile shaking it enough to preserve the interest of whatever might be on the other end. My skepticism stayed with me right to the last. I don't know what I expected to see come out of there—perhaps a snapping turtle, or some pretentious crayfish from the Cape of Good Hope, or possibly a clawless Spanish *langosta*. But suddenly out into the sunlight—hanging on to the wire and snapping at it like a fence cutter—came several pounds of glistening, mottled, dark blue-green lobster, in shape and appearance identical to the most expensive creature in Penobscot Bay. Donald seemed a little surprised when I said the resemblance was so close, but he believed me, and was impressed. He had apparently been skeptical, too.

"When I fished lobsters, I used creels and went out every day in a boat," he said. "I didn't have a boat big enough to stand the winter weather. I never did it all the year round. We baited the creels with saithe and mackerel. I had a partner. The boat was mine. We worked eighty creels. On our best days, we got sixty or seventy lobsters. Ordinarily, we would get about thirty." He had the wire deep in another cavern, and soon he was engaged in a patient fight with another lobster. When we started home, we had three of them. I told Donald that the smallest of the three would be worth somewhere between ten and fifteen shillings, over the counter, in Maine, and that the biggest one—the first caught—would be worth well over a pound. He said that the lobsters in our hands (he had wrapped their claws with string) were worth a great deal more than that, since they can bring as much as a pound per pound nowadays to the lobsterman himself, let alone the storied sums they command in the retail markets of London. In his own day, he had got only three shillings sixpence per pound. He had shipped the lobsters, in boxes, to Oban, or sometimes direct to Billingsgate, in London. He had to keep them alive for as long as a month while he waited for suitable transport to the mainland. Of the proceeds, a share went to the boat, a share to the gear, and a share to each partner. Working from May to November, Donald made about fifteen pounds a week. Anything under nine inches long went back into the sea, as did any lobster with spawn. He said that he had given up lobster fishing in 1957, when his father turned eighty and decided to stop working the croft. Since then, Donald went on, no one on Colonsay has fished lobsters commercially. The people don't fish for much of anything else there, either. In fact, they give the impression that they have, if not an active distaste for the sea, at least a thorough-going indifference to it. There are no commercial fishermen in the population. Cut off out there in the ocean, the people of Colonsay lead rural, agrarian landlocked lives, growing their roots and vegetables and looking after their poultry and livestock, meanwhile turning their backs to the water whenever possible, and in summer ignoring the island's splendid beaches. They eat fish rarely. Some years ago, the postmaster bought a deep freeze, in which he keeps a stock of frozen foods for sale. When fish *is* eaten on Colonsay, the freezer is where it comes from. The brand is Birdseye. For an islander of Colonsay, it was a most unusual and in a sense original thing that Donald Gibbie did when, for ten years, he worked at taking lobsters from the sea.

With our wives, we ate the three lobsters from Ardskenish after boiling them in sea water for twenty minutes, cracking them, and dipping the meat in drawn butter. The McNeills, who had tasted lobster only in bits with other foods, were interested in trying the New England method. However, I think both of them were appalled to see the equivalent of six or seven pounds sterling just vanish from the table after a bath in butter, but they said they found the lobsters delicious—as did my wife and I. The claw meat was a little sweeter than the claw meat of a Maine lobster. The rest was undifferentiable from its American counterpart. On the table as well was pure Highland malt whisky from Speyside, and it was just right with the Scottish lobster.

Given the view that most of the islanders seem to take of the sea, it is not surprising that Donald Gibbie barely knows how to swim.

During the war, when he was working in the mines in Fife, he once went to a public swimming pool in Dunfermline, and while he was paddling around there he somehow caught his toe below a hand rail and nearly drowned. He says that that put him off swimming forever. In a boat, though, he is unafraid of the ocean. He has had any number of small boats, and in them he has never hesitated to make long voyages, usually alone, to explore other islands, and he will even flirt with the Strait of Corryvreckan, eighteen miles east of Colonsay. Corryvreckan is a whirlpool celebrated in the history and legends of the Hebrides. Its spectral sucking and hissing can be heard from great distances over the water, and it has swallowed bigger boats than Donald Gibbie's. I once asked him what he would do if wind or wave ever separated him from his boat on one of his explorations, and he said, with an explosive laugh, "Well, I guess I'd drown."

Donald's experience with boats on the sea derives from something more than lobster fishing. He also worked for many years as a ferryman for MacBrayne's, the company that operates the mail boat to Colonsay. The mail boat calls three times a week, and the voyage from the mainland takes five hours. The island is absolutely dependent on the little steamer, the Lochiel, but until very recently, when the Argyll County Council built the Colonsay pier, the Lochiel had no place to tie up. It used to drop anchor some distance offshore, and a small boat, skippered by Donald Gibbie, would go out to pick up and deliver mail, passengers, and cargo. Frequently the ocean was so violent that the Lochiel would heave to for a while and wait; then, if it became clear that the ferry had no chance of surviving an attempt to make the connection, the Lochiel would go back to the mainland. When this happened, a small crowd of disappointed islanders and incomers, anxious to receive or send goods, and inn guests, due home from their island vacations, would abuse Donald Gibbie, since most of them had even less regard for the sea than he did. "When inn guests were particularly arrogant," he told me, "I used to take them out a short distance, until they were thoroughly shaken up and soaking wet. They were happy enough to return to shore." These ferries were not impressive vessels, probably no more so than the boat in which Mrs. Macneil and her infant son John of the Ocean arrived from Barra. When Donald started with MacBrayne's, in the late nineteen-forties, as assistant ferryman, he learned some of his seamanship on a ferry he describes as "a thirty-footer with an old Kelvin poppet fifteen-horse petrol paraffin engine—just to get near it, you had to have your wits about you." But he never lost any cargo, not so much as a pipe cleaner, in seventeen years of ferrying people, cattle, sheep, mail, automobiles, and sometimes extraordinarily bulky cargo.

There was one aspect of all this that forced him literally into the sea. Cattle, like autos, were swung over the ferry in slings depending from a small crane, then were lowered to the deck. The slings were placed under the bellies of the animals, and their legs hung down on either side. Donald stood in his boat and waited for each cow as she swung out over his head. It is not hard to envision how frightened a cow might be, hanging in a sling from a crane over a boat that was pitching and rolling at the edge of an apparently limitless expanse of roiling water. In two cases out of three, the tails of the cattle would rise and yesterday's cud would drop on Donald Gibbie. "You just had to forget that they had an opening at the other end," he told me. There was no going home for a bath after one of these cattle trips. There was nothing to do but jump into the sea beside the boat—in winter, often enough, in the almost total darkness of the mornings. Now, in the course of things, he has become the pier master, responsible for the operations of a long platform of white concrete that reaches out to deep water, and from which cattle can walk onto the Lochiel. After our own voyage to Colonsay, over green and foaming waters in a wind that made tears run down our cheeks, the first person we saw was Donald Gibbie, standing there on his pier in the lee of Cnoc na Faire Mor (Big Lookout Hill), in his Wellington boots, his dungarees, his heavy gray pullover, and his brown-and-tan knitted cap, with his hands clasped behind his back, a frown on his face, and a look of felt responsibility in his eyes.

A few nights ago, when the McNeills asked us to come over to their house for a wee dram by the fire, I found myself telling them about American weddings and any number of peculiar rituals that sometimes complement the basic rites. Donald seemed particularly amused to learn that a few hours after my wife and I were married, in 1957, I had been surrounded by a cordon of friends—overmuscled, post-adolescent males with flaring nostrils—and, after a valiant struggle, had been pinned shirtless to the floor of an upstairs room at something called the Woman's Club of Ridgewood. There, despite continued resistance on my part, a set of messages—not in code—was written all over my chest, back, and shoulders, in four shades of lipstick.

The McNeills responded to my story with one of their own. On the evening before a Colonsay wedding, they told me, all the chickens to be used in the next day's wedding feast are plucked in the bride's house by the friends and families of the betrothed, and the feathers are piled high in the middle of the room. The size of the pile is determined by the number of expected guests, and in their case the daughter of a crofter was about to marry the son of another crofter, and nearly every islander of Colonsay was related to one of the two families, so the pile of feathers was enormous. After the last chicken had been plucked, Donald stripped to the waist and prepared to do battle—as tradition required—against all the other men of roughly his age, with the hill of feathers as the battleground. Donald put up a good fight but was soon overwhelmed and, struggling violently, was pinned down by four others and all but buried in the feathers. He held his breath as long as he could, but finally he could hold it no longer, and inhaled. He said that he took in two lungfuls of pinfeathers and very nearly died right there. He came up purple, rapidly fading to gray—hacking, heaving, unable to find new breath. But enough oxygen finally got through the pinfeathers, and he was on his feet when he was married. The year was 1957.

That was also the year when Gilbert McNeill, who has since died, stopped working the croft and turned it over to his son. A true crofter, Donald has told me, works only part time on his croft, and turns to other resources to round out his income. For this reason, Donald puts in only about seventy hours a week working on the croft. He grows beef and mutton, and he has ninety breeding ewes and seven breeding cows. The laird's bull is available, at one pound sterling per visit. To feed his animals, Donald grows oats, turnips, hay, and potatoes. The family eats the potatoes, too, and if there is a surplus it is sold. The croft has ten or twelve chickens, mainly for eggs and rarely for the pot. One of the breeding cows doubles as a milk cow, so the McNeills make their own butter and their own crowdy (a form of cheese). Assessors for Her Majesty's Government have decided that the food the croft produces for the McNeills' own table is worth sixty pounds sterling a year, and Donald pays tax on that figure as income. He and Margaret also collect winkles, limpets, lobsters, clams, and mussels from the shore. They even go fishing once in a while. They eat rabbits, too. ("I remember when there was very little bought meat coming into any house on the island. Everyone ate rabbit, but for some time now the myxomatosis has put people off.") Deep in rabbit burrows, shelducks lay their eggs, and the McNeills sometimes collect and eat the eggs. They also eat the eggs of eider ducks, oyster catchers, and gulls—and often enough they eat the eider ducks, too, and shelducks, mallards, and pheasants. The pheasant population of Colonsay is probably ten times the human population, and one comes to recognize some of the pheasants individually, always foraging in pairs, models of fidelity, aging gracefully together, sometimes all the way to the table. Once in a while, but rarely, Donald takes his shotgun and goes off to shoot a wild goat—never for sport but just for the meat. Goats were originally brought to Colonsay because it was known that they would assert territorial rights to the highest ground, thus keeping sheep away from the crags and contributing to their safety. The goats have long since gone completely wild, but their effect on the sheep is still the same. The McNeills also collect watercress from the streams, they make nettle soup, and they eat sea kale. But they do all this only in part to supplement their income. They do it, as well, because they get pleasure from it. Most of the food they eat comes either from grocers on the mainland who send out boxes of provisions on the Lochiel to fill private orders or from the small island store, whose sign, "The Shop," painted in white letters on the side of the green building, is the only sign on Colonsay.

The McNeills collect and burn a great deal of driftwood, to save coal. In winter, they go to the tidal pools of the Ardskenish Peninsula and gather winkles, which they can ship to the mainland and sell for two pounds a hundredweight. There are about seven thousand winkles in a hundredweight. On even a casual walk along the shore, Donald's eyes are always alert for a find of any sort. One day when we made a circuit of Ardskenish together, he came back with a boat hook, a large basket, a scrub brush, a stainless-steel bolt, a Norwegian plastic fishing float the size of a big balloon, and perhaps a dozen grapefruit-size aluminum floats of the type that a fishing boat uses to support a net. The floats bring two pounds a hundredweight. At home, the McNeills waste nothing. When their old steel teapot develops a leak, Donald plugs up the hole with a wood screw. I once picked up the teapot and looked inside. The points of fourteen screws intruded.

Margaret counts on the yield from winkle sales to give her the extra and special things she looks forward to having—a new rug, for example. She experienced a particularly bitter setback a couple of years ago when, after she had gathered winkles and shipped them to the mainland all through the winter, the firm to which the Lochiel had been delivering the winkles went bankrupt, and for the winter's work she collected nothing at all. There is some hazard, also, in shipping animals over the water, and none of this risk is assumed by the owners of the Lochiel. Before anyone can set foot or place goods on a MacBrayne's boat, a risk note must be signed freeing the company from all responsibility. After that, it's full steam ahead and hope for the best. A few years ago, the Lochiel, with a third mate at the helm, swung into West Loch Tarbert, near the mainland end of its route, lost the channel in a mist, crashed into a rock, lurched across the narrow sea loch and crashed into another rock, and then, with water pouring into her hold, made a desperate but unsuccessful attempt to get to the West Loch Tarbert pier, a few yards short of which she sank in twenty feet of water, stern in the air, bow down, with the surface of the sea loch lapping at the windows of the wheelhouse. Unfortunately, there were on the foredeck forty sheep that belonged to Donald Gibbie. They all drowned. The loss to him was two hundred and fifty pounds, the equivalent of the savings of four good years —a good year being one in which the net income of the croft, including the government subsidies he gets for his sheep and cattle, is about a hundred and fifty pounds.

For his work at the pier—about twenty hours a week—Donald gets four hundred and sixty-eight pounds a year from MacBrayne's. He is also the Colonsay constable, a job that takes almost no time and pays nothing, unless he can show loss of earning. And he is a coast-watcher for the Coast Guard. During big storms, he sits in a radio shack on Maol Chlibhe (the Bare Cliff) prepared to fire signal rockets and to call in compass bearings if he should see a ship in distress, and for this service he is paid thirty-three and six an hour. Adding all things together, the McNeills make the equivalent of about fifteen hundred dollars a year.

Not long after Donald took over the croft, he began applying to the Crofting Commission for the right to fence off his part of the common grazing—his soamings on the hill. The Crofting Commission, which was set up soon after the first crofting act, has the jurisdiction over crofters that was once arbitrarily exercised by the lairds. To get permission to fence off his own part of the common grazing, a crofter has to show cause —and showing cause usually has to do with irresolvable difficulties with the crofters sharing the hill. But in Donald Gibbie's case I imagine that whatever cause he was able to show may have been less significant to him than the sense of independence he wanted to gain. At all events, he won out, and his croft and his grazing land are now integral and unshared, and he has run his fences far up the slopes of the Brindled Pinnacle. He has a hundred and forty-one acres in all, with seas breaking on two sides of it, high meadows, good water (from a deep well now), and good soil. His potatoes and oats win prizes in the island's annual competitions. And he also has his two houses, two byres, an implement shed (in the ruins of still another family house, a predecessor of the two now standing), a barn, and a stable. The doorways are painted red, and the walls of most of the buildings, low and compact, are of deep-gray Colonsay stone. For someone who loves this place as much as he obviously does, there could be no other in the world, and it is not hard to see why he would not leave it. His apparent affection for independence, however, rests uneasily on a paradox of his time. Protected and secured by the Crofters' Holdings Act, he has tenure on the land of his father and his grandfathers, and the rent he pays for all his land and buildings is only forty-five pounds a year—about a hundred and twenty dollars. If the croft were available to him to buy outright, he could not afford it. So his modified vassalage under the laird, though it may conflict with his hunger for personal freedom, is not something that he could readily give up. "One feels that one is neither a proper crofter nor a proper landholder, sort of style" is the way he put it once. Parliament, concerned only that no repetition of the Highland clearances should ever occur, has preserved certain fragments of the Middle Ages in something like a gigantic block of clear plastic, and inside it is Donald Gibbie. The laird, for that matter, is in there, too, set, as is Donald Gibbie, within what has become the grand anachronism of the Highlands. "Some crofters don't work their crofts," Donald said. "They have a cow, a few sheep. That is all. My father was always one for working the croft. When I took it over, I kept it going. It's not right to let the land be neglected. I'm quite happy here. I make out, so long as the shore's handy, and such like. But if you expect many things in life, crofting isn't the way to get them. Crofting cannot keep up with the times. Most people expect more than the bare necessities of living now. And crofting is not a livelihood. It's an existence."

Between the two houses of the croft is a shed full of driftwood and coal. We collect driftwood frequently and pile it up in the shed, because we burn a great deal of it ourselves, particularly at night. The coal, which is brought out twice a year from the mainland in boats called puffers, costs twelve pounds a ton in its cheapest form—two-foot floes of it, like cakes of black ice. In the early mornings, I go outside and break up the coal with an axe. One bucketful is enough to give the stove in the kitchen a good start for the day. Ordinarily, the ashes are dead in the morning, because I am mediocre at preserving fire through the night. So I shake down the ashes, remove them, build a new fire, and take the ashes out to a rusted steel drum, where both families also throw the remains from the table. A cat and a rooster are always near the drum. If ashes go into it, they don't move. If garbage goes into it, the cat jumps in first and spends ten minutes inside. Then he jumps out, half gray with ash, and the rooster jumps in—thus the hierarchy of the croft.

The stove not only has a cooking surface and an oven but also heats a water tank and, often most important, emits some radiant heat in a house in which the temperature in the other rooms is usually around forty-five degrees at the beginning and end of the day. Colonsay has a consistent marine climate. The temperature rarely goes above sixty or below freezing at any time of the day or the year. The island is on the latitude of northern Labrador, Kodiak, and Novosibirsk, but the Gulf Stream peters out nearby, and a good thick Scottish pullover is all one needs here, perhaps two or more in winter. Each morning, until the stove has been going for a while no one else in my family will get up. Fortunately, we also have a bottled-gas hot plate, and I make tea for them— Melrose's Tartan Tips Tea—while they, wrapped in their blankets, females all, aged two to thirty-two, wait. Then they come into the kitchen and eat Jaffajuice grapefruit segments, toast and Chivers thick-cut marmalade, Scott's porridge or Kellogg's Rice Krispies, and cream from the McNeills' milk cow. After breakfast, the older two children go off with the McNeills' children to school.

The school day begins at nine-thirty—in a low, gray, roughcast building that has only one classroom. The hour is so late because of the distances that some of the children have to travel. Wee Ian, of Balnahard, whose age is twelve, has to drive a tractor three and a half miles to a point where the school bus can pick him up. The school bus is driven by Charlie McKinnon the Motor Hirer, whose route is limited by Colonsay's single paved road, which is little more than a loop through the center of the island. The school's enrollment—twenty-three in all—is heavily unbalanced toward the earlier grades. Six children are in Primary 1, four in Primary 2. The teacher, Miss Walker, says, "At the moment, there are so many wee tiny ones that I never seem to get beyond the reading, writing, and arithmetic." There are no blackboards, because blackboards would be pointless in a schoolroom that contains children of ten ages. Miss Walker writes work on paper for each student, then moves from desk to desk. "Please, Miss. Please, Miss, I am stuck," someone calls out, and Miss Walker goes to that one to give help. "I've been feeling my way to find the best way with this group," Miss Walker has told me. "I haven't found it yet. You've got to give quite a bit of attention to the wee-est ones at the moment. If I notice that someone isn't picking something up, I try to make time to go and help that person." Now, after some weeks, she has said that she is pleased with the work of my two older daughters, because each of them—the one in Primary 4, the other in Primary 2—is reading exactly at the Highland standard for her level, and one of them is right where she should be in counting, while the other is only slightly sub-par. I, for my part, am much impressed that the public-school system of Princeton, New Jersey, which once harbored me and is now, at home, responsible for the education of my children, seems to measure up to the level of an education on Colonsay.

At half past ten each morning, Miss Walker serves milk, with which the children eat biscuits they bring from home. She mixes the milk from powder that comes from a subdivision of the Argyll County Council, on the mainland. In their homes, Colonsay children drink milk of unsurpassable quality from cows on their crofts and farms, but at ten-thirty in the morning they drink powdered milk from Dunoon, to conform to regulations established to insure the good health of the children of Argyll. Then they run around outside—if the weather is all right—for a fifteen-minute period called "the interval." Back at their desks, they turn to the study of the English language, each writing in his own jotter, some of the young ones going through the "First Introductory English Workbook."

Multiple choice: "Instead of *large,* we could say (small) (big) (wee)."

Attention wanders. Discipline slips out of control. There is an event of insubordination. Miss Walker takes the offending boys into another room and straps them. Two boys once ran away from such a scene and fled overland. Miss Walker went after them in her automobile and brought them back to the strap.

Primary 4 is writing in its jotters. "Saint Patrick of Ireland was born in Dumbarton, Scotland," the children write. "While he was still a boy, he moved to the side of the Solway Firth." A little later, they write the story of the tanning of leather: "Each skin is split into two pieces. The grain leather is the hair side. The suede leather is the flesh side." Now they have a go at their McDougall's Semi-Vertical Copy Books. "No gain

without pain," they write three times. "Eisleben: the birthplace of Luther
. . . Frankfort: birthplace of Goethe . . . Kasanlik produces attar of
roses."

English is the language of the school, and the children hear Gaelic
only at home. The school once used Gaelic in all its extracurricular
aspects and English in the classroom. The children of incomers used to
learn Gaelic within one year, but now they don't learn it at all, and this
saddens Donald Gibbie. Unless someone comes into his home who
speaks only English, Donald speaks Gaelic there throughout the day. So
does Margaret. Their children understand, but answer in English. Donald thinks in Gaelic, even when he is speaking English. "The English of
the isles is pure and good," he told me. "It's not pukka English, you
know, but it's the King's English. The English of the isles is good because
it is the second language and has been learned in school."

It is, in fact, often said that the purest English spoken in the world
is spoken in the Highlands. Tangled brogues and syntactical impurities
sometimes misassociated with the Highlanders are the monopoly of the
Lowland Scots. Idiomatic peculiarities in the Highlands are kept mainly
in the Gaelic, the native tongue, and the acquired one, English, runs
almost pure. A certain Gaelic tone and a certain Gaelic rhythm filter
through into the English of the Highlanders, and the sounds of their
voices carrying the words of the Sassenach are so beautiful that one
almost resents having to hear the language anywhere else. In Gaelic,
*Sasunn* is England. And a *Sasunnach* is an Englishman. The words are
apparently never used as compliments. When Dr. Johnson travelled
through the islands, in the summer of 1773, he decided that both the
islanders and their language were rude and barbaric, but he knew no
Gaelic, and no judgment of his could have disturbed the self-assurance
of the people of the Hebrides, who knew, as one Gaelic dictionary has
put it, that "in the islands of Argyll every word is pronounced just as
Adam spoke it."

The school day breaks at twenty minutes to one for dinner: stews,
roast beef, roast pork, potatoes, vegetables, steam puddings, dumplings,
fruit and custard—whatever is on the menu from Dunoon. At twenty
minutes to one each day, all the schoolchildren in Argyll sit down to the
same meal. A cook prepares it from supplies shipped out by the County
Council. History follows, and geography, and a half hour of the Bible
and another half hour of nature study. "Or," Miss Walker says, "we just
go out for a wee walk and see the wild flowers"—daisies, celandines, sea

pinks, heath orchis, pheasant's-eyes, wild iris, whin, broom, meadow rue. When my daughters came home from school one day, one said to me, "Daddy, we say prayers at school. What do you think of that? Did you do that when you were a little boy in school?"

"Yes, I think I did."

"On Colonsay?"

"In Princeton."

"In Princeton? You're kidding."

"No, I'm telling you the truth. You're late today. What time is it?"

"It's just a wee bit past four."

I sat one noon on a cliff near the top of Ben Oronsay, which rises prominently from the edge of The Strand, the amphibious acreage that separates Oronsay from Garvard and Balaromin Mor. In cold rain and cold sunshine, I ate a piece of lamb, some Islay Mini-Dunlop cheese, shortbread, and white chocolate, and looked to the south across a thousand acres of grazing land, flat and green and as isolated as Balnahard. The grazing, covered with sheep and cattle, was framed by converging rocky shorelines that met in a distant point, the end of the island. Beyond the tip, a small following drop, was Eilean nan Ron (Seal Island). Gray seals by the hundred are born there in late summer. It was among the skerries around this islet that the last Colonsay chief was found in hiding —his presence announced by seagulls screaming above his head—on the day that he was taken across The Strand to Balaromin Mor and killed. Just below the cliffs of Ben Oronsay, in shelter from northerly winds, a priory was built in the Middle Ages, and its chapels, halls, and cloisters are only partly gone. Stones were taken from the priory in more recent times for use in the construction, on adjacent ground, of Oronsay farmhouse and its steadings. As I looked down from the cliff, I saw, among the ruins of some of the most interesting ecclesiastical structures in the Hebrides, a man and two sheep dogs—the dogs black and lupine, part wolf, or so they seemed, and part collie. The man had a crook in his hand, a visored tweed cap on his head: Andrew Oronsay. I had not met him, but as he moved around below me, I remembered the things I had heard about him.

When people talk about Andrew Oronsay, the stories usually reflect their considerable regard for the diversity of his skills and talents, and the finesse with which he applies them. Affectionately remembered is the day when Andrew almost drowned the factor—Findlay the Factor, who is no longer on the island. It is recalled, as well, that Andrew was an expert in unarmed combat during the Second World War. He is said to be an excellent Highland dancer. And during the bygone era of the annual sheep-dog trials—the dogs had to go through three sets of gates, around their owners, and into pens—Andrew Oronsay's dogs traversed the course so fast and so faultlessly that they always won and eventually made the competition irrelevant. As a speaker of two tongues, Andrew Oronsay is credited with eloquence in both, and in Gaelic or English he is said to be as facile with coarse words as with smooth ones. The summer guests at the inn in Scalasaig tend to be energetic women in their fifties and sixties, mainly from Glasgow and Edinburgh, with powdery hair and walking sticks; and almost all of them sooner or later visit Oronsay Priory. When these women tire of looking at Celtic crosses and beautiful tombstones with hinds and hounds and swords and galleys and twining ivy in relief, they look at Andrew Oronsay. They lean on stone fences or stand in the doorway of his threshing shed and sometimes attempt to communicate with him as he performs the business of his farm. Some of Andrew's friends say that although he is ordinarily a polite and gracious man he does not like people watching him as he works, and when people do watch him he swears lightly at first, letting the words patter around just under his breath, and then, after a time, he gets the words up there on his breath at a high mutter, and, with a little more time, a little more watching, the language rises and eventually breaks into a thoroughgoing crescendo that drives all the women back up the road, stilting along like scared blue herons.

One other talent is frequently mentioned. In any place as small and remote as Colonsay, it is unusual in modern times to find someone who can play the great Highland bagpipes even competently, let alone well, and it is thus almost unbelievable that there lives on the island—in a population of a hundred and thirty-eight—a piper of the magnitude of Andrew Oronsay. He once lived on the mainland, and although he is too modest to admit it he is said to have played at the launching of the R.M.S. Queen Elizabeth, at Clydebank, and to have been singled out for congratulations by the Queen Mother. Pipers have genealogies, lines of pedagogical ancestry, that are as important to them as bloodlines may be to others. A piper schooled in classical *piobaireachd*—or *ceol mor,* the purest expression of Highland bagpipe music—can listen to another piper and say accurately who his teachers were and who, in turn, taught the teachers. A Scottish bagpiper might be traced to, say, the Macintyres of Atholl or to the Rankins of Duart and Coll, but he can have among his aesthetic forebears no greater men than the MacCrimmons of Skye, hereditary pipers to the MacLeods of MacLeod. Donald Mor MacCrimmon, born in 1570, taught his son, Patrick Mor MacCrimmon, who taught *his* son, Patrick Og MacCrimmon, who felt that his father and grandfather were guilty of ever-increasing excessive embellishment and therefore purified what he had learned by stripping it down to classical standards that have stood for nearly three hundred years. Pipers, in the era of the clans, were so important that they were given servants to carry the pipes. Patrick Og MacCrimmon taught John Dall Mackay of Gairloch, a blind piper ( *"dall"* means "blind") who died in 1754, eight years after Culloden and as many years after the playing of the great Highland bagpipes had been declared an act of treason. John Dall Mackay had already taught his son, Angus, and this Angus Mackay, treason immaterial, later taught John Mackay of Raasay, who was born in 1767, twenty-one years after Culloden. John Mackay of Raasay, who was a clansman but not any sort of immediate relative of his teacher, passed along his craft and art to his son, Angus Mackay. By now, piping was in open and ceremonial revival, with much made of it by the Highland Society of London, in memory of the clans. Felix Mendelssohn was imitating the sound of the pipes in his "Scotch Symphony." And Angus Mackay eventually became piper to Queen Victoria. He also went insane, and finally drowned himself in an asylum. ("There are," someone once said to me, "a lot of wee stories about them all.") One of the first to record the *ceol mor* in staff notation, Angus Mackay had also been the teacher of Donald Cameron. Donald Cameron taught Alexander Cameron, who taught John MacDougall Gillies, who taught Robert Reid, who taught Andrew Oronsay.

I made my way down from the cliff to meet him. He was a short man with a round, weather-reddened face. He looked youthful, although his hair was gray. He had a mustache. His eyes were blue and quick and bright, but they turned aside at times in shyness. When I introduced myself to him, he spoke in an extraordinarily soft voice and said that he was glad that I had come for a wee visit, for he had heard of me from his brother-in-law, Donald Garvard, and also from Donald Gibbie. "You're wet and cold," he said. "You must come in and dry off and have a cup of tea."

The legs of my trousers were soaked from the high heather and the patches of mushy ground that I had gone through on my way up Ben

Oronsay. The water had gone down inside my boots. I was shivering, so I followed him without trying to disclaim what he said. I told him that I thought his sheep dogs, which circled us as we walked, were fine-looking animals.

"They're intelligent, anyway," he said. "You can speak to them and tell them there are three sheep in a certain place, and they will go and get them. But the price of their intelligence is that every so often they go mad and kill sheep. Not terribly long ago, two of them—not these two —killed forty in one night."

The path he followed curved along the low stone fence of the graveyard by the priory church, whose walls were still standing, with tufts of grass growing high above the ground from chinks in the rotting stone. The church was roofless, like most of the other buildings, but the mullions in its principal window were still intact, and they divided three lanciform lights, tall and slim. In the graveyard were two Celtic crosses. Andrew said that one cross dated only to the sixteenth century but that the other had been carved in the ninth century. Bits of headstones and tombstones were scattered all over the graveyard, having become disengaged long since from the turf that covered the bones they once commemorated. "This place is full of your people," Andrew said. "Would you like to see the best stones? They were taken away and put under shelter." He crossed to the far side of the priory and went into a building that had once been the barn and byre, and had been given a new roof some forty years ago so that the slabs of the dead could be preserved there. The tombstones were spaced out on the floor in long rows, each stone about six feet long and covered with carving in relief. Andrew showed me the one that he thought was the most beautiful. It was the tombstone of the chief who was killed by the MacLean arrow in the cave —or "black gully"—that still bears his name. The stone showed a stag surrounded by dogs, and a griffin, and below that a sword garlanded with foliage, and below that a galley in full sail. Andrew said that the ship and the sword had traditionally represented the Lords of the Isles, and *only* the Lords of the Isles—something that no man of Colonsay had ever come near to being. "But at the time of this one's death," he said, "there was some dubiety as to who actually was the Lord of the Isles, so he nipped in smartly and put the galley and the sword on his tombstone."

I told Andrew that even in recent times there had been people in my family who would do things like that.

"Are there many Highland people in your area?" he said.

I thought of some people I had known—Roger MacLean, Audrey MacPherson, Laura MacMillan, Russ McNeill, David McAlpin, Robbie Campbell, Jim Cameron, Corning Chisholm, Ruth Mackay, Godfrey MacDonald—and I said, "Some, I guess. To tell you the truth, I have never really thought of them that way."

Five pictures hung on the walls of Andrew's sitting room. Two, in handsome frames, were of sheep. A third, even more handsomely mounted, was a portrait of a sheep dog. The two others were striking photographic reproductions of rubbings from Oronsay tombstones, including the one of the chief who had tried to nip in on the Lordship of the Isles. Andrew gave me woollen socks and a pair of trousers, and when I had changed from my own socks and trousers his wife spread them over a chair by a coal fire to dry. Flora Oronsay, a solid and attractive woman, had the auburn hair of her brother, Donald Garvard, and the same easygoing, affable manner. Flora and Andrew were married in 1947, I would eventually learn, and the wedding party crossed at low tide to Oronsay for the reception and stayed for twelve hours, wandering back across The Strand at the next low tide, weaving and swaying in the heavy mists in the small hours of the morning. For five years, Flora and Andrew had run The Shop, in Scalasaig, and had then taken over at Oronsay, where, now, the sole inhabitants are the two of them and her mother, Ina Oronsay, a strong and constantly grinning woman of ninety. They live on some fourteen hundred acres, cut off by hill and tide, and when I first visited them the two women had not crossed The Strand, had not gone even to Garvard, let alone to Scalasaig, for the better part of a year.

Flora and Ina Oronsay set dinner on the kitchen table. The tea Andrew had mentioned was supplemented by eggs, sausages, pancakes, scones, and round slices of bread that had been baked in a tubular tin, which had once held the dried milk that is shipped from the mainland to the school. The women of Colonsay are bakers of great skill, and they have to be, because they are so far from the nearest baker's shop. In any Colonsay house, at least six meals are served each day, and into the people and their visitors go an incredible number of drop scones, blueberry scones, oven scones, girdle scones, potato scones, pancakes, spongecakes, creamcakes, oatcakes, chocolate cakes, mince pies, Madeira cakes, rock cakes, and clootie-dumpling fruitcakes. That particular day, I tried to excuse myself by saying that I had only recently eaten my lunch, but that made no impression, and I was soon inflated with scones.

While we ate, I asked Andrew if he found island farming profitable enough, and he told me that it was all right but nothing more, that he had six hundred and thirty sheep, thirty cows, and a bull, and that his sales of calves and lambs had brought him thirteen hundred pounds the previous year. "It is easy to be romantic about the Highlands," he said. "People from the mainland come here in the summer and say what a free and open country life it is, but when they come here for a winter and get a little mud up their backs, the romantic part of it is all over. It's difficult to keep people interested in the islands."

I remarked that his pastures looked beautiful just now.

"It's rough-grazing," he said. "The word 'pasture' to me conveys something more succulent than what we have here."

Toward the end of the meal, his wife asked me, "Do many Highland people live where you do?"

I told her what I had earlier told Andrew.

Andrew said, "Do many pipers live near you?"

And I said, "No. We hear them in parades once in a while, and in Scottish shows in Madison Square Garden."

"The Black Watch played the pipes in President Kennedy's funeral," he said. "I have heard a record of it, and they did not play well."

After a moment, I said, "As a matter of fact, I haven't heard any pipers on Colonsay."

"I used to play," he said. "But I don't play much anymore."

"I've been told that you are quite good," I said.

"Och, they tell stories," Andrew said. "I haven't played in months —years."

Flora and Ina Oronsay laughed. I said I hoped to hear a piper sometime.

"Would you like a wee tune?" he said, looking past me and into the floor.

From another room he brought his pipes, and he assembled them in the kitchen, the metal surfaces of each one being as clear as mirrors. They fitted together with lathed threads, like the tubes of some precision instrument, which, in a sense, they were. Andrew then filled the bag with air and stepped into the stone-surfaced courtyard outside his kitchen door. The sun was shining again. The first sound was a giant monotone

—the basic air release—and it was a sound that seemed big enough to scatter clouds. The melody rode over the top, high lingering notes coming so slowly that they seemed to be growing from the pipes. Andrew, with a look of pained concentration, turned slowly as he played, clockwise, his face in sun and then in shadow. He was playing "Over the Sea to Skye," and when he finished that he played "The Road to the Isles." A scruffy black-and-white cat crouched beside him. His shepherd's crook leaned against the garden wall behind him.

When he had finished, we went back to the sitting room, where he disassembled the pipes and, while he did so, told me that the bagpipe as an instrument had not changed since the seventeenth century, that the high era of bagpipe composition had passed before 1800, and that the Courts of Justice had once ruled that a man carrying bagpipes was a man carrying a weapon—so inspiring was the music of the pipers to the clans in battle. He said that *ceol mor* consists of traditionally structured themes and groundwork, to which individuals attach their own variations, and that young pipers often exasperate him because they leave out fundamental elements. He showed me his basic text of *piobaireachd, The Kilberry Book of Ceol Mor.* As I turned the pages slowly, he hummed some of the tunes that went by, and the tunes he was humming were so sad, beautiful, lilting, and melodic that I found myself wondering if, when these themes emerged from the great Highland bagpipes, Andrew could hear something that I could not. My ear is not a good one for the sound of the pipes. The possibility crossed my mind that there might be some congenital difference in the architecture of our ears. Perhaps he had a double, a triple, a braided auditory nerve that evolution had prepared for the piper alone. My ear, on the other hand, was more than receptive to the sound of the names of the great *ceol-mor* tunes that were now passing before me on the pages of the book, and I remember thinking that if I was deprived of some of the magic of the sound of the pipes I could hear at least the roll of the titles—"The Lament for Red Hector of the Battles," "MacDonald of Kinlochmoidart's Lament," "Salute on the Birth of Rory Mor MacLeod," "The Glen Is Mine," "In Praise of Morag," "Clanranald's Salute," "Lady Margaret MacDonald's Salute," "The Battle of the Pass of Crieff," "The Battle of the Bridge of Perth," "The Lament for Donald Ban MacCrimmon," "The Sound of the Waves Against the Castle of Duntroon."

I had crossed to Oronsay as the tide was going out, and it was now time for me to leave. From his house, Andrew can tell by watching a certain point on the western shoreline how much time a visitor has before it is too late to recross The Strand to Balaromin Mor. He said he would give me a ride partway on his tractor, and asked if I would like to have a look inside the church and the cloisters before I left. The church was floored with turf and a ram was grazing there. Andrew said that it was generally thought that St. Columba had established the priory in the sixth century, and that most of the present structures had been built on the same site by John, Lord of the Isles, in the fourteenth. Grass grew deep in the cloisters, among three rows of triangular arches and one row of semicircular arches, serene and intact. As we were going out, Andrew bent over and picked up a human occipital bone. "One of yours, I expect," he said, and handed it to me. Holding it, I felt nothing more than, perhaps, an affectionate curiosity. Since that day, though, I have found that that moment in the cloister has not left my mind, and that the touch of the grasses, the wet cool of the air, and even the inscriptions on the arches— *"Celestinus Canonicus Huius Operis"*—are more distinct in memory than they seemed to be at the time. I set the occipital piece on a ledge in the cloister wall where there was a small pile of other human bones. "Tidying up a bit," Andrew said.

"Yes, tidying up," I said, and we went to the tractor.

He let me off at a place in the middle of The Strand where a stone cross had once stood, engulfed half the time, but half the time appearing as a sign to anyone who sought sanctuary at the priory. Fugitives from metropolitan Colonsay were beyond pursuit and in utter safety once they passed what became known as the Sanctuary Cross. Only a few broken stones, arranged in the flat sand in the shape of a cross, marked the area now. I said goodbye to Andrew beside these stones, and he turned the tractor around and started back, his tires spraying the perceptibly rising water. The stones of the cross were covered with mussels. I collected as many as I could hold or fit into my pockets and the hood of my rain gear, then ran to beat the tide. We made *moules marinière* that night with malt whisky.

I have volunteered to help the laird prepare his launch for use by a group of marine biologists from the University of Glasgow and the British Museum. In earlier explorations, the scientists have discovered beneath the waters off Colonsay the largest laminaria forest they have ever seen—sequoias of seaweed so dense that men can move among them only in single file along the bottom of the sea. Within these forests they have found a tiny red alga of a type previously seen only in the waters of California, and today, as soon as the launch is ready, they will return to the rubbery wilderness to renew and perhaps to expand their discoveries. The air temperature at the moment is forty-two degrees and the water temperature is exactly the same. There is a strong wind. The sea is choppy. The biologists are up in the inn checking over their equipment —underwater cameras, lanterns, wet-suits—and the laird is in the open-sided shed at the edge of Port na Feamainn (Seaweed Harbor), where his launch has been wedged in storage through the winter. He wears a baggy and partly shredded crimson pullover, tattered plus fours, and frayed leather shoes that are covered with worms of dried paint. He is assisted by Dougie McGilvray, an unredundant hand from the home farm, and Dougie has with him a tractor, which he is maneuvering into position between the shed and the water. The launch is perhaps twenty-five feet long, has a large rust-covered inboard engine, and appears to be planted in the shed, an inertia of tons. It is unimaginable that a tractor of the size of Dougie's could ever pull it out of there. The laird collects bruised and rotting timbers for use as impromptu rollers. He kicks props away from the gunwales of the launch. He pauses and points out a dory just up the beach—one of his dories—that has a staved-in hull plank. "That's the sort of thing that bothers this particular laird," he says. "The boat was left in the open, and that is what happened." When it is repaired, the laird is the one who will do the job. All his life—that is, during all his summers from boyhood, here on Colonsay—he has been a fixer and builder of boats. He is a general carpenter as well. He repairs the furniture in Colonsay House. He describes himself as "an artisan *manqué*." Two or three nights ago, after a dinner of sherried broth, mutton, and several bottles of Burgundy, he showed me, in a roomful of tools and planking, the boat he is working on at the moment—a sailing dinghy. While he talked, he picked up a chisel and shaved away lightly at its bowpiece and gunwales. As he worked, he said, among other things, "I love this place, and in a few years, when the children are older, I want to come live here, and I also want to die here." Now, by Seaweed Harbor, it is beginning to rain, and the rain is ice-cold. The tide is low and turning. Dougie has the tractor in position, and the laird loops a sorry-looking rope between the tractor and the launch, which will emerge, if at all, stern first. One of the scientists approaches along the shore, wearing boots, denim trousers, a black slicker. "I'm terribly sorry, but I shan't be able to introduce you to this chap," the laird says. "I've forgotten his name." The arriving figure turns out to be a woman. She is a distinguished don. The other marine biologists, whose ages vary widely, join us as well. Several young men are in wet-suits and ready to dive. The whole seaweed team is impatient. The tractor roars, and lunges toward the water. The launch moves, its rudder bracket cutting down into the sand and heavy gravels of the shore. The rudder bracket is nearly rusted through, so this essentially clumsy operation has got to be delicate. The laird, with strength surprising even for a man his size, rams a plank into the gravel and under the keel of the launch, and pries up the stern, while the rest of us stuff the impromptu rollers into place. The tractor erupts again, and the launch moves another foot. The laird pries it up. The rain is coming down hard, and on the wind it is coming at an angle that stings. Fifteen minutes go by, and now the tractor is so close to the water that it is useless. Dougie removes it. Everyone heaves at the gunwales to move the launch farther. "We should avoid going in to the left there, if we can," the laird says. "They sort of blew up some rocks here once, to deepen the harbor. That area is full of primordial ooze." Finally, the launch rests on props in shallow water. The incoming tide will float it. The biologists load up, and the laird miraculously starts the rusted engine. But there is a hole in the exhaust. The laird goes off to a small building on the harborside where he keeps nautical supplies. The place is full of oarlocks, anchors, paints, ropes. He rummages for a Jubilee clip —an adjustable steel band secured by a screw—and while he does so he confides to me that his appreciation of the spirit of scientific inquiry has made him feel not entirely comfortable about the fact that he is renting the launch to the scientists for an attractive price. The clip he finds is rusty, but it will do. Back on the beach, the seaweed people are standing around restlessly, smoking. They wanted to get going an hour ago. Sitting in the launch with rain driving horizontally into his face, his long hair hanging down in strings all about his head, the laird bears down on the Jubilee clip's screw. He says, "This screw hasn't moved since God was a boy." The screwdriver slips, and its point goes into and almost through a finger of his left hand. Blood wells up and runs across his fingers and the palm of his hand, mixing with rain and diesel oil. "There I go, trying to screw myself instead of the boat," he says. After much effort, he tightens the clip. The engine is covered with gore. The diving team and its surface dons are ready to go. As the tide washes up around them, the laird keeps handing them small pieces of frayed rope and used hardware that might serve well in an emergency. The laird's right hand is almost as red from cold as his left hand is with blood. It is still raining. The launch begins to move under power. "Goodbye," the laird calls. "I admire you more than I can possibly say. The thought of diving today fills me with the utmost gloom."

There is a graveyard just in front of Donald Gibbie's croft, in Kilchattan, and this for many years has been the island's main burial ground. On a low, flat, and unadorned tombstone beside the graveyard's southern wall are the words "Donald Third Baron Strathcona and Mount Royal, 1891–1959." He was the old laird, and the only laird in modern times to be buried on Colonsay. It was, of course, his wish. His mother, who held the title before him, and his grandfather, the First Baron Strathcona and Mount Royal, had not really been much in evidence on the island they owned. But the old laird apparently looked upon solitude as a form of capital, and the largest share of it he had in his life was on Colonsay. He was a tall, spare man. Alone, he would go to the coastline of uninhabited Balavetchy, where he built with his own hands over a period of years a stone pier for small boats of the type that his oldest son, Euan, was forever making and sailing. "The island had been a place where the family went for a long picnic once a year," Euan now says. "My father increasingly regarded it as his home. Nearly all my boyhood recollections are here. We came here, absolutely always, for the summer. I bathed like a maniac in all weather, made boats, sailed, shot grouse." Euan, who would eventually wonder if the twentieth century could ever completely reach Colonsay, meanwhile watched its tentative approaches: the first telephone, in 1940; the first automobile, in 1947; electricity, in 1952.

Euan was born in 1923, in London. After his Eton years and one year at Trinity College, Cambridge, he went to McGill University, in Montreal, where he earned a degree in engineering. He is a director of various small manufacturing companies, the chief of which is Tallon, Ltd., a maker of ball-point pens, and before his life was altered by the death of his father and his own accession to the peerage, he was an employee, for seven years, of Urwick, Orr & Partners, Ltd., a management-consulting firm in Newcastle, for which he specialized in lavatory valves, foundation garments, and oil seals. Now in Bath he lives in an attractive but unprepossessing segment of an eighteenth-century crescent that he helped to restore. His wife, whom he married in 1954, is a daughter of the Twelfth Earl Waldegrave. Her name is Jinny, and she is pretty and quick, slim, dark-haired, girlish, bright-eyed. She has a wash of freckles. She is the manager of the Schola Cantorum, the university choir of Oxford. She helps her husband with his chairmanship of the annual Bath Festival and looks after their six children, the youngest of whom—Emma and Andrew—are twins. Her capacity for nonchalance seems about equal to the laird's. "Both of us take the peerage business quite lightly," she said one evening. "Euan has no strong atavistic feelings as a laird. He is not the traditional, native, Scottish laird. His great-grandfather was a Scot, but he is English, and even among his Eton-Cambridge friends he is most untypical. He has done things they would consider unthinkable. He went to McGill, and, worse, during the war he went into the Navy and ignored the Guards."

"I drove a motor torpedo boat with singular lack of distinction," said the laird.

She said, "You were wounded in the bottom, darling."

On his mother's side, the laird is descended not only from Jeremiah Colman, the mustard king, but also from Nell Gwyn, the orange wench. During the Restoration, young women carrying baskets of oranges used to stand near the stage in London theatres, face the audience, and sell oranges at sixpence apiece and themselves for a little more. The girls were known as Orange Girls, and they worked under the administration of women called Orange Molls. Nell Gwyn, a beautiful and illiterate Orange Girl, became a minor actress and the mistress of King Charles II. "Anybody may know she has been an orange wench by her swearing," said the Duchess of Portsmouth. Nell Gwyn died when she was thirty-seven, but she lived to see her son made Duke of St. Albans. "My mother's line included the bluest of illegitimate bluebloods—the Duke of St. Albans," the laird has told me. On his father's side, the laird is descended from North American Indians. One of his great-great-grandmothers was a full-blooded Cree. His great-grandfather Donald Smith, of Forres, Morayshire, Scotland, married a half-Indian girl in the Canadian wilderness, performing the ceremony himself, in the absolute absence of clergy. Smith, who would become the First Baron Strathcona and Mount Royal, was, in the words of a biographer, a child of parents "by no means greatly blessed with this world's goods"—the second son of a village merchant. He grew up in a house that resembled, in its essentials, the houses of the crofters of Colonsay and of the Highlands in general. He went to a school that had been established for children of "necessitous parents," and when he was eighteen he signed on as a clerk with the Hudson's Bay Company and was sent to a trading post on the St. Lawrence River. He spent five years there and fifteen more in Labrador, and rose from clerk to trader to chief trader to chief factor to chief executive officer of the Hudson's Bay Company in Canada, head-quartered in Montreal. In time, he became High Commissioner for Canada and, as a member of the Canadian Parliament, author of the Smith Liquor Act, which prohibited the sale and use of alcoholic drinks in the Northwest Territories. To help enforce the act, he wrote the recommendation that resulted in the creation of the Northwest Mounted Police. He also became a founding director of the Canadian Pacific. By his colleagues' acknowledgment, it was largely through his perseverance that the great railway was completed across the Rockies. He was by now the richest man in Canada. White beard flowing, he drove the final spike —at Craigellachie, in British Columbia, November 7, 1885. The spike is now on Colonsay, in a small showcase in the laird's house, and there is a groove in it where iron has been removed so that bits of the spike could be set among the diamonds in the brooches of various Strathcona women. On a wall close by is the family crest and coat of arms. The heraldry—"gules, on a fesse argent . . ."—includes a demi-lion rampant over a hammer and spike, four men paddling a canoe, a beaver gnawing a maple tree, and, over all, the Strathcona motto: "Perseverance."

Showing me all this one day, the laird said that his great-grandfa-ther, after a time as chancellor of McGill University, had returned to Britain as a representative of Canada. "Home with his fortune, he sort of thought the time had come for an estate and a peerage," the laird went on. "So he bought Glencoe." Anciently a MacDonald territory and the scene of the worst massacre in the era of the clans, Glencoe became the seat of the family until 1930, when it was sold. Meanwhile, Queen Victoria had obliged with the peerage, and Donald Smith became, in full title, Baron Strathcona and Mount Royal of Glencoe in the County of Argyll and Montreal in the Province of Quebec. "Strathcona" was mere linguistic prestidigitation—another way of saying "Glencoe." Colonsay was acquired as a kind of afterthought. Smith had loaned some money to the last McNeill laird of Colonsay, and when McNeill died, Smith gave an additional sum to McNeill's heirs and took over the island, for an aggregate of forty-four thousand pounds. The first Lord Strathcona's only child was a daughter, and through something called a "special remainder," cordially dispensed by the Crown, permission was granted that his title pass to her. Thus the second Baron was a woman. Her husband, R. J. B. Howard, was a Canadian physician. Their grandson Euan Howard is the Fourth Baron Strathcona and Mount Royal, and Colonsay's present laird.

The laird, with his legs stretched out, is sitting, sipping whisky, on a low bench before a log fire at Colonsay House in late evening, his wife beside him. He has been considering, with only minor signs of emotion, the fact that he is the least popular man on the island he owns. He accepts this as inevitable, if not pleasant. He is sorry, but he cannot accept the anachronism he stepped into when he became laird in 1959. It is an odd summer place indeed that includes a hundred and thirty-eight dependent people. Embalmed in law, the crofting system of the Highlands is borne forward ever more incongruously toward the twenty-first century, perfectly protecting people from the terrors of the eighteenth century while isolating them from the twentieth. One crofter pays the laird six pounds' rent a year, another forty; the average is fifteen. "Rents here at the moment are lower than they were in 1905. The Depression pushed them down. Rent is fixed by the Scottish Land Court, which will add a pound or two in rent for thousands in improvements." One cotter lives free, another pays five pounds a year, another pays seven. Their houses could be rented to summer people for fifty pounds. Houses that were put up for thirty-five hundred pounds rent for fifteen a year. The whole of Machrins farm—three thousand acres and two houses, one of which has nine bedrooms—rents for four hundred pounds a year. Neil Darroch said his chimney was smoking and asked for a cowl. A cowl would cost fifty-five shillings. Darroch's annual rent is less than that. "When I inherited, the estate was losing more than ten thousand pounds a year. The rent income was two thousand pounds and we were spending well above twelve thousand around the island, and that does not include money spent on our own house and gardens. The people regarded it as axiomatic that we would provide work. Finally, in 1965, we said, 'To hell with all this,' and began creating redundancies, applying for increases in rents, not replacing people who retired or died. We have given the electrical generator plants to the people to run and maintain. It's actually a permanent, interest-free loan. If anyone is going to sell the generators and have a wild weekend in Glasgow, I want it to be me. We used to have a gamekeeper and a forestry staff, but we've packed that up for the moment. Now we are close to washing our face, but it's been at the sacrifice of the economic balance of the island. I blame my own family for getting the people into the situation they are in now. My father's benevolence was misplaced. It is not easy, or practical, to maintain a paradise. People complain about broken skylights and let the rain pour into their houses while they wait for the estate to repair the damage. Waiting for the estate, they leave windows unpainted, and the windows rot out. For sixty years, these people have never been made to do repairs which legitimately belong to them. One wants to educate them to have enough pride to stand on their own feet. They've got to put their fair share into the pot. Donald Gibbie would be a bad example, because from what you tell me he has got the message already. Most of the people here are very lazy, and they are two-faced, in a nice way. They have great charm. They're happy-go-lucky. They're well educated. They always like to give you the answer you want to hear. This sometimes makes them seem to be downright liars, which they are; I would ask you to bear this in mind. Colonsay has an ancient feudal society which basically wants to go on being feudal, provided they can find someone who wants to play at—and finance—being a feudal baron. The term 'laird' is slightly fey and old-fashioned. I am the landlord and the proprietor. These are the facts. I let houses to the other people. The island is my property. All the people live in houses that belong to me. It's a perfectly modern contractual situation. Offhand, I can't think of any ancient rights which are vested in the owner of Colonsay. The paternalistic and benevolent landlord cannot go on being as paternalistic and benevolent as he used to be, and this calls into question the viability of the whole community. The curious thing about our situation is that it is happening on an island. If I lived in Fort William and had to make the odd man redundant, he could find work nearby. My position here would be even more of an incongruity than it is were it not based on a deep tradition. The tradition, however, is becoming less and less tenable. It's frightfully tempting to say, 'To hell with these bloody idle so-and-sos,' but one must remember that for sixty years they have been cosseted. They are entitled to be a little sore when they are dragged screaming into the twentieth century. It's a dicey business for *me!*"

Wherever the laird goes, whether he is hauling a boat out of Loch a' Sgoltaire or walking along Kiloran Bay, he is surrounded by his jumping, nattering, extroverted children. He and his wife walk in the deep parallel ruts of the long driveway to Colonsay House, each holding one of Andrew's hands and swinging the little boy high in the air with every second stride. The laird and his wife have many times stayed up until three in the morning, painting, sweeping, glazing if necessary, to get cottages ready for summer rentals. Their daughter Caroline, who is eight years old, has been living with a housekeeper here for several months now, so that she can go to the island school. Down by the harbor in Scalasaig is a strange shack that consists of four impromptu walls and a vaulted roof that is actually an overturned dory. The laird built it when he was young. The inverted dory is in the most public place on the island and serves, to my eye, at least, as a kind of reminder that when it comes to building codes or zoning, on whatever level, the whole zone is the laird's. Kiloran, the area he generally keeps to, is as different from the rest of the island as the laird is from its people. The vale of Kiloran is completely surrounded by high hills, which interrupt the winds from all directions. On an island that is assaulted by the storms of the North Atlantic, Kiloran is a glen of privileged protection, and it is so lush that people travel from other continents to see it. The earlier Strathcona lairds developed gardens in Kiloran that are among the best in the west of Scotland, known mainly for their profusions of rhododendron. Palm trees were introduced there long ago (the air temperature seldom goes below forty), and they are tall and healthy, growing beside Colonsay House. The house was built in 1722, on the site of the graveyard of an abbey that once stood in Kiloran. Human bones sometimes surface in the gardens. Once French Provincial and symmetrical, the building has been given so many additions that it is now miscellaneous. It has twenty bedrooms, each with a name painted on its door—Balnahard, Garvard, Balaromin Mor—and a billiard room and a library, all high-ceilinged and musty and cavernous. Edward VII came to Kiloran and planted a tree. The Britannia dropped anchor in Kiloran Bay several years ago and the present Royal Family had a picnic there with the laird and his family. When the Queen has a picnic, she brings her own food. The laird was her guest for lunch. She had come to see Kiloran Bay, three-quarters of a mile of gold-white crescent sand, said to be the finest beach in the Hebrides. Once a year, a chartered cruise ship, dazzling white from bow to stern, stops at Colonsay so that members of the National Trust for Scotland can see the island for themselves. The ship has too deep a draft for the pier. Sailors bring the passengers ashore in power launches, and most of the men aboard are dressed in great blazing kilts, and the women wear tartan bonnets and assertive tartan skirts. The laird is there to greet them. He wears the baggiest tweed suit in the United Kingdom, with plus fours and a waistcoat, and on his feet are old, weather-beaten shoes. The suit, resplendently frayed, nobly tattered, appears to have been cut in 1905. He cleans his pipe and spills dottle all over his waistcoat. The dottle blends with several generations of ash already there. He appears to be cheerfully resigned to being an exhibit of the Hebrides. Somehow, he has not compromised. He is pure Sassenach and all laird.

# Encounters with the Archdruid

The designer's logo for this volume shows three delta triangles perched on a line above a fulcrum of one triangle: ▲▲▲. That equation starkly depicts McPhee's own plan for the book, to set a single figure against three adversaries, each time in a place appropriate to their "encounter."

He developed this strategy before finding his protagonist, the archspokesman for wilderness preservation and former director of the Sierra Club, David Brower. After years of distinguished work as an outdoorsman and publisher, Brower had gradually turned to intense political activism—and in the process lost his majority support on the Sierra Club board. Ousted from his directorship, he formed two new organizations —the John Muir Institute for Environmental Studies, and Friends of the Earth—and continued to lobby for the curtailment of modern technology.

McPhee located three antagonists for Brower, each an advocate of his bêtes noires—mines, resorts, dams—and then arranged to have Brower meet the opponents on disputed turf, where they could argue while traversing spectacular scenery. The plan was a bit formulaic; it resembled Boswell's jostling of Dr. Johnson into conversations of quotable prose. But McPhee surmounts that risk by adopting an air of absolute impartiality on the issues he dramatizes. For every point Brower scores on the beauties of wildness, his opponents respond with sensible defenses of progress. And the four personalities only rumple these issues, since Brower is no mere Druid, a worshipper of trees, nor are his adversaries simply out to exploit the land.

This selection is the third and final encounter, originally entitled "A River," which pits Brower against Floyd Dominy during a voyage down the Colorado River. The story exemplifies how facts lend themselves to McPhee's imaginative handling: the lake, river, dam, and raft become his emblems of rigidity or flexibility, expressing a scale of values without forcing him to "take a position" on these controversial issues.—*WLH*

---

Floyd Elgin Dominy raises beef cattle in the Shenandoah Valley. Observed there, hand on a fence, his eyes surveying his pastures, he does not look particularly Virginian. Of middle height, thickset, somewhat bandy-legged, he appears to have been lifted off a horse with block and tackle. He wears bluejeans, a white-and-black striped shirt, and leather boots with heels two inches high. His belt buckle is silver and could not be covered over with a playing card. He wears a string tie that is secured with a piece of petrified dinosaur bone. On his head is a white Stetson.

Thirty-five years ago, Dominy was a county agent in the rangelands of northeastern Wyoming. He could not have come to his job there at a worse time. The Great Drought and the Great Depression had coincided, and the people of the county were destitute. They were not hungry —they could shoot antelope and deer—but they were destitute. Their livestock, with black tongues and protruding ribs, were dying because of lack of water. Dominy, as the agent not only of Campbell County but of the federal government, was empowered to pay eight dollars a head for these cattle—many thousands of them—that were all but decaying where they stood. He paid the eight dollars and shot the cattle.

Dominy was born on a farm in central Nebraska, and all through his youth his family and the families around them talked mainly of the vital weather. They lived close to the hundredth meridian, where, in a sense more fundamental than anything resulting from the events of United States history, the West begins. East of the hundredth meridian, there is enough rain to support agriculture, and west of it there generally is not. The Homestead Act of 1862, in all its promise, did not take into account this ineluctable fact. East of the hundredth meridian, homesteaders on their hundred and sixty acres of land were usually able to fulfill the dream that had been legislated for them. To the west, the odds against them were high. With local exceptions, there just was not enough water. The whole region between the hundredth meridian and the Rocky Mountains was at that time known as the Great American Desert. Still beyond the imagination were the ultramontane basins where almost no rain fell at all.

Growing up on a farm that had been homesteaded by his grandfather in the eighteen-seventies, Dominy often enough saw talent and energy going to waste under clear skies. The situation was marginal. In some years, more than twenty inches of rain would fall and harvests would be copious. In others, when the figure went below ten, the family lived with the lament that there was no money to buy clothes, or even sufficient food. These radical uncertainties were eventually removed by groundwater development, or reclamation—the storage of what water there was, for use in irrigation. When Dominy was eighteen years old, a big thing to do on a Sunday was to get into the Ford, which had a rumble seat, and go out and see the new dam. In his photo album he put pictures of reservoirs and irrigation projects. ("It was impressive to a dry-land farmer like me to see all that water going down a ditch toward a farm.") Eventually, he came to feel that there would be, in a sense, no West at all were it not for reclamation.

In Campbell County, Wyoming, the situation was not even marginal. This was high, dry country, suitable only for free-ranging livestock, not for farming. In the best of years, only about fourteen inches of rain might fall. "Streams ran water when the snow melted. Otherwise, the gulches were dry. It was the county with the most towns and the fewest people, the most rivers with the least water, and the most cows with the least milk in the world." It was, to the eye, a wide, expansive landscape with beguiling patterns of perspective. Its unending buttes, flat or nippled, were spaced out to the horizons like stone chessmen. Deer and antelope moved among them in herds, and on certain hilltops cairns marked the graves of men who had hunted buffalo. The herbage was so thin that forty acres of range could reasonably support only one grazing cow. Nonetheless, the territory had been homesteaded, and the homesteaders simply had not received from the federal government enough land for enough cattle to give them financial equilibrium as ranchers, or from the sky enough water to give them a chance as farmers. They were going backward three steps for each two forward. Then the drought came.

"Nature is a pretty cruel animal. I watched the people there—I mean good folk, industrious, hardworking, frugal—compete with the rigors of nature against hopeless odds. They would ruin their health and still fail." Without waiting for approval from Cheyenne or Washington, the young county agent took it upon himself to overcome nature if the farmers and ranchers could not. He began up near Recluse, on the ranch of a family named Oedekoven, in a small bowl of land where an intermittent stream occasionally flowed. With a four-horse Fresno—an ancestral bulldozer—he moved earth and plugged the crease in the terrain where the water would ordinarily run out and disappear into the ground and the air. He built his little plug in the classic form of the earth-fill dam —a three-for-one slope on the water side and two-for-one the other way. More cattle died, but a pond slowly filled, storing water. The pond is still there, and so is Oedekoven, the rancher.

For two and a half years, Dominy lived with his wife and infant daughter in a stone dugout about three miles outside Gillette, the county seat. For light they used a gasoline lantern. For heat and cooking they had a coal-burning stove. Dominy dug the coal himself out of a hillside. His wife washed clothes on a board. On winter mornings when the temperature was around forty below zero, he made a torch with a rag and a stick, soaked it in kerosene, lighted it, and put it under his car. When the car was warm enough to move, Dominy went off to tell ranchers and farmers about the Corn-Hog Program ("Henry Wallace slaughtering piglets to raise the price of ham"), the Wheat Program (acreage control), or how to build a dam. "Campbell County was my kingdom. When I was twenty-four years old, I was king of the God-damned county." He visited Soda Well, Wild Cat, Teckla, Turnercrest —single-family post offices widely spaced—or he followed the farmers and ranchers into the county seat of the county seat, Jew Jake's Saloon, where there was a poker game that never stopped and where the heads of moose, deer, elk, antelope, and bighorn sheep looked down on him and his subjects, feet on the rail at 9 A.M. Dominy had his first legitimate drink there. The old brass rail is gone—and so is Dominy—but the saloon looks just the same now, and the boys are still there at 9 A.M.

There was an orange scoria butte behind Dominy's place and an alfalfa field in front of it. Rattlesnakes by the clan came out of the butte in the spring, slithered around Dominy's house, and moved on into the alfalfa for the summer. In September, the snakes headed back toward the butte. Tomatoes were ripe in Dominy's garden, and whenever he picked some he first took a hoe and cleared out the rattlesnakes under the vines. Ranchers got up at four in the morning, and sometimes Dominy was outside honking his horn to wake them. He wanted them to come out and build dams—dams, dams, dams. "I had the whole county stirred up. We were moving! Stockpond dam and reservoir sites were supposed to be inspected first by Forest Service rangers, but who knows when they would have come? I took it upon myself to ignore these pettifogging minutiae." Changing the face of the range, he polka-dotted it with ponds. Dominy and the ranchers and farmers built a thousand dams in one year, and when they were finished there wasn't a thirsty cow from Jew Jake's

Saloon to the Montana border. "Christ, we did more in that county in one year than any other county in the country. That range program really put me on the national scene."

In the view of conservationists, there is something special about dams, something—as conservation problems go—that is disproportionately and metaphysically sinister. The outermost circle of the Devil's world seems to be a moat filled mainly with DDT. Next to it is a moat of burning gasoline. Within that is a ring of pinheads each covered with a million people—and so on past phalanxed bulldozers and bicuspid chain saws into the absolute epicenter of Hell on earth, where stands a dam. The implications of the dam exceed its true level in the scale of environmental catastrophes. Conservationists who can hold themselves in reasonable check before new oil spills and fresh megalopolises mysteriously go insane at even the thought of a dam. The conservation movement is a mystical and religious force, and possibly the reaction to dams is so violent because rivers are the ultimate metaphors of existence, and dams destroy rivers. Humiliating nature, a dam is evil—placed and solid.

"I hate all dams, large and small," David Brower informs an audience.

A voice from the back of the room asks, "Why are you conservationists always against things?"

"If you are against something, you are for something," Brower answers. "If you are against a dam, you are for a river."

When Brower was a small boy in Berkeley, he used to build dams in Strawberry Creek, on the campus of the University of California, piling up stones in arcs convex to the current, backing up reservoir pools. Then he would kick the dams apart and watch the floods that returned Strawberry Creek to its free-flowing natural state. When Brower was born—in 1912—there was in the Sierra Nevada a valley called Hetch Hetchy that paralleled in shape, size, and beauty the Valley of the Yosemite. The two valleys lay side by side. Both were in Yosemite National Park, which had been established in 1890. Yet within three decades—the National Park notwithstanding—the outlet of Hetch Hetchy was filled with a dam and the entire valley was deeply flooded. Brower was a boy when the dam was being built. He remembers spending his sixth birthday in the hills below Hetch Hetchy and hearing stories of the battle that had been fought over it, a battle that centered on the very definition of conservation. Should it mean preservation of wilderness or wise and varied use of land? John Muir, preservationist, founder of the young Sierra Club, had lost this bitter and, as it happened, final struggle of his life. It had been a battle that split the Sierra Club in two. Fifty-five years later, the Sierra Club would again divide within itself, and the outcome of the resulting battle would force the resignation of its executive director, David Brower, whose unsurprising countermove would be to form a new organization and name it for John Muir.

Not long after Brower's departure from the Sierra Club and his founding of the John Muir Institute, I went to Hetch Hetchy with him and walked along the narrow top of the dam, looking far down one side at the Tuolumne River, emerging like a hose jet from the tailrace, and in the other direction out across the clear blue surface of the reservoir, with its high granite sides—imagining the lost Yosemite below. The scene was bizarre and ironic, or so it seemed to me. Just a short distance across the peaks to the south of us was the Yosemite itself, filled to disaster with cars and people, tens of thousands of people, while here was the Yosemite's natural twin, filled with water. Things were so still at Hetch Hetchy that a wildcat walked insolently across the road near the dam and didn't even look around as he moved on into the woods. And Brower—fifty-six years old and unshakably the most powerful voice in the conservation movement in his country—walked the quiet dam. "It was not needed when it was built, and it is not needed now," he said. "I would like to see it taken down, and watch the process of recovery."

During the years when Brower was developing as a conservationist, many of his most specific and dramatic personal accomplishments had to do with proposed dams. Down the tiers of the Western states, there are any number of excellent damsites that still contain free-flowing rivers because of David Brower—most notably in the immense, arid watershed of the Colorado. Anyone interested, for whatever reason, in the study of water in the West will in the end concentrate on the Colorado, wildest of rivers, foaming, raging, rushing southward—erratic, headlong, incongruous in the desert. The Snake, the Salmon, the upper Hudson—all the other celebrated white torrents—are not in the conversation if the topic is the Colorado. This is still true, although recently (recently in the long span of things, actually within the past forty years) the Colorado has in places been subdued. The country around it is so dry that Dominy's county in Wyoming is a rain forest by comparison. The states of the basin need water, and the Colorado is where the water is. The familiar story of contention for water rights in the Old West—Alan Ladd shooting it out with Jack Palance over some rivulet God knows where—has its mother narrative in the old and continuing story of rights to the waters of the Colorado. The central document is something called the Colorado River Compact, in which the basin is divided in two, at a point close to the Utah-Arizona line. The states of the Upper Basin are allowed to take so much per year. The Lower Basin gets approximately an equal share. And something gratuitous is passed on to Mexico. The Colorado lights and slakes Los Angeles. It irrigates Arizona. The odd thing about it is that all its writhings and foamings and spectacular rapids lead to nothing. The river rises in the Rockies, thunders through the canyons, and is so used by mankind that when it reaches the Gulf of California, fourteen hundred miles from its source, it literally trickles into the sea. The flow in the big river and in its major tributaries—the Green, the Yampa, the Escalante, the San Juan, the Little Colorado—is almost lyrically erratic, for the volume can vary as much as six hundred per cent from one year to the next. The way to control that, clearly enough, is storage, and this is accomplished under programs developed and administered by the federal Bureau of Reclamation. The Bureau of Reclamation, all but unknown in the American East, is the patron agency of the American West, dispenser of light, life, and water to thirty million people whose gardens would otherwise be dust. Most of the civil servants in the Bureau are Westerners—from the dry uplands as well as the deserts of the Great Basin. They have lived in the problem they are solving, and they have a deep sense of mission. There are many people in the Bureau of Reclamation—perhaps all nine thousand of them—who hope to see the Colorado River become a series of large pools, one stepped above another, from the Mexican border to the Rocky Mountains, with the headwaters of each succeeding lake lapping against the tailrace of a dam. The river and its tributaries have long since been thoroughly surveyed, and throughout the basin damsites of high quality and potentiality stand ready for river diversion, blast excavation, and concrete. Three of these sites are particularly notable here. One is near the juncture of the Green and the Yampa, close to the Utah-Colorado border. The two others are in northern Arizona—in the Grand Canyon. A fourth site would belong in this special list if it were still just a site, but a dam is actually there, in northernmost Arizona, in Glen Canyon. David Brower believes that the dam in Glen Canyon represents the greatest failure of his life. He cannot think of it without melancholy, for he sincerely believes that its very existence is his fault. He feels that if he had been more aware, if he had more adequately prepared himself for his own kind of mission, the dam would not be there. Its gates closed in 1963, and it began backing up water a hundred and eighty-six miles into Utah. The reservoir is called Lake Powell, and it covers country that Brower himself came to know too late. He made his only trips there—float trips on the river with his children—before the gates were closed but after the dam, which had been virtually unopposed, was under construction. Occasionally, in accompaniment to the talks he gives around the country, Brower shows an elegiac film about Glen Canyon, "the place no one knew." That was the trouble, he explains. No one knew what was there. Glen Canyon was one of the two or three remotest places in the United States—far from the nearest road, a hundred and twenty-five miles from the nearest railhead. The film records that the river canyon and its great trellis of side canyons was a deep and sometimes dark world of beauty, where small streams had cut gorges so profound and narrow that people walking in them were in cool twilight at noon, and where clear plunges of water dropped into pools surrounded with maidenhair fern in vaulted grottoes with names like Cathedral in the Desert, Mystery Canyon, Music Temple, Labyrinth Canyon. With all their blue-and-gold walls and darkly streaked water-drip tapestries, these places are now far below the surface of Lake Powell. "Few people knew about these canyons," Brower says quietly. "No one else will ever know what they were like."

The lost worlds of Utah notwithstanding, if conservationists were to label their heroes in the way the English label their generals, David Brower would be known as Brower of the Colorado, Brower of the Grand Canyon. In the early nineteen-fifties, he fought his first major campaign—in his capacity as the first executive director of the Sierra Club—against the dam that the Bureau of Reclamation was about to build near the juncture of the Green and the Yampa. The reservoir would have backed water over large sections of Dinosaur National Monument. In the view of Brower, the Sierra Club, and conservationists generally, the integrity of the National Park system was at stake. The Dinosaur Battle, as it is called, was a milestone in the conservation movement. It was, to begin with, the greatest conservation struggle in half a century —actually, since the controversies that involved the damming of Hetch Hetchy and led to the debates that resulted in the creation, in 1916, of the National Park Service. The Dinosaur Battle is noted as the first time that all the scattered interests of modern conservation—sportsmen, ecologists, wilderness preservers, park advocates, and so forth—were drawn together in a common cause. Brower, more than anyone else, drew them together, fashioning the coalition, assembling witnesses. With a passing wave at the aesthetic argument, he went after the Bureau of Reclamation with facts and figures. He challenged the word of its engineers and geologists that the damsite was a sound one, he suggested that cliffs would dissolve and there would be a tremendous and cataclysmic dam failure there, and he went after the basic mathematics underlying the Bureau's proposals and uncovered embarrassing errors. All this was accompanied by flanking movements of intense publicity—paid advertisements, a film, a book—envisioning a National Monument of great scenic, scientific, and cultural value being covered with water. The Bureau protested that the conservationists were exaggerating—honing and bending the truth—but the Bureau protested without effect. Conservationists say that the Dinosaur victory was the birth of the modern conservation movement—the turning point at which conservation became something more than contour plowing. There is no dam at the confluence of the Green and the Yampa. Had it not been for David Brower, a dam would be there. A man in the public-relations office of the Bureau of Reclamation one day summed up the telling of the story by saying, "Dave won, hands down."

There are no victories in conservation, however. Brower feels that he can win nothing. There is no dam at the Green and the Yampa now, but in 2020 there may be. "The Bureau of Reclamation engineers are like beavers," he says. "They can't stand the sight of running water." Below the Utah-Arizona border, in Marble Gorge, a part of the Grand Canyon, there is likewise no dam. The story is much the same. The Bureau of Reclamation had the dam built on paper, ready to go. A battle followed, and Brower won, hands down. In the Lower Granite Gorge, another part of the Grand Canyon, there is also no dam, and for the same reason. These Grand Canyon battles were the bitterest battles of all. The Bureau felt that Brower capitalized on literary hyperbole and the mystic name of the canyon. He implied, they said, that the dams were going to fill the Grand Canyon like an enormous bathtub, and that the view from the north rim to the south rim would soon consist of a flat expanse of water. Brower's famous advertising campaigns reached their most notable moment at this time. He placed full-page ads in *The New York Times* and the *San Francisco Chronicle,* among other places, under the huge headline "SHOULD WE ALSO FLOOD THE SISTINE CHAPEL SO TOURISTS CAN GET NEARER THE CEILING?" Telegrams flooded Congress, where the battle was decided. The Bureau cried foul, saying that it was intending to inundate only a fraction of one per cent of what Brower was suggesting. The Internal Revenue Service moved in and took away from the Sierra Club the tax-deductibility of funds contributed to it. Contributions to lobbying organizations are not tax-deductible, and the ads were construed as lobbying. The Sierra Club has never recovered its contributions-deductible status, but within the organization it is felt—by Brower's enemies as well as his friends—that the Grand Canyon was worth it. There are no dams in the Grand Canyon, and in the Bureau of Reclamation it is conceded that there will not be for at least two generations. The defeat of the high dams is frankly credited, within the Bureau, to David Brower. "He licked us." "He had all the emotions on his side." "He did it singlehanded."

Popular assumptions to the contrary, no federal bureau is completely faceless—and, eyeball to eyeball with David Brower, there was a central and predominant figure on the other side of these fights, marshalling his own forces, battling in the rooms of Congress and in the canyon lands of the West for his profound and lifelong belief in the storage of water. This was the Bureau's leader—Floyd E. Dominy, United States Commissioner of Reclamation.

In the District of Columbia, in the labyrinthine fastnesses of the Department of the Interior, somewhere above Sport Fisheries and Wildlife and beyond the Office of Saline Water, there is a complex of corridors lined with murals of enormous dams. This is Reclamation, and these are its monuments: Flaming Gorge Dam, Hungry Horse Dam, Hoover Dam, Glen Canyon Dam, Friant Dam, Shasta Dam, Vallecito Dam, Grand Coulee Dam. I remember the day that I first saw these murals. In the moist and thermoelectric East, they seemed exotic, but hardly more so than the figure to whom the corridors led, the man in the innermost chamber of the maze. The white Stetson was on a table near the door. Behind a magisterial desk sat the Commissioner, smoking a big cigar. "Dominy," he said, shaking hands. "Sit down. I'm a public servant. I don't have any secrets from anybody."

He wore an ordinary Washington suit, but capital pallor was not in his face—a hawk's face, tanned and leathery. He had dark hair and broad shoulders, and he seemed a big man—bigger than his height and weight would indicate—and powerful but not forbidding. "Many people have said of me that I never meet a stranger," he said. "I like people. I like taxi-drivers and pimps. They have their purpose. I like Dave Brower, but I don't think he's the sanctified conservationist that so many people think he is. I think he's a selfish preservationist, for the few. Dave Brower hates my guts. Why? Because I've *got* guts. I've tangled with Dave Brower for many years."

On a shelf behind Dominy's desk, in the sort of central and eye-catching position that might be reserved for a shining trophy, was a scale model of a bulldozer. Facing each other from opposite walls were portraits of Richard M. Nixon and Hoover Dam. Nixon's jowls, in this milieu, seemed even more trapeziform than they usually do. They looked as if they, too, could stop a river. Seeing that my attention had been caught by these pictures, Dominy got up, crossed the room, and stood with reverence and devotion before the picture of Hoover Dam. He said, "When we built that, we—Americans—were the only people who had ever tried to put a high dam in a big river." He said he remembered as if it were his birthday the exact date when he had first seen—as it was then called—Boulder Dam. He had taken a vacation from Campbell County, Wyoming, and driven, with his wife, into the Southwest, and on January 2, 1937, reached the Arizona-Nevada border and got his first view of the dam as he rounded a curve in the road descending toward the gorge of the Colorado. "There she was," he said, looking at the picture in his office. "The first major river plug in the world. Joseph of Egypt learned to store food against famine. So we in the West had learned to store water." He went on to say that he felt sure that—subconsciously, at least—the outline of his career had been formed at that moment. He had begun by building dams seven feet high, and he would one day build dams seven hundred feet high.

The rancher Fred Oedekoven, on whose place Dominy built his first dam, is nearly eighty years old. A tall man, bent slightly forward, he lives in a peeled-log house on the land he homesteaded when he was twenty. I met him once, when I was in the county, and talked with him in the sitting room of his house. Two pictures hung on the walls. One was of Jesus Christ. The other was the familiar calendar scene of the beautiful lake in Jackson Hole, Wyoming, with the Grand Tetons rising in the background. Jackson Lake, as it is called, was built by the Bureau of Reclamation. "When Dominy come here, he took aholt," Oedekoven said. "I hated to see him go. They wanted him to go to Washington, D.C., to go on this water-facilities program, and I advised him to do it, for the advancement. He really clumb up in life."

Dominy had stayed up there as well, becoming the longest-running commissioner in the Department of the Interior. Appointed by Eisenhower, he adapted so well to the indoor range that he was able to keep his position—always "at the pleasure of the President, without term of office"—through two Democratic Administrations, and now he was, in his words, "carrying the Nixon hod." He winked, sat down on the edge of his desk, and pronounced his absorbing code: "Never once have I made a decision against my will if it was mine to make." He had learned to plant creative ideas in senators' and congressmen's minds ("Based on your record, sir, we assume . . ."), when to be a possum, and when to spring like a panther (" 'You get out of my office,' I said. The average bureaucrat would have been shaking, but I wasn't the least bit scared. No member of Congress is going to make me jump through hoops. I've never lost my cool in government work unless I thought it was to my advantage"). He had given crucial testimony against the proposed Rampart Dam, on the Yukon River, arguing that it was too much for Alaska's foreseeable needs; Rampart Dam would have flooded an area the size of Lake Erie, and Dominy's testimony defeated it. He had argued for federal—as opposed to private—power lines leading away from his big dams, thus irritating the special interests of senators and congressmen from several states. "I have been a controversial bastard for many years," he explained, lighting another cigar. Dominy knew his business, though, and he could run a budget of two hundred and forty-five million dollars as if he were driving a fast bus. He had cut down the Bureau's personnel from seventeen thousand to ten thousand. And he had built his stupendous dams. On the wall of his office there was also a picture of Dominy—a bold sketch depicting his head inside a mighty drop of water. It seemed more than coincidence that in an age of acronyms his very initials were FED.

Dominy switched on a projector and screened the rough cut of a movie he had had prepared as an antidote to the Sierra Club's filmed elegy to the inundated canyons under Lake Powell. Dominy's film was called "Lake Powell, Jewel of the Colorado," and over an aerial shot of its blue fjords reaching into the red desert a narrator said, "Through rock and sand, canyon and cliff, through the towering formations of the sun-drenched desert, the waters of the Colorado River pause on their way to the sea." Water skiers cut wakes across the water.

"Too many people think of environment simply as untrammelled nature," Dominy commented. "Preservation groups claim we destroyed this area because we made it accessible to man. Six hundred thousand people a year use that lake now."

The film showed a Navajo on horseback in a blazing-red silk shirt. "Into his land came Lake Powell, which he has woven into his ancient ways," said the narrator.

"Right," said Dominy. "Now people can fish, swim, water-ski, sun-bathe. Can't you imagine going in there with your family for a weekend, getting away from everybody? But Mr. Brower says we destroyed it."

"The canyon lay isolated, remote, and almost unknown to the outside world," said the narrator, "until"—and at that moment a shot of the red walls of Glen Canyon came on the screen, and suddenly there was a great blast and the walls crumbled in nimbuses of dust. Ike had pressed a button. Bulldozers followed, and new roads, and fifty thousand trucks. Cut to dedication of dam, ten years later. "I am proud to dedicate such a significant and beautiful man-made resource," said Lady Bird Johnson. "I am proud that man is here."

Dominy blew smoke into the scene as Lady Bird dissolved. "The need for films of this kind, for public information, is great, because of those who would have all forests and rivers remain pristine," he said. "People ignore facts and play on emotions."

There were more scenes of the blue, still water, lapping at high sandstone cliffs—panoramic vistas of the reservoir. An airplane now appeared over the lake—twin-engine, cargo. "Watch this," Dominy said. "Just watch this." What appeared to be a contrail paid out behind the plane—a long, cloudy sleeve that widened in the air. "Trout!" Dominy said. "Trout! Those are fingerling trout. That's how we put them in the lake."

Montages of shots showed the half-filled lateral canyons—Forgotten Canyon, Cascade Canyon, Reflection Canyon, Mystery Canyon—with people swimming in them, camping beside them, and singing around fires. "In this land, each man must find his own meanings," said the narrator. "Lake Powell, Jewel of the Colorado, offers the opportunity."

"Reclamation is the father of putting water to work for man—irrigation, hydropower, flood control, recreation," Dominy said as he turned on the lights. "Let's *use* our environment. Nature changes the environment every day of our lives—why shouldn't *we* change it? We're part of nature. Just to give you a for-instance, we're cloud-seeding the

Rockies to increase the snowpack. We've built a tunnel under the Continental Divide to send water toward the Pacific that would have gone to the Atlantic. The challenge to man is to do and save what is good but to permit man to progress in civilization. Hydroelectric power doesn't pollute water and it doesn't pollute air. You don't get any pollution out of my dams. The unregulated Colorado was a son of a bitch. It wasn't any good. It was either in flood or in trickle. In addition to creating economic benefits with our dams, we regulate the river, and we have created the sort of river Dave Brower dreams about. Who are the best conservationists—doers or preservationists? I can't talk to preservationists. I can't talk to Brower, because he's so God-damned ridiculous. I can't even reason with the man. I once debated with him in Chicago, and he was shaking with fear. Once, after a hearing on the Hill, I accused him of garbling facts, and he said, 'Anything is fair in love and war.' For Christ's sake. After another hearing one time, I told him he didn't know what he was talking about, and said I wished I could show him, I wished he would come with me to the Grand Canyon someday, and he said, 'Well, save some of it, and maybe I will.' I had a steer out on my farm in the Shenandoah reminded me of Dave Brower. Two years running, we couldn't get him into the truck to go to market. He was an independent bastard that nobody could corral. That son of a bitch got into that truck, busted that chute, and away he went. So I just fattened him up and butchered him right there on the farm. I shot him right in the head and butchered him myself. That's the only way I could get rid of the bastard."

"Commissioner," I said, "if Dave Brower gets into a rubber raft going down the Colorado River, will you get in it, too?"

"Hell, yes," he said. "Hell, yes."

Mile 130. The water is smooth here, and will be smooth for three hundred yards, and then we are going through another rapid. The temperature is a little over ninety, and the air is so dry that the rapid will feel good. Dominy and Brower are drinking beer. They have settled into a kind of routine: once a day they tear each other in half and the rest of the time they are pals.

Dominy is wearing a blue yachting cap with gold braid, and above its visor in gold letters are the words "LAKE POWELL." His skin is rouge brown. His nose is peeling. He wears moccasins, and a frayed cotton shirt in dark, indeterminate tartan, and long trousers secured by half a pound of silver buckle. He has with him a couple of small bags and a big leather briefcase on which is painted the great seal of the Bureau of Reclamation—snow-capped mountains, a reservoir, a dam, and irrigated fields, all within the framing shape of a big drop of water. Dominy has been discoursing on the multiple advantages of hydroelectric power, its immediacy ("When you want it, you just throw a switch") and its innocence of pollution.

"Come on now, Dave, be honest," he said. "From a conservationist's point of view, what is the best source of electric power?"

"Flashlight batteries," Brower said.

Brower is also wearing an old tartan shirt, basically orange, and faded. He wears shorts and sneakers. The skin of his legs and face is bright red. Working indoors and all but around the clock, he has been too long away from the sun. He protects his head with a handkerchief knotted at the corners and soaked in the river, but his King Lear billowing white hair is probably protection enough. He travels light. A miniature duffelbag, eight inches in diameter and a foot long—standard gear for the river—contains all that he has with him, most notably his Sierra Club cup, without which he would be incomplete.

Dominy and Brower are both showing off a little. These organized expeditions carry about a dozen people per raft, and by now the others are thoroughly aware of the biases of the conservationist and the Commissioner. The people are mainly from Arizona and Nevada—schoolteachers, a few students, others from the U.S. Public Health Service. On the whole, I would say that Dominy so far has the edge with them. Brower is shy and quiet. Dominy is full of Irish pub chatter and has a grin as wide as the river.

Cans of beer are known as sandwiches in this red, dry, wilderness world. No one questions this, or asks the reason. They just call out "Sandwich, please!" and a can of Coors comes flying through the air. They catch the beer and drink it, and they put the aluminum tongues inside the cans. I threw a tongue in the river and was booed by everyone. No detritus whatever is left in the canyon. Used cans, bottles—all such things—are put in sacks and go with the raft all the way. The beer hangs in the water in a burlap bag from the rear of the raft, with Cokes and Frescas. The bag is hauled onto the raft before a heavy rapid but rides through the lighter ones.

The raft consists of, among other things, two neoprene bananas ten yards long. These pontoons, lashed to a central rubber barge, give the over-all rig both lateral and longitudinal flexibility. The river sometimes leaps straight up through the raft, but that is a mark of stability rather than imminent disaster. The raft is informal and extremely plastic. Its lack of rigidity makes it safe.

This is isolation wilderness: two or three trails in two hundred miles, otherwise no way out but down the river with the raft. Having seen the canyon from this perspective, I would not much want to experience it another way. Once in a rare while, we glimpse the rims. They are a mile above us and, in places, twelve miles apart. All the flat shelves of color beneath them return the eye by steps to the earliest beginnings of the world—from the high white limestones and maroon Hermit Shales of Permian time to the red sandstones that formed when the first reptiles lived and the vermillion cliffs that stood contemporary with the earliest trees. This Redwall Limestone, five hundred feet thick, is so vulnerable to the infiltrations of groundwater that it has been shaped, in the seas of air between the canyon rims, into red towers and red buttes, pillars, caverns, arches, and caves. The groundwater runs for hundreds of miles between the layers of that apparently bone-dry desert rock and bursts out into the canyon in stepped cascades or ribbon falls. We are looking at such a waterfall right now, veiling away from the Redwall, high above us. There is green limestone behind the waterfall, and pink limestone that was pressed into being by the crushing weight of the ocean at the exact time the ocean itself was first giving up life—amphibious life—to dry land. Beneath the pink and green limestones are green-gray shales and dark-brown sandstones—Bright Angel Shale, Tapeats Sandstone—that formed under the fathoms that held the first general abundance of marine life. Tapeats Sea was the sea that compressed the rock that was cut by the river to create the canyon. The Tapeats Sandstone is the earliest rock from the Paleozoic Era, and beneath it the mind is drawn back to the center of things, the center of the canyon, the cutting plane, the Colorado. Flanked by its Bass Limestones, its Hotauta Conglomerates, its Vishnu Schists and Zoroaster Granites, it races in white water through a pre-Cambrian here and now. The river has worked its way down into the stillness of original time.

Brower braces his legs and grips one of the safety ropes that run along the pontoons. He says, "How good it is to hear a living river! You can almost hear it cutting."

Dominy pulls his Lake Powell hat down firmly around his ears. He has heard this sort of thing before. Brower is suggesting that the

Colorado is even now making an ever deeper and grander Grand Canyon, and what sacrilege it would be to dam the river and stop that hallowed process. Dominy says, "I think most people agree, Dave, that it wasn't a river of this magnitude that cut the Grand Canyon."

Brower is too interested in the coming rapid to respond. In this corridor of calm, we can hear the rapid ahead. Rapids and waterfalls ordinarily take shape when rivers cut against resistant rock and then come to a kind of rock that gives way more easily. This is not the case in the Grand Canyon, where rapids occur beside the mouths of tributary creeks. Although these little streams may be dry much of the year, they are so steep that when they run they are able to fling considerable debris into the Colorado—sand, gravel, stones, rocks, boulders. The debris forms dams, and water rises upstream. The river is unusually quiet there —a lakelike quiet—and then it flows over the debris, falling suddenly, pounding and crashing through the boulders. These are the rapids of the Grand Canyon, and there are a hundred and sixty-one of them. Some have appeared quite suddenly. In 1966, an extraordinarily heavy rain fell in a small area of the north rim, and a flash flood went down Crystal Creek, dumping hundreds of tons of rock into the river at Mile 99. This instantly created the Crystal Rapids, one of the major drops in the Colorado. In rare instances—such as the rapid we are now approaching —the river has exposed resistant pre-Cambrian rock that contributes something to the precipitousness of the flow of white water. The roar is quite close now. The standing waves look like blocks of cement. Dominy emits a cowboy's yell. My notes go into a rubber bag that is tied with a string. This is the Bedrock Rapid.

We went through it with a slow dive and climb and a lot of splattering water. We undulated. The raft assumed the form of the rapid. We got very wet. And now, five minutes later, we are as dry and warm as if we were wearing fresh clothes straight out of a dryer. And we are drinking sandwiches.

We have a map that is seven inches high and fifty feet long. It is rolled in a scroll and is a meticulously hand-done contemporary and historical portrait of the Colorado River in the Grand Canyon. River miles are measured from the point, just south of the Utah line, where the Paria River flows into the Colorado—the place geologists regard as the beginning of the Grand Canyon. As the map rolls by, it records who died where. "Peter Hansbrough, one of two men drowned, Mile 24, Tanner

Wash Rapids, 1889. . . . Bert Loper upset, not seen again, Mile 24, 1949. . . . Scout found and buried in talus, Mile 43, 1951. . . . Roemer drowned in Mile 89, 1948." The first known run of the river was in 1869, and the second shortly thereafter—both the expeditions of Major John Wesley Powell—and even by 1946 only about a hundred people had ever been through the canyon by river. With the introduction of neoprene rafts—surplus from the Second World War—the figure expanded. Five hundred a year were going through by the middle nineteen-sixties, and the number is now in the low thousands.

"As long as people keep on taking out everything that they bring in, they're not going to hurt the Grand Canyon," Brower says. "Rule No. 1 is 'Leave nothing—not even a dam.' "

Dominy does not hear that. He is busy telling a pretty young gym teacher from Phoenix that he played sixty minutes a game as captain of the ice-hockey team at the University of Wyoming. "I liked the speed. I liked the body contact. I developed shots the defense couldn't fathom."

Dominy is in his sixtieth year and is planning an early retirement, but he looks fifty, and it is not at all difficult to imagine him on a solo dash down the ice, slamming the Denver Maroons into pulp against the boards and breaking free to slap the winning shot into the nets. He once did exactly that. He has the guts he says he has, and I think he is proving it now, here on the Colorado. He may be an athlete, but he can't swim. He can't swim one stroke. He couldn't swim across a goldfish pond. And at this moment it is time for us to put things away and pull ourselves together, because although we are scarcely dry from the Bedrock Rapid, the crescendoing noise we hear is Deubendorff, an officially designated "heavy rapid," one of the thirteen roughest in the canyon. Brower goes quiet before a rapid, and he is silent now. He says he is not much of a swimmer, either. We all have life vests on, but they feel as if they would be about as effective against these rapids as they would be against bullets. That is not true, though. Once in a great while, these rafts turn over, and when they do the people all end up bobbing in the calmer water at the foot of the rapid like a hatful of spilled corks. Riding a rigid boat, Seymour Deubendorff was claimed by this rapid on the Galloway-Stone expedition, in 1909. This we learn from our map. Looking ahead, we see two steep grooves, a hundred and fifty yards apart, that have been cut into the south wall of the river gorge. They are called Galloway Canyon and Stone Canyon, and the streams in them are not running now, but each has thrown enough debris into the river to make a major rapid, and together they have produced Deubendorff. Directly in front of us, a mile ahead and high against the sky, is a broad and beautiful Redwall mesa. The river disappears around a corner to the left of it. Meanwhile, the big, uncompromising mesa seems to suggest a full and absolute stop, as if we were about to crash into it in flight, for spread below it in the immediate foreground is a prairie of white water.

There is a sense of acceleration in the last fifty yards. The water is like glass right up to where the tumult begins. Everything is lashed down. People even take hats and handkerchiefs off their heads and tie them to the raft. Everyone has both hands on safety ropes—everyone but Dominy. He giggles. He gives a rodeo yell. With ten smooth yards remaining, he lights a cigar.

There is something quite deceptive in the sense of acceleration that comes just before a rapid. The word "rapid" itself is, in a way, a misnomer. It refers only to the speed of the white water relative to the speed of the smooth water that leads into and away from the rapid. The white water is faster, but it is hardly "rapid." The Colorado, smooth, flows about seven miles per hour, and, white, it goes perhaps fifteen or, at its whitest and wildest, twenty miles per hour—not very rapid by the standards of the twentieth century. Force of suggestion creates a false expectation. The mere appearance of the river going over those boulders—the smoky spray, the scissoring waves—is enough to imply a rush to fatality, and this endorses the word used to describe it. You feel as if you were about to be sucked into some sort of invisible pneumatic tube and shot like a bullet into the dim beyond. But the white water, though faster than the rest of the river, is categorically slow. Running the rapids in the Colorado is a series of brief experiences, because the rapids themselves are short. In them, with the raft folding and bending—sudden hills of water filling the immediate skyline—things happen in slow motion. The projector of your own existence slows way down, and you dive as in a dream, and gradually rise, and fall again. The raft shudders across the ridgelines of water cordilleras to crash softly into the valleys beyond. Space and time in there are something other than they are out here. Tents of water form overhead, to break apart in rags. Elapsed stopwatch time has no meaning at all.

Dominy emerged from Deubendorff the hero of the expedition to date. Deubendorff, with two creeks spitting boulders into it, is a long rapid for a Grand Canyon rapid—about three hundred yards. From top to bottom, through it all, Dominy kept his cigar aglow. This feat was something like, say, a bumblebee's flying through a field of waving wheat at shock level and never once being touched. Dominy's shirt was soaked. His trousers were soaked. But all the way down the rapid the red glow of that cigar picked its way through the flying water from pocket to pocket of air. Actually, he was lucky, and he knew it. "Lucky Dominy," he said when we moved into quiet water. "That's why they call me Lucky Dominy." The whole raftload of people gave him an organized cheer. And he veiled his face in fresh smoke.

We have now moved under and by the big mesa. Brower watched it silently for a long time, and then softly, almost to himself, he quoted Edith Warner: " 'This is a day when life and the world seem to be standing still—only time and the river flowing past the mesas.' "

Wild burros stand on a ledge and look at us from above, right. All burros are on the right, all bighorns on the left. Who knows why? We have entered the beauty of afternoon light. It sharpens the colors and polishes the air.

Brower says, "Notice that light up the line now, Floyd. Look how nice it is on the barrel cactus."

"Gorgeous," says Dominy.

The river is in shadow, and we have stopped for the night where a waterfall arcs out from a sandstone cliff. This is Deer Creek Falls, and it is so high that its shafts of plunging water are wrapped in mist where they strike a deep pool near the edge of the river. The campsite is on the opposite bank. Brower has half-filled his Sierra Club cup with water and is using it as a level with which to gauge the height of the falls. His measuring rod is his own height at eye level. Sighting across the cup, he has painstakingly climbed a talus slope behind us, adding numbers as he climbed, and he is now a small figure among the talus boulders at the level of the lip of the waterfall across the river. He calls down that the waterfall is a hundred and sixty feet high. With the raft as a ferry, we crossed the river an hour or so ago and stood in the cool mist where the waterfall whips the air into wind. We went on to climb to the top of the fall and to walk above the stream through the gorge of Deer Creek. The creek had cut a deep, crenellated groove in the sandstone, and for several hundred yards, within this groove, we moved along a serpentine ledge high above the water, which made a great deal of sound below, within the narrow walls of the cut. Brower walked along the ledge—it was sometimes only a foot wide—as if he were hurrying along a sidewalk. At the beginning, the ledge was perhaps fifty feet above the foaming creek, and gradually, up the gorge, the ledge and the creek bed came closer together. Brower just strode along, oblivious of the giddy height. In that strange world between walls of rock, a butterfly flickered by, and he watched it with interest while his feet moved surely forward, never slowing. "Viceroy," he said.

I am afraid of places like that, and my legs were so frozen that I couldn't feel the ledge underfoot. I suggested that we stop and wait for Dominy, who had started later and had said he would catch up. This would obviously provide a good rest, because where Dominy comes from the narrowest ledge is at least three hundred miles wide, and I thought if he was still coming along this one he was probably on his hands and knees. Just then, he came walking around a shoulder of the rock face, balanced above the gorge, whistling. We moved on. Where the ledge met the creek bed, the walls of the gorge widened out and the creek flowed in clear, cascading pools among cactus flowers and mariposa lilies under stands of cottonwood. A scene like that in a context of unending dry red rock is unbelievable, a palpable mirage. Brower walked in the stream and, after a while, stopped to absorb his surroundings. Dominy, some yards behind, had an enamelled cup with him, and he dipped it into the stream. Lifting it to his lips, he said, "Now I'll have a drink of water that has washed Dave Brower's feet."

The water was cold and very clear. Brower scooped some for himself, in his Sierra Club cup. "Any kind of water in country like this is good, but especially when man isn't hogging it for his own use," he said.

Watercress grew around the plunge pools of the short cascades—watercress, growing in cool water, surrounded by thousands of square miles of baking desert rock. Brower took a small bunch in his hand. Bugs were crawling all over it, and he carefully selected leaves and ate them, leaving the bugs behind. "I don't mind sharing my cress with them," he said. "I hope they don't mind sharing it with me."

Brower's snack appealed to Dominy. He waded into the same pool, picked two handfuls of cress, and ate them happily, bugs and all. "Paradise," he said, looking around. "Paradise."

Half obscured in the stream under a bed of cress was the distinctive shimmer of a Budweiser can. Brower picked it up, poured the water out of it, and put it in his pocket.

"When people come in, you can't win," Dominy said, and Brower looked at him with both approval and perplexity.

Inside Dominy's big leather briefcase is a bottle of Jim Beam, and now, at the campsite, in the twilight, with the sun far gone over the rimrocks, we are going to have our quotidian ration—and Dominy is a generous man. After dinner, if patterns hold, he and Brower will square off for battle, but they are at this moment united in anticipation of the bourbon. Big steaks are ready for broiling over the coals of a driftwood fire. There is calm in the canyon. The Commissioner steps to the river's edge and dips a half cup of water, over which he pours his whiskey. "I'm the nation's waterboy," he says. "I need water with my bourbon."

Over the drinks, he tells us that he once taught a German shepherd to climb a ladder. We believe him. He further reminisces about early camping trips with his wife, Alice. They were in their teens when they married. He was state Master Counsellor for the Order of DeMolay, and she was the Queen of Job's Daughters. They had married secretly, and she went with him to the University of Wyoming. "We lived on beans and love," he said. "Our recreation was camping. We went up into the Snowy Range and into the Laramie Peak country, where there was nothing but rattlesnakes, ticks, and us. We used to haul wood down from the mountains to burn for heat in the winter."

Jerry Sanderson, the river guide who has organized this expedition, calls out that dinner is ready. He has cooked an entire sirloin steak for each person. We eat from large plastic trays—the property of Sanderson. Brower regularly ignores the stack of trays, and now, when his turn comes, he steps forward to receive his food in his Sierra Club cup. Sanderson, a lean, trim, weathered man, handsome and steady, has seen a lot on this river. And now a man with wild white hair and pink legs is holding out a four-inch cup to receive a three-pound steak. Very well. There is no rapid that can make Sanderson's eyes bat, so why should this? He drapes the steak over the cup. The steak covers the cup like a sun hat. Brower begins to hack at the edges with a knife. Brower in wilderness eats from nothing but his Sierra Club cup.

10 P.M. The moon has moved out in brilliance over the canyon rim. Brower and Dominy are asleep. Dominy snores. Just before he began to snore, he looked at the moon and said, "What's the point of going there? If it were made of gold, we couldn't afford to go get it. Twenty-three billion dollars for landings on the moon. I can't justify or understand that. One, yes. Half a dozen, no. Every time they light a roman candle at Cape Canaveral, they knock four hundred million off other projects, like water storage."

Tonight's fight was about siltation. When Brower finished his steak, he looked across the river at the flying plume of Deer Creek Falls and announced to all in earshot that Commissioner Dominy wished to fill that scene with mud, covering the riverbed and the banks where we sat, and filling the inner gorge of the Colorado right up to within fifty feet of the top of the waterfall.

"That's God-damned nonsense," Dominy said.

Brower explained quietly that rivers carry silt, and that silt has to go somewhere if men build dams. Silt first drops and settles where the river flows into still water at the heads of reservoirs, he said. Gradually, it not only fills the reservoir but also accumulates upstream from the headwaters, and that might one day be the story here at Deer Creek Falls, for Dominy wanted to create a reservoir that would begin only seven miles downstream from our campsite.

"They said Hoover Dam was going to silt up Lake Mead in thirty years," Dominy said. "For thirty years, Lake Mead caught all the God-damned silt in the Colorado River, and Hoover has not been impaired."

"No, but when Mead is low there are forty miles of silt flats at its upper end, and they're getting bigger."

"Not appreciably. Not with Lake Powell three hundred miles upstream."

"Yes, Lake Powell will fill up first."

"When? Tell me *when?*" Dominy was now shouting.

"In a hundred to two hundred years," Brower said quietly.

"That's crap! The figures you work with aren't reliable."

"They come from reliable people."

"Nonsense."

"Oh."

The Colorado, Brower reminded us, used to be known as Old Red. This was because the river was full of red mud. It would never have been possible for Dominy to dip his cup in it in order to get water to go with his bourbon unless he wished to drink mud as well. On arriving at a campsite, rivermen used to fill their boats with water, so that the mud would settle to the bottom of the boats and they would have water for drinking and cooking. Except after flash floods, the Colorado in the Grand Canyon is now green and almost clear, because Lake Powell is catching the silt, and Glen Canyon Dam—fifteen miles upstream from the beginning of the Grand Canyon—is releasing clean water. "Emotionally, people are able to look only two generations back and two generations forward," Brower said. "We need to see farther than that. It is absolutely inevitable, for example, that Lake Powell and Lake Mead will someday be completely filled with silt."

"Nonsense, nonsense, complete nonsense. First of all, we will build silt-detention dams in the tributaries—in the Paria, in the Little Colorado. And, if necessary, we will build more."

"Someday the reservoirs have to fill up, Floyd."

"I wouldn't admit that. I wouldn't admit one inch!"

"Someday."

"*Some*day! Yes, in geologic time, maybe. Lake Powell *will* fill up with silt. I don't know how many thousands of years from now. By then, people will have figured out alternative sources of water and power. That's what I say when you start talking about the geologic ages."

Brower then began to deliver a brief lecture on the phenomenon of aggradation—the term for the final insult that follows when a reservoir is full of silt. Aggradation is what happens to the silt that keeps on coming down the river. The silt piles up and, in a kind of reverse ooze, reaches back upstream many miles, following an inclined plane that rises about eighteen inches per mile—a figure reckoned from the site of the now mud-packed and obsolete dam.

Brower was scarcely halfway through sketching that picture when Dominy ended his contributions with a monosyllabic remark, walked away, put on his pajamas, delivered to the unlistening moon his attack on the space program, and, forgetting Brower and all the silt of years to come, fell asleep. He sleeps on his back, his feet apart, under the mesas.

5 A.M. The sky is light. The air temperature is eighty degrees. Brower sleeps on his side, his knees drawn up.

7 A.M. Eighty-eight degrees. We will soon be on the river. Dominy is brushing his teeth in the green Colorado. Sam Beach, a big, bearded man from White Plains, New York, just walked up to Dominy and said, "I see God has given us good water here this morning."

"Thank you," Dominy said.

And Brower said to Beach, "I imagine that's the first time you ever heard Him speak."

And Beach said, "God giveth, and God taketh away."

What seemed unimaginable beside the river in the canyon was that all that wild water had been processed, like pork slurry in a hot-dog plant, upstream in the lightless penstocks of a big dam. Perspective is where you find it, though, and with this in mind Dominy had taken Brower and me, some days earlier, down into the interior of his indisputable masterpiece, the ten-million-ton plug in Glen Canyon. We had seen it first from the air and then from the rim of Glen Canyon, and the dam had appeared from on high to be frail and surprisingly small, a gracefully curving wafer wedged flippantly into the river gorge, with a boulevard of blue water on one side of it and a trail of green river on the other. No national frontier that I can think of separates two worlds more dissimilar than the reservoir and the river. This frontier has a kind of *douane* as well, administered by men who work in a perfectly circular room deep inside the dam. They wear slim ties and white short-sleeved shirts. They make notes on clipboards. They sit at desks, and all around them, emplaced in the walls of the room, are gauges and dials, and more gauges and dials. To get to this control room, we rode about five hundred feet down into the dam in an elevator, and as we descended Dominy said, "People talk about environment. We're doing something about it." His eyes gleamed with humor. He led us down a long passageway and through a steel door. The men inside stood up. From the devotional look in their eyes, one might have thought that Marc Mitscher had just walked into the engine room of the carrier Lexington on the night after the Battle of the Philippine Sea. This was, after all, the man they called the Kmish. Throughout Reclamation, Dominy was known as the Kmish. Standing there, he introduced each man by name. He asked the elevation of Lake Powell.

"Three thousand five hundred and seventy-seven point two zero feet, sir."

Dominy nodded. He was pleased. When the level of the surface is lowered, a distinct band, known to conservationists as "the bathtub ring," appears along the cliff faces that hold the reservoir. Three thousand five hundred and seventy-seven point two zero would eliminate that, and a good thing, too, for on this day—one hundred years to the sunrise since the day Major Powell reached Glen Canyon on his first expedition—Lake Powell was to be dedicated.

"What are we releasing?" Dominy asked.

"Four thousand three hundred and fifty-six point zero cubic feet per second, sir."

"That's about normal," Dominy said. "Just a little slow."

At their consoles, turning knobs, flicking switches, the men in the control room continually create the river below the dam. At that moment, they were releasing something like fourteen hundred tons of water every ten seconds—or, in their terminology, one acre-foot.

"We have eight generating units," Dominy went on. "When we want to make peaking power, we turn them up full and send a wall of water downstream. The rubber rafts operate with licenses, and the guides know the schedule of releases."

Dominy then took us all the way down—down in another elevator, down concrete and spiral stairways, along ever-deeper passageways and down more stairways—until we were under the original bed of the Colorado and at the absolute bottom of the dam, seven hundred and ten feet below the crest. "I don't want Dave Brower to be able to say he didn't see everything," Dominy said—and I could not help admiring him for it, because the milieu he had taken us into could easily be misunderstood. Water was everywhere. Water poured down the spiral staircases. It streamed through the passageways. It fell from the ceilings. It ran from the walls. In some places, sheets of polyethylene had been taped to the concrete. At the bottom, Glen Canyon Dam is three hundred feet thick, but nearly two hundred miles of reservoir was pressing against it, and it had cracked. The Colorado was pouring through. "We may have to get some Dutch boys in here with their thumbs," Dominy said. "The dam is still curing. It hasn't matured yet. So we aren't doing much of anything about this now. We will soon. We have a re-injectionable grouting system; it's an idea I picked up in Switzerland. The crack water is declining anyway. The crack may be sealing itself. It's not serious. You just cannot completely stop the Colorado River."

Brower seemed unable to decide whether he should be shocked by the crack in the dam or impressed by the unvanquishable river. Stalactites had formed on the ceilings of the passageways. I reached up and broke one off. "Don't let Dave Brower see you do that," Dominy said. "You're interrupting nature." Obviously in love with his dam, he scrambled all over it. "When a dam is being built, the concrete is *placed,* not poured," he said, rubbing a hand over a smooth interior wall. "The concrete is barely wet—too dry for pouring. It's put in place with vibrators. We regularly take core samples and send them to Denver for testing —to see if the contractor is meeting specifications. Dave, just to cement our friendship, I'm going to have a pair of bookends made from some of those old core samples for you. Nothing could support a set of Sierra Club books better than a couple of pieces of Glen Canyon Dam. Would you accept that?"

"I'll accept the bookends," Brower said. "Thank you very much, Floyd."

Under the generator room, Dominy led us onto a steel platform inches away from a huge, shining steel generator shaft. The shaft was spinning at who knows how many revolutions per minute, yet the platform around it was scarcely trembling. "Balance," he said proudly. "The secret is balance. In Russia, these platforms vibrate so much they practically knock you down. I know. I've stood on them there." He pointed out sections of giant pipe—penstocks—that contained the Colorado in its passage from reservoir to riverbed. The mighty rapids of the Grand Canyon were now inside that pipe.

Dominy opened a door that led to a strange exterior space—a wide, flat area at the base of the main wall of the dam. Six hundred feet of acutely angled concrete—white and dazzling in the sun—soared up from this level, where Dominy, for purely aesthetic reasons, had somehow imported tons of soil and had planted a smooth and elegant lawn. He called it "the football field," and it was more than large enough to hold one. When visitors peer over the crest of the dam, they look far down its white face to this incongruous lawn, unique in the cosmetics of high dams. From the lawn itself, the thought of the great wall of water on the other side of the dam is unnerving, but no more so than the ten acres of concave concrete up which the eye is led to fragments of red cliff where power-line towers claw at off-plumb angles into a blue swatch of sky. "You don't really appreciate this dam unless you're down on the transformer deck looking up," Dominy said. "Looking down is no way to look at life. You've got to be looking up. Suicides come down that wall sometimes. They don't realize how unvertical it is. When they're found at the bottom, there isn't a God-damned bit of flesh left on them."

Brower said, "My advice to suicides is 'If you've got to go, take Glen Canyon Dam with you.' "

"Read *Desert Solitaire,*" Dominy said. "Page 165. The guy who wrote it is way ahead of you."

I eventually bought a copy of *Desert Solitaire,* and found that on page 165 its angry author—Edward Abbey—imagines "the loveliest explosion ever seen by man, reducing the great dam to a heap of rubble in the path of the river. The splendid new rapids thus created we will name Floyd E. Dominy Falls. . . ."

On an overlook not far from the dam, Lake Powell was dedicated by men, white and red, who addressed much of what they said to an unseen enemy, assuming that he was a thousand miles away; he happened to be standing right there. "The Sierra Club to the contrary, I *like* dams," said Governor John Williams of Arizona. When the dam was begun, Williams was a radio announcer, and it was he who broadcast the play-by-play of the original blasting ceremony.

"The Sierra Club notwithstanding, this is a beautiful lake," said Governor Calvin Rampton of Utah, sweeping an arm toward the reservoir. Red cliff walls met the dark-blue water, big buttes stood high in the background, and above it all—immense and alone in the distance—was sacred Navajo Mountain. Far below the overlook, boats wove patterns on the water. Skiers cut crescent wakes. Bunting hung from the speakers' platform in symbolic blue and brown—blue for Lake Powell and brown for the old Colorado.

"A conservationist is one who is content to stand still forever," said Raymond Nakai, of Window Rock, the head of the Navajo Tribal Council. "Major Powell would have approved of this lake. May it ever be brimmin' full." Brower remained silent, but was having difficulty doing so. It was not hard to guess his thoughts. Major Powell—explorer, surveyor, geographer—was not alive to say how he might feel, in English or Navajo.

Then Dominy spoke. "Dave Brower is here today," he said, and the entire ceremony almost fell into the reservoir. "Brower is not here in an official capacity but as my guest," Dominy went on. "We're going to spend several days on Lake Powell, so I can convert him a little. Then we're going down the river, so he can convert me."

Mile 141. We are in a long, placid reach of the river. The Upset Rapid is eight miles downstream, but its name, all morning, has been a refrain on the raft. People say it as if they were being wheeled toward it on a hospital cart. We have other rapids to go through first—the Kanab Rapid, the Matkatamiba Rapid—but everyone has been thinking beyond them to Upset.

"According to the *River Guide,* there hasn't been a death in the Upset Rapid for a little over two years," someone joked.

"The map says Upset is very bad when the water is low."

"How is the water, Jerry?"

"Low."

"Under today's controlled river, we're riding at the moment on last Sunday's releases," Dominy explained. "This is as low as the river will get under controlled conditions. Tomorrow, Monday's conditions will catch up with us, so things will improve."

"Thank you very much, Commissioner, but what good will Monday's releases do us today?"

"Let's camp here," someone put in.

"It's ten-thirty in the morning."

"I don't care."

"The river has its hands tied, but it's still running," said Brower. "If the Commissioner gets very wet today, it's his own fault."

Jerry Sanderson has cut the engine—a small, cocky outboard that gives the raft a little more speed than the river and is supposed to add some control in rapids. We drift silently.

Brower notices a driftwood log, bleached and dry, on a ledge forty feet above us. "See where the river was before you turned it off, Floyd?"

"I didn't turn it off, God damn it, I turned it on. Ten months of the year, there wasn't enough water in here to boil an egg. My dam put this river in business."

Dominy begins to talk dams. To him, the world is a tessellation of watersheds. When he looks at a globe, he does not see nations so much as he sees rivers, and his imagination runs down the rivers building dams. Of all the rivers in the world, the one that makes him salivate most is the Mekong. There are chances in the Mekong for freshwater Mediterraneans—huge bowls of topography that are pinched off by gunsight passages just crying to be plugged. "Fantastic. Fantastic river," he says, and he contrasts it with the Murrumbidgee River, in New South Wales, where the Australians have spent twenty-two years developing something called the Snowy Mountains Hydroelectric Scheme—"a whole lot of effort for a cup of water." Brower reminds Dominy that dams can break, and mentions the disaster that occurred in Italy in 1963. "That dam didn't break," Dominy tells him. "That dam did *not* break. It was nine hundred feet high. Above it was a granite mountain with crud on top. The crud fell into the reservoir, and water splashed *four hundred feet* over the top of the dam and rushed down the river and killed two thousand people. The dam is still there. It held. Four hundred feet of water over it and it held. Of course, it's useless now. The reservoir is full of crud."

"Just as all your reservoirs will be. Just as Lake Powell will be full of silt."

"Oh, for Christ's sake, Dave, be rational."

"Oh, for Christ's sake, Floyd, *you* be rational."

"Have you ever been *for* a dam, Dave? Once? Ever?"

"Yes. I testified in favor of Knowles Dam, on the Clark Fork River, in Montana. I saw it as a way to save Glacier National Park from an even greater threat. Tell me this, Floyd. Have you ever built a dam that didn't work?"

"Yes, if you want to know the truth. I'm not afraid to tell you the truth, Dave. On Owl Creek, near Thermopolis, Wyoming. Geologic tests were done at one point in the creek and they were O.K., and then the dam was built some distance upstream. We learned a lesson. Never build a dam except exactly where tests are conducted. Cavities developed under the dam, also under the reservoir. Every time we plug one hole, two more show up. Plugs keep coming out. The reservoir just won't fill. Someday I'll tell you another story, Dave. I'll tell you about the day one of our men opened the wrong valve and flooded the *inside* of Grand Coulee Dam."

"I've heard enough."

Dominy and Brower call for sandwiches, open them, and dutifully drop the tongues inside. Brower now attacks Dominy because a dam project near Ventura, California, is threatening the existence of thirty-nine of the forty-five remaining condors in North America. "We've got to get upset about the condor," Brower tells him. "No one likes to see something get extinct."

"The condor was alive in the days of the mastodons," Dominy says. "He is left over from prehistoric times. He can't fly without dropping off something first. He is so huge a kid with a BB gun can hit him. He's in trouble, dam or no dam. If you give him forty thousand acres, he's still in trouble. He *is* in trouble. His chances of survival are slim. I think it would be nice if he survived, but I don't think this God-damned project would have any real bearing on it."

Dominy draws deeply on his beer. He takes off his Lake Powell hat, smooths his hair back, and replaces the hat. I wonder if he is thinking of the scale-model bulldozer in his office in Washington. The bulldozer happens to have a condor in it—a rubber scale-model condor, sitting in the operator's seat.

Dominy's thoughts have been elsewhere, though. "Who was that old man who tried to read poetry at Kennedy's Inaugural? With the white hair blowing all over the place."

"Robert Frost."

"Right. He and I went to Russia together. I was going to visit Russian dams, and he was on some cultural exchange, and we sat beside each other on the plane all the way to Moscow. He talked and talked, and I smoked cigars. He said eventually, 'So you're the dam man. You're the creator of the great concrete monoliths—turbines, generators, stored water.' And then he started to talk poetically about me, right there in the plane. He said, 'Turning, turning, turning . . . creating, creating . . . creating energy for the people . . . for the people. . . .'

"Most of the day, Frost reminisced about his childhood, and he asked about mine, and I told him I'd been born in a town so small that the entrance and exit signs were on the same post. Land as dry and rough as a cob. You'll never see any land better than that for irrigating. God damn, she lays pretty. And he asked about my own family, and I told him about our farm in Virginia, and how my son and I put up nine hundred and sixty feet of fence in one day. I told my son, 'I'll teach you how to work. You teach yourself how to play.' "

We have been through the Kanab Rapid—standing waves six feet high, lots of splash—and we are still wet. It is cold in the canyon. A cloud —a phenomenon in this sky—covers the sun. We are shivering. The temperature plunges if the sun is obscured. The oven is off. Clothes do not quickly dry. Fortunately, the cloud seems to be alone up there.

Mile 144.8. "Here we are," Brower says. He has the map in his hand. Nothing in the Muav Limestone walls around us suggests that we are anywhere in particular, except in the middle of the Grand Canyon. "We are entering the reservoir," Brower announces. "We are now floating on Lake Dominy."

"Jesus," mutters Dominy.

"What reservoir?" someone asks. Brower explains. A dam that Dominy would like to build, ninety-three miles downstream, would back still water to this exact point in the river.

"Is that right, Commissioner?"

"That's right."

The cloud has left the sun, and almost at once we feel warm again. The other passengers are silent, absorbed by what Brower has told them.

"Do you mean the reservoir would cover the Upset Rapid? Havasu Creek? Lava Falls? All the places we are coming to?" one man asks Dominy.

Dominy reaches for the visor of his Lake Powell hat and pulls it down more firmly on his head. "Yes," he says.

"I'd have to think about that."

"So would I."

"I would, too."

Our fellow-passengers have become a somewhat bewildered—perhaps a somewhat divided—chorus. Dominy assures them that the lake would be beautiful, like Powell, and, moreover, that the Hualapai Indians, whose reservation is beside the damsite, would have a million-dollar windfall, comparable to the good deal that has come to the Navajos of Glen Canyon. The new dam would be called Hualapai Dam, and the reservoir—Brower's humor notwithstanding—would be called Hualapai Lake.

"I'm prepared to say, here and now, that we should touch nothing more in the lower forty-eight," Brower comments. "Whether it's an island, a river, a mountain wilderness—nothing more. What has been left alone until now should be left alone permanently. It's an extreme statement, but it should be said."

"That, my friend, is debatable."

The others look from Brower to Dominy without apparent decision. For the most part, their reactions do not seem to be automatic, either way. This might seem surprising among people who would be attracted, in the first place, to going down this river on a raft, but nearly all of them live in communities whose power and water come from the Colorado. They are, like everyone, caught in the middle, and so they say they'll have to think about it. At home, in New Jersey, I go to my children's schoolrooms and ask, for example, a group of fourth graders to consider a large color photograph of a pristine beach in Georgia. "Do you think there should be houses by this beach, or that it should be left as it is?" Hands go up, waving madly. "Houses," some of the schoolchildren say. Others vote against the houses. The breakdown is fifty-fifty. "How about this? Here is a picture of a glorious mountain in a deep wilderness in the State of Washington. There is copper under the mountain." I list the uses of copper. The vote is close. A black child, who was for houses on the beach, says, "Take the copper." I hold up the Sierra Club's Exhibit-Format book *Time and the River Flowing* and show them pictures of the Colorado River in the Grand Canyon. Someone wants to build a dam in this river. A dam gives electricity and water—light and food. The vote is roughly fifty-fifty.

After Brower ran his ad about the flooding of the Sistine Chapel, Dominy counterattacked by flying down the Colorado in a helicopter,

hanging by a strap from an open door with a camera in his hand. He had
the pilot set the helicopter down on a sandbar at Mile 144.8, and he took
a picture straight down the river. The elevation of the sandbar was
eighteen hundred and seventy-five feet above sea level. Taking pictures
all the way, Dominy had the pilot fly at that exact altitude down the river
from the sandbar to the site of Hualapai Dam. ("That pilot had the
God-damned props churning right around the edge of that inner-gorge
wall, and he was *noivous,* but I made him stay there.") At the damsite,
the helicopter was six hundred feet in the air. Dominy took his collection
of pictures to Congress. "Brower says we want to ruin the canyon. Let's
see whether we're going to ruin it," he said, and he demonstrated that
Hualapai Lake, for all its length, would be a slender puddle hidden away
in a segment of the Grand Canyon that was seven miles wide and four
thousand feet deep. No part of the lake would be visible from any public
observation point in Grand Canyon National Park, he told the congressmen. "Hell, I know more about this river than the Park Service, the
Sierra Club, and everyone else," he says, finishing the story. "I took my
pictures to Congress because I thought that this would put the ball in
their court, and if they wanted to field it, all right, and if they wanted
to drop it, that was all right, too."

We have gone through Matkatamiba and around a bend. Jerry
Sanderson has cut the motor again, and we are resting in the long
corridor of flat water that ends in the Upset Rapid. There is a lot of talk
about "the last mile," the low water, "the end of the rainbow," and so
on, but this is just fear chatter, dramatization of the unseen.

"Oh, come on, now. One of these rafts could go over Niagara Falls."

"Yes. With no survivors."

Brower hands Dominy a beer. "Here's your last beer," he says. It
is 11 A.M., and cool in the canyon. Another cloud is over the sun, and
the temperature is seventy-seven degrees. The cloud will be gone in
moments, and the temperature will go back into the nineties.

"Here's to Upset," Brower says, lifting his beer. "May the best man
win."

The dropoff is so precipitous where Upset begins that all we can see
of it, from two hundred yards upstream, is what appears to be an agglom-
eration of snapping jaws—the leaping peaks of white water. Jerry cannot
get the motor started. "It won't run on this gas," he explains. "I've tried
river water, and it won't run on that, either." As we drift downstream,
he works on the motor. A hundred and fifty yards. He pulls the cord.

No sound. There is no sound in the raft, either, except for the *psss* of a can being opened. Dominy is having one more beer. A hundred yards. Jerry starts the motor. He directs the raft to shore. Upset, by rule, must be inspected before the running.

We all got off the raft and walked to the edge of the rapid with Sanderson. What we saw there tended to erase the thought that men in shirtsleeves were controlling the Colorado inside a dam that was a hundred and sixty-five river miles away. They were there, and this rapid was here, thundering. The problem was elemental. On the near right was an enormous hole, fifteen feet deep and many yards wide, into which poured a scaled-down Canadian Niagara—tons upon tons of water per second. On the far left, just beyond the hole, a very large boulder was fixed in the white torrent. High water would clearly fill up the hole and reduce the boulder, but that was not the situation today.

"What are you going to do about this one, Jerry?"

Sanderson spoke slowly and in a voice louder than usual, trying to pitch his words above the roar of the water. "You have to try to take ten per cent of the hole. If you take any more of the hole, you go in it, and if you take any less you hit the rock."

"What's at the bottom of the hole, Jerry?"

"A rubber raft," someone said.

Sanderson smiled.

"What happened two years ago, Jerry?"

"Well, the man went through in a neoprene pontoon boat, and it was cut in half by the rock. His life jacket got tangled in a boat line, and he drowned."

"What can happen to the raft, Jerry?"

"Oh, parts of them sometimes get knocked flat. Then we have to stop below the rapid and sew them up. We have a pump to reinflate them. We use Dacron thread, and sew them with a leather punch and a three-inch curved needle. We also use contact adhesive cement."

"Wallace Stegner thinks this river is dead, because of Glen Canyon Dam, but I disagree," Brower said. "Just look at it. You've got to have a river alive. You've just got to. There's no alternative."

"I prefer to run this rapid with more water," Sanderson said, as if for the first time.

"If you want to sit here twenty-four hours, I'll get you whatever you need," said Dominy.

Sanderson said, "Let's go."

We got back on the raft and moved out into the river. The raft turned slightly and began to move toward the rapid. "Hey," Dominy said. "Where's Dave? Hey! We left behind one of our party. We're separated now. Isn't he going to ride?" Brower had stayed on shore. We were now forty feet out. "Well, I swear, I swear, I swear," Dominy continued, slowly. "He isn't coming with us." The Upset Rapid drew us in.

With a deep shudder, we dropped into a percentage of the hole—God only knows if it was ten—and the raft folded almost in two. The bow and the stern became the high points of a deep V. Water smashed down on us. And down it smashed again, all in that other world of slow and disparate motion. It was not speed but weight that we were experiencing: the great, almost imponderable, weight of water, enough to crush a thousand people, but not hurting us at all because we were part of it—part of the weight, the raft, the river. Then, surfacing over the far edge of the hole, we bobbed past the incisor rock and through the foaming outwash.

"The great outdoorsman!" Dominy said, in a low voice. "The great outdoorsman!" He shook water out of his Lake Powell hat. "The great outdoorsman standing safely on dry land wearing a God-damned life jacket!"

The raft, in quiet water, now moved close to shore, where Brower, who had walked around the rapid, stood waiting.

"For heaven's sake, say nothing to him, Floyd."

"Christ, I wouldn't think of it. I wouldn't dream of it. What did he do during the war?"

The raft nudged the riverbank. Dominy said, "Dave, why didn't you ride through the rapid?"

Brower said, "Because I'm chicken."

*A Climber's Guide to the High Sierra* (Sierra Club, 1954) lists thirty-three peaks in the Sierra Nevada that were first ascended by David Brower. "*Arrowhead.* First ascent September 5, 1937, by David R. Brower and Richard M. Leonard. . . . *Glacier Point.* First ascent May 28, 1939, by Raffi Bedayan, David R. Brower, and Richard M. Leonard . . . . *Lost Brother.* First ascent July 27, 1941, by David R. Brower. . . ." Brower has climbed all the Sierra peaks that are higher than fourteen thousand feet. He once started out at midnight, scaled the summit of Mount Tyndall (14,025) by 3 A.M., reached the summit of Mount Williamson (14,384) by 7 A.M., and was on top of Mount Barnard (14,003) at noon. He ate his lunch—nuts, raisins, dried apricots—and he went to sleep. He often went to sleep on the high peaks. Or he hunted around for ice, removing it in wedges from cracks in the granite, sucking it to slake his thirst. If it was a nice day, he would stay put for as much as an hour and a half. "The summit is the anticlimax," he says. "The way up is the thing. There is a moment when you know you have the mountain by the tail. You figure out how the various elements go together. You thread the route in your mind's eye, after hunting and selecting, and hitting dead ends. Finally, God is good enough. He built the mountain right, after all. A pleasant surprise. If you don't make it and have to go back, you play it over and over again in your mind. Maybe this would work, or that. Several months, a year, or two years later, you do it again." When Brower first tried to climb the Vazquez Monolith, in Pinnacles National Monument, he was stopped cold, as had been every other climber ever, for the face of the monolith was so smooth that Brower couldn't even get off the ground. Eventually, someone else figured out how to do that, but, as it happened, was stopped far shy of the summit. When Brower heard about this, he went to his typewriter, wrote a note identifying himself as the first man to ascend Vazquez Monolith, and slipped the note into a small brass tube. In his mind, he could see his route as if he were carrying a map. He went to Pinnacles National Monument, went up the Vazquez Monolith without an indecisive moment, and, on top, built a cairn around the brass tube. When Brower led a group to Shiprock in 1939, at least ten previous climbing parties had tried and failed there. Shiprock is a seven-thousand-foot monadnock that looks something like a schooner rising in isolation from the floor of the New Mexican desert. Brower studied photographs of Shiprock for many months, then planned an ornately complicated route —about three-quarters of the way up one side, then far down another side, then up a third and, he hoped, final side, to the top. That is how the climb went, without flaw, start to finish. Another brass tube. "I like mountains. I like granite. I particularly like the feel of the Sierra granite. When I climbed the Chamonix Aiguilles, the granite felt so much like the granite in the Yosemite that I felt right at home. Once, in the Sierra, when I was learning, I was going up the wall of a couloir and I put both hands and one knee on a rock. The rock moved, and fell. It crashed seventy-five feet below. One of my hands had shot upward, and with two fingers I caught a ledge. I pulled myself up, and I sat there on that ledge and thought for a long while. Why was I that stupid—to put that much faith in one rock? I have an urge to get up on top. I like to get up there and see around. A three-hundred-and-sixty-degree view is a nice thing to have. I like to recognize where I've been, and look for routes where I might go."

Mile 156. Already the talk is of Lava Falls, which lies twenty-four miles ahead but has acquired fresh prominence in the aftermath of Upset. On the table of rated rapids—copies of which nearly everyone is at the moment studying—categories run from "Riffle" through "Heavy" to "Not Recommended." Upset was a "Heavy" rapid, like Deubendorff. In the "Not Recommended" category there is only Lava Falls.

"Do you agree with that, Jerry?"

Sanderson grins with amusement, and speaks so slowly he seems wistful. "It's the granddaddy of them all," he says. "There's a big drop, and a lot of boulders, and several holes like the one at Upset. You have to look the rapid over carefully, because the holes move."

In the stillness of a big eddy, the raft pauses under an overhanging cliff. Lava Falls fades in the conversation. Twenty-four miles is a lot of country. Through a cleft that reaches all the way down through the overhanging cliff a clear green stream is flowing into the river. The cleft is so narrow that the stream appears to be coming straight out of the sandstone. Actually, it meanders within the cliff and is thus lost to view. The water is so clear that it sends a pale-green shaft into the darker Colorado. The big river may no longer be red with silt, but it carries enough to remain opaque. In the small stream, the pebbles on the bottom are visible, magnified, distinct. "Dive in," Brower suggests. "See where it goes."

Brower and I went into the stream and into the cliff. The current was not powerful, coming through the rock, and the water was only four feet deep. I swam, by choice—the water felt so good. It felt cool, but it must have been about seventy-five degrees. It was cooler than the air. Within the cliff was deep twilight, and the echoing sound of the moving water. A bend to the right, a bend to the left, right, left—this stone labyrinth with a crystal stream in it was moment enough, no matter where it ended, but there lay beyond it a world that humbled the mind's eye. The walls widened first into a cascaded gorge and then flared out to become the ovate sides of a deep valley, into which the stream rose in tiers of pools and waterfalls. Some of the falls were only two feet high, others four feet, six feet. There were hundreds of them. The pools were as much as fifteen feet deep, and the water in them was white where it plunged and foamed, then blue in a wide circle around the plunge point, and pale green in the outer peripheries. This was Havasu Canyon, the immemorial home of the Havasupai, whose tribal name means "the people of the blue-green waters." We climbed from one pool to another, and swam across the pools, and let the waterfalls beat down around our shoulders. Mile after mile, the pools and waterfalls continued. The high walls of the valley were bright red. Nothing grew on these dry and flaky slopes from the mesa rim down about two-thirds of the way; then life began to show in isolated barrel cactus and prickly pear. The cacti thickened farther down, and below them was riverine vegetation—green groves of oak and cottonwood, willows and tamarisk, stands of cattail, tall grasses, moss, watercress, and maidenhair fern. The Havasupai have lived in this place for hundreds, possibly thousands, of years, and their population has remained stable. There are something like two hundred of them. They gather nuts on the canyon rim in winter and grow vegetables in the canyon in summer. They live about twelve miles up Havasu Creek from the Colorado. Moss covered the rocks around the blue-and-green pools. The moss on dry rock was soft and dense, and felt like broadloom underfoot. Moss also grew below the water's surface, where it was coated with travertine, and resembled coral. The stream was loaded with calcium, and this was the physical explanation of the great beauty of Havasu Canyon, for it was the travertine—crystalline calcium carbonate—that had both fashioned and secured the all but unending stairway of falls and pools. At the downstream lip of each plunge pool, calcium deposits had built up into natural dams, and these travertine dams were what kept Havasu Creek from running freely downhill. The dams were whitish tan, and so smooth and symmetrical that they might have been finished by a mason. They were two or three feet high. They sloped. Their crests were flat and smooth and with astonishing uniformity were about four inches thick from bank to bank. Brower looked up at the red canyon walls. He was sitting on the travertine, with one foot in a waterfall, and I was treading the green water below him. He said, "If Hualapai Dam had been built, or were ever built, this place where you are swimming would be at the bottom of a hundred feet of water." It was time to go back to the Colorado. I swam to the travertine dam at the foot of the pool, climbed up on it and dived into the pool below it, and swam across and dived again, and swam and dived—and so on for nearly two miles. Dominy was waiting below. "It's fabulous," he said. "I know every river canyon in the country, and this is the prettiest in the West."

Mile 171. Beside the minor rapids at Gateway Canyon, we stop, unload the raft, and lay out our gear before settling down to drinks before dinner. Brower is just beyond earshot. Dominy asks me again, "What did Dave do during the war?"

I tell him all I happen to know—that Brower trained troops in climbing techniques in West Virginia and Colorado, and that he later went with the 10th Mountain Division to Italy, where he won the Bronze Star.

Dominy contemplates the river. Brower goes to the water's edge and dips his Sierra Club cup. He will add whiskey to the water. "Fast-moving water is a very satisfying sound," Dominy says to him. "There is nothing more soothing than the sound of running or falling water."

"The river talks to itself, Floyd. Those little whirls, the sucks and the boils—they say things."

"I love to see white water, Dave. In all my trips through the West over the years, I have found moving streams with steep drops to them the most scenic things of all."

Over the drinks, Brower tells him, "I will come out of this trip different from when I came in. I am not in favor of dams, but I am in favor of Dominy. I can see what you have meant to the Bureau, and I am worried about what is going to happen there someday without you."

"No one will ever say that Dominy did not tell anyone and everyone exactly what he thinks, Dave."

"I've never heard anything different, Floyd."

"And, I might say, I've never heard anything different about you."

"I needed this trip more than anyone else."

"You're God-damned right you did, with that white skin."

Dominy takes his next drink out of the Sierra Club cup. The bottle of whiskey is nearly empty. Dominy goes far down into his briefcase and brings out another. It is Jim Beam. Dominy is fantastically loyal to Jim Beam. At his farm in Virginia a few weeks ago, he revived a sick calf by shooting it with a hypodermic syringe full of penicillin, condensed milk, and Jim Beam. Brower says he does not believe in penicillin.

"As a matter of fact, Dave Brower, I'll make a trip with you any time, anywhere."

"Great," Brower mutters faintly.

"Up to this point, Dave, we've won a few and lost a few—each of us. Each of us. Each of us. God damn it, everything Dave Brower does is O.K.—tonight. Dave, now that we've buried the hatchet, you've got to come out to my farm in the Shenandoah."

"Great."

To have a look at the map of the river, Dominy puts on Brower's glasses. Brower's glasses are No. 22s off the counter of F. W. Woolworth in San Francisco. Dominy rolls the scroll back to the Upset Rapid.

"How come you didn't go through there, Dave?"

"I'm chicken."

"Are you going to go through Lava Falls?"

"No."

"No?"

"No, thank you. I'll walk."

Upstream from where we sit, we can see about a mile of straight river between the high walls of the inner gorge, and downstream this corridor leads on to a bold stone portal. Dominy contemplates the scene. He says, "With Hualapai Dam, you'd really have a lake of water down this far."

"Yes. A hundred and sixty feet deep," notes Brower.

"It would be beautiful, and, like Lake Powell, it would be better for *all* elements of society."

"There's another view, and I have it, and I suppose I'll die with it, Floyd. Lake Powell is a drag strip for power boats. It's for people who won't do things except the easy way. The magic of Glen Canyon is dead. It has been vulgarized. Putting water in the Cathedral in the Desert was like urinating in the crypt of St. Peter's. I hope it never happens here."

"Look, Dave. I don't live in a God-damned apartment. I didn't grow up in a God-damned city. Don't give me the crap that you're the only man that understands these things. I'm a greater conservationist than you are, by far. I do things. I make things available to man. Unregulated, the Colorado River wouldn't be worth a good God damn to anybody. You conservationists are phony outdoorsmen. I'm sick and tired of a democracy that's run by a noisy minority. I'm fed up clear to my God-damned gullet. I had the guts to come out and fight you bastards. You're just a bunch of phonies and you'll stoop to any kind of

God-damned argument. That's why I took my pictures. You were misleading the public about what would happen here. You gave the impression that the whole canyon was going to be inundated by the reservoir. Your weapon is emotion. You guys are just not very God-damned honorable in your fights."

"I had hoped things would not take this turn, Floyd, but you're wrong."

"Do you want to keep this country the way it is for a handful of people?"

"Yes, I do. Hualapai Dam is not a necessity. You don't even want the water."

"We mainly want the power head, but the dam would be part of the over-all storage project under the Colorado Compact."

"The Colorado Compact was not found on a tablet written on Mount Sinai. Hualapai Dam is not necessary, and neither was Glen Canyon. Glen Canyon Dam was built for the greater good of Los Angeles."

"You're too intelligent to believe that."

"You're too intelligent not to believe that."

"For Christ's sake, be objective, Dave. Be reasonable."

"Some of my colleagues make the error of trying to be reasonable, Floyd. Objectivity is the greatest threat to the United States today."

Mile 177, 9:45 A.M. The water is quite deep and serene here, backed up from the rapid. Lava Falls is two miles downstream, but we have long since entered its chamber of quiet.

"The calm before the storm," Brower says.

The walls of the canyon are black with lava—flows, cascades, and dikes of lava. Lava once poured into the canyon in this segment of the river. The river was here, much in its present form. It had long since excavated the canyon, for the volcanism occurred in relatively recent time. Lava came up through the riverbed, out from the canyon walls, and even down over the rims. It sent the Colorado up in clouds. It hardened, and it formed a dam and backed water two hundred miles.

"If a lava flow were to occur in the Grand Canyon today, Brower and the nature lovers would shout to high heaven that a great thing had happened," Dominy said, addressing everyone in the raft. "But if a man builds a dam to bring water and power to other men, it is called desecration. Am I right or wrong, Dave? Be honest."

"The lava dam of Quaternary time was eventually broken down by the river. This is what the Colorado will do to the Dominy dams that are in it now or are ever built. It will wipe them out, recover its grade, and go on about its business. But by then our civilization and several others will be long gone."

We drift past an enormous black megalith standing in the river. For eighty years, it was called the Niggerhead. It is the neck of a volcano, and it is now called Vulcan's Forge. We have a mile to go. Brower talks about the amazing size of the crystals on the canyon walls, the morning light in the canyon, the high palisades of columnar basalt. No one else says much of anything. All jokes have been cracked twice. We are just waiting, and the first thing we hear is the sound. It is a big, tympanic sound that increasingly fills the canyon. The water around us is dark-green glass. Five hundred yards. There it is. Lava Falls. It is, of course, a rapid, not a waterfall. There is no smooth lip. What we now see ahead of us at this distance appears to be a low whitewashed wall.

The raft touches the riverbank. Sanderson gets out to inspect the rapid, and we go, too. We stand on a black ledge, in the roar of the torrent, and look at the water. It goes everywhere. From bank to bank, the river is filled with boulders, and the water smashes into them, sends up auroras of spray, curls thickly, and pounds straight down into bomb-crater holes. It eddies into pockets of lethal calm and it doubles back to hit itself. Its valleys are deeper and its hills are higher than in any other rapid in North America. The drop is prodigious—twenty-six feet in a hundred yards—but that is only half the story. Prospect Creek, rising black-walled like a coal chute across the river, has shoved enough rock in here to stop six rivers, and this has produced the preëminent rapid of the Colorado.

When Dominy stepped up on the ledge and into the immediacy of Lava Falls, he shouted above the thunder, "Boy, that's a son of a bitch! Look at those *rocks!* See that hole over there? Jesus! Look at that one!"

Brower said, "Look at the way the water swirls. It's alive!"

The phys.-ed. teacher said, "Boy, that could tear the hell out of your bod."

Brower said, "Few come, but thousands drown."

Dominy said, "If I were Jerry, I'd go to the left and then try to move to the right."

Lava protruded from the banks in jagged masses, particularly on the right, and there was a boulder there that looked like an axe blade. Brower said, "I'd go in on the right and out on the left."

My own view was that the river would make all the decisions. I asked Sanderson how he planned to approach what we saw there.

"There's only one way to do it," he said. "We go to the right."

The raft moved into the river slowly, and turned, and moved toward the low white wall. A hundred yards. Seventy-five yards. Fifty yards. It seems odd, but I did not notice until just then that Brower was on the raft. He was, in fact, beside me. His legs were braced, his hands were tight on a safety rope, and his Sierra Club cup was hooked in his belt. The tendons in his neck were taut. His chin was up. His eyes looked straight down the river. From a shirt pocket Dominy withdrew a cigar. He lighted it and took a voluminous drag. We had remaining about fifteen seconds of calm water. He said, "I might bite an inch off the end, but I doubt it." Then we went into Lava Falls.

Water welled up like a cushion against the big boulder on the right, and the raft went straight into it, but the pillow of crashing water was so thick that it acted on the raft like a great rubber fender between a wharf and a ship. We slid off the rock and to the left—into the crater-scape. The raft bent like a V, flipped open, and shuddered forward. The little outboard—it represented all the choice we had—cavitated, and screamed in the air. Water rose up in tons through the bottom of the raft. It came in from the left, the right, and above. It felt great. It covered us, pounded us, lifted us, and heaved us scudding to the base of the rapid.

For a moment, we sat quietly in the calm, looking back. Then Brower said, "The foot of Lava Falls would be two hundred and twenty-five feet beneath the surface of Lake Dominy."

Dominy said nothing. He just sat there, drawing on a wet, dead cigar. Ten minutes later, however, in the dry and baking Arizona air, he struck a match and lighted the cigar again.

# The Deltoid
# Pumpkin Seed

Bizarre, sometimes tragic events checker the history of aviation in New Jersey. Charles and Anne Lindbergh built their estate at Somerville to be near a test facility; their son's kidnapping and murder exiled them from America for years. The Hindenburg, largest rigid airship ever built, crashed and burned at Lakehurst; that ended the use of dirigibles for passenger service. In his radio version of *War of the Worlds*, Orson Welles landed "Martians" at Grover's Mill—a hamlet just south of Princeton—and panicked thousands of listeners into fleeing the imaginary spacecraft.

Thirty years later, fecund minds still work on New Jersey's airfields, designing and testing experiments like the Aereon, a hybrid of airship and airplane. The craft has an aerodynamic configuration, yet is bloated with a chamber for lifting gas. While perfectly sound in theory, its working prototypes look strange, cost plenty, and fly only when handled with Mozartian dexterity. Aereon's proponents are equally odd-lot: they include a minister with portfolio but no congregation; a model builder who has chronic airsickness; and a pilot whose cool would fluster most computers. Working in comical secrecy, since Aereon's shape only commands attention, the crew eventually tests its craft successfully—and then finds the world unready to buy.

*The Deltoid Pumpkin Seed* is an entertaining book, for McPhee works his characters into a suspenseful plot, yet he also has the courage to override these conventional aims and press for something more. To some readers, his motion may seem almost aerobatic, rolling between alternate moments of doubt and joy, then diving into the loops and stalls of digression, circling the main subject for a while. If not deliberate, the method is appropriate; it provides an experimental mode for this story about testing and experimentation. These selections depict three flights

233

of the "deltoid pumpkin seed," the first as a model and the others as a manned aircraft, Aereon 26.—*WLH*

---

After Aereon had been a going corporation for more than eight years, it had not yet flown anything higher than the bounce that might happen when a model hit a stone. This was around the end of 1967, a particularly depressed area in the company's history. Previously, in another configuration, there had been an eighty-foot Aereon that had never left the ground and had rolled over in a gust of wind, more or less destroying itself. Moving on (more cautiously) into the deltoid form, the company built a four-foot plastic Aereon equipped with a noisy, powerful little gasoline engine. This version—Aereon 4—displayed absolutely no inclination to fly. It was tested at Lakehurst Naval Air Station, within a short distance of the historic swatch of ground where the German rigid airship Hindenburg had burned thirty years before. The model hobbled all over Lakehurst, and occasionally raced at high speed, but it never so much as tilted its nose into the air. Small crowds of investors, directors, and other onlookers were sometimes present. One observer whispered to Miller, "If I were a stockholder in your company, I'd worry about the engineer." Less than a year earlier, Miller had become Aereon's president, and now as his fortunes melted his spirits subsided, too. He was a study in gloom, in Princeton one day, when a friend of his whose work was also in aeronautics happened to see him at a simulated eighteenth-century tavern called the King's Court, where Miller was having lunch. The friend asked what was the matter. Miller confessed his troubles. "The models go rocketing up and down the field, but they won't even budge off the ground," he said. "They're too heavy, plain and simple, and there are problems with the radio control."

"Call John Kukon," the other man said. "K-u-k-o-n. He builds models for the university. There's no one better. Maybe he'll help you."

Miller called Kukon and introduced himself. Aereon's office was then in a hangar at Mercer County Airport, about ten miles west of Princeton. Kukon's house was not far from there. Sure, he would be happy to come have a talk. Why not after work tonight?

When Kukon kept the appointment, Miller told him of the company's difficulties and showed him sketches of the deltoid pumpkin seed. There were no detailed plans and never had been. Kukon examined the sketches and offered a suggestion. Before continuing the four-foot model series, Aereon might do well to start over again—with a model, say, around two feet long. It would be simpler—it could be rubber-powered —and it would probably serve just as well to indicate in a rudimentary way the performance characteristics of an aircraft shaped like the one in the sketch.

Miller considered the idea, and then asked, "Will you build it?"

"Sure, why not have a try?"

"How long would that take?"

Kukon looked around the hangar, and paused to think, while Miller reflected on the sorry history of his company: formed in the nineteen-fifties, now getting on toward the end of the sixties, its closets cluttered with former presidents, with records of a million spent dollars, and with broken aircraft, in various sizes, that had proved to be penguins all. Now here was still another beginning, almost from scratch—new departure, new delay. What difference, though, could another couple of months make after eight and a half years? He asked again, "How long will you need?"

Kukon said, "Will it be all right if I bring it here the day after tomorrow?"

Kukon was twenty-nine years old. He had started building gasoline-powered flying model airplanes when he was seven. Year after year, he built miscellaneously—indoor models, outdoor models, gliders, stunt models, and combat models that fought in the air. He was fifteen when he decided to specialize. He had joined the Academy of Model Aeronautics—the organization that regulates and administers flying-model competitions of regional and national scope—and his choice was whether to fly figure eights in front of judges or to fly for pure speed. "A stopwatch doesn't lie," he told himself. "It doesn't have any personality." So he elected to concentrate in the field of controlling speed. When he tried a competition for the first time, he placed third among thirty contestants, and he felt drawn to what he was doing as never before. He took a paper route to help pay for materials. Afternoons, almost without exception, he came home from high school and immediately went to the basement to build and build and build—Class A's, Class B's, Class C's, proto-speeds, jets. He lived in Fords, New Jersey, outside Perth Amboy, where control-line exhibitions regularly took place in Waters Stadium on the Fourth of July. Kukon would be in there every year, exhibiting his Ringmasters, his scale-model Cessnas, his little P-51s—in dust and smoke and the rampant noise of V-1 scale-model pulse-jet engines. You could hear them seven miles away. He went to a contest somewhere every Sunday—to Wilmington and Baltimore, to airports and fairgrounds, to naval bases, to the Grumman plant at Bethpage, Long Island. The planes were hand-launched. Kukon's father—a cook at a home for disabled veterans in Menlo Park—was his crewman. Once the plane was in the air, Kukon, holding the control line, would jam his wrist into a yoke (a thing that looked like an oarlock) that was set into the top of a short steel pole. The plane would race around in circles on the end of the line while Kukon, rapidly circling the pole, determined the plane's altitude by manipulating a monoline control system with his left hand. Classes were a matter of engine size, and the bigger the engine the longer the control line—forty-two feet, fifty-two and a half feet, sixty feet, seventy feet. The official stopwatch started after three laps. The timed distance was always a half mile. The planes were required to fly at an altitude of fifteen feet or less. The place to be, though, was close to the ground, because of a phenomenon known in aeronautics as ground effect. Ground effect, or the ground cushion, as it is sometimes called, is not fully understood but is somehow related to wingspan. An airplane in flight—any plane, from a small model to a 747—is in the ground cushion when its altitude measures less than the spread of its wings. Sitting on the cushion, the plane gets added lift without the penalty of drag. So Kukon—risking complete destruction of his models, which flew well over a hundred miles per hour—learned to fly them within two inches of the ground. He won three hundred and fifty trophies. He once set two national records in a single week—one in Maryland and the other at the New York *Mirror* Model Flying Fair at Floyd Bennett Field. Two thousand contestants were there, most of them adults. Kukon was nineteen. Flying started at dawn, and all day long Kukon won prizes. His Class C plane flew nine miles per hour faster than the national record. Kukon and his father went home in their twenty-year-old Chevrolet with five trophies, five radios, four wristwatches, a set of tools, two cases of Coca-Cola, a box of silverware, three wallets, and a cookstove. An accident that happened at Johnsville Naval Air Development Center, near Philadelphia, caused Kukon to decide to give up control-line speed flying forever. Sitting on a box with a stopwatch in his hand, he was monitoring a run by one of his regular opponents, a doctor from the medical faculty of Temple University. The engine, prop, landing gear, and other attached parts of the doctor's plane—a two-pound package in all—broke away from the fuselage and projectiled toward Kukon's head. Just then a young boy stepped in front of Kukon. At eighteen thousand revolutions per minute, the wild engine went into the boy's kidney, nearly killing him. Kukon cancelled all his competitive plans. He had little time, anyway, for much but work and study. After high school, he had enrolled at the Academy of Aeronautics at LaGuardia Airport, where he got his Airframe and Powerplant credentials, the badge of the licensed mechanic. He had been about to go to work at Newark Airport as a mechanic for American Airlines when a friend told him about a job at Princeton that seemed unbelievable. The university actually paid people to build models. They had a unique test facility called the Long Track, a narrow building seven hundred and sixty feet long, where they worked with designs for low-speed aircraft. Soon Kukon was building models at Princeton which cost contracting companies as much as eighty-five thousand dollars; for example, a four-engine vertical-lift model whose wing could rotate through a ninety-degree arc so that the engines would point forward or up, as the pilot chose. Doing consulting work, he built a model tube train. The tube was two thousand feet long. The train was driven by counter-rotating propellers. It shot through the tube at two hundred miles per hour. For all the diversions of his work, though, Kukon's thoughts, in the months that followed the accident at Johnsville, were drawn repeatedly to one trophy, its image sharp in his mind. It was a staggeringly big trophy, an elaborate gold sculpture in late aerobaroque. It was almost as tall as Kukon—a giant gold cup, fourteen inches from rim to rim, and it had a gold lid, on top of which was a gold airplane. It was given for the over-all best performance at a model contest held annually at Westchester County Airport, in White Plains. The trophy belonged to the Westchester Exchange Club, and not to the winner. There was a provision, however, that should anyone ever win it three years in a row that person could keep it permanently. There had never been a three-time winner. Kukon had won the trophy the year before. He had also won it the year before that. This fact tormented his decision to retire. He kept thinking about that stupendous cup with its gold filigree and its gold airplane. In the end, inevitably, he decided to go back into control-line speed for one more day. When the day came, he moved around the airfield from flying circle to flying circle, from class to class, and put his various planes through their lariat flights, always on the edge of record speeds. There were so many contestants that Kukon had time only for one flight in each class he entered, although the rules technically allowed him three. By late afternoon, though, he was beginning to relax into the expectation that the big trophy was on its way to Fords, for he had flown five events and his times were the best in each. Nothing less would do, because in the contest as a whole there were many events—speed events, free-flight events—and even a single second place could eliminate a contender for the high-point trophy. By the rules, all flying would cease at 6 P.M. At five-fifteen, someone beat Kukon's Class A time by one-tenth of a second. With luck, he could try once more. He put his number in at the judges' table and began the wait for a final turn in the Class A circle. Several others were ahead of him. It seemed likely that the contest would close before he could get into the circle. Half an hour went by, while Kukon chewed the ends of his fingers. The nails had long since been bitten back so far he could not reach them. At ten minutes to six, his number came up. Kukon opened his fuel box. He made his own fuels. Fuel bought in a store was castor oil and alcohol, and Kukon was far past that. In his fuel, only five per cent was alcohol. The rest was high-energy material in various blends—propylene oxide, nitromethane. In the fuel box were four bottles, four blends. Each bottle was wrapped in carpeting. Blend 4 had never been used. Kukon had never actually expected to use it. He had conceived of it as a fuel for a situation of extreme and unusual emergency. Its characteristics were that it would almost certainly destroy the engine that burned it, but meanwhile the engine would develop enough thrust to drive a sparrow to the moon. Kukon entered the circle with his Class A plane and poured Blend 4 into the engine. By the rules of the competition, he had three minutes to get the plane into the air. The engine seemed not so much to start as to explode. Its force immediately broke the propeller. Kukon ran to his equipment box for another propeller, and, with his hands shaking, tried to get it mounted before his time ran out. When he finished the job, he had twenty seconds left. He started the engine again. This time the propeller did not break. The airplane, screaming, bolted into the air. Kukon could barely hold on to the control line. He could not pirouette fast enough to keep pace with the plane. It was all he could do to get his wrist into the yoke. Class A planes are small, as control-line speed models go, and no one in the world had ever flown one a hundred and fifty miles an hour. Kukon's model got right down onto the deck, deep in the ground cushion. An audio tachometer covered the run and showed that the engine was doing thirty thousand revolutions per minute. The plane ate up its half mile at an average speed of 150.013 miles per hour. Then it flew on and on and on. It flew six miles. There is no way to shut off one of those engines in the air. When the plane landed, the motor was extraordinarily hot but undamaged.

Forty-eight hours after his first meeting with Miller, Kukon returned to Mercer County Airport with a twenty-inch Aereon in a cardboard box. Using one-thirty-second-inch balsa sheet—following the sketches, working essentially from scratch, from blueprints that developed in his imagination—he had made a double root rib as a keel, two tip ribs, and two more ribs to complete the structure. He had covered it with tissue paper that had come out of a shoebox. To the trailing edge of the delta he had glued a pair of vertical balsa fins. Unlike its successors —the 7 and the 26—this smallest of Aereons had no anhedrals, no horizontal tail fins. Kukon said, "You don't need them indoors—no gusts." Its motor was a single twenty-inch loop of rubber band. For landing, it had wire skids. And for sheer jazz he had painted a red streak down the axis of the delta, top and bottom. Miller and others gathered around him. Kukon held the wingless aerobody in his hand, gave the rubber two hundred turns, and arrested the pusher prop in his fingers. He looked around the big hangar. The place was full of posts and girders and airplanes, including a two-engine Grumman Gulfstream. Kukon himself had never flown anything larger than a model, and he apparently never would. The few times he had ridden in small aircraft, he had turned gray and become sick. He had once made plans to take flying lessons but changed his mind after a ride in a small plane made him sick for two days. He had never flown in a commercial airliner. He had, however, become an aeronautical engineer. At night, after work at Princeton, he had commuted for several years to the Polytechnic Institute of Brooklyn, where he earned his degree. Now, in the Mercer County hangar, he studied the situation some more, and then he breathed on the elevons and the fins of the Aereon to warp them just so, to work the wood, to set a turning radius for the flight. He let the aerobody go. Its propeller whirring, it began to move, to fly, and it climbed out over the wings of the Gulfstream. It moved in a wide ascending circle toward the roof of the hangar, skimming under the girders and by the posts. It levelled off. In a steady state of flight—the first and only flight in the long history of the Aereon Corporation—it circled the hangar three times, high overhead. Then it made its descent and landed at Kukon's feet.

In the pumpkin-seed configuration, helium would be ineffective at any length that was much under a hundred and fifty feet. So helium was not included in the tests of the 7 and the 26. They would have to get up there on their own—without wings, without lifting gas—and ratify the computer that had created them. Then the way would open to the behemoths. The 7 was tested for the fourteenth, and last, time on September 2, 1970, near Princeton. Monroe Drew was not invited. He was in Trenton—eleven miles, and many light-years, away. John Fitzpatrick was in Neshaminy, pumping Esso. Drew and Fitzpatrick by now were like old Russian premiers. They had been there once, but no one quite remembered them. When Miller had become president of the company in 1967, he replaced Drew's overt and provocative optimism with a hair shirt of caution and secrecy. Something called the Technical Advisory Group replaced Fitzpatrick. The image of Aereon flew by night, and Miller dedicated himself to building a different impression. He found his consultants, in the main, in the Department of Aerospace and Mechanical Sciences of Princeton University. Putman, the aerodynamicist, was one of these, as was Kukon, and Olcott had been trained there. The evening of September 2nd was heavy with the heat of the day. Air was moving, but barely. Everyone wore a sports shirt but Olcott, who was dressed in a plain brown suit and did not remove his jacket or tie. The advisory group formed a circle around the 7, at the head of the runway. "Today's outing must be a success or a complete failure," Putman said. "We are here to make a flight. And to get a flight—to get out of ground effect and make a circuit of the field—we are willing to risk totalling the 7."

To salvage the aircraft, Kukon had worked for a week, steadily and far into the night, in a shop near Princeton. The work had been done so skillfully that the others had to think to remember which side had been crushed by Putman's car. The orange silk glistened with fresh, clear butyrate dope. Kukon showed no trace of concern for the 7's immediate future. It was part of his routine to build with uncompromising care devices that might be destroyed in an instant. He did say, however, "If I can't get above six feet, I may just set it back down in the grass."

Olcott said to Kukon, "In trying to get out of ground effect, try not to do it too quickly. Let the vehicle go out at a shallow angle. Don't raise the nose so much that you start to lose air speed." Within a few days —everything going well—Olcott was expected to get into Aereon 26 and fly it. He had been flying it for the last couple of days on a computer. Now he wanted to see if the model would reflect or contradict what he had learned. He wanted to see how it would behave when it got out of ground effect, among other things, and what sort of roll angle would be best for a turn, what the diameter of the turn would be, and how much elevator deflection would be needed to fly at a given altitude as a function of center-of-gravity location. He said, "Try one control input at a time, John. First try pitch excursions. I don't want anything gross. Just small things. So we can see what's happening. Try coördinated rolls. I think the vehicle may have N delta A, adverse yaw, a little more than predicted, and the only way to take care of that would be with rudder. So you may have a problem with just-aileron rolls. I think where this vehicle can get in trouble is that it can become grossly uncoördinated. If you let the sideslip build up quite a little, I think you'll find that it becomes unmanageable. In the 26, I'm going to try very hard to keep everything coördinated, to keep that ball right in the center. The simulations indicate that life remains manageable when the ball is in the center, but if the ball gets way out, if the sideslip angle builds up, life can become very difficult."

"Gentlemen, I think we ought to do it," Putman said.

"O.K.," said Kukon.

The engine started—small, rear-mounted, earsplitting—and the 7 taxied around, limbering up. Everybody got into Putman's convertible. As before, Putman would drive in close formation with the aircraft, but when it went into the air he was to stop. Kukon sat on the convertible's trunk, his feet dangling into the rear seat, his Logictrol transmitter in his lap. Miller was beside him with his Super 8. Olcott was in front. Kukon advanced the throttle. The aerobody and the automobile raced side by side. Putman called out, "Twenty! Twenty-five! Thirty! Thirty-two!" At thirty-seven miles per hour, the 7 took off.

The wreckage this time was total and irreparable. Small pieces of Styrofoam, balsa wood, piano wire, and orange silk were scattered across a dirt road and into a cornfield. No remark showing disappointment or dismay was made by anyone. They all got out of Putman's car, stood in the middle of the orange and white debris, and talked about what had happened. Miller's movie camera, clicking as if it were packed with tree frogs, committed each fragment to film. Olcott looked reflectively at the bits and the pieces, the Styrofoam spread out like snow in the late, slanting light. He spoke at length with Kukon, and as he did so he flew his own hand, in various pitch attitudes and aileron rolls, in the air before him. Now and again, he grinned. The 7 had at least *flown* to its final destination. It had flown high and, for a while, straight.

Putman said, "We haven't seen anything shockingly unusual on this outing. I don't think the 7 had stability problems. I think it had control-effectiveness problems and trim problems. Any power problems, John?"

"No. Here's the story, and it's very strange," Kukon said, speaking rapidly and supporting his words with gestures. "The aerobody lifted off very gradually. Then it seemed to settle. I gave it more up-elevator. It sort of got a little soggy. I gave it more up-elevator. It climbed a little —to three or four feet—and I gave it more up-elevator, which was probably two-thirds of what I had. I held that elevator, and the aerobody very gradually started to settle. At that point, I had to make a decision. Was I going to throttle back and set it down, or go all the way? I decided to go all the way. I throttled back just a little bit, though—three notches. And when I throttled back, the whole thing levelled off and climbed. It surprised the hell out of me. When I saw that, I gave it full throttle and full up-elevator. It kept on climbing. I felt a very strong trim change when it moved out of ground effect."

"In ground effect you need a lot less elevon?" Putman said.

"Exactly."

"The proximity of the ground gave you a more positive angle of attack?" Olcott said.

"Right."

"O.K.," said Putman. "This would indicate to me that we need a more nose-up elevator after we get out of ground effect. With the more nose-up elevator, if the separation and scale effects are severe, your aileron effectiveness will accordingly go to pot. So you may have a lot less aileron effectiveness out of ground effect *not* due to the fact that you are out of ground effect but due to the fact that you need more elevator."

"Close to the ground, everything was sensitive," Kukon said. "I had a lot of power. I could put it where I wanted. Everything was terrific. Even the rudders were more effective. Once I got a little higher, though, it was as if I was trying to hold a long rubber band that was hooked into the controls."

"There's a distributed lift effect," Putman said. "It might be less severe on a full-scale machine. I don't think it is something that we can do anything about at this point, but ground effect is the major unknown area that is going to give us problems."

"After it had climbed out, I tried the ailerons a little bit, and they were responsive to low roll angles," Kukon went on. "Everything seemed O.K. But then the aerobody rolled sharply to the left. I gave it some right aileron. This was at fourteen feet of altitude. I gave it some more right aileron, and it really wasn't responding. Then I gave it some rudder, and, boy, did it respond! That was the first time I used rudder, and it just zipped right around and straightened itself out. I neutralized the ailerons and neutralized the rudder. That's when the aerobody went up to forty feet. Flying straight. Everything fine. Until I tried to turn around. I rolled it over with a little bit of aileron. It held there pretty well, but then it started to slip off to the left. I straightened out the ailerons. Nothing happened. The amount of roll that I was allowed on the whole flight was essentially zero. I mean, just a little bit and it was already too much. I gave it a little more right aileron. Nothing happened. I gave it full right aileron. Nothing happened. I gave it full right rudder, and it wasn't enough—full right and full right! There was no way I could get out of it. It was over too far. It spiralled down."

"That seems very close to what we learned in the computer simulations," Olcott said.

"If you ever get to that point, there's no way out," Kukon said.

"The thing is not to get to that point," said Olcott. "With this aircraft we have to be very careful that we don't let things get too far out of trim."

"I agree."

"Because by the time we got that second rudder input—"

"It would be too late."

"—we would have gone too far. Do you have any notion what might happen if we did not use the ailerons but just the rudders?"

"I think the vehicle would be uncontrollable," Kukon said. "Because the motion I got out of pure rudder was a wild thing. The whole flight was very difficult. I was working pretty hard, I thought, even during the straight portion. One puff, one gust, one very small disturbance, and I'd have lost the whole ballgame right there. That one time I put in full rudder was almost a panic control."

"John, thank you," Olcott said. "Thank you for that flight."

"I'm sorry I couldn't get it a little better around for you, but that was the best I could do," said Kukon.

"Flying the 26, we'll have a lot more information at our command than you had flying the 7—a lot more abort opportunities," said Olcott. "The whole philosophy of the 26 is that we're not going into any unknown area quickly. We'll go in small, manageable steps—so we can always back out. I'm not going to force the 26 to do anything it doesn't want to do. I don't intend to force it into the air. It has to fly into the air. Meanwhile, the 7 has told us a heck of a lot. The 7 supports the simulator study. There is no glaring conflict. It indicates that N delta A is a little higher than predicted and that L delta A might be just a little less than predicted, but we've got a consistent set of data." Olcott unbuttoned his jacket. A lock of hair had fallen across his forehead. He paused a moment and looked down into the wreckage, but he was not really seeing it. "That flight was worth its weight in gold, John," he said finally. "We have a way of approaching the 26. We've identified a risk. Now we want to say, 'If we can keep it small, we can handle it.' I think we ought to go to NAFEC. I think we ought to go into an attempted lift-off Friday morning."

On Saturday evening, September 5, 1970, John Olcott and his wife gave a dinner party at their home, in Basking Ridge, thirty miles north of Princeton. Beforehand, Olcott dialled the Aereon Corporation's number and spoke with an answering service. He gave his name, and waited while it was checked against a list. Rain and wind had delayed the first attempt to fly the 26. Now the message was "Good weather tomorrow morning. The winds will be south-southwest three to six knots at 6 A.M., building up to six to ten knots by 8 A.M." Aereon had reserved dawn to eight Sunday on the big runway at NAFEC. The guests came. Olcott prepared drinks. He did not want to be a killjoy, so he privately mixed himself water on the rocks with an olive. He revealed nothing of his plans until after dinner, when he said he was sorry but he had to work early the next morning; and abruptly he went to bed. He got up at three, and although he was on his way to a remote and all but deserted airfield, he dressed in a blue button-down shirt, a dark-blue narrow tie, gray flannel slacks, and a blue-white-and-yellow madras jacket. By three-thirty, he was moving south in his Karmann Ghia—Interstate 287, the New Jersey Turnpike, the Garden State Parkway. At seventy miles per hour, glued to the banked turns, he was going about as fast as Aereon 26 would ever go or was ever meant to go. He moved under stars through mile after mile of dark-corridor forest on the eastern perimeter of the Pine Barrens. He crossed over the Mullica River, shot through the vacant streets of Pomona, and went on through a countryside of open fields and stands of pine to a set of gates in the high chain-link and barbed-wire fencing that surrounded the flat immensity of NAFEC. Inside, he drove on for another mile or so, until windowless walls seventy feet high loomed up black before him against the barely graying sky. He parked the Karmann Ghia at the corner of Lindbergh Drive and Firehouse Lane. Carrying his flying boots and his test pilot's note pad—his jump suit over one arm—he walked toward the big building. He went through a small door in an acre of wall, like a mouse going home.

More cars came into NAFEC—small auroras moving in through the darkness and blinking out near the big hangar: William Miller from Princeton, William Putman from Staten Island, Charles Mills from Toms River. Mills, a German teacher in a high school on the outskirts of Trenton, had once been Air Operations Officer at Lakehurst Naval Air Station. He was now an Aereon consultant. He had been a celebrated pilot of naval airships. When the airships, just before the Navy abandoned them, gave ironic proof of themselves flying out of South Weymouth, Massachusetts, in the middle nineteen-fifties, it was Mills who piloted the most dangerous flights. He rigged up closed-circuit television so he could watch ice coating up on his Z.P.G.s—big ships, three hundred and forty-three feet long—until he had as much as five tons of it weighing down his leading edges, his propellers, his control wires, and his windshield. Then he would hunt for the worst of a storm. Mills had the feel of the airships, of the wind and the weather. His responses were quick, and he knew how to use them. He had an athlete's sense of anticipation. An airship moved cyclically in pitch and yaw. Anticipated lead time was the middle of the art. When the nose was going down, the moment was right for some down elevator to check the up cycle that was coming later on. Pilots who did not feel this could let their ships stand on end or slide, giddily, sideways. Mills liked to take the Z.P.G.s out onto the triangle of runways at South Weymouth and slide around on his landing gear with the precision of a figure skater, upwind, downwind, crosswind—strange exercise, a waltzing cow. Watching all this from an engineering office, Lieutenant Commander John Fitzpatrick, who did not overestimate other men's abilities, came to regard Mills as "a master of lighter-than-air flying." To show just how much strain a dirigible could withstand, Mills deliberately flew one carrying eight thousand pounds of ice into a front of warm air, and somehow—through touch, verve, whatever—emerged safely on the far side of an aerial avalanche. For that flight, he was given the Harmon Trophy. Mills now opened the small door in the big wall and stepped into the brightly lighted interior of the NAFEC hangar, where single-engine, twin-engine, and four-engine aircraft were spaced out on fifty thousand square feet of smooth concrete, and where reciprocating engines, out of their nacelles, had been set up on mounts and looked like big women in curlers.

"Hello, Charlie."

"Hello, Charlie. Did you have any trouble getting up this morning?"

"Negative."

Aereon 26 was in the central foreground, bright orange and lustrous, fat, sleek, and implausible, with its black stripes, its black markings, its nose-mounted Pitot boom pricking forward a full six feet. This boom, from which a little stub-winged airspeed indicator hung like a model rocket, was about the only added feature that made the 26 different from the 7—other than, of course, its scale. Everett Linkenhoker was crawling around inside the 26, completing its final preflight checkout. He had been there most of the night.

Mills put his head in through the hatch—a squarish head, with short hair, blue eyes, reading glasses hanging from a cord around his neck. "Hello, Link."

"Charlie." Linkenhoker spoke around a toothpick, without really looking up. His hands were on the airframe. His eyes were moving from weld to weld. He was a short man, heavy in the cheeks, heavy in the middle, a quiet, contemplative man, inventive within his realm. He had light-blue eyes under bifocal lenses, and sandy-blond hair that had gone partly to strings. When Mills had been Air Operations Officer at Lakehurst, Linkenhoker had been a petty officer there, rigging airships.

In volume, Aereon 26 was twenty times as capacious as light airplanes of the same length. At eleven hundred and forty pounds, it weighed about half as much. If its structure had been formed from sheet-metal jigs, the way modern airplanes are built, Linkenhoker would have been able to move around quite easily inside it, but Aereon had had no sheet-metal-working equipment nor the money to buy it. What the company did have was Linkenhoker, a Heliarc welder, and in building the airframe he had used neither a bolt nor a rivet. The 26 had a totally welded tubular structure, consisting of many hundreds of slender aluminum rods compiled in intricate rhomboids, trapezoids, triangles. Drenched now in filtered orange light, the interior of the 26 seemed to have been composed rather than engineered. Or it might have been some prize-winner's discovery in organic chemistry—a novel molecule magnified eight hundred billion times. These aluminum tubes had been salvaged by Linkenhoker from the wreckage of the triple-hulled Aereon, as had most of the 26's instruments: the cylinder-head temperature meter, the free-air temperature meter, the altimeter, the artificial horizon. Piper

Aircraft asked thirty-two hundred dollars for a big Pitot boom of the type Aereon wanted (with a yaw instrument, an angle-of-attack instrument), and that was beyond Aereon's means, so Linkenhoker borrowed a set of plans and made the boom himself. He built the fuel tank—ten gallons—out of new sheet aluminum, and he mounted it to the aluminum rods in the exact center of gravity. To make landing gear, he bought at an auto store some half-inch-diameter bungee shock cords—the things that keep suitcases from falling off roof racks—and he cut them into pieces eleven and a half inches long, bunching up six for each main gear and four for the nose gear, attaching them to landing-gear tripods with aircraft wire and U-shackles. He foraged at small airports until he found an appropriate wreck and from it took the 26's brakes. He found the plastic cockpit canopy on a decaying glider. One day there was an odd and tragic accident at Red Lion Airport. A mechanic flew off in a Cessna to another airport to pick up a case of oil. It was a bumpy day. The Cessna had dual seats, dual controls. Returning, the mechanic put the case of oil on the empty seat beside him. He was on final, approaching the Red Lion runway, when the plane hit a bump and the heavy package jumped off the seat and rammed the stick forward. The Cessna plunged to the ground, nose first. The mechanic was killed. Linkenhoker took the seat that the oil had been on and emplaced it in the cockpit of the 26. To this pattern of aircraft construction by junk collage there was one exception, the control system—rudders, elevons, cables, hardware—all of which was new. The engine, though, was the same four-cylinder, horizontally opposed, two-cycle McCullough that had powered the triple-hulled Aereon.

Linkenhoker used tools from his workbench at home. He cut metal with a wood saw. "It's pretty hard for people to believe—this back-yard project," he said at one point. "When you try to describe the shop that you've been working from and the tools that you've been using, people smile with a gentle little smile and turn away to keep from hurting your feelings. I've had my doubts. I've felt somewhat insecure. It doesn't worry me any. This is the type of work I like to do. It's in the airship field, which is the only thing that I really know. This is a stepping stone to future airships. Just how big a part it will play I haven't the slightest idea. I wouldn't even try to prophesy." He had been in naval aviation for twenty years, almost always in airships, sometimes flying as a crewman, doing structure and envelope rigging, on patrol from Maine to Brazil. He had gone into the Navy straight from high school in Covington, Virginia, where his father was supervisor of a machine room in a paper mill. The young sailor developed expansive feelings about the future possibilities of lighter-than-air, and with the others—the other helium heads—he gradually became disillusioned and, ultimately, bitter in the feeling that the Navy had sold them out. "Any form of aviation must be experimented with," he would say afterward. "L.T.A. experimentation was absolutely nothing. All through the Second World War they should have been experimenting, but they were flying the same type of airship up till the very last. This is a touchy subject. It was strictly a one-sided affair. We were down to twenty ships by 1953. Nothing new was cranked into the picture; it just had to reach its end." When the Navy gave up airships, Linkenhoker gave up the Navy. He had nowhere to go where he might have faintly cared to go except to the Goodyear Tire & Rubber Co., which kept a few blimps alive, like the whooping cranes in the New Orleans zoo. The Goodyear blimps carried fields of light bulbs through which rippled advertising messages to America in the night. Linkenhoker was ready to settle for that—to travel from city to city, away from his family, as airborne maintenance man in a hovering billboard—rather than lose touch forever with airships. He was virtually packed for Akron when Admiral Rosendahl called him and suggested he go to Aereon. It had taken him six years to build the triple hull, and three more to build the 26.

Charlie Mills pulled his head out of the hatch, and Linkenhoker went on with his inspection, experiencing a refreshed sensation of relief that Mills was no longer the test program's test pilot, as Mills had been once, at Red Lion. When the 26 had made its first taxi runs, two years earlier, it had no skin. Rolled out into the open, it was a jungle gym even beyond the imagination of children, and it moved up and down the Red Lion runway at forty-two miles per hour through fresh snow, with Mills dressed in an astronaut's puffy flying suit, perched in the front, like a bird on a naked branch, his feet sticking forward into a cold wind. The ship without skin could not possibly leave the ground. What worried Linkenhoker and everyone else was what might happen when the aerobody was covered with cloth. It had become apparent that, given half a chance, Mills might shrug off the plotted prudence of the test program, eschew the developing counsel of engineers and computers, turn up the engine, take the stick in his hand, and—wings or no wings—bolt for the sky. "There are two ways to test," Mills had said. "One is slow, gingerly, step by step. That way consumes time and money. The other approach is short-time, high-risk. With the 26, the best procedure is to fly it. That's what pilots are for—to take risks." Linkenhoker covered the ship with airplane cloth, and Miller told him to paint it Princeton orange. Linkenhoker went to Shick Auto Supplies in Trenton, and said he wanted Princeton orange. "Mack Truck orange is what we've got here," the man said, and Linkenhoker said that would do. To save weight, he applied only one coat. He used no primer and only five coats of dope instead of the normal nine or ten. When Charlie Mills was about to enter the cockpit to perform another taxi test, Miller, visibly nervous, took him aside and said to him, "Charlie, you are not to fly the 26." Hundreds of items had to be proved out, in many taxi tests, before a first flight could even be contemplated. The replacement cost of the 26—time and materials only—was about a hundred and fifty thousand dollars.

"Wilco," said Charlie, and down the runway he went and took a little jump into the air. The wheels rose only an inch or two off the ground, but Miller aged ten years and Linkenhoker bit his toothpick in half.

Now, at NAFEC, standing among the expectants around the 26, Mills said, "Had I been running the railroad, it would probably be a wrecked aircraft by now." There were appreciative grins. No one spoke up to disagree. Linkenhoker, out of sight inside the ship, thought of the catastrophe that might have occurred because "Charlie wanted just to jump it into the air and try a go-round." Linkenhoker liked Mills well enough, and unreservedly admired his skill in airships, but he sensed the complexities within Mills—fast assessments, speed-drying interests— and, although he could never feel it was his place to say so, he preferred seeing other characteristics in the cockpit of the 26. Olcott was modern, circumspect—more mathematics, no flair. Olcott had already taxied the 26 more than a hundred miles. "I like the cut of his—his attitude," Linkenhoker would say. "His matter-of-fact reasoning. There never seems to be a need for words between Olcott and me. There's an understanding there that doesn't need words. I know what I have to do, and he knows what he has to do."

Olcott had changed his clothes. His jump suit was green. His flying boots, actually construction worker's boots, were new ones from Sears, Roebuck. He put on a white plastic helmet marked "U.S. Air Force." Briefing, he said to everyone present, "We're going to try a lift-off in ground effect, a short hop; and, if that works out, we'll try a lift-off and a prolonged straight and level flight, still in ground effect." The memory that the 7, repeatedly trying to do just that, had porpoised, oscillated, jackrabbited, and finished its days in smithereens had clearly been screwed into a remote corner of Olcott's mind. His computer—at his firm, Aeronautical Research Associates of Princeton—had helped him do this. The computer, full of equations of motion that mathematically detailed the performance characteristics of the 26, had been refreshed with the data gathered on the final flight of the 7. Olcott had then spent four days flying the computer, moving an actual control stick that changed the variables of the equations. Voltmeters plugged into the computer could be read as airspeed indicator, pitch-attitude indicator, rate-of-climb indicator, turn-and-bank indicator, altimeter, and so forth. Moving the stick, Olcott had tried one variable at a time—roll damping, roll rate, pitch damping, vertical acceleration, horizontal acceleration, control sensitivity. Basic truths of the deltoid Aereons were uncovered or confirmed. The initial response from up-elevator would be a pitch change and not an altitude change, for example. While an ordinary airplane turns principally with ailerons, the primary control in the aerobody was apparently the rudder. If power was reduced, the nose would go up—also the reverse of what happens with a conventional plane. One way to get the 26 into a takeoff attitude might be to reduce power. In any case, the stick was not to be used to force the aircraft into the air.

Linkenhoker emerged from the 26 and said he thought everything was ready. Olcott said, finally, "I hope no one will be disappointed in what they see today. Nothing sensational will happen—I trust."

Holding a handle that was attached to the nosewheel gear, Linkenhoker began to tow the 26 like a huge wagon toward the hangar doors. A loud buzzer sounded as power came on and the doors began to part. Boeing 707s had often rolled through those doors with no clearance problem whatever. The 26, whose trailing-edge control surfaces had extended backward beyond original intentions, was twenty-seven feet seven inches long (Pitot boom excluded). Behind its pinpoint nose, it widened to a breadth of twenty-four feet across the tail. So the big doors opened scarcely a crack, and the 26 went out into the night.

Lights of the airfield, blue and red, spaced out through the dark to the horizon. Airplanes parked on the apron formed high silhouettes behind the 26, black on deep gray—a giant Globemaster, its engines hanging like teats; a Boeing 720, slick as the night; a couple of Convairs; a DC-7; an Aero Commander; a DC-3. A bar of light from the aperture in the hangar fell across the 26. Olcott climbed through the hatch and into the seat, his white helmet appearing to be almost phosphorescent within the plastic bubble. He strapped himself in. He strapped his note pad to his right thigh. Now that he was aboard, cast-iron weights were removed from the nose, and a Detecto bathroom scale was slipped under the nosewheel, read, and removed. Dawn began, pushing pink streaks upward, painting out the eastern stars. Venus stayed. Gray lightened and turned into high pale blue, with white bits of cirrus in it. The pinks flared. The dark airplanes on the apron turned silver and cold. White stucco buildings now stood out across the airfield flatness. One of these was a firehouse. Its doors opened and fire trucks began to move toward situations on the runway. Red as blood, they had enormous gold numerals on their sides, the figure 6, the figure 8. A red fire car, sedan of the chief, sprinted cross-country toward the 26, stopped nearby, and waited, its roof light revolving and flashing. Station wagons drew up carrying flagstaffs and large, flapping orange-and-red checked flags. One station wagon was Linkenhoker's Dodge, which he would drive. The other was the airport operations car of NAFEC—roof light turning, flashing, now red, now yellow. All vehicles were equipped to radio the NAFEC tower. Olcott lowered over his eyes the glare shield of his crash helmet. Putman leaned in through the hatch. Bits of conversation drifted out.

"Fifty-six knots calibrated is the best rate-of-climb speed," Olcott said.

"I concur."

"Alpha R is seven point six. Delta E flight is eight point four."

"I read it nearer ten point zero."

"O.K."

"You could have a three-point lift-off. Do you understand what I'm saying?"

"Yes."

Putman, aerodynamicist, who had never flown or cared to fly, was trim and handsome, with rich dark hair that was now tumbling across his forehead. He was wearing a blue shirt and a gray sweater that had a hole in one elbow. His trousers were vertical candy stripes—blue, white, and gold. A comb protruded from a hip pocket. Putman had built models all through his youth—Fort Smith, Arkansas (he was an undertaker's son), Phillips Andover Academy, Princeton University. He never tried to fly the models he built. What mainly attracted him about airplanes was their incredibly beautiful appearance, airplanes as pinnacles in the aesthetics of function. He was thirty-six now, advanced-degreed and academic: Princeton Department of Aerospace and Mechanical Sciences. His wife had once filled in a coupon that brought an Encyclopaedia Britannica salesman to their door. The salesman was Paul Shein, Aereon's treasurer. Putman bought the encyclopedia, and Shein drew Putman into Aereon as a consultant.

"I'm basing fifty-two indicated as fifty-six calibrated," Olcott said. "Fifty-two indicated gives me a reasonable takeoff solution."

Putman said, "Very well."

"The first run will be without rotation. The second run will include a rotation at a forty-seven-knot takeoff solution. The third run will be a go."

"Jack, you're wise to select to do the rotation at a lower speed," said Putman.

Olcott said, "The only thing I'm concerned about is staying on the front side of the power curve."

"O.K., then?"

"O.K. I'm all set."

Linkenhoker, at the rear, stood on a two-step steel ladder and put his hands on the propeller, which had a forty-eight-inch diameter. A self-starter would be dead weight in the air, an impossible luxury at this level of the aerobody's development. Linkenhoker shouted, "Contact!"

From the nose, Olcott shouted, "Contact!"

Linkenhoker pulled down hard on the propeller. It turned a quarter turn and nothing happened. He tried again. Nothing. Again. Nothing. Again. Nothing. He shouted, "Full throttle!"

"Full throttle!"

Four more tries. Nothing. Linkenhoker paused, and rubbed his head against his shoulder. He primed the carburetor. He tried six more times. The engine did not so much as cough. Miller displayed signs of nervousness. Mills, who had a stopwatch in his hand, looked impatient. Putman folded his arms and waited. Linkenhoker seemed annoyed—nothing more. There was very little he did not know about motors.

"Do you think it will start, Link?"

"Of course it will start. It's a gasoline engine, isn't it?"

Reaching high, he jerked the prop down with all his weight and muscle. Nothing. In quick succession, he heaved at it five more times. Once, it eructed slightly; but that was all. Linkenhoker's hair was becoming damp with sweat. "Switch off!" he shouted.

"Switch off!"

"You want more priming gas, Link?"

"No, I want some more breath." Linkenhoker suddenly looked vulnerable, as if he, not Olcott, were the man in danger. He was near fifty and not, by appearance, in condition for this much of a workout. "Switch on!"

"Switch on!"

Five more tries. Nothing.

"Half throttle!"

"Half throttle!"

One more try. Nothing. A gill of primer. Another heave. The engine started. It sounded exactly like a chain saw. It sprayed noise off the high walls of the hangar, killing talk. Olcott closed the hatch and called the NAFEC tower. There was no response. His radio was inadequate. He opened the hatch. Could someone else please call the tower for him? Soon, in the NAFEC operations car, a thumb went up. Olcott raised a thumb in acknowledgment, and the 26 began to move out past the big silent jets. Linkenhoker drove Miller and Mills to the main runway, and they got out on the turf at the edge, midway between the ends—Mills, the consultant, with his stopwatch; Miller, the president, maintaining the corporate records with his Nikon Super 8. The station wagon sped away. Hundreds of seagulls were holding some sort of meeting on Taxiway Bravo, parallel to the big runway, and Linkenhoker's Dodge scattered them as he hurried to join the 26 and the other vehicles in time for the first run.

The dawn air was cold. Mills wore a suède jacket, old khaki trousers, old flying boots. Miller wore his Navy flight jacket, which had been issued to him twenty-five years before. His past seemed somewhat at odds with his theological present—the Master of Theology whose time-and-a-half labors for Aereon were virtually equalled by his continuing church work, as, for example, a leader of the Children's Sand and Surf Mission, in Ship Bottom, New Jersey. Large block lettering on his flight jacket said "ATTACK 35," on an emblem in which a fire-breathing flying red dragon was riding a torpedo. Miller, however, had long since reconciled the divergences in his cosmography; witness a psalm he had once contributed, as a Naval Reserve fighter pilot, to the *Bulletin* of the Officers' Christian Union of the United States of America:

Savior, you have launched me, and you will bring me aboard,
    I shall never land short.

I can never land short of your flight-deck;
  short of your elevators are the deep waters of death.
The black waves you have stilled;
  you have overcome them that I may land in heaven.
I shall never land short, for you, my Savior, have launched me,
  and you will surely bring me in.


The sun, now a deep-red full circle lifting from the horizon, was halved by a wafer of cloud that appeared black against the red and against the pinks and blues of the sky. The stars were gone. The air was sharply clear. A six-knot breeze had been predicted for this hour, but even that had failed to develop. "We must thank the Lord," said Miller. "This day is providential. He has given us perfect conditions. Clear. Dry. Dead calm." Fearing observation, Miller scanned the peripheries of NAFEC—the chain-link fencing, the automobiles moving on exterior roads. The ones that moved slowly made him nervous.

The 26 crescendoed, wheels rolling firm on the ground, in a high-speed taxi run. In single file, the station wagons, the car of the fire chief, and a fire engine raced down the taxiway—flags flying, lights flashing and whirling—keeping pace with the 26. These five vehicles were the only moving things in the huge level acreage of NAFEC. At the far end, Olcott turned the 26 around. Having neither seen nor felt anything that he did not expect, he decided that that was enough taxiing and he was ready to fly. He went over his checklist. Both boost pumps on. Twenty-one minutes of fuel consumed. Controls O.K. Very simple. Forget nothing. Next, he reviewed his plan for rotation—the moment when an aircraft, on the ground and rolling, lifts its nosewheel and assumes an angle of attack from which, with added acceleration, it will rise into the air. He would rotate at fifty-two knots with an elevator deflection of thirty degrees. This should produce an angle of attack of eight degrees for initial lift-off. In flight, the angle of attack would increase to ten degrees. He would hold that attitude, flying the aircraft. He looked out through the clear-plastic canopy at the other vehicles all around him like sheep dogs, protection itself, watching, waiting for his move, within his philosophy of small increments, of small and careful steps one at a time, toward a new level. He looked at the NAFEC operations car and raised his right thumb. The tower was told. A thumb went up in the car. Olcott accelerated to full throttle.

On the windscreen before him were two horizontal strips of black plastic tape, one above the other, like an equals sign. The upper tape was on the line of sight between Olcott's eyes and the horizon. The other tape was ten degrees lower. Gaining speed, he scanned his indicators: airspeed, angle of attack, control position, revolutions per minute. At fifty-two knots he deflected the elevators and watched the horizon descend, steadily, fairly rapidly, just as it should do, from the one tape almost to the other. In rotation. Angle of attack: eight degrees. One hand on the throttle, the other on the stick, he held things just where they were, and he began to ask himself questions. How much stick force is necessary? Is there sway? Is it heavy on the main wheels? Is it spongy? He was feeling his way toward the first indication of lift-off. He thought of nothing else and noticed nothing else—not Mills beside the runway, smoking a cigarette, his stopwatch running; nor Miller, following the aerobody with the Super 8 like a duck hunter; nor the file of automobiles, bouncing and lurching at high speed over the ground swells of the taxiway, racing to stay with him, while engineers within them narrated the scene into spinning cassettes. He asked himself if the 26 was responding. Did it have a mind of its own? Did it tend to stay where he put it? He sought motion cues. Vibration. Acceleration. Runway shock. There was now no runway shock. Fifty-six knots, and the 26 was airborne.

Putman, riding in Linkenhoker's car, said, "I see daylight! I see daylight under the wheels! Estimated angle, ten degrees." Linkenhoker chewed his toothpick, drove the car, and said nothing. Miller, by the runway, shooting film steadily, did not dare to expect anything after eleven years. The moment brought to his mind an image, as he later put it, "of long bedraggled nights at Mercer County Airport, with dead flies on the floor, Linkenhoker working late, night after night—a whole fragile structure brought to focus: torn between ultimate trust that all things work together for good for those who are the called (my own overarching awareness of the providence of God) and authentic human stress." Mills grinned, standing there in his old flying boots, his reading glasses dangling from his neck. As the 26 came at him and went past him, he said, "Steady as a rock. I haven't seen an Aereon fly that steady since the old rubber-band model."

The 26, as the computer had said it would, moved its own angle of attack, after takeoff, from eight to ten degrees and firmly held it there. No wild oscillations for this ship. No need to manhandle it. Everything seemed to Olcott to be on nice, manageable terms. The 26 had slid into the air. Felt just like that. It eased into the air. In the right lateral-directional sense, it sat there. It was very soft. It felt very smooth. He reduced power. Kept everything else the same. Felt for the ground. Maintain the body attitude, he told himself. Feel for ground contact. He was concerned about ballooning into the air. He searched for the first indication that the wheels were on the ground. He asked himself, Is the pitch effect right? The runway gave him his answer. Main wheels down. Power change. Adjust for attitude change. Roll out. He came to the end of the runway. He turned the nosewheel. The 26 spun around, and sat still, pointing back into the airspace it had come out of, having its day as a falcon, spreading the wings it did not have.

It had flown a thousand feet at an altitude of twenty-four inches.

Mills said, almost to himself, "What a beautiful flight!" Watching it, he had multiplied the size, the altitude, and the range of what he had seen. He had seen a rigid airship, with new proportions, new missions, flying not a thousand feet but a thousand miles. The rest was detail. Work it out, men; on the double. Mills might have been an admiral if the lighter-than-air program had survived. One of his last acts in the Navy had been to write a thesis for the War College called "Airships— Renaissance or Requiem." Then, like many others, he faded into the sycamores of a small New Jersey town—a picket fence, a frame house, big airships visible, if nowhere else, in pictures on his study wall. He kept a bottle of Windex on his desk. He cleaned his glasses with Windex, the better to see the pictures of the blimps. "This was the M. The sweetest ship that ever flew. Look at that long car—a hundred and seventeen feet; in effect, a dorsal fin. She's more stable in yaw than any other airship I've ever flown. This is me at the controls. And here's an idea we had—a helicopter pad on top of an airship. We actually had it half built. If new airships were constructed today, we would have a line waiting to use them tomorrow, for radar calibrations, for atmospheric samplings, for ecological surveys, for airfreight. Airships used to use goldbeater's skin (ox intestines) for gas cells. Engines were built at eight pounds per horsepower. Now we could do three-quarters of a pound per horsepower. Think what could be done with modern materials. We came to an untimely end." He pressed the stopwatch. Olcott, a mile away from him, was starting another run.

Don't step out of the straight and narrow, Olcott told himself. Don't get carried away. False confidence can attend the second run, so this is where I have to be careful. Then he drove the 26 up an invisible ramp until it was ten feet off the ground, where it remained in level flight without a quibbling motion while he diverted his attention to collecting data. After flying two thousand feet, he landed, smooth as talc. Pausing, making notes, he almost quit for the day, because he wondered if he had become overconfident. Deciding that he had not, he took off again. This time, he allowed his left hand to leave the controls, and with it he clicked pictures. (A camera was mounted above his left shoulder and focussed on the instrument panel.) The flight was again perfect, nose high, ten feet up, three thousand feet from lift-off to touchdown. Mills clicked his watch, and said to Miller, "Don't stop now, Bill. Don't, for heaven's sake, stop now. Have the test go on. Conditions are right. Everything is right. Do the next phase now."

"I'll speak to Jack," Miller said, but there was really no need to. He could already hear Olcott saying, "I want to go into unknown areas on my terms, with no surprises." In fact, the 26 was already moving toward the hangar. Miller and Mills walked across the runway, and for what had happened Miller silently offered thanks to the Lord. The heel of one of Mills' boots came off and settled like a coin on the asphalt. He picked it up, and took off the boot, and walked with one shoe off and one shoe on, attempting repairs. "All my eight thousand hours of flight are in these shoes," he said. "All my eight thousand hours of flight." With his fist he punched the heel back on. "Don't stop now, Bill. Do the next phase now."

Miller was swelling with exuberance, but Calvin within him would not let it brim over. On the apron beside the hangar, Miller suggested that Olcott and Linkenhoker pose for photographs with the ship the one had built and the other had flown. Olcott looked uncomfortable. Linkenhoker—much too shy for show business—blushed, bent his head forward, took hold of the 26 by the nose, and dragged it into the hangar. The debriefing, held around a table in the NAFEC cafeteria, was in its way like the debriefing after the last, and most spectacular, crash of the 7. Everyone's voice was flat. The discussion was totally technical. Neither joy nor dismay had relevance there. Developed facts were what mattered. "The sequence was to accelerate on the ground with the controls faired," Olcott was saying. "The controls felt a little mushy, but they're responsive. I had no difficulty setting the angle of attack. The landing was accomplished by maintaining the same angle of attack and reducing the power. Letting the 26 settle at that attitude is just the way to do it."

"We need a ratio of predicted to actual values, and then we can decide how far to back off the tab," Putman said.

Olcott nodded in agreement. "I would say we're right where we ought to be," he said. "Tuesday morning, we'll explore prolonged hops in transition out of ground effect, and prolonged hops out of ground effect."

Afterward, Olcott gave me a lift back to Princeton in his Karmann Ghia. "We're exploring relatively unknown areas," he said at one point. "It's not an airship. It's not an airplane. It's what Bill Putman says it is: an original concept—something like the lifting bodies that NASA tested for reëntry vehicles to land on land. When we lifted off today, it was just a very, very small step into an unknown region, and we had been there before in the piloted analogue simulation. I felt no big heartbeats or adrenalin inputs. The first flight was a normal extension of what we had done beforehand. No quick judgments. Right on plan. I didn't want to dump on Miller's elation, but for me it was business as usual. No hurrahs. The thing that pleases me is that we were able to predict what would happen. If the predictions were correct this time, we can have more confidence in other predictions to come, when we try to take the vehicle a little farther." Olcott suddenly showed alarm, a trace of panic, the only trace of panic I was ever to see in him. His gasoline gauge was riding on "Empty," and had been for who knows how many miles. He drove on for ten minutes, a little tight in the lips. "I do this often," he said. "I just forget." An Amoco station saved him. Sitting there beside the pumps, he took out a notebook and recorded the current mileage and the replacement volume of the gasoline.

Miller had long since discovered the hole in the fence between religion and superstition. All week long, as he worried and as he watched the weather, he looked for omens. When he learned that a major reunion of American airship men would be held at Lakehurst on June 26 and 27 next, he shivered with hopeful presentiment. The aircraft registration number of Aereon 26, boldly painted on its side, was N2627. The weather forecast for Saturday, March 6th, was more than promising. All the mechanical work Olcott had asked for had been done. So word went out on Friday, through the Aereon answering service, that the test group should meet at NAFEC at five-thirty the following morning. Reaching into a pocket, Miller took out his daily appointment book. It was called the Success Agenda Seven-Star Diary, and it included a fortune message for each day. Turning the page, Miller read the message for March 6, 1971. It said, "The mocker's arrow turns back like a boomerang."

Jack Olcott and his wife, Hope, happened to be giving a dinner party

March 5th, as they had on the night before the first lift-off, six months before. Olcott mixed himself an aquatini—water with an olive in it—and after dinner he passed cordials around and said to his guests, "I hope you won't consider me rude, and I hope I won't break up the conversation, but I have a very early morning appointment and I have to retire for the night." He got up at four, and took fifteen minutes to dress, choosing a blue blazer, a blue-and-gold button-down striped shirt, his royal-blue tie with fleurs-de-lis, gray flannel trousers, and a pair of defeated, broken-down loafers with flapping soles. In the blazer's lapel was a small set of wings, emblematic of his membership in the secret society of Quiet Birdmen. At four-thirty, he parked his car at Morristown Airport, and shovelled an aging snowdrift from the apron of a T-hangar. He rolled out a Beechcraft Travelair, climbed in, and took off. His route south passed above McGuire Air Force Base. The McGuire approach controller said to him, "Are you going home late or getting up early?" Olcott gave the controller a straight answer. Crossing the Pine Barrens, he ate a box breakfast that his wife had packed—crullers and coffee, meat-loaf sandwiches. At five-thirty, he raised the galactic blue lights of NAFEC.

The big hangar was crowded. The 26 was nestled like an orange-dyed egg between the wing and tail fin of a Convair 880, a four-engine commercial jet roughly the size of a 707 or a DC-8. Around the 26 was a nonagon of gold nylon cord, strung among nine wooden stanchions. Linkenhoker, inside the barricade, was finishing up the preflight inspection. ("I had one major thing in my mind," he said later. "How might I feel if through some fault in the aircraft it cracked up and we lost a man? This was the foremost thought in my mind the whole time we were down there. I know one thing now: I'll never be placed in a position where I have to take complete responsibility for a man's life again. The design was good, but, nevertheless, the over-all putting together of the aircraft was mine, and that presented a hell of a feeling, I'll tell you. I thought, Here we are using an unaccepted structure and an uncertified engine, and we have low prior knowledge of the vehicle's flight characteristics. It presented a rather dismal picture in my mind. Fortunately, we were so damned busy—the buildup to the tests was so great—that I didn't have much time to think.") Everything seemed right with the aircraft and its engine—eleven hundred and one pounds minus Olcott, center of gravity fifty point three five per cent, examined and ready to go. Linkenhoker began to remove the gold cord. John Kukon, who had no official role to perform, had got up in the middle of the night and come to NAFEC anyway, unable to resist seeing this particular outing. Olcott, now in his test-pilot clothes, slot pockets bristling with stubby pencils, was telling Kukon stories about experimental airplanes he had known and interesting troubles they had had. There had been one in India, for example, "with a classical aileron wing-bending flutter problem" that always developed at just so many miles per hour. Olcott would accelerate the plane until he got a nice, pronounced flutter going. With a high-speed camera he would take pictures of the flutter. He also told a story about a plane that had recently crashed in a bizarre way, yielding three survivors. If these were parables, they were to Olcott himself subliminal. His manner was, as always, calm and precise. He asked Kukon what he thought about the popping in the engine. Small power plants like that were not unlike model-aircraft engines, about which there was very little that Kukon did not know. Kukon told him not to worry. The 26 had a two-cycle engine, like a chain saw or an outboard, developing a great deal of horsepower for its weight. Two-cycle engines run on combined gas and oil, lubricating themselves as they go along, and just the right amount of air has to be mixed with this fuel to produce maximum horsepower. If the mixture is too lean, horsepower declines, and—more important—the engine can develop too much heat and destroy itself. If the mixture is too rich, horsepower declines also, but the engine functions well. One sign of a rich mixture is that the engine occasionally, harmlessly, pops. Olcott was used to flying four-cycle engines, and that, of course, was another story altogether. Popping in a four-cycle engine could be a symptom of catastrophic trouble. With a two-cycle engine, though, the best ratio for the fuel-air mixture was just a little way over on the safe side of the power peak—popping now and again, like corn on a stove.

Olcott thanked Kukon and said he felt relieved of that problem. The tall, telescopic doors moved apart. The Aereon was rolled toward the breaking day. Emerging from beneath the Convair 880, the 26 seemed small to the point of absurdity, with its little chain-saw-type engine mounted above the rear like a horsefly sitting on the head of a pin. Minuscule beside the giant airplane, the Aereon was hard to imagine at full scale, but if it ever grew to its ultimate conceptual dimensions it would not be able to insert into this big hangar a great deal more than its nose, for it would be the size of the Hindenburg and the Graf Zeppelin placed together in the shape of a T, with superstructure filled in to form an immense rigid delta. A couple of dozen Convair 880s could fit inside it. Linkenhoker, standing on an iron stool, primed the Aereon's engine, and tugged at a blade of the new propeller. The engine eventually coughed, ignited, and racketed against the walls of NAFEC. Olcott closed the hatch, radioed for permission to move, and routinely went up Taxiway Bravo toward the head of the runway.

For stopwatch timing and for photography, Miller, Putman, and others were delivered by station wagon to various points on the airfield. Fire and crash vehicles were operating on both sides of the runway this time—yellow lights, red lights flashing everywhere. The morning was pale blue, clear, and fine. The sun was above the horizon, its light streaming to the west. "This is a day the Lord has made," Miller said. "Let us rejoice and be glad in it. It's just ideal. No wind. Dry. Clear. This day is a gift." Olcott was facing west, at the head of the runway. Cleared, he accelerated, rotated, and lifted into the air. He climbed to forty feet and levelled off. He tried a coördinated bank and gentle turn to the left. It went well. He did the same to the right. The 26 responded as he had expected it would. It did not seem to have a tendency to roll excessively. The roll damping was light. He got a promising sense of the roll-control effectiveness of the vehicle. Reducing power over the seven-thousand-foot markers, he descended, landed, and taxied to the turnaround block at the runway's western end. The brief flight had been Olcott's warmup. He now felt that he had the vehicle all around him. NAFEC had asked him to take off to the east if he ever intended to leave the airspace of the runway, because the terrain at the eastern end of the NAFEC reservation had a dirt road winding through it and was particularly accessible to fire trucks and crash vehicles. Olcott was now facing east. He called the tower and said this was Aereon 2627 requesting permission to lift off and make a circuit of the field. Two miles of broad runway reached out before him. The parallel taxiway, where the fire trucks would race him, was to his right. To the right of the taxiway and a little more than halfway down was the great dark block of the NAFEC hangar, its near wall lined with tiers of offices behind shining plate-glass windows that reflected the low rays of the sun. The fire trucks and other cars were lined up and ready. Olcott showed them a raised thumb, moved the engine up to four thousand revolutions per minute, and left the head of the runway. He watched the black tape marks on his windshield, rotated, established his angle of attack, and went into the air. He climbed to forty feet. This time, however, he did not level off. Still in a position to abort the flight with ease, still in an environment he had been in many times before, he now had to decide whether the rate of climb was sufficient to warrant an advance to where he had not been. He had hoped for a rate of climb of two hundred, or even two hundred and fifty, feet per minute, but the engine was running flat out and he was getting a hundred and fifty. He figured that a hundred feet per minute, or less, would be so marginal that he would have to go down. This was, for sure, the inverse frontier—an exploration of the lower, most economical limits of aerodynamic possibility. Some commercial jets climb six thousand feet per minute. He watched the rate-of-climb indicator. It was holding at one hundred and fifty, positive rate of climb—positive enough for him to decide to stay with it. He put in a little rudder and made a slight right turn. Moving obliquely, he would add something to the time when he would be near enough to the runway to get to it if the engine failed. He was flying directly toward the NAFEC hangar, however, and NAFEC sternly told him to head somewhere else at once. He was about eighty feet in the air. If his engine failed, he could not have hit the NAFEC building even if he tried. The building was half a mile away. The 26 had a glide ratio of about five to one. From that altitude, the 26 could not have glided more than four hundred feet before scraping the ground. Moreover, the 26 was so light that if it had hit the building head on it might have had difficulty breaking the glass. Olcott corrected his turn, though, and continued to climb slowly to the east. It was like driving a station wagon stuffed with cordwood up the side of a mountain in first gear. He was getting there. He knew he would make it over the hill. Meanwhile, there was nothing to do but be patient. He reached a hundred feet, a hundred and fifty feet, two hundred feet, all the while reminding himself: Do not change anything. Stay at this airspeed. Hold the controls with constant pressure. Let the vehicle do the work. These tests are important, they must be concluded. You knew all along that the vehicle was never going to behave like a homesick angel. It just wasn't going to climb like that. Within the margins of our considerations was a poor rate of climb.

The 26 was almost over the end of the runway, and was two hundred and fifty feet in the air. Seen from the ground and from a mile behind, it appeared to be a small black diamond moving into the sun. "Fantastic!" John Kukon said. "It's got a lot higher nose attitude than I expected, but if that's the way it is, so be it."

Olcott was now about to try the first significant turn the 26 had ever made. He could not with certainty predict what would happen. He did not have the altitude he had planned for, and he had to ask himself a lot of questions. He had to keep looking for and selecting places where he might set the Aereon down if the engine stopped, or if much of anything else went wrong. You can't wait until the engine quits to decide how to handle the situation. It's too late then. You have to know what you're going to do before you have to do it. So you are continually saying to yourself: What will I do if this happens? What will I do if that happens? If the engine quits now, I'll put the stick forward to make sure I'm going downhill, like the boy on a bicycle who doesn't want to pedal anymore. He's got to be pointed downhill or he'll topple over. Get the nose down. Establish the glide. Keep the airspeed the same, so you have control. Then go into one of those preselected landing spots. The engine is the primary consideration. Stability is the secondary consideration. The Aereon is not a broom balancing on the palm of your hand. It is a stable vehicle. Nevertheless, you do not yet know to what extent it is stable. As long as you don't disturb anything—as long as you move into any control input very slowly and smoothly—the chances are that you'll never upset the dynamics of the vehicle so drastically that you cannot cope with it. I am two hundred and fifty feet over the end of the runway. If the engine fails here, there is no way I can turn around and get back into the runway. If I were to try, I'd probably lose control of the aircraft. So what do I do? Where would I go? The dirt road. It is sort of a hard dirt road. I believe I could get in there. Maybe damage the nose gear but not do too much harm. I could negotiate that landing.

He went into the turn. He made it shallow, because he had never been in one before. His mind raced with the conditions and problems of the turn, addressing himself, addressing the aircraft. Let's take it nice and easy. Let's not depart too much from what we've done before. Here we go. This is the first time we've really got a sustained angle of bank. Really a turn. We know from the computer simulations that if the angle of bank gets a little too high, and the rudders are not coördinated just right, the vehicle will want to continue to the left and will be difficult to control. That would be disconcerting at low altitude. There's a straight-forward way out, with use of rudders and manipulation of the stick.

He had taped one end of a bit of black yarn to the outside of the cockpit canopy, and now he watched it closely. Air should always be flowing straight back, no matter what maneuver the aircraft might be making. If the yarn were to move sidewise, the 26 would be going into a yaw. The yarn was straight. The sideslip angle was zero—just what it was supposed to be.

The 26, continuing to climb, had turned through an arc of ninety degrees and was heading north. Olcott no longer needed the dirt road. If trouble developed now, he could probably get around to the runway, heading west, if he had to. It was like trying to cross a stream from one bare rock to the next bare rock, trying not to fall in. Meanwhile, in addition to and above all else, he was supposed to be collecting test data. What is the rate of climb now? What is the indicated airspeed? What is the angle of attack? What is the control-position transducer saying? How am I doing? How am I doing relative to what I want to be doing? How much will this turn hurt the rate of climb?

The 26 completed its wide arc to a hundred and eighty degrees and was headed west, parallel to, but considerably north of, the runway. The rate of climb had remained steady. The ship was four hundred feet up now, and it continued to rise until Olcott levelled off, as he had planned to, at five hundred feet. Data now flowed from the instruments. The maximum speed, full throttle, was sixty-four knots—a little better than Olcott had expected. He planned his route over the western end of the reservation, telling himself not to fly over the houses there, because that was not good professional technique in an aircraft that had a limited flight history and a configuration that had never flown before. I'll just have to go into the shrubbery if anything happens here, he told himself, but he swung into a perfect hundred-and-eighty-degree turn and was now pointed again into the sun. He was five hundred feet over the broad white stripes from which he had begun his takeoff. He had completed a circuit of the field.

"Wow!" Miller said, shooting straight up with his Nikon Super 8. "This is fantastic!" The fire trucks stopped running around. All the ground vehicles stopped. Everyone watched the sky.

Olcott now had the Atlantic Ocean spread before him, wide marshes and bays, the skyline of Atlantic City to his right, Absecon Bay straight ahead, and to the left the Brigantine National Wildlife Refuge. Almost below him was the Garden State Parkway, a superior alternative to the dirt road as an emergency landing strip. Northbound or southbound, the 26 could blend right in with the cars there, if necessary, at an identical speed. Olcott found the scope of his view extraordinary, because there were no wings around him to impede it.

Olcott again circled the field, this time reducing his airspeed to fifty-nine knots to see how the 26 would handle there. Then he went around again, at fifty-two knots, and again, at fifty. Each circuit was about eight miles.

"It's slowly sinking in," Miller said. "He's not going to come down."

In subsequent days, Olcott would fly the 26 right out to the end of its engine time. It would be tracked by NAFEC's theodolite, yielding, for two hundred dollars an hour, precise airspeed data. Olcott would do Dutch rolls and steady sideslips, kicking out hard with his rudders. He would do aileron rolls to the right, aileron rolls to the left, rudder kicks right, rudder kicks left, as if he were practicing swimming. He would climb, slow down, dive, speed up—a fundamental longitudinal mode, the phugoid motion. Investigating the phugoid, he would go into a steady sideslip and then "put in a doublet—just to get the thing excited."

"That's how we lost one of the Aereon 4s," Linkenhoker would say, biting a toothpick, watching from the ground, and then, perhaps because he was unable just to stay there and watch, Linkenhoker would jump into a Piper Cherokee and chase the 26 into the sky. I went with him. The 26 seemed to float beside us, over the field, pinewoods, the parkway—with tidal estuaries, salt marshes, and the sea beyond. Shafts of sunlight sprayed down from behind clouds in which the sun kept appearing as a silver disc, and, moving in and out of these palisades of light, the 26 went into smooth roll angles and controlled yaws—part airplane, part airship, floating, flying, settling in to landings light and slow. "Aereon is great," said NAFEC's chief executive officer. "Just look at it and you can see the potential. What made New York great? What made Chicago great? The carrying of freight." One could almost see New Yorks and Chicagos springing up under the slow-moving shadow of the Aereon as it flew. A subtler and perhaps more durable endorsement had come from NAFEC beforehand, however, on the day of the first circuit of the field. Flying on and on—the first circuiting flight lasted more than half an hour—Olcott looked up at one point to see a Starlifter approaching the field. The two aircraft—one weighing eleven hundred pounds, the other weighing seventy tons—were more or less on a collision course. "Tell them to give me plenty of room," Olcott said to the tower. "I cannot tolerate their wake." The tower told the Starlifter to turn right, go south, and keep on going south indefinitely. "The traffic on your left," the tower explained, "is an aerobody—a wingless vehicle—proceeding northwest."

# Pieces of the Frame

"Travels in Georgia" (1975) is McPhee's first *New Yorker* profile of a female subject, Carol Ruckdeschel of Atlanta, Georgia. Her life and working habits defy most simple labels. She is a field zoologist, an ecology activist, a protector of landscape and guardian of animals, alive or dead. She is young, free, handsome, and wild; not a "new woman" so much as one with ancient missions. She fears no serpents, can live without men, takes things apart to see how they are made. Carol will dare, touch, and taste anything, even the clay from a buffalo lick. She is a trusting, resourceful creature, like those she loves, and her example urges us to care but half as much.

Carol is a Georgian. She might have grown up anywhere, but one of McPhee's quiet points is that people and places in Georgia have a special affinity for each other, a relation too often missing from American life. The lesser characters confirm this theme: Sam Candler has shied from the life of a wealthy socialite and chosen instead to ramble back roads and study swamps. Pulling in the opposite direction is Jimmy Carter, a country boy who captured the governor's mansion in Atlanta. Georgians are an independent lot, as varied as the ground they occupy.

McPhee's journey with Carol and Sam makes a great loop through Georgia, touching its mountains, piedmont, and coastal plain. Yet the trip also "tended to mock the idea of a state—as an unnatural subdivison of the globe," for the bogs and creeks of Georgia are places without political boundaries, embracing values beyond the simple legalities of city life. People constantly threaten Georgia's wild places, but McPhee cannot bring himself to paint them as simple villains. Chap Causey, the dragline operator who reams a river, is a "world class" performer; the dozen folks who live in Georgia's remotest, most beautiful place have an ornery aesthetic of their own: "Lyrical in its effrontery to fact, the name of the valley was Tate City." On his own travels, McPhee cuts to the same line of balance, lyrical in one moment and the ironic "little Yankee bastard" in another.—*WLH*

---

# *Travels in Georgia*

I asked for the gorp. Carol passed it to me. Breakfast had been heavy with cathead biscuits, sausage, boiled eggs, Familia, and chicory coffee, but that was an hour ago and I was again hungry. Sam said, "The little Yankee bastard wants the gorp, Carol. Shall we give him some?" Sam's voice was as soft as sphagnum, with inflections of piedmont Georgia.

"The little Yankee bastard can have all he wants this morning," Carol said. "It's such a beautiful day."

Although Sam was working for the state, he was driving his own Chevrolet. He was doing seventy. In a reverberation of rubber, he crossed Hunger and Hardship Creek and headed into the sun on the Swainsboro Road. I took a ration of gorp—soybeans, sunflower seeds, oats, pretzels, Wheat Chex, raisins, and kelp—and poured another ration into Carol's hand. At just about that moment, a snapping turtle was hit on the road a couple of miles ahead of us, who knows by what sort of vehicle, a car, a pickup; run over like a manhole cover, probably with much the same sound, and not crushed, but gravely wounded. It remained still. It appeared to be dead on the road.

Sam, as we approached, was the first to see it. "D.O.R.," he said. "Man, that is a big snapper." Carol and I both sat forward. Sam pressed hard on the brakes. Even so, he was going fifty when he passed the turtle.

Carol said, "He's not dead. He didn't look dead."

Sam reversed. He drove backward rapidly, fast as the car would go. He stopped on the shoulder, and we all got out. There was a pond beyond the turtle. The big, broad head was shining with blood, but there was, as yet, very little blood on the road. The big jaws struck as we came near, opened and closed bloodily—not the kind of strike that, minutes ago, could have cut off a finger, but still a strike with power. The turtle was about fourteen inches long and a shining hornbrown. The bright spots on its marginal scutes were like light bulbs around a mirror. The neck lunged out. Carol urged the turtle, with her foot, toward the side of the road. "I know, big man," she said to it. "I know it's bad. We're not tormenting you. Honest we're not." Sam asked her if she thought it had a chance to live and she said she was sure it had no chance at all. A car, coming west, braked down and stopped. The driver got out, with some effort and a big paunch. He looked at the turtle and said, "Fifty years old if he's a day." That was the whole of what the man had to say. He got into his car and drove on. Carol nudged the snapper, but it was too hurt to move. It could only strike the air. Now, in a screech of brakes, another car came onto the scene. It went by us, then spun around with squealing tires and pulled up on the far shoulder. It was a two-tone, high-speed, dome-lighted Ford, and in it was the sheriff of Laurens County. He got out and walked toward us, all Technicolor in his uniform, legs striped like a pine-barrens tree frog's, plastic plate on his chest, name of Wade.

"Good morning," Sam said to him.

"How y'all?" said Sheriff Wade.

Carol said, "Would you mind shooting this turtle for us, please?"

"Surely, Ma'am," said the sheriff, and he drew his .38. He extended his arm and took aim.

"Uh, Sheriff," I said. "If you don't mind . . ." And I asked him if he would kindly shoot the turtle over soil and not over concrete. The sheriff paused and looked slowly, with new interest, from one of us to another: a woman in her twenties, good-looking, with long tawny hair, no accent (that he could hear), barefoot, and wearing a gray sweatshirt and brown dungarees with a hunting knife in the belt; a man (Sam) around forty, in weathered khaki, also without an accent, and with a full black beard divided by a short white patch at the chin—an authentic, natural split beard; and then this incongruous little Yankee bastard telling him not to shoot the road. Carol picked up the turtle by its long, serrated tail and carried it, underside toward her leg, beyond the shoulder of the highway, where she set it down on a patch of grass. The sheriff followed with his .38. He again took aim. He steadied the muzzle of the pistol twelve inches from the turtle. He fired, and missed. The gun made an absurdly light sound, like a screen door shutting. He fired again. He missed. He fired again. The third shot killed the turtle. The pistol smoked. The sheriff blew the smoke away, and smiled, apparently at himself. He shook his head a little. "He should be good," he said, with a nod at the turtle. The sheriff crossed the road and got into his car. "Y'all be careful," he said. With a great screech of tires, he wheeled around and headed on west.

Carol guessed that the turtle was about ten years old. By the tail, she carried it down to the edge of the pond, like a heavy suitcase with a broken strap. Sam fetched plastic bags from the car. I found a long two-by-ten plank and carried it to the edge of the water. Carol placed the snapper upside down on the plank. Kneeling, she unsheathed her hunting knife and began, in a practiced and professional way, to slice around the crescents in the plastron, until the flesh of the legs—in thick steaks of red meat—came free. Her knife was very sharp. She put the steaks into a plastic bag. All the while, she talked to the dead turtle, soothingly, reassuringly, nurse to patient, doctor to child, and when she reached in under the plastron and found an ovary, she shifted genders with a grunt of surprise. She pulled out some globate yellow fat and tossed it into the pond. Hundreds of mosquito fish came darting through the water, sank their teeth, shook their heads, worried the fat. Carol began to remove eggs from the turtle's body. The eggs were like ping-pong balls in size, shape, and color, and how they all fitted into the turtle was more than I could comprehend, for there were fifty-six of them in there, fully finished, and a number that had not quite taken their ultimate form. "Look at those eggs. Aren't they beautiful?" Carol said. "Oh, that's sad. You were just about to do your thing, weren't you, girl?" That was why the snapper had gone out of the pond and up onto the road. She was going to bury her eggs in some place she knew, perhaps drawn by an atavistic attachment to the place where she herself had hatched out and where many generations of her forebears had been born when there was no road at all. The turtle twitched. Its neck moved. Its nerves were still working, though its life was gone. The nails on the ends of the claws were each an inch long. The turtle draped one of these talons over one of Carol's fingers. Carol withdrew more fat and threw a huge hunk into the pond. "Wouldn't it be fun to analyze *that* for pesticides?" she said. "You're fat as a pig, Mama. You sure lived high off the hog." Finishing the job—it took forty minutes—Carol found frog bones in the turtle. She put more red meat into plastic sacks and divided the eggs. She kept half for us to eat. With her knife she carefully buried the remaining eggs, twenty-eight or so, in a sandbank, much as the mother turtle might have been doing at just that time. Carol picked away some leeches from between her fingers. The leeches had come off the turtle's shell. She tied the sacks and said, "All right. That's all we can say grace over. Let's send her back whence she came." Picking up the inedible parts—plastron, carapace, neck, claws—she heaved them into the pond. They hit with a slap and sank without bubbles.

As we moved east, pine trees kept giving us messages—small, hand-painted signs nailed into the loblollies. "HAVE YOU WHAT IT TAKES TO

MEET JESUS WHEN HE RETURNS?" Sam said he was certain he did not. "JESUS WILL NEVER FAIL YOU." City limits, Adrian, Georgia. Swainsboro, Georgia. Portal, Georgia. Towns on the long, straight roads of the coastal plain. White-painted, tin-roofed bungalows. Awnings shading the fronts of stores—prepared for heat and glare. Red earth. Sand roads. Houses on short stilts. Sloping verandas. Unpainted boards.

"D.O.R.," said Carol.

"What do you suppose that was?"

"I don't know. I didn't see. It could have been a squirrel."

Sam backed up to the D.O.R. It was a brown thrasher. Carol looked it over, and felt it. Sam picked it up. "Throw him far off the road," Carol said. "So a possum won't get killed while eating him." Sam threw the bird far off the road. A stop for a D.O.R. always brought the landscape into detailed focus. Pitch coming out of a pine. Clustered sows behind a fence. An automobile wrapped in vines. A mailbox. "Donald Foskey." His home. Beyond the mailbox, a set of cinder blocks and on the cinder blocks a mobile home. As Sam regathered speed, Carol turned on the radio and moved the dial. If she could find some Johnny Cash, it would elevate her day. Some Johnny Cash was not hard to find in the airwaves of Georgia. There he was now, resonantly singing about his Mississippi Delta land, where, on a sharecropping farm, he grew up. Carol smiled and closed her eyes. In her ears—pierced ears—were gold maple leaves that seemed to move under the influence of the music.

"D.O.R. possum," Sam said, stopping again. "Two! A grown one and a baby." They had been killed probably ten minutes before. Carol carried the adult to the side of the road and left it there. She kept the baby. He was seven inches long. He was half tail. Although dead, he seemed virtually undamaged. We moved on. Carol had a clipboard she used for making occasional notes and sketches. She put the little possum on the clipboard and rested the clipboard on her knees. "Oh, you sweet little angel. How could anybody run over *you?*" she said. "Oh, I just love possums. I've raised so many of them. This is a great age. They are the neatest little animals. They love you so much. They crawl on your shoulder and hang in your hair. How people can dislike them I don't understand." Carol reached into the back seat and put the little opossum into a container of formaldehyde. After a while, she said, "What mystifies me is: that big possum back there was a male."

Bethel Primitive Baptist Church. Old Canoochee Primitive Baptist Church. "THE CHURCH HAS NO INDULGENCES." A town every ten miles, a church—so it seemed—every two. Carol said she frequently slept in church graveyards. They were, for one thing, quiet, and, for another, private. Graham Memorial Church of the Nazarene.

Sam and Carol both sat forward at the same moment, alert, excited. "D.O.R. Wow! That was something special. It had a long yellow belly and brown fur or feathers! Hurry, Sam. It's a good one." Sam backed up at forty miles an hour and strained the Chevrolet.

"What is it? What is it?"

"It's a piece of bark. Fell off a pulpwood truck."

The approach to Pembroke was made with a sense of infiltration—Pembroke, seat of Bryan County. "Remember, now, we're interested in frogs," Sam said, and we went up the steps of Bryan County Courthouse. "We understand there is a stream-channelization project going on near here. Could you tell us where? We're collecting frogs." It is hard to say what the clerks in the courthouse thought of this group—the spokesman with the black-and-white beard, the shoeless young woman, and their silent companion. They looked at us—they in their pumps and print dresses—from the other side of a distance. The last thing they might have imagined was that two of the three of us were representing the state government in Atlanta. The clerks did not know where the channelization was going on but they knew who might—a woman in town who knew everything. We went to see her. A chicken ran out of her house when she opened the screen door. No, she was not sure just where we should go, but try a man named Miller in Lanier. He'd know. He knew everything. Lanier was five miles down the track—literally so. The Seaboard Coast Line ran beside the road. Miller was a thickset man with unbelievably long, sharp fingernails, a driver of oil trucks. It seemed wonderful that he could get his hands around the wheel without cutting himself, that he could deliver oil without cutting the hose. He said, "Do you mind my asking why you're interested in stream channelization?"

"We're interested in frogs," Sam said. "Snakes and frogs. We thought the project might be stirring some up."

Miller said, "I don't mind the frog, but I want no part of the snake."

His directions were perfect—through pine forests, a right, two lefts, to where a dirt road crossed a tributary of the Ogeechee. A wooden bridge there had been replaced by a culvert. The stream now flowed through big pipes in the culvert. Upriver, far as the eye could see, a riparian swath had been cut by chain saws. Back from the banks, about fifty feet on each side, the overstory and the understory—every tree,

bush, and sapling—had been cut down. The river was under revision. It
had been freed of meanders. It was now two yards wide between vertical
six-foot banks; and it was now as straight as a ditch. It had, in fact,
become a ditch—in it a stream of thin mud, flowing. An immense yellow
machine, slowly backing upstream, had in effect eaten this river. It was
at work now, grunting and belching, two hundred yards from the culvert.
We tried to walk toward it along the bank but sank to our shins in black
ooze. The stumps of the cut trees were all but covered with mud from
the bottom of the river. We crossed the ditch. The dredged mud was
somewhat firmer on the other side. Sam and I walked there. Carol waded
upcurrent in the stream. The machine was an American dragline crane.
The word "American" stood out on its cab in letters more than a foot
high. Its boom reached up a hundred feet. Its bucket took six-foot bites.
As we approached, the bucket kept eating the riverbed, then swinging
up and out of the channel and disgorging tons of mud to either side.
Carol began to take pictures. She took more and more pictures as she
waded on upstream. When she was fifty feet away from the dragline, its
engine coughed down and stopped. The sudden serenity was oddly disturbing. The operator stepped out of the cab and onto the catwalk. One
hand on the flank of his crane, he inclined his head somewhat forward
and stared down at Carol. He was a stocky man with an open shirt and
an open face, deeply tanned. He said, "Howdy."

"Howdy," said Carol.

"You're taking some pictures," he said.

"I sure am. I'm taking some pictures. I'm interested in the range
extension of river frogs, and the places they live. I bet you turn up some
interesting things."

"I see some frogs," the man said. "I see lots of frogs."

"You sure know what you're doing with that machine," Carol said.
The man shifted his weight. "That's a *big* thing," she went on. "How
much does it weigh?"

"Eighty-two tons."

"Eighty-two *tons?*"

"Eighty-two tons."

"Wow! How far can you dig in one day?"

"Five hundred feet."

"A mile every ten days," Sam said, shaking his head with awe.

"Sometimes I do better than that."

"You live around here?"

"No. My home's near Baxley. I go where I'm sent. All over the state."

"Well, sorry. Didn't mean to interrupt you."

"Not 't all. Take all the pictures you want."

"Thanks. What did you say your name was?"

"Chap," he said. "Chap Causey."

We walked around the dragline, went upstream a short way, and sat down on the trunk of a large oak, felled by the chain saws, to eat our lunch—sardines, chocolate, crackers, and wine. Causey at work was the entertainment, pulling his levers, swinging his bucket, having at the stream.

If he had been at first wary, he no doubt had had experience that made him so. All over the United States, but particularly in the Southeast, his occupation had become a raw issue. He was working for the Soil Conservation Service, a subdivision of the United States Department of Agriculture, making a "water-resource channel improvement"—generally known as stream channelization, or reaming a river. Behind his dragline, despite the clear-cutting of the riverine trees, was a free-flowing natural stream, descending toward the Ogeechee in bends and eddies, riffles and deeps—in appearance somewhere between a trout stream and a bass river, and still handsomely so, even though it was shaved and ready for its operation. At the dragline, the recognizable river disappeared, and below the big machine was a kind of reverse irrigation ditch, engineered to remove water rapidly from the immediate watershed. "How could anyone even conceive of this idea?" Sam said. "Not just to do it, but even to *conceive* of it?"

The purpose of such projects was to anticipate and eliminate floods, to drain swamps, to increase cropland, to channel water toward freshly created reservoirs serving and attracting new industries and new housing developments. Water sports would flourish on the new reservoirs, hatchery fish would proliferate below the surface: new pulsations in the life of the rural South. The Soil Conservation Service was annually spending about fifteen million dollars on stream-channelization projects, providing, among other things, newly arable land to farmers who already had land in the Soil Bank. The Department of Agriculture could not do enough for the Southern farmer, whose only problem was bookkeeping. He got money for keeping his front forty idle. His bottomland went up in value when the swamps were drained, and then more money came for not farming the drained land. Years earlier, when a conservationist had been someone who plowed land along natural contours, the Soil Conservation Service had been the epicenter of the conservation movement, decorated for its victories over erosion of the land. Now, to a new generation that had discovered ecology, the S.C.S. was the enemy. Its drainage programs tampered with river mechanics, upsetting the relationships between bass and otter, frog and owl. The Soil Conservation Service had grown over the years into a bureau of fifteen thousand people, and all the way down at the working point, the cutting edge of things, was Chap Causey, in the cab of his American dragline, hearing nothing but the pounding of his big Jimmy diesel while he eliminated a river, eradicated a swamp.

After heaving up a half-dozen buckets of mud, Causey moved backward several feet. The broad steel shoes of the crane were resting on oak beams that were bound together in pairs with cables. There were twelve beams in all. Collectively, they were called "mats." Under the crane, they made a temporary bridge over the river. As Causey moved backward and off the front pair of beams, he would reach down out of the sky with a hook from his boom and snare a loop of the cable that held the beams. He snatched them up—they weighed at least half a ton—and whipped them around to the back. The beams dropped perfectly into place, adding a yard to Causey's platform on the upstream side. Near the tree line beyond one bank, he had a fuel tank large enough to bury under a gas station, and every so often he would reach out with his hook and his hundred-foot arm and, without groping, lift the tank and move it on in the direction he was going. With his levers, his cables, his bucket, and hook, he handled his mats and his tank and his hunks of the riverbed as if he were dribbling a basketball through his legs and behind his back. He was deft. He was world class. "I bet he could put on a baby's diapers with that thing," Sam said.

Carol said, "See that three-foot stump? I sure would like to see him pull *that* out." She gestured toward the rooted remains of a tree that must have stood, a week earlier, a hundred and fifty feet high. Causey, out of the corner of his eye, must have seen the gesture. Perhaps he just read her mind. He was much aware that he was being watched, and now he reached around behind him, grabbed the stump in his bucket, and ripped it out of the earth like a molar. He set it at Carol's feet. It towered over her.

After a modest interval, a few more buckets of streambed, Causey shut off the dragline and stopped for an adulation break. Carol told him he was fabulous. And she meant it. He was. She asked him what the name of the stream was. He said, "To tell you the truth, Ma'am, I don't rightly know."

Carol said, "Do you see many snakes?"

"Oh, yes, I see lots of snakes," Causey said, and he looked at her carefully.

"What kinds of snakes?"

"Moccasins, mainly. They climb up here on the mats. They don't run. They never run. They're not afraid. I got a canoe paddle in the cab there. I kill them with the paddle. One day, I killed thirty-five moccasins. People come along sometimes, like you, visitors, come up here curious to see the digging, and they see the dead snakes lying on the mats, and they freeze. They refuse to move. They refuse to walk back where they came from."

If Causey was trying to frighten Carol, to impress her by frightening her, he had picked the wrong person. He might have sent a shot or two of adrenalin through me, but not through Carol. I once saw her reach into a semi-submerged hollow stump in a man-made lake where she knew a water snake lived, and she had felt around in there, underwater, with her hands on the coils of the snake, trying to figure out which end was the front. Standing thigh-deep in the water, she was wearing a two-piece bathing suit. Her appearance did not suggest old Roger Conant on a field trip. She was trim and supple and tan from a life in the open. Her hair, in a ponytail, had fallen across one shoulder, while her hands, down inside the stump, kept moving slowly, gently along the body of the snake. This snake was her friend, she said, and she wanted Sam and me to see him. "Easy there, fellow, it's only Carol. I sure wish I could find your head. Here we go. We're coming to the end. Oh, damn. I've got his tail." There was nothing to do but turn around. She felt her way all four feet to the other end. "At last," she said. "How are you, old fellow?" And she lifted her arms up out of the water. In them was something like a piece of television cable moving with great vigor. She held on tight and carried her friend out of the lake and onto the shore.

At Carol's house, Sam and I one night slept in sleeping bags on the floor of her study beside Zebra, her rattlesnake. He was an eastern diamondback, and he had light lines, parallel, on his dark face. He was young and less than three feet long. He lived among rocks and leaves in a big glass jar. "As a pet, he's ideal," Carol told us. "I've never had a diamondback like him before. Anytime you get uptight about anything, just look at him. He just sits there. He's so great. He doesn't complain. He just waits. It's as if he's saying, 'I've got all the time in the world. I'll outwait you, you son of a bitch.' "

"He shows you what patience is," Sam said. "He's like a deer. Deer will wait two hours before they move into a field to eat."

In Carol's kitchen was the skin of a mature diamondback, about six feet long, that Sam and Carol had eaten in southwest Georgia, roasting him on a stick like a big hot dog, beside the Muckalee Creek. The snake, when they came upon him, had just been hit and was still alive. The men who had mortally wounded the snake were standing over it, watching it die. A dump truck full of gravel was coming toward the scene, and Carol, imagining the truck running over and crushing the diamondback, ran up to the men standing over it and said, "Do you want it?" Surprised, they said no. "No, *Ma'am!*" So she picked up the stricken snake, carried it off the road and back to the car, where she coiled it on the floor between her feet. "Later, in a gas station, we didn't worry about leaving the car unlocked. Oh, that was funny. We do have some fun. We ate him that night."

"What did he taste like?" I asked her.

"Taste like? You know, like rattlesnake. Maybe a cross between a chicken and a squirrel."

Carol's house, in Atlanta, consisted of four small rooms, each about ten feet square—kitchen, study, storage room, bedroom. They were divided by walls of tongue-and-groove boards, nailed horizontally onto the studs. A bathroom and vestibule were more or less stuck onto one side of the building. She lived alone there. An oak with a three-foot bole stood over the house like an umbrella and was so close to it that it virtually blocked the front door. An old refrigerator sat on the stoop. Around it were the skulls of a porpoise, a horse, a cow, and a pig. White columns adorned the façade. They were made of two-inch iron pipe. Paint peeled from the clapboard. The front yard was hard red clay, and it had some vestigial grasses in it (someone having once tried a lawn) that had not been mowed for possibly a decade. Carol had set out some tomatoes among the weeds. The house stood on fairly steep ground that sloped through woods to a creek. The basement was completely above grade at the rear, and a door there led into a dim room where Carol's red-tailed hawk lived. He was high in one corner, standing on a pipe. I had never been in the immediate presence of a red-tailed hawk, and at sight of him I was not sure whether to run or to kneel. At any rate, I could not have taken one step nearer. He was two feet tall. His look was incendiary. Slowly, angrily, he lifted and spread his wings, reached out a yard and a half. His talons could have hooked tuna. His name was Big Man. His spread-winged posture revealed all there was to know about him: his beauty—the snowy chest, the rufous tail; his power; his afflic-tion. One of his wings was broken. Carol had brought him back from near death. Now she walked over to him and stood by him and stroked his chest. "Come on, Big Man," she said. "It's not so bad. Come on, Big Man." Slowly, ever so slowly—over a period of a minute or two—the wide wings came down, folded together, while Carol stroked his chest. Fear departed, but nothing much changed in his eyes.

"What will he ever do?" I asked her.

She said, "Nothing, I guess. Just be someone's friend."

Outside the basement door was a covered pen that housed a rooster and a seagull. The rooster had been on his way to Colonel Sanders' when he fell off a truck and broke a drumstick. Someone called Carol, as people often do, and she took the rooster into her care. He was hard of moving, but she had hopes for him. He was so new there he did not even have a name. The seagull, on the other hand, had been with her for years. He had one wing. She had picked him up on a beach three hundred miles away. His name was Garbage Belly.

Carol had about fifteen ecosystems going on at once in her twenty-by-twenty house. In the study, a colony of dermestid beetles was eating flesh off the pelvis of an alligator. The beetles lived in a big can that had once held forty pounds of mincemeat. Dermestids clean bones. They do thorough work. They all but simonize the bones. Carol had obtained her original colony from the Smithsonian Institution. One of her vaulting ambitions was to be able to identify on sight any bone that she happened to pick up. Also in the can were the skulls of a water turkey, a possum, and a coon.

The beetles ate and were eaten. Carol reached into the colony, pulled out a beetle, and gave it to her black-widow spider. The black widow lived in a commercial mayonnaise jar. Carol had found her in the basement while cleaning it up for Big Man. The spider's egg was getting ready to hatch, and when it did thousands like her would emerge into the jar. Efficiently, the black widow encased the beetle in filament gauze that flowed from her spinnerets.

Carol then fed dermestids to her turtles. She had three galvanized tubs full of cooters and sliders, under a sunlamp. "They need sun, you know. Vitamin D." She fed dermestids to her spotted salamander, and to her gray tree frog. Yellow spots, polka dots, on black, the salamander's coloring was so simple and contrasting that he appeared to be a knick-knack from a gift shop, a salamander made in Japan. The tree frog lived in a giant brandy snifter, furnished with rocks and dry leaves. With his latex body and his webbed and gummy oversize hands, he could walk right up the inside of his brandy snifter, even after its shape began to tilt him backward, then lay a mitt over the rim and haul himself after and walk down the outside. He could walk straight up a wall; and he did that, while digesting his beetle. He had been with Carol three years. He was a star there in her house. No mayonnaise jar for him. He had the brandy snifter. It was all his and would be as long as he lived.

Notebooks were open on Carol's desk, a heavy, kneehole desk, covered with pens, Magic Markers, brushes, pencils, drawing materials. The notebooks had spiral bindings and were, in part, diaries.

17 April. Okefenokee. Caught two banded water snakes, one skink. . . .

18 April. To King's Landing. Set three line traps baited with peanut butter, caught a rather small moccasin AGKISTRODON coming from under shed. Put out ninety-five set hooks baited with pork liner. To gator hole. Tried to use shocker, after putting up seines across exit. No luck!

19 April. D.O.R. *Natrix rigida,* glossy water snake; *Farancia abacura,* mud snake; *Elaphe guttata guttata,* corn snake. . . .

21 April. S.W. Georgia. D.O.R. vulture, ½ mi. E. Leary, Hwy 62, Calhoun County. Fresh. Possum D.O.R. nearby. . . .

The notebooks were also, in part, ledgers of her general interests.

Dissolve mouse in nitric acid and put him through spectrophotometer—can tell every element.

A starving snake can gain weight on water.

Gray whales are born with their bellies up and weigh a ton, and when they are grown they swim five thousand miles to breed in shallow lagoons and eat sand and stand on their tails and gravity-feed on pelagic crabs.

And the notebooks were, in part, filled with maps and sketches. Making a drawing of something—a mermaid weed, the hind foot of an opossum, the egg case of a spotted salamander, a cutaway of a deer's heart—was her way of printing it into her memory. The maps implied stories. They were of places too specific—too eccentric, wild, and minute—to show up as much of anything on other maps, including a topographical quadrangle. They were of places that Carol wanted to remember and, frequently enough, to find again.

12 May. Caught *Natrix erythrogaster flavigaster,* red-bellied water snake 9:30 A.M. Saw quite a large gator at 9:35. Ten feet. Swarm of honeybees 25 feet up cypress at edge of creek. Large—six-foot—gray rat snake in oak tree over water. *Elaphe obsoleta spiloides.* Tried unsuccessfully to knock it into canoe. Finally climbed tree but snake had gone into hole in limb. . . .

26 June. Sleep on nest where loggerhead laid eggs Cumberland Island, to protect eggs from feral hogs. Return later find that hog has eaten eggs. Shoot hog. . . .

27 August. Oconee River. Saw *Natrix* wrestling with a catfish in water. *Natrix* was trying to pull fish out on bank. Snake about 2½ feet. Fish 8 inches. Snake finally won. Didn't have heart to collect snake as he was so proud of fish and wouldn't let go even when touched. Camped by railroad bridge. Many trains. Found catfish on set hook, smoked him for supper. . . .

The rods of the vertebrate eye provide scotopic vision—sight in dim light. Nocturnal animals that also go out in daylight need slit eyes to protect the rods. Crocodiles. Seals. Rattlesnakes. Cottonmouths.

13 June. North Georgia. Oh, most glorious night. The fireflies are truly in competition with the stars! At the tops of the ridges it is impossible to tell them apart. As of old, I wished for a human companion. On the banks of a road, a round worm was glowing, giving off light. What a wonderful thing it is. It allows us to see in the darkness.

Above the desk, tacked to a wall, was the skin of a bobcat—D.O.R. two miles west of Baxley, Highway 341. "I was excited out of my mind when we found him," Carol said. "He was the best D.O.R. ever. It was late afternoon. January. He was stiff, but less than a day old. Bobcats move mostly at night. He was unbloody, three feet long, and weighed twenty-one pounds. I was amazed how small his testicles were. I skinned him here at home. I tanned his hide—salt, alum, then neat's-foot oil. He had a thigh like a goat's—so big, so much beautiful meat. I boiled him. He tasted good—you know, the wild taste. Strong. But not as strong as a strong coon."

Zebra lifted his head, flashed his fangs, and yawned a pink yawn. This was the first time in at least a day that Zebra had moved. Carol said the yawn meant he was hungry. Zebra had had his most recent meal

seven weeks before. Carol went over to the gerbil bin to select a meal for
Zebra. "Snakes just don't eat that much," she said, shaking her head in
dismay over the exploding population of gerbils. She tossed one to a cat.
She picked up another one, a small one, for Zebra. "Zebra eats every
month or two," she went on. "That's all he needs. He doesn't do anything. He just sits there." She lifted the lid of Zebra's jar and dropped
the gerbil inside. The gerbil stood still, among the dry leaves, looking.
Zebra did not move. "I'm going to let him go soon. He's been a good
friend. He really has. You sometimes forget they're deadly, you know.
I've had my hand down inside the jar, cleaning it out, and suddenly
realized, with cold sweat, that he's poisonous. Ordinarily, when you see
a rattlesnake you are on guard immediately. But with him in the house
all the time I tend to forget how deadly he is. The younger the snake,
the more concentrated the venom."

The gerbil began to walk around the bottom of the big glass jar.
Zebra, whose body was arranged in a loose coil, gave no sign that he was
aware of the gerbil's presence. Under a leaf, over a rock, sniffing, the
gerbil explored the periphery of Zebra's domain. Eventually, the gerbil
stepped up onto Zebra's back. Still Zebra did not move. Zebra had been
known to refuse a meal, and perhaps that would happen now. The gerbil
walked along the snake's back, stepped down, and continued along the
boundary of the base of the jar, still exploring. Another leaf, another
stone, the strike came when the gerbil was perhaps eight inches from
Zebra's head. The strike was so fast, the strike and the recovery, that it
could not really be followed by the eye. Zebra lanced across the distance,
hit the gerbil in the heart, and, all in the same instant, was back where
he had started, same loose coil, head resting just where it had been resting
before. The gerbil took three steps forward and fell dead, so dead it did
not even quiver, tail out straight behind.

Sam had once told me how clumsy he thought rattlesnakes were,
advising me never to walk through a palmetto stand third in a line,
because a rattlesnake, said Sam, takes aim at the first person, strikes at
the second, and hits the third. After watching Zebra, though, I decided
to go tenth in line, if at all. Carol seemed thoughtful. "I've had copper-
heads," she said. "But I'm not really that much on snakes. I'm always
worrying that someday I'll come home and find the jar turned over and
several dead cats lying around on the floor." That night, on the floor in
my sleeping bag, I began to doze off and then imagined rolling over and
knocking Zebra out of his jar. The same thought came to me when I

started to doze off again. I spent most of the night with my chin in my hands, watching him through the glass.

There was a baby hawk in a box in the kitchen, and early in the morning he began to scream. Nothing was going to quiet him except food. Carol got up, took a rabbit out of the refrigerator, and cut it up with a pair of scissors. It had been a rabbit D.O.R. The rabbit was twice the size of the hawk, but the hawk ate most of the rabbit. There followed silence, bought and paid for. In the freezer, Carol had frogs' legs, trout, bream, nighthawk, possum, squirrel, quail, turtle, and what she called trash fish. The trash fish were for Garbage Belly. The destiny of the other items was indistinct. They were for the consumption of the various occupants of the house, the whole food chain—bird, amphibian, beast and beetle, reptile, arachnid, man. A sign over the kitchen sink said "EAT MORE POSSUM," black on Chinese red.

In the bedroom was a deerskin. "I saw blood on the trail," Carol said. "I knew a deer wouldn't go uphill shot, so I went down. I found it. It wasn't a spike buck, it was a slickhead. It had been poached. I poached it from the poacher." On the walls were watercolors and oils she had done of natural scenes, and three blown-up photographs of Johnny Cash. A half-finished papier-mâché head of Johnny Cash was in her bedroom as well, and other pieces of her sculpture, including "Earth Stars," a relief of mushrooms. Carol looked reverently at the photographs and said that whenever she had had depressing and difficult times she had turned to Johnny Cash, to the reassurances in the timbre of his voice, to the philosophy in his lyrics, to his approach to life. She said he had more than once pulled her through.

Carol grew up in Rochester, New York, until she was twelve, after that in Atlanta. Her father, Earl Ruckdeschel, worked for Eastman Kodak and managed the Atlanta processing plant. She was an only child. Animals were *non grata* at home, so she went to them. "You have to turn to something. There was a lot of comfort out there in those woods. Wild creatures were my brothers and sisters. That is why I'm more interested in mammals than anything else. They're warm-blooded. Fish are cold-blooded. You can't snuggle up with a fish." Her parents mortally feared snakes, but she never did. Her father once made her a snake stick. Her mother told her, many times a month and year, that it was not ladylike to be interested in snakes and toads. Carol went to Northside High in Atlanta. After high school, for five years, she worked at odd jobs—she fixed car radios, she wandered. Then she went to Georgia State University, studied biology, and married a biologist there. He was an authority on river swamps, an ecologist—a tall, prognathous, slow-speaking scientific man. His subspecialty was cottonmouths. He had found an island in the Gulf that had a cottonmouth under every palmetto, and he lived for a time among them. He weighed and measured them one by one. He was a lot older than Carol. She had taken his course in vertebrate zoology. The marriage did not really come apart. It evaporated. Carol kept going on field trips with him, and she stayed on at Georgia State as a biological researcher. The little house she moved into could not have been better: low rent, no class, high privacy, woods, a creek. And it was all her own. A cemetery was across the street. She could sleep there if she wanted to get out of the house. On Mother's Day, or whenever else she needed flowers, she collected bouquets from among the graves. From time to time, she wandered away. She had a white pickup truck and a German shepherd. His name was Catfish, and he was "all mouth and no brains." Carol and Catfish slept on a bale of hay in the back of the truck, and they went all over, from the mountains to the sea. They fished in the mountains, hunted in the sand hills, set traps in the Okefenokee Swamp. She began collecting specimens for the Georgia State University research collection. Most she found dead on the road. Occasionally, she brought new specimens into the collection, filling in gaps, but mainly she replenished exhausted supplies—worn-out pelts and skulls. There was always a need. An animal's skin has a better chance against a Goodyear tire than it does against the paws of a college student. She had no exclusive specialty. She wanted to do everything. Any plant or creature, dead or alive, attracted her eye.

She volunteered, as well, for service with the Georgia Natural Areas Council, a small office of the state government that had been established to take an inventory of wild places in Georgia worth preserving, proclaiming, and defending. While she travelled around Georgia picking up usable D.O.R.s for the university, she appraised the landscape for the state, detouring now and again into river swamps to check the range of frogs. Sam Candler, who also worked for the Natural Areas Council, generally went with her. Rarely, they flew in his plane. For the most part, they were on the road. Sam had a farm in Coweta County. He had also spent much of his life in the seclusion of Cumberland Island, off the Georgia coast. He was a great-grandson of the pharmacist who developed and at one time wholly owned the Coca-Cola Company, so he could have been a rampant lion in social Atlanta, but he would have preferred to wade blindfolded through an alligator swamp with chunks of horse-meat trussed to his legs. He wanted to live, as he put it, "close to the earth." He knew wilderness, he had been in it so much, and his own outlook on the world seemed to have been formed and directed by his observations of the creatures that ranged in wild places, some human, some not. Sam had no formal zoological or ecological training. What he brought to his work was mainly a sense of what he wanted for the region where he had lived his life. He had grown up around Atlanta, had gone to Druid Hills Grammar School and to Emory University and on into the Air Force. He had lived ever since on the island and the farm. His wife and their four children seemed to share with him a lack of interest in urban events. The Natural Areas Council had been effective. It had the weight of the government behind it. Georgia was as advanced in this respect as, say, Indiana, Illinois, Iowa, and New Jersey, where important conservancy work was also being accomplished on the state-government level, and far more advanced than most other states. There was much to evaluate. Georgia was, after all, the largest state east of the Mississippi River, and a great deal of it was still wild. Georgia forests, mountains, swamps, islands, and rivers—a long list of sites of special interest or value —had become Registered Natural Areas. Sam and Carol had done the basic work—exploring the state, following leads, assessing terrain, considering vegetation and wildlife, choosing sites, and persuading owners to register lands for preservation.

Sam had been a friend of mine for some years, and when he wrote to say that he was now travelling around the state collecting skulls and pelts, eating rattlesnakes, preserving natural areas, and charting the ranges of river frogs, I could not wait until I could go down there and see. I had to wait more than a year, though, while finishing up some work. I live in Princeton, New Jersey, so I flew from Newark when the day came, and I nearly missed the plane. Automobiles that morning were backed up at least a mile from the Newark Airport tollbooths (fourteen tollbooths, fourteen lanes), and the jam was just as thick on the paid side as it was on the unpaid side—thousands and thousands of murmuring cars, moving nowhere, nowhere to move, shaking, vibrating, stinking, rattling, *Homo sapiens* D.O.R. I got out of my car and left it there, left it, shamefully, with a high-school student who was accepting money to drive it home, and began to make my way overland to the terminal. I climbed up on bumpers and over corrugated fences and ducked under huge green signs. I went around tractor trailers and in front of buses.

Fortunately, Sam had told me to bring a backpack. Carrying a suitcase through that milieu would have been like carrying a suitcase up the Matterhorn. Occasionally, I lost direction, and once I had to crawl under a mastodonic truck, but I did get through, and I ran down the cattle-pen corridors of the airport and, with a minute to go, up the steps and into the plane—relieved beyond measure to be out of that ruck and off to high ground and sweet air, taking my chances on the food. Sam and Carol met me, and we went straight to the mountains, stopping all the way for D.O.R.s. That night, we ate a weasel.

In a valley in north Georgia, Carol had a cabin that was made of peeled logs, had a stone fireplace, and stood beside a cold stream. We stayed there on the first night of a journey that eventually meandered through eleven hundred miles of the state—a great loop, down out of the river gorges and ravine forests of the mountains, across the granitic piedmont and over the sand hills and the red hills to the river swamps and pine flatwoods of the coastal plain. Sam had a canoe on the top of the car. We slept in swamps and beside a lake and streams. Made, in part, in the name of the government, it was a journey that tended to mock the idea of a state—as an unnatural subdivision of the globe, as a metaphor of the human ego sketched on paper and framed in straight lines and in riparian boundaries behind an unalterable coast. Georgia. A state? Really a core sample of a continent, a plug in the melon, a piece of North America. Pull it out and wildcats would spill off the high edges. Alligators off the low ones. The terrain was crisscrossed with geological boundaries, mammalian boundaries, amphibian boundaries—the range of the river frogs. The range of the wildcat was the wildcat's natural state, overlaying segments of tens of thousands of other states, one of which was Georgia. The State of Georgia. Governor Jimmy Carter in the mansion in Atlanta.

The first thing Sam and Carol wanted to assess on this trip was a sphagnum bog in Rabun County, off the north side of the Rabun Bald (4,696 feet). The place seemed marginal to me, full of muck and trout lilies, with swamp pinks in blossom under fringe trees and smooth alders, but Sam and Carol thought it ought to be registered, and they sought out the owner, a heavy woman, greatly slow of speech, with a Sears, Roebuck tape measure around her neck. She stood under a big white pine by the concrete front porch of her shingled house on a flinty mountain farm. Sam outlined the value of registering a natural area for preservation beyond one's years. She looked at him with no expression and said, "We treasure the bog." He gave her an application. ("Being aware of the high responsibility to the State that goes with the ownership and use of a property which has outstanding value in illustrating the natural history of Georgia, we morally agree to continue to protect and use this site for purposes consistent with the preservation of its natural integrity.") Perhaps she could consider it with her husband and his brothers and nephews when they came home. One day soon, he would stop back to talk again. She said, "We likes to hunt arrowheads. We treasure the bog."

The D.O.R.s that first day included a fan belt Sam took for a blacksnake—jammed on his brakes, backed up to see—and a banana peel that Carol identified, at first glimpse, as a jumping mouse. Eager was the word for them. They were so much on the hunt. "It is rare for specimens to be collected this way," Carol said. "Most people are too lazy. Or they're hung up on just frogs or just salamanders, or whatever, and they don't care about other things. Watching for D.O.R.s makes travelling a lot more interesting. I mean, can you imagine just *going* down the road?"

We went around a bend in a mountain highway and the road presented Carol with the find of the day. "D.O.R.!" she said. "That was a good one. That was a *good* one! Sam, hurry back. That was a weasel!"

Sam hurried back. It was no banana peel. It was exactly what Carol said it was: *Mustela frenata,* the long-tailed weasel, dead on the road. It was fresh-killed, and—from the point of view of Georgia State University—in fine condition. Carol was so excited she jumped. The weasel was a handsome thing, minklike, his long body a tube roughly ten by two, his neck long and slender. His fur was white and yellow on the underside and dark brown on his back. "What a magnificent animal!" Carol said. "And hard as hell to trap. Smell his musk. The scent glands are back here by the tail." While backing up after seeing him, she had hoped against hope that he would be a least weasel—smallest of all carnivores. She had never seen one. The least weasel diets almost exclusively on tiny, selected mice. This one would have eaten almost anything warm, up to and including a rabbit twice his size. Carol put him in an iced cooler that was on the back seat. The cooler was not airtight. Musk permeated the interior of the car. It was not disturbing. It was merely powerful. Carol said they had once collected a skunk D.O.R. They had put it in a plastic bag within a plastic bag within four additional plastic bags. The perfume still came through.

Carol's valley resisted visitors. It was seven miles from a paved road.

It was rimmed with mountains. It was the coldest valley in Georgia. A trout stream cascaded out of the south end. Ridges pressed in from east and west. The north was interrupted by a fifty-five-hundred-foot mountain called Standing Indian. Standing Indian stood in North Carolina, showing Georgia where to stop. The valley was prize enough. Its floor was flat and green with pastureland and shoots of new corn. Its brooks were clear. Now, in May, there would be frost across the fields in the morning, heavy and bright, but blossoms were appearing on the dogwoods and leaves on the big hardwoods—only so far up the mountains, though; it was still winter on Standing Indian, stick-figure forests to the top. Sam had flown over this whole area, minutely, in his Cessna—Mt. Oglethorpe to the Chattooga River, Black Rock Mountain to the Brasstown Bald. He said there was no valley in Georgia like this one in beauty or remoteness. It was about two miles long and a half mile wide. Its year-round population was twelve. Someone else, somewhere else, would have called it by another name, but not here. Lyrical in its effrontery to fact, the name of the valley was Tate City. On our way in, we stopped to see Arthur and Mammy Young, its senior residents. Their house, until recently, had had so many preserves stacked on boards among the rafters that the roof sagged. Their outhouse straddled a stream. Their house, made of logs, burned to the ground one day when they were in town, eighteen miles away. Now they lived in a cinderblock hut with a pickup truck outside, fragments of machinery lying on the ground, hound dogs barking. The Youngs were approaching old age, apparently with opposite metabolisms, he sinewy, she more than ample, after sixty years of cathead biscuits. Inside, Arthur rolled himself a cigarette and sat down to smoke it beside his wood-burning stove. Near him was a fiddle. Sam said that Arthur was a champion fiddler. Arthur went on smoking and did not reach for the fiddle. He exchanged news with Carol. Christ looked down on us from pictures on each wall. The room had two kerosene lanterns, and its windows were patched with tape. "I always wished I had power, so I could iron," Mammy said. "When I had kids. Now I don't care." Dusk was near and Carol wanted time in the light, so we left soon and went on up the valley, a mile or so, to her log cabin.

A wooden deck reached out from the cabin on stilts toward the stream. The place had been cut out of woods—hemlock, ironwood, oak, alder, dogwood, rhododendron. A golden birch was standing in a hole in the center of the deck. Carol got out the weasel and set him, paws up, on the deck. Sam unpacked his things and set a bottle of The Glenlivet near the weasel, with three silver cups. I added a bottle of Talisker. Sam was no bourbon colonel. He liked pure Highland malt Scotch whisky. Carol measured the weasel. She traced him on paper and fondled his ears. His skull and his skin would go into the university's research collection. She broke a double-edged Gillette blade in half the long way. "Weasels are hard to come by, hard to scent, hard to bait," she said. "We've tried to trap a least weasel. We don't even have one. I hate to catch animals, though. With D.O.R.s, I feel great. We've got the specimen and we're making use of it. The skull is the most important thing. The study skin shows the color pattern."

With a simple slice, she brought out a testicle; she placed it on a sheet of paper and measured it. Three-quarters of an inch. Slicing smoothly through the weasel's fur, she began to remove the pelt. Surely, she worked the skin away from the long neck. The flesh inside the pelt looked like a segment of veal tenderloin. "I lived on squirrel last winter," she said. "Every time you'd come to a turn in the road, there was another squirrel. I stopped buying meat. I haven't bought any meat in a year, except for some tongue. I do love tongue." While she talked, the blade moved in light, definite touches. "Isn't he in perfect shape?" she said. "He was hardly touched. You really lose your orientation when you start skinning an animal that's been run over by a Mack truck." From time to time, she stopped for a taste of The Glenlivet, her hand, brown from sun and flecked with patches of the weasel's blood, reaching for the silver cup. "You've got to be careful where you buy meat anyway. They inject some animals with an enzyme, a meat tenderizer, before they kill them. *That* isn't any good for you." Where the going was difficult, she moistened the skin with water. At last it came away entire, like a rubber glove. She now had the weasel disassembled, laid out on the deck in cleanly dissected parts. "I used to love to take clocks apart," she said. "To see how they were built. This is the same thing. I like plants and animals and their relationship to the land and us. I like the vertebrates especially." The weasel's tailbone was still in the skin. She tugged at it with her teeth. Pausing for a sip, she said that sometimes you just had to use your mouth in her line of work, as once when she was catching cricket frogs. She had a frog in each hand and saw another frog, so she put one frog into her mouth while she caught the third. Gradually, the weasel's tailbone came free. She held it in her hand and admired it. "Some bones are real neat," she said. "In the heart of a deer, there's a bone. And not between the ventricles, where you'd expect it. Some animals have bones in their penises—raccoons, for example, and weasels." She removed the bone from the weasel's penis. It was long, proportionately speaking, with a hook at the penetrating end. It was called a baculum, she said, which meant "rod" in Latin. She would save it. Its dimensions were one way to tell the weasel's age. Baculums are also involved in keying differences in species. Sam said he kept a raccoon's baculum in his wallet because it made a great toothpick. He got out his wallet and displayed his great toothpick. Carol turned the pelt inside out and folded the forepaws in an X, standard procedure with a study skin. She covered it with a deep layer of salt and packed it away.

The dusk was deep then. Carol had finished working almost in the dark. The air was cold. It was on its way to thirty. Sam had a fire going, inside, already disintegrating into coals. The smell of burning oak was sweet. We went into the cabin. Carol put the weasel on the tines of a long fork and roasted it over the coals.

"How do you like your weasel?" Sam asked me.

"Extremely well done," I said.

Carol sniffed the aroma of the roast. "It has a wild odor," she said. "You *know* it's not cow. The first time I had bear, people said, 'Cut the fat off. That's where the bad taste is.' I did, and the bear tasted just like cow. The next bear, I left the fat on."

The taste of the weasel was strong and not unpleasant. It lingered in the mouth after dinner. The meat was fibrous and dark. "It just goes to show you how good everything is," said Carol. "People who only eat cows, pigs, sheep, chickens—boy, have those people got blinders on! Is that tunnelization! There's one poisonous mammal in the United States: the shorttailed shrew. And you can even eat that."

Sam built up the fire.

"How can you be sure that something is not too old?" I asked.

"My God, if you can't tell if it's bad, what's the difference?" said Carol.

Sam said, "If it tastes good, don't knock it."

"People don't make sense," Carol said. "They hunt squirrels, but they wouldn't consider eating a squirrel killed on the road. Only once have I ever had competition for a D.O.R. A man wanted a squirrel for his black servant, and we had a set-to in the road."

There were double-deck bunks in the corners of the room. The corners were cold. We pulled three mattresses off the bunks and put them down side by side before the fire. We unrolled our three sleeping bags.

It had been a big day; we were tired, and slept without stirring. Sam dreamed in the night that he was eating his own beard.

With a load of honey and cathead biscuits, gifts of Mammy Young, we went down out of the valley in the morning, mile after mile on a dirt road that ran beside and frequently crossed the outlet stream, which was the beginnings of the Tallulah River. Some twenty miles on down, the river had cut a gorge, in hard quartzite, six hundred feet deep. Warner Brothers had chosen the gorge as the site for the filming of a scene from James Dickey's novel, *Deliverance*. This mountain land in general was being referred to around the state as *"Deliverance* country." The novel seemed to have been the most elaborate literary event in Georgia since *Gone With the Wind*. *Deliverance* was so talked about that people had, for conversational convenience, labelled its every part ("the owl scene," "the banjo scene"). It was a gothic novel, a metaphysical terror novel, the structural center of which involved four men going through the rapids of a mountain river in canoes. They were attacked. The action climax occurred when one of the canoemen scaled the wall of a fantastically sheer gorge to establish an ambush and kill a mountain man. He killed him with a bow and arrow. Carol and Sam, like half the people in Atlanta and a couple of dozen in Hollywood, called this "the climb-out scene," and they took me to see where Warners would shoot. The six-hundred-foot gorge was a wonder indeed, clefting narrowly and giddily down through the quartzite to the bed of the river that had done the cutting. Remarkably, though, no river was there. A few still pools. A trickle of water. Graffiti adorned the rock walls beside the pools. There was a dam nearby, and, in 1913, the river had been detoured through a hydropower tunnel. Steel towers stood on opposite lips of the chasm, supported by guy wires. A cable connected the towers. They had been built for performances of wire walkers, the Flying Wallendas. Nearby was the Cliffhanger Café. A sign said, "Enjoy Coca-Cola. See it here, free. Tallulah Gorge. 1200 feet deep." The Georgia Natural Areas Council looked on. Too late to register that one. The eye of the Warner Brothers camera would, however, register just what it wanted to select and see, and it would move up that wall in an unfailing evocation of wilderness. I was awed by the power of Dickey. In writing his novel, he had assembled *"Deliverance* country" from such fragments, restored and heightened in the chambers of his imagination. The canoes in his novel dived at steep angles down breathtaking cataracts and shot like javelins through white torrents among blockading monoliths. If a canoe were ten inches long and had men in it three inches high, they might find such conditions in a trout stream, steeply inclined, with cataracts and plunge pools and rushing bright water falling over ledges and splaying through gardens of rock. Dickey must have imagined something like that and then enlarged the picture until the trout stream became a gothic nightmare for men in full-size canoes. A geologically maturer, less V-shaped stream would not have served. No actual river anywhere could have served his artistic purpose—not the Snake, not the Upper Hudson, not even the Colorado—and least of all a river in Georgia, whose wild Chattooga, best of the state's white-water rivers, has comparatively modest rapids. The people of the *Deliverance* mountains were malevolent, opaque, and sinister. Arthur and Mammy Young.

There were records of the presence of isolated cottonmouths on Dry Fork Creek, in wild, forested piedmont country east of Athens. Dry Fork Creek, a tributary of a tributary of the Savannah River, was about halfway between Vesta and Rayle, the beginning and the end of nowhere. We searched the woods along the creek. It would not have been at all unusual had we found the highland moccasin (the copperhead) there, for this was his terrain—*Agkistrodon contortrix contortrix.* What we were looking for, though, was the water moccasin (the cottonmouth), inexplicably out of his range. Cottonmouths belong in the coastal plain, in the rice fields, in the slow-moving rivers—*Agkistrodon piscivorus piscivorus.* Seeing a cottonmouth in a place like this would be a rare experience, and Carol fairly leaped into the woods. For my part, I regretted that I lacked aluminum boots. Carol was wearing green tennis shoes. Sam's feet were covered with moccasins. Carol rolled every log. She lifted anything that could have sheltered a newt, let alone a snake. By the stream, she ran her eye over every flat rock and projecting branch. Always disappointed, she quickly moved on. Sam sauntered beside her. The flood plain was beautiful under big sycamores, water oaks, maples: light filtering down in motes, wet leaves on the ground, cold water moving quietly in the stream. But the variety of tracks she found was disturbingly incomplete. "There, on that sandbar—those are possum tracks. Possums and coons go together, but that's just possum right there, no way about it. And that is not right. There shouldn't be a bar like that with no coon tracks on it, even if the water goes up and down every night. Possums can live anywhere. Coons can't. Coon tracks signify a healthy place. I don't much like this place. It's been cut over. There are no big dead trees." One big dead tree with a cottonmouth under it would have changed that, would have glorified Dry Fork Creek for Carol, coons or no coons—*piscivorus piscivorus* caught poaching, out of his territory, off the edge of his map, beyond his range. I felt her disappointment and was sorry the snakes were not there. "Don't be disappointed," she said. "When we go down the Cemocheckobee, cottonmouths will show us the way."

Buffalo disappeared from Georgia in early Colonial time. William Bartram noted this when he visited the colony and wrote *Travels in Georgia and Florida, 1773–74.* Bartram, from Philadelphia, was the first naturalist to describe in detail the American subtropics. After his book reached London, sedentary English poets cribbed from his descriptions (Wordsworth, for example, and Coleridge). Ten miles south of Dry Fork Creek, Sam, Carol, and I crossed Bartram's path. In Bartram's words, "We came into an open Forest of Pines, Scrub white Oaks, Black Jacks, Plumb, Hicory, Grapes Vines, Rising a sort of Ridge, come to a flat levill Plain, and at the upper side of this, levell at the foot of the hills of the great Ridge, is the great Buffiloe Lick, which are vast Pits, licked in the Clay, formerly by the Buffiloes, and now kept smoothe and open by Cattle, deer, and horses, that resort here constantly to lick the clay, which is a greesey Marle of various colours, Red, Yellow & white, & has a sweetish taste, but nothing saltish that I could perceive." Bartram was describing what is now Philomath, Georgia 30659—a one-street town consisting of thirty houses and a buffalo lick. Philomath was established, early in the nineteenth century, as a seat of learning—hence the name. The town was the address of an academy whose students, in time, vanished like the buffalo. Now it was a place of preeminent silence under big oaks, and as we glided into town we were the only thing that moved. Ninety blacks, fifty whites lived there, but no one was out in the midday shade. The almost idling engine was the only sound. In an L-shaped elegant clapboard house, built in 1795, lived Dorothy Daniel Wright. Sam and Carol, having read Bartram's description and having determined that the buffalo lick was still intact, wanted to see it and, they hoped, to register it as a Georgia Natural Area. Miss Wright was the person to see. It was her lick. She was in her upper sixties. Her hair was white and swept upward, and crowned with a braided gold bun. Her welcome was warm. She showed us the lick. Cattle and deer had licked it slick all through her girlhood, she said. Now it was covered with grass, some hawthorn and sumac, and dominated by an immense, outreaching laurel oak. Carol squatted flat-footed, knees high, and dug with her hands for various colors of clay. She ate some blue clay, and handed pieces to me and Sam. It was sweet, bland, alkaline, slightly chewy. "My first thought was 'soapy,' " she said. "I expected it to get stronger, but it didn't. The final thought was 'sweetness.' " She put a bit more in her mouth and ate it contemplatively. There was, apparently, no sodium chloride in this ground. Phosphate, sodium, and calcium are what the buffalo licked. Where did they get their salt? "Twelve miles away there was salt," Miss Wright said. "Twelve miles is nothin' to a buffalo roamin' around. Between the two licks, they got all the minerals they needed for their bovine metabolism." Miss Wright had taught biology and chemistry in various high schools for forty-three years. She was eager to register the Great Buffalo Lick Natural Area, which had once been a boundary-line landmark separating the Georgia colony from the territory of the Creeks and Cherokees. She took us home to a lunch of salad and saltines. Into the salad went mushrooms, violets, and trout lilies that Carol had gathered in the mountains the day before.

Leaving Philomath, heading south, Sam commented how easy and pleasant that experience had been and how tense such encounters could sometimes be. He talked about a redneck peanut farmer in south Georgia, owner of a potential Natural Area. This redneck had taken one look at Sam's beard and had seemed ready to kill him then and there.

"What is a redneck, Sam?"

"You know what a redneck is, you little Yankee bastard."

"I want to hear your definition."

"A redneck is a fat slob in a pickup truck with a rifle across the back. He hates 'niggers.' He would rather have his kids ignorant than go to school with colored. I guess I don't like rednecks. I guess I've known some."

"Some of my best friends are rednecks," Carol said.

D.O.R. blacksnake, five miles south of Irwinton—old and bloated. "I'll just get it off the road, so its body won't be further humiliated," Carol said. Across a fence, a big sow was grunting. Carol carried the snake to the fence. She said, "Here, piggy-poo, look what I've got for you." She tossed the snake across the fence. The sow bit off the snake's head and ate it like an apple.

"Interesting," Carol said, "that we can feed a rotten snake to something we in turn will eat."

I said I would rather eat the buffalo lick.

Carol said, "I'll tell you the truth, I've had better clay."

We were out of the piedmont and down on the coastal plain, into the north of south Georgia. The roadside ads were riddled with bullet holes. "PREPARE TO MEET JESUS CHRIST THE LORD." "WE WANT TO WIPE OUT CANCER IN YOUR LIFETIME." "WE CANNOT ACCEPT TIRES THAT HAVE BEEN CAPPED AS TRADE-INS."

Johnny Cash was back. Indians were now his theme. He was singing about a dam that was going to flood Seneca land, although the Senecas had been promised title to their land "as long as the moon shall rise." Cash's voice was deeper than ever. He sounded as if he were smoking a peace pipe through an oboe. Carol hugged herself. "As long . . . as the moon . . . shall rise . . . As long . . . as the rivers . . . flow."

"DON'T LOSE YOUR SOUL BY THE MARK OF THE BEAST."

We ate muskrat that night in a campsite on flat ground beside Big Sandy Creek, in Wilkinson County, innermost Georgia—muskrat with beans, chili powder, onions, tomatoes, and kelp. "I have one terrible handicap," Carol said. "I cannot follow a recipe." The muskrat, though, was very good. Carol had parboiled it for twenty minutes and then put it through a meat grinder, medium grind. Firewood was scarce, because the area was much used by fishermen who were prone to build fires and fish all night. Carol went up a tall spruce pine, and when she was forty feet or so above the ground she began to break off dead limbs and throw them down. She had to throw them like spears to clear the living branches of the tree. Pine burns oily, but that would not matter tonight. The muskrat was in a pot. Sam and I built up the fire. He pitched a tent.

To pass time before dinner, I put the canoe into the river and paddled slowly downstream. Carol called to me from the tree, "Watch for snakes. They'll be overhead, in the limbs of trees." She was not warning me; she was trying to raise the pleasure of the ride. "If you don't see the snake, you can tell by the splash," she went on. "A frog splash is a concentrated splash. A snake splash is a long splat." Gliding, watching, I went a quarter of a mile without a splash or a splat. It was dusk. The water was growing dark. I heard the hoot of a barred owl. Going back against the current, I worked up an appetite for muskrat.

After dinner, in moonlight, Sam and Carol and I got into the canoe and went up the river. A bend to the left, a bend to the right, and we penetrated the intense darkness of a river swamp that seemed to reach out unendingly. We could only guess at its dimensions. Upland swamps occur in areas between streams. River swamps are in the flood plains of rivers, and nearly all the streams in the Georgia coastal plain have them.

They can be as much as six miles wide, and when the swamps of two or more big rivers connect, the result can be a vast and separate world. The darkness in there was so rich it felt warm. It was not total, for bars and slats of moonlight occasionally came through, touched a root or a patch of water. Essentially, however, everything was black: black water, black vegetation—water-standing maples, cypress—black on black. Columnar trunks were all around us, and we knew the channel only by the feel of the current, which sometimes seemed to be coming through from more than one direction. Here the black water sucked and bubbled, roiled by, splashed through the roots of the trees. Farther on, it was silent again. Silent ourselves, we pushed on into the black. Carol moved a flashlight beam among the roots of trees. She held the flashlight to her nose, because the eye can see much more if the line of sight is closely parallel to the beam. She inspected minutely the knobby waterlines of the trees. Something like a sonic boom cracked in our ears. "Jesus, what was that?"

"Beaver."

The next two slaps were even louder than the first. Carol ignored the beaver, and continued to move the light. It stopped. Out there in the obsidian was a single blue eye.

"A blue single eye is a spider," she said. "Two eyes is a frog. Two eyes almost touching is a snake. An alligator's eyes are blood red."

Two tiny coins now came up in her light. "Move in there," she said. "I want that one."

With a throw of her hand, she snatched up a frog. It was a leopard frog, and she let him go. He was much within his range. Carol was looking for river frogs, pig frogs, carpenter frogs, whose range peripheries we were stalking. She saw another pair of eyes. The canoe moved in. Her hand swept out unseen and made a perfect tackle, thighs to knees. This was a bronze frog, home on the range. Another pair of eyes, another catch, another disappointment—a bullfrog. Now another shattering slap on the water. Another. The beaver slapped only when the canoe was moving upstream. The frog chorus, filling the background, varied in pitch and intensity, rose and fell. Repeatedly came the hoot of the barred owl.

Sam dipped a cup and had a drink. "I feel better about drinking water out of swamps than out of most rivers," he said. "It's filtered. No one ever says a good word for a swamp. The whole feeling up to now has been 'Fill it in—it's too wet to plow, too dry to fish.' Most people stay out of swamps. I love them. I like the water, the reptiles, the amphibians. There is so much life in a swamp. The sounds are so different. Frogs, owls, birds, beavers. Birds sound different in swamps."

"You see a coon in here and you realize it's his whole world," Carol said.

"It's a beautiful home with thousands of creatures," Sam said.

With all this ecological intoxication, I thought they were going to fall out of the canoe.

"Life came out of the swamps," Sam said. "And now swamps are among the last truly wild places left."

We went back downstream. Tobacco smoke was in the air over the river. Occasionally, on the bank, we saw an orange-red glow, momentarily illuminating a black face. Fishing lines, slanting into the stream, were visible against the light of small fires. The canoe moved soundlessly by, and on into the darkness. "The groids sure love to fish," Sam murmured. The moon was low. It was midnight.

Now, at noon, a hundred miles or so to the southeast and by another stream, we were sitting on the big felled oak, pouring out the last of the wine, with Chap Causey moving toward us a foot at a time in his American dragline crane. He swung a pair of mats around behind him and backed up a bit more, and as he went on gutting the streambed the oak began to tremble. It must have weighed two or three tons, but it was trembling and felt like an earthquake—time to move. Carol picked up a piece of dry otter scat. She bounced it in the palm of her hand and looked upcurrent at the unaltered stream and downcurrent into the new ditch. She said, "You can talk about coons' being able to go off into the woods and eat nuts and berries, because they're omnivores. But not this otter. He's finished." She broke open the scat. Inside it were fishbones and hair—hair of a mouse or hair of a young rabbit. There were fish otoliths as well, two of them, like small stones. She flung it all into the stream. "He's done for," she said, and waved goodbye to Chap Causey.

On down the dirt road from the stream-channelization project, we saw ahead a D.O.R.

"Looks like a bad one," Carol said.

Sam stopped. "Yes, it's a bad one," he said. "Canebrake. Do you want to eat him?"

Carol leaned over and looked. "He's too old. Throw him out of the road, the poor darlin'. What gets me is that some bastard is proud of having run over him. When I die, I don't want to be humiliated like that."

Sam threw the rattlesnake out of the road. Then we headed south-west through underdeveloped country, almost innocent of towns—Alma, Douglas, Adel, Moultrie, a hundred miles from Alma to Moultrie.

D.O.R. king snake, blue jay, sparrow hawk, wood thrush, raccoon, catbird, cotton rat. The poor darlin's. Threw them out of the road.

A.O.R. hobo—man with a dog. "Oh, there's a good guy," Carol said as we passed him. "He has a dog and a bedroll. What else do you need?"

D.O.R. opossum. Cook County. Three miles east of Adel. Carol spoke admiringly of the creature flexibility of the opossum. Among the oldest of mammals, the possum goes all the way back to Cretaceous time, she said, and, like people, it has never specialized, in a biological sense. "You can specialize yourself out of existence. Drain the home of the otter. The otter dies. The opossum, though, can walk away from an ecological disaster. So much for that. Try something else. He eats any-thing. He lives almost anywhere. That's why the possum is not extinct. That's why the possum has been so successful." One place this particular possum was never going to walk away from was Georgia Highway 76. Technology, for him the ultimate ecological disaster, had clouted him at seventy miles an hour.

Between Moultrie and Doerun, in the watershed of the Ochlock-onee, was a lake in a pine grove surrounded by fifty acres of pitcher plants. They belonged to a couple named Barber, from Moultrie, who had read about the Natural Areas Council and had offered their pitcher plants to posterity. Sam and Carol, posterity, would accept. This was the largest colony of pitcher plants any of us was ever likely to see. Bright-green leaves, ruddy blooms, they glistened in the sun and nodded in the breeze and reached out from the lakeshore like tulips from a Dutch canal. Barber cut one off at the base and held up a leaf—folded upon itself like a narrow goblet, half full of water. The interior was lined with bristles, pointing downward. In the water were dozens of winged crea-tures, some still moving, most not. Barber had interrupted a handsome meal. His pitcher plants, in aggregate, could probably eat a ton of bugs a day. Sam said he sure was pleased to be able to make the pitcher plants a Georgia Natural Area. Carol saw a tiny water snake. She picked it up. It coiled in her hand and snapped at her. She talked gently to it until it settled down. "Are you going to be good now?" she said. She opened her hand, and the snake sat there, placidly, on her palm. The Barbers did not seem charmed. They said nothing and did not move. Carol set down the snake. It departed, and so did the Barbers. They went back to

Moultrie in their air-conditioned car, leaving us their lake, their pines, their pitcher plants.

We jumped into the lake with a bar of soap and scrubbed ourselves up for dinner. In places, the lake was warm from the sun and in places cold from springs. We set up the tent and built a fire. The breeze was cool in the evening in the pines. Carol's stomach growled like a mastiff. She said that when she was hungry she could make her stomach growl on cue. It growled again. She had a tape recorder in the car. Sam got it and recorded the growls, which seemed marketable. He said they could scare away burglars. We fried beefsteaks and turtle steaks under a gibbous moon. We buried the fossils of pleasure: three cow bones and a bottle that had held The Glenlivet. Frogs were hooting. There were no owls. We slept like bears.

At six in the morning, we got into the canoe and moved slowly around the lake. Sam cast for bass. He could flick his lure seventy feet and drop it on a pine needle. He could lay it under stumps with the delicacy of an eyedropper, or drive it, if he wanted to, halfway down the lake. He caught two bass. One wrapped itself hopelessly into a big waterlogged multiple branch. We pulled the branch up out of the water. The bass had himself woven into it like a bird in a cage. Under the blue sky and star-burst clusters of longleaf pine—pitcher plants far as you could see, the lake blue and cool—we cooked the bass in butter and ate it with fried turtle eggs. Then we fried salt-risen bread in the bass butter with more turtle eggs and poured Tate City honey over the bread. Chicory coffee with milk and honey. Fish-crackling off the bottom of the pan.

The yolk of a turtle egg cooks readily to a soft, mushy yellow. The albumen, though, pops and bubbles and jumps around the pan, and will not congeal. No matter how blazing the heat beneath it may be, the white of the egg of the snapping turtle will not turn milky and set. It will jump like a frog and bounce and dance and skitter all over the pan until your patience snaps or the fire dies. So you give up trying to cook it. You swallow it hot and raw.

D.O.R. cat. D.O.R. dog. Near the Mitchell County line. Carol sighed, but no move was made to stop. We were heading west on 37 to check out a river that the Natural Areas Council had been told was like no other in Georgia. Florida was only forty miles away. The terrain was flat and serene between the quiet towns—Camilla, Newton, Elmodel.

Cattle stood on light-green grassland under groves of dark pecans. Sometimes the road was a corridor walled with pines. Sometimes the margins opened out into farms, then closed down toward small cabins, more palisades of pine.

D.O.R. gray squirrel. "We could eat him," Carol said.

"We've got enough food," said Sam.

More pines, more pecans, more farms, a mild morning under a blue-and-white sky. Out of the sky came country music—the Carter Sisters, Johnny Cash, philosophy falling like hail: "It's not easy to be all alone, but time goes by and life goes on . . . for after night there comes a dawn. Yes, time goes by and life goes on."

D.O.R. fox squirrel. Baker Country. He was as warm as in life, and he was in perfect shape. Kneeling in the road, Carol held out his long, feathery silver-gray tail so that it caught the sunlight. "There aren't many things prettier than that," she said. "Makes a human being sort of jealous not to have a pretty tail like that." Gently, she brushed the squirrel and daubed blood from his head. He looked alive in her hands. She put him in a plastic bag. The ice was low. We stopped at the next icehouse and bought twenty-five pounds.

D.O.R. nighthawk, fresh as the squirrel. Carol kept the hawk for a while in her lap, just to look at him. He could have been an Aztec emblem—wings half spread, head in profile, feathers patterned in blacks and browns and patches of white. Around the mouth were stiff bristles, fanned out like a radar screen, adapted for catching insects.

D.O.R. box turtle.

D.O.R. loggerhead shrike.

D.O.R. gas station. It was abandoned, its old pumps rusting; beside the pumps, a twenty-year-old Dodge with four flat tires.

D.O.R. cottonmouth. Three miles east of Bluffton. Clay County. Finding him there was exciting to Carol. We were nearing the Cemocheckobee, the river we had come to see, and the presence of one cottonmouth here on the road implied crowded colonies along the river. There was no traffic, no point in moving him immediately off the road. Carol knelt beside him. "He was getting ready to shed. He would have been a lot prettier when he had," she said. The skin was dull olive. Carol felt along the spine to a point about three-quarters of the way back and squeezed. The dead snake coiled. "That is what really frightens some people," she said. She lifted the head and turned it so that we could see, between the mouth and the nostrils, the deep pits, sensory organs, through which the striking snake had homed on his targets. Slowly, Carol opened the creature's mouth. The manuals of herpetology tell you not to do that, tell you, in fact, not to touch a dead cottonmouth, because through reflex action a dead one can strike and kill a human being. Now a fang was visible—a short brown needle projecting down from the upper jaw. "You have to be very careful not to scratch your finger on one of those," Carol said. She pressed with her fingertips behind the eyes, directly on the poison sacs, and a drop of milky fluid fell onto a stick she held in her other hand. Four more drops followed, forming a dome of venom. "That amount could kill you," she said, and she pressed out another drop. "Did you know that this is where they got the idea for the hypodermic syringe?" Another drop. "It has to get into the bloodstream. You could drink all you want and it wouldn't hurt you." She placed the cottonmouth off the road. Carol once milked honeysuckle until she had about two ounces, which she then drank. The fluid was so concentratedly sweet it almost made her sick.

Carol's purse fell open as we got back into the car, and out of it spilled a .22-calibre revolver in a case that looked much like a compact. Also in the purse was a Big Brother tear-gas gun, flashlight bulbs, chapstick, shampoo, suntan lotion, and several headbands. Once, when she was off in a swamp frogging and salamandering, a state trooper came upon the car and—thinking it might be an abandoned vehicle—rummaged through it. He found the purse and opened it. He discovered the pistol, the chapstick, the shampoo, et cetera, and a pink garter belt and black net stockings. He might have sent out a five-state alert, but Carol just then emerged from the swamp. She was on her way, she told him, to make a call on Kimberly-Clark executives in an attempt to get them to register some forest and riverbank land with the Natural Areas Council, and for that mission the black net stockings would be as useful as the pistol might be in a swamp or the chapstick in a blistering sun. "Yes, Ma'am." The visit to the Kleenex people was successful, as it happened, and the result was the Griffin's Landing Registered Natural Area, fifty acres—a series of fossil beds on the Savannah River containing by the many thousands *Crassostrea gigantissima*, forty-million-year-old oysters, the largest that ever lived.

Down a dirt road, across a railroad track, and on through woods that scraped the car on both sides, Sam worked his way as far as he could toward the river's edge. We took down the canoe, and carried it to the water. The Cemocheckobee was a rejuvenated stream. Widening its valley, long ago, it had formed relaxed meanders, and now, apparently, the land was rising beneath it, and the river had speeded up and was cutting deeply into the meanders. The current was strong—nothing spectacular, nothing white, but forceful and swift. It ran beneath a jungle of overhanging trees. The river was compact and intimate. The distance from bank to bank was only about thirty feet, so there could be no getting away from the trees. "I'd venture to say we'll see our share of snakes today," Carol exulted. "Let's go! This is cottonmouth country!" Carol shoved up the sleeves of her sweatshirt over her elbows. Sam went to the car and got a snakebite kit.

I had thought I might be apprehensive about this part of the journey. I didn't see how I could help but be. Now I realized that I was having difficulty walking toward the river. "Sam," I said, "wouldn't you prefer that I paddle in the stern?" I had put in many more hours than he had in canoes on rivers, so it seemed only correct to me that Sam should sit up in the bow and fend off branches and cottonmouths while I guided the canoe from the commanding position in the rear.

"I'll go in the stern," said Sam. "Carol will go in the middle to collect snakes. You go in the bow." So much for that. It was his canoe. I got in and moved to the bow. They got in, and we shoved off.

The canoe found the current, accelerated, went downstream fifty feet, and smashed into a magnolia branch. I expected cottonmouths to strike me in both shoulders and the groin. But the magnolia proved to be snakeless. We shot on through and downriver. We could not avoid the overhanging branches. The current was too fast and there were too many of them. Once or twice a minute, we punched through the leafy twigs reaching down from a horizontal limb. But I began to settle down. There weren't any snakes, after all—not in the first mile, anyway. And things Carol was saying made a difference. She said, for example, that snakes plop off branches long before the canoe gets to them. She also said that cottonmouths rarely go out onto branches. They stay back at the river's edge and in the swamps. Snakes on branches are, in the main, as harmless as licorice. Bands of tension loosened and began to drop away. I looked ahead. At the next bend, the river was veiled in a curtain of water oak. I was actually hoping to see a snake hit the surface, but none did. We slipped through and into the clear.

This was heavy current for a river with no white water, and when we rested the river gave us a fast drift. Scenes quickly changed, within the steep banks, the incised meanders, against backgrounds of beech and laurel, white oak, spruce pine, Venus maidenhair and resurrection fern. We came upon a young coon at the foot of a tree. He looked at us with no apparent fear. We pulled in to the bank. "Hey, there, you highstepper, you," Carol said. "Get up that tree!" The coon put a paw on the tree and went up a foot or two and looked around. "Why aren't you afraid?" Carol went on. "Are you O.K., cooner?" The raccoon's trouble—probably—was that he had never seen a human. He was insufficiently afraid, and Carol began to worry about him. So she got out of the canoe and went after him. The coon moved up the tree fifteen feet. The tree was a slender maple. Carol started up it like a rope climber. The coon stayed where he was. Carol said, "I'm not climbing the tree to make him jump out. I'll just go high enough to let him know he ought to be afraid of people." When she got near him, the coon scrambled to the high branches, where he hung on to one and swayed. Carol stopped about twenty feet up. "Hey, coon! We're no good. Don't you know that?" she called to him. Then she slid on down. "Let that be a lesson to you!" she called from the bottom.

We moved on downstream, passing blue-tailed skinks and salamanders, animal tracks on every flat. A pair of beavers dived into the water and went around slapping the surface, firing blanks. Carol saw the mouth of their den, and she got out of the canoe, climbed the bank, and stuck her head inside. She regretted that she had not brought a flashlight with her. We moved on. We passed a banded snake sitting on a limb. He produced mild interest. Fear was gone from me. It had gone off with the flow of the river. There was a light splash to the right—as if from a slide, not a dive. No one saw what made it. "Otter," Carol said. "Pull in to the opposite bank—over there. Quickly!" We stopped the canoe, and held on to bush stems of the riverbank and waited. Nothing happened. The quiet grew. "The otter will come up and look at us," Carol said. We waited. Smooth, the river moved—never the same, always the same. No otter. "He is an extraordinarily intelligent and curious animal," Carol said. "He could go off somewhere, if he wanted to, just to breathe. But he wants to see us. He will not be able to stand it much longer. He will have to come up." Up came a face, chin on the water—dark bright eyes in a dark-brown head, small ears, wide snout: otter. His gaze was direct and unflinching. He looked at us until he had seen his fill; then he went back under. "Wouldn't you like to live in this creek?" Carol said. "You'd never get lonely. Wouldn't you like to play with the otter?"

A waterfall, about twelve feet high, poured into the river from the left. Two hundred yards downstream, another fall dropped into the river from the right. The feeder streams of the Cemocheckobee were not cutting down as fast as the river itself, and these hanging tributaries poured in from above, all the way down. We now moved through stands of royal fern under big sycamores and big beeches, and past another waterfall. "This is otter, beaver, coon heaven," Carol said. Her only disappointment was the unexpected scarcity of snakes. She said she had seen more than her share of "magnolia-leaf snakes" that day. Her imagination, charged with hope and anticipation, could, and frequently did, turn magnolia leaves into snakes, green upon the branches. I found myself feeling disappointed, too. Only one lousy banded snake. The day was incomplete.

Sam said the threat to this river was the lumber industry. Logging was going on in the forests on both sides, and he would try to persuade the lumbermen to register the river—and its marginal lands—before the day came when it would be too late. While he was speaking, I saw a snake on a log at the water's edge, and pointed to it, interrupting him.

"Is that a banded snake?"

"That is not a banded snake," Carol said.

"Is it a bad one?"

"It's a bad one, friend."

"Well, at last. Where have you been all day?"

He had been right there, of course, in his own shaft of sun, and the sight of a shining aluminum canoe with three figures in it was not going to cause him to move. Moving back was not in his character. He would stay where he was or go toward something that seemed to threaten him. Whatever else he might be, he was not afraid. He was a cottonmouth, a water moccasin. Carol was closer to him than I was, and I felt no fear at all. Sam, in the stern, was closest of all, because we were backing up toward the snake. I remember thinking, as we moved closer, that I preferred that they not bring the thing into the canoe, but that was the sum of my concern; we were ten miles downstream from where we had begun. The moccasin did not move. We were now right next to it. Sam reached toward it with his paddle.

"Rough him up a little to teach him to beware of humans," Carol said. "But don't hurt him."

Under the snake Sam slipped the paddle, and worked it a bit, like a spatula, so that the snake came up onto the blade. Sam lifted the cottonmouth into the air. Sam rocked the paddle. "Come on," he said. "Come on, there. Open your mouth so John can see the cotton."

"Isn't he magnificent?" Carol said. "Set him down, Sam. He isn't going to open his mouth."

Sam returned the moccasin to the log. The canoe moved on into a gorge. The walls of the gorge were a hundred feet high.

The Cemocheckobee was itself a feeder stream, ending in the Chattahoochee, there in southwestern Georgia, at the Alabama line. An appointment elsewhere with the Chattahoochee—a red-letter one for Sam and Carol—drew us back north. The Chattahoochee is Georgia's most prodigious river. Atlanta developed where railheads met the river. The Chattahoochee rises off the slopes of the Brasstown Bald, Georgia's highest mountain, seven miles from North Carolina, and flows to Florida, where its name changes at the frontier. It is thereafter called the Appalachicola. In all its four hundred Georgia miles, what seems most remarkable about this river is that it flows into Atlanta nearly wild. Through a series of rapids between high forested bluffs, it enters the city clear and clean. From parts of the Chattahoochee within the city of Atlanta, no structures are visible—just water, sky, and woodland. The circumstance is nostalgic, archaic, and unimaginable. It is as if an unbefouled Willamette were to flow wild into Portland—Charles into Boston, Missouri into Omaha, Hudson into New York, Delaware into Philadelphia, James into Richmond, Cuyahoga into Cleveland (the Cuyahoga caught fire one day, and fire engines had to come put out the blazing river). Atlanta deserves little credit for the clear Chattahoochee, though, because the Chattahoochee is killed before it leaves the city. It dies between Marietta Boulevard and South Cobb Drive, just below the Atlanta Water Intake, at the point where thirty-five million gallons of partially treated sewage and forty million gallons of raw sewage are poured into the river every day. A short distance below that stand two enormous power plants, whose effluent pipes raise the temperature of the river. A seven-pound brown trout was caught recently not far above the Water Intake. It is difficult to imagine what sort of fin-rotted, five-legged, uranium-gilled, web-mouthed monster could live in the river by Georgia Power. Seen from the air (Sam showed it to me once in his plane), the spoiling of the Chattahoochee is instant, from river-water blue to sewer ochre-brown, as if a pair of colored ribbons had been sewn together there by the city.

Now a sewer line was projected to run upstream beside the river to fresh subdivisions that would bloom beyond the city's perimeter highway. The sewer would not actually be in the water, but, unless it could be tunnelled or not built at all, it would cause the clear-cutting of every tree in a sixty-foot swath many miles long. A segment of the sewer was already under construction. The Georgia Natural Areas Council was among the leadership in an effort to put down this specific project and at the same time to urge a bill through the legislature that would protect permanently the river and its overview. Sam had asked Jimmy Carter to come get into a canoe and shoot the metropolitan rapids and see for himself the value and the vulnerability of the river. Carter was willing. So, in three canoes, six of us put in under the perimeter highway, I-285, and paddled into Atlanta.

Sam had Carter in his bow. Carter might be governor of Georgia but not of Sam's canoe. Carol and I had the second canoe. In the third was a state trooper, who had a pistol on his hip that could have sunk a frigate. In the stern was James Morrison, of the federal government, the Bureau of Outdoor Recreation's man in Atlanta. He wore wet-suit bootees and rubber kneepads and seemed to be ready to go down the Colorado in an acorn.

The current was strong. The canoes moved smartly downstream. Carter was a lithe man, an athletic man in his forties—at home, obviously enough, in boats. He was wearing a tan windbreaker, khaki trousers, and white basketball shoes. He had a shock of wind-tossed sandy hair. In the course of the day, he mentioned that he had grown up in Archery, Georgia, by a swamp of the Kinchafoonee and the Choctawhatchee. He and his friend A. D. Davis, who was black, had built a twelve-foot bateau. "When it rained and we couldn't work in the fields, we went down to the creek and set out set hooks for catfish and eels, and we drifted downstream in the bateau hunting ducks with a shotgun. We fished for bass and red-bellies, and we waded for jack. The bateau weighed eighty pounds. I could pick it up." Archery was three miles west of Plains, a crossroads with a short row of stores and less than a thousand people. Sam, Carol, and I had passed through Plains—in fifteen seconds —on our way north. An enormous red-lettered sign over the stores said, "PLAINS, GEORGIA, HOME OF JIMMY CARTER." Carter had played basketball at Plains High School, had gone on to Annapolis and into nuclear submarines, and had come back to Plains in 1953 to farm peanuts and to market them for himself and others, businesses he continued as he went on into the legislature and upward to become governor. The career of his boyhood friend had been quite different. The last Carter had heard of A. D. Davis, Davis was in jail for manslaughter.

Now, on the Chattahoochee, the Governor said, "We're lucky here in Georgia that the environment thing has risen nationally, because Georgia is less developed than some states and still has much to save." With that, he and Sam went into the largest set of rapids in the city of Atlanta. The rip was about a hundred yards long, full of Vs confusing to the choice, broad ledges, haystacks, eddies, and tumbling water. They were good rapids, noisy and alive, and strong enough to flip a canoe that might hit a rock and swing broadside.

In the shadow of a two-hundred-foot bluff, we pulled out on a small island to survey the scene. Carol said the bluff was a gneiss and was full of garnets. The Governor had binoculars. With them, he discovered a muskrat far out in the river. The muskrat was gnawing on a branch that had been stopped by a boulder. "He's sniffin' around that little old limb on top of that rock," Carter said. "Maybe he's eating the lichens off it. Look, there's another. Who owns the land here?"

"Various people," Morrison said. "Some are speculators. A lot of it is owned by Alfred Kennedy."

"Kennedy?"

"A director of the First National Bank," Carol said.

"Is he a good guy, so far as conservancy goes?"

"From what I hear, he's too busy making money."

"Sometimes it's better to slip up on people like that," Carter told her. "Rather than make an issue of it right away." He spoke in a low voice, almost shyly. There was a touch of melancholy in his face that disappeared, as it did frequently, when he grinned. A trillium caught his eye. He asked her what it was, and she told him. "And what's that?" he said.

"Dog hobble," Carol said. "*Leucothoë.* Look here." She pointed at the ground. "A coon track."

The canoes moved on, and the next stop was a visit with a fisherman who was casting from the bank. He was middle-aged and weathered, a classical, prototype fisherman, many years on the river. He was wreathed in smiles at sight of the Governor. I looked hard at Sam, but nothing in his face indicated that he had planted the man there. The fisherman, Ron Sturdevant, showed the Governor a Kodacolor print of a twenty-three-inch rainbow he had recently caught right here under this bluff. "I guess

I'm glad I met you," Sturdevant said. "I'm glad you're taking this trip. I'm worried about the river."

"I hope we can keep it this way," Carter said.

We climbed from the river through a deep wood of oaks and big pines to a cave in which families of Cherokees had once lived. It was about a hundred feet up. The view swept the river, no structures visible. "Who owns this place?"

Sam said, "Alfred Kennedy."

"And he hasn't even slept here," said Carol.

"Have you slept here, Carol?" the Governor asked her.

"Many times," she told him. "With a dog named Catfish."

Morrison said, "There's gold here, around the Indian cave. It's never been mined."

"That would be a good way to keep this place undisturbed," Carter said. "To announce that there was gold up here."

Back on the river, he used his binoculars while Sam paddled. He saw four more muskrats and an automobile, upside down in the water, near the far bank. He also saw a turtle.

"What kind is it?" Carol asked him.

"If I knew what kind it was, I could tell you." He handed the binoculars across to her, too late.

"I've been down through here and seen fifteen turtles with bullet holes in their shells," Carol told him.

"What kind?" Carter said.

"Cooters and sliders."

There was a racket of engines. Out of nowhere came two motorcyclists riding *in* the river. A mile or so later, we took out, beside an iron bridge. Carol said she had washed her hair any number of times under that bridge.

The Governor invited us home for lunch. The mansion was new— a million-dollar neo-Palladian Xanadu, formal as a wedding cake, and exquisitely landscaped. Carol and Sam and I were ropy from a thousand miles of mountains, rivers, and swamps. None of us had changed clothes in nearly a week, but we would soon be eating grilled cheese sandwiches at a twenty-foot table under a crystal chandelier. The Governor, for that matter, did not look laundered anymore—mud on his trousers, mud on his basketball shoes. We parked in back of the mansion. A backboard, hoop, and net were mounted there. A ball sat on the pavement. Before going in, we shot baskets for a while.

"The river is just great," the Governor said, laying one in. "And it ought to be kept the way it is. It's almost heartbreaking to feel that the river is in danger of destruction. I guess I'll write a letter to all the landowners and say, 'If you'll use some self-restraint, it'll decrease the amount of legal restraint put on you in the future.' I don't think people want to incur the permanent wrath of the governor or the legislature."

"I've tried to talk to property owners," Carol said. "To get them to register their land with the Natural Areas Council. But they wouldn't even talk to me."

The Governor said, "To be blunt about it, Carol, why would they?"

The Governor had the ball and was dribbling in place, as if contemplating a property owner in front of him, one-on-one. He went to the basket, shot, and missed. Carol got the rebound and fed the ball to Sam. He shot. He missed, too.

# Pieces of the Frame

"The Search for Marvin Gardens" is a counterpoint to "Travels in Georgia," a portrait of urban blight in Atlantic City, once the resort kingdom of the New Jersey shore. The piece has a virtuoso air. It tells of history gone sour, a story of "deep and complex decay" boldly set within the frame of Monopoly, a parlor game whose rules are a primer in heartless, irrational economics. As its name suggests, Monopoly is capitalism par excellence, "chess on a Wall Street level." Its champions are masters of the quick kill, players of the same perilous game that built and destroyed Atlantic City. Since Monopoly was invented by a frequent visitor to the resort, the game board has an array of local place names: Boardwalk, Park Place, Marvin Gardens.

In building his story, McPhee neatly sandwiches two accounts: an imaginary best-of-seven match with an anonymous opponent, and a concurrent trip through the devastated streets of Atlantic City. The game's familiar elements—going to jail, buying hotels, extracting rents—detonate ironic bombshells in the city, which "looks like Metz in 1919, Cologne in 1944." His juxtapositions of these two scenes, and their multiple planes of history, memory, or geography, are always quick, sharp, and caustic. The crosscutting produces a formal tour de force, reminiscent of Faulkner's *As I Lay Dying,* a story equally funny and mordant. McPhee's diamond-hard, only half-joking style brings him as close as he wishes to overt political statement. Monopoly is a game of undeserved wins and losses, and so was Atlantic City. His search reveals that one of the few neighborhoods to survive is Marvin Gardens, a middle-class sanctuary lying south of the Boardwalk, well beyond the city limits.—*WLH*

# The Search for
# Marvin Gardens

Go. I roll the dice—a six and a two. Through the air I move my token, the flatiron, to Vermont Avenue, where dog packs range.

The dogs are moving (some are limping) through ruins, rubble, fire damage, open garbage. Doorways are gone. Lath is visible in the crumbling walls of the buildings. The street sparkles with shattered glass. I have never seen, anywhere, so many broken windows. A sign —"Slow, Children at Play"—has been bent backward by an automobile. At the lighthouse, the dogs turn up Pacific and disappear. George Meade, Army engineer, built the lighthouse—brick upon brick, six hundred thousand bricks, to reach up high enough to throw a beam twenty miles over the sea. Meade, seven years later, saved the Union at Gettysburg.

I buy Vermont Avenue for $100. My opponent is a tall, shadowy figure, across from me, but I know him well, and I know his game like a favorite tune. If he can, he will always go for the quick kill. And when it is foolish to go for the quick kill he will be foolish. On the whole, though, he is a master assessor of percentages. It is a mistake to underestimate him. His eleven carries his top hat to St. Charles Place, which he buys for $140.

The sidewalks of St. Charles Place have been cracked to shards by through-growing weeds. There are no buildings. Mansions, hotels once stood here. A few street lamps now drop cones of light on broken glass and vacant space behind a chain-link fence that some great machine has in places bent to the ground. Five plane trees—in full summer leaf, flecking the light—are all that live on St. Charles Place.

Block upon block, gradually, we are cancelling each other out—in the blues, the lavenders, the oranges, the greens. My opponent follows a plan of his own devising. I use the Hornblower & Weeks opening and the Zuricher defense. The first game draws tight, will soon finish. In 1971, a group of people in Racine, Wisconsin, played for seven hundred and sixty-eight hours. A game begun a month later in Danville, California, lasted eight hundred and twenty hours. These are official records, and they stun us. We have been playing for eight minutes. It amazes us that Monopoly is thought of as a long game. It is possible to play to a complete, absolute, and final conclusion in less than fifteen minutes, all within the rules as written. My opponent and I have done so thousands of times. No wonder we are sitting across from each other now in this best-of-seven series for the international singles championship of the world.

On Illinois Avenue, three men lean out from second-story windows. A girl is coming down the street. She wears dungarees and a bright-red shirt, has ample breasts and a Hadendoan Afro, a black halo, two feet in diameter. Ice rattles in the glasses in the hands of the men.

"Hey, sister!"

"Come on up!"

She looks up, looks from one to another to the other, looks them flat in the eye.

"What for?" she says, and she walks on.

I buy Illinois for $240. It solidifies my chances, for I already own Kentucky and Indiana. My opponent pales. If he had landed first on Illinois, the game would have been over then and there, for he has houses built on Boardwalk and Park Place, we share the railroads equally, and we have cancelled each other everywhere else. We never trade.

In 1852, R. B. Osborne, an immigrant Englishman, civil engineer, surveyed the route of a railroad line that would run from Camden to Absecon Island, in New Jersey, traversing the state from the Delaware River to the barrier beaches of the sea. He then sketched in the plan of a "bathing village" that would surround the eastern terminus of the line. His pen flew glibly, framing and naming spacious avenues parallel to the shore—Mediterranean, Baltic, Oriental, Ventnor—and narrower transsecting avenues: North Carolina, Pennsylvania, Vermont, Connecticut, States, Virginia, Tennessee, New York, Kentucky, Indiana, Illinois. The place as a whole had no name, so when he had completed the plan Osborne wrote in large letters over the ocean, "Atlantic City." No one ever challenged the name, or the names of Osborne's streets. Monopoly was invented in the early nineteen-thirties by Charles B. Darrow, but

Darrow was only transliterating what Osborne had created. The railroads, crucial to any player, were the making of Atlantic City. After the rails were down, houses and hotels burgeoned from Mediterranean and Baltic to New York and Kentucky. Properties—building lots—sold for as little as six dollars apiece and as much as a thousand dollars. The original investors in the railroads and the real estate called themselves the Camden & Atlantic Land Company. Reverently, I repeat their names: Dwight Bell, William Coffin, John DaCosta, Daniel Deal, William Fleming, Andrew Hay, Joseph Porter, Jonathan Pitney, Samuel Richards—founders, fathers, forerunners, archetypical masters of the quick kill.

My opponent and I are now in a deep situation of classical Monopoly. The torsion is almost perfect—Boardwalk and Park Place versus the brilliant reds. His cash position is weak, though, and if I escape him now he may fade. I land on Luxury Tax, contiguous to but in sanctuary from his power. I have four houses on Indiana. He lands there. He concedes.

Indiana Avenue was the address of the Brighton Hotel, gone now. The Brighton was exclusive—a word that no longer has retail value in the city. If you arrived by automobile and tried to register at the Brighton, you were sent away. Brighton-class people came in private railroad cars. Brighton-class people had other private railroad cars for their horses—dawn rides on the firm sand at water's edge, skirts flying. Colonel Anthony J. Drexel Biddle—the sort of name that would constrict throats in Philadelphia—lived, much of the year, in the Brighton.

Colonel Sanders' fried chicken is on Kentucky Avenue. So is Clifton's Club Harlem, with the Sepia Revue and the Sepia Follies, featuring the Honey Bees, the Fashions, and the Lords.

My opponent and I, many years ago, played 2,428 games of Monopoly in a single season. He was then a recent graduate of the Harvard Law School, and he was working for a downtown firm, looking up law. Two people we knew—one from Chase Manhattan, the other from Morgan, Stanley—tried to get into the game, but after a few rounds we found that they were not in the conversation and we sent them home. Monopoly should always be *mano a mano* anyway. My opponent won 1,199 games, and so did I. Thirty were ties. He was called into the Army, and we stopped just there. Now, in Game 2 of the series, I go immediately to jail, and again to jail while my opponent seines property. He is dumbfoundingly lucky. He wins in twelve minutes.

Visiting hours are daily, eleven to two; Sunday, eleven to one; evenings, six to nine. "NO MINORS, NO FOOD, Immediate Family Only Allowed in Jail." All this above a blue steel door in a blue cement wall in the windowless interior of the basement of the city hall. The desk sergeant sits opposite the door to the jail. In a cigar box in front of him are pills in every color, a banquet of fruit salad an inch and a half deep —leapers, co-pilots, footballs, truck drivers, peanuts, blue angels, yellow jackets, redbirds, rainbows. Near the desk are two soldiers, waiting to go through the blue door. They are about eighteen years old. One of them is trying hard to light a cigarette. His wrists are in steel cuffs. A military policeman waits, too. He is a year or so older than the soldiers, taller, studious in appearance, gentle, fat. On a bench against a wall sits a good-looking girl in slacks. The blue door rattles, swings heavily open. A turnkey stands in the doorway. "Don't you guys kill yourselves back there now," says the sergeant to the soldiers.

"One kid, he overdosed himself about ten and a half hours ago," says the M.P.

The M.P., the soldiers, the turnkey, and the girl on the bench are white. The sergeant is black. "If you take off the handcuffs, take off the belts," says the sergeant to the M.P. "I don't want them hanging themselves back there." The door shuts and its tumblers move. When it opens again, five minutes later, a young white man in sandals and dungarees and a blue polo shirt emerges. His hair is in a ponytail. He has no beard. He grins at the good-looking girl. She rises, joins him. The sergeant hands him a manila envelope. From it he removes his belt and a small notebook. He borrows a pencil, makes an entry in the notebook. He is out of jail, free. What did he do? He offended Atlantic City in some way. He spent a night in the jail. In the nineteen-thirties, men visiting Atlantic City went to jail, directly to jail, did not pass Go, for appearing in topless bathing suits on the beach. A city statute requiring all men to wear full-length bathing suits was not seriously challenged until 1937, and the first year in which a man could legally go bare-chested on the beach was 1940.

Game 3. After seventeen minutes, I am ready to begin construction on overpriced and sluggish Pacific, North Carolina, and Pennsylvania. Nothing else being open, opponent concedes.

The physical profile of streets perpendicular to the shore is something like a playground slide. It begins in the high skyline of Boardwalk hotels, plummets into warrens of "side-avenue" motels, crosses Pacific, slopes through church missions, convalescent homes, burlesque houses, rooming houses, and liquor stores, crosses Atlantic, and runs level through the bombed-out ghetto as far—Baltic, Mediterranean—as the eye can see. North Carolina Avenue, for example, is flanked at its beach end by the Chalfonte and the Haddon Hall (908 rooms, air-conditioned), where, according to one biographer, John Philip Sousa (1854–1932) first played when he was twenty-two, insisting, even then, that everyone call him by his entire name. Behind these big hotels, motels—Barbizon, Catalina—crouch. Between Pacific and Atlantic is an occasional house from 1910—wooden porch, wooden mullions, old yellow paint—and two churches, a package store, a strip show, a dealer in fruits and vegetables. Then, beyond Atlantic Avenue, North Carolina moves on into the vast ghetto, the bulk of the city, and it looks like Metz in 1919, Cologne in 1944. Nothing has actually exploded. It is not bomb damage. It is deep and complex decay. Roofs are off. Bricks are scattered in the street. People sit on porches, six deep, at nine on a Monday morning. When they go off to wait in unemployment lines, they wait sometimes two hours. Between Mediterranean and Baltic runs a chain-link fence, enclosing rubble. A patrol car sits idling by the curb. In the back seat is a German shepherd. A sign on the fence says, "Beware of Bad Dogs."

Mediterranean and Baltic are the principal avenues of the ghetto. Dogs are everywhere. A pack of seven passes me. Block after block, there are three-story brick row houses. Whole segments of them are abandoned, a thousand broken windows. Some parts are intact, occupied. A mattress lies in the street, soaking in a pool of water. Wet stuffing is coming out of the mattress. A postman is having a rye and a beer in the Plantation Bar at nine-fifteen in the morning. I ask him idly if he knows where Marvin Gardens is. He does not. "HOOKED AND NEED HELP? CONTACT N.A.R.C.O." "REVIVAL NOW GOING ON, CONDUCTED BY REVEREND H. HENDERSON OF TEXAS." These are signboards on Mediterranean and Baltic. The second one is upside down and leans against a boarded-up window of the Faith Temple Church of God in Christ. There is an old peeling poster on a warehouse wall showing a figure in an electric chair. "The Black Panther Manifesto" is the title of the poster, and its message is, or was, that "the fascists have already decided in advance to murder Chairman Bobby Seale in the electric chair." I pass an old woman who carries a bucket. She wears blue sneakers, worn through. Her feet spill out. She wears red socks, rolled at the knees. A white handkerchief, spread over her head, is knotted at the corners. Does she know where Marvin Gardens is? "I sure don't know," she says, setting down the bucket. "I sure don't know. I've heard of it somewhere, but I just can't say where." I walk on, through a block of shattered glass. The glass crunches underfoot like coarse sand. I remember when I first came here—a long train ride from Trenton, long ago, games of poker in the train—to play basketball against Atlantic City. We were half black, they were all black. We scored forty points, they scored eighty, or something like it. What I remember most is that they had glass backboards—glittering, pendent, expensive glass backboards, a rarity then in high schools, even in colleges, the only ones we played on all year.

I turn on Pennsylvania, and start back toward the sea. The windows of the Hotel Astoria, on Pennsylvania near Baltic, are boarded up. A sheet of unpainted plywood is the door, and in it is a triangular peephole that now frames an eye. The plywood door opens. A man answers my question. Rooms there are six, seven, and ten dollars a week. I thank him for the information and move on, emerging from the ghetto at the Catholic Daughters of America Women's Guest House, between Atlantic and Pacific. Between Pacific and the Boardwalk are the blinking vacancy signs of the Aristocrat and Colton Manor motels. Pennsylvania terminates at the Sheraton-Seaside—thirty-two dollars a day, ocean corner. I take a walk on the Boardwalk and into the Holiday Inn (twenty-three stories). A guest is registering. "You reserved for Wednesday, and this is Monday," the clerk tells him. "But that's all right. We have *plenty* of rooms." The clerk is very young, female, and has soft brown hair that hangs below her waist. Her superior kicks her.

He is a middle-aged man with red spiderwebs in his face. He is jacketed and tied. He takes her aside. "Don't say 'plenty,' " he says. "Say 'You are fortunate, sir. We have rooms available.' "

The face of the young woman turns sour. "We have all the rooms you need," she says to the customer, and, to her superior, "How's that?"

Game 4. My opponent's luck has become abrasive. He has Board-walk and Park Place, and has sealed the board.

Darrow was a plumber. He was, specifically, a radiator repairman who lived in Germantown, Pennsylvania. His first Monopoly board was a sheet of linoleum. On it he placed houses and hotels that he had carved from blocks of wood. The game he thus invented was brilliantly conceived, for it was an uncannily exact reflection of the business milieu at large. In its depth, range, and subtlety, in its luck-skill ratio, in its sense of infrastructure and socio-economic parameters, in its philosophical characteristics, it reached to the profundity of the financial community. It was as scientific as the stock market. It suggested the manner and means through which an underdeveloped world had been developed. It was chess at Wall Street level. "Advance token to the nearest Railroad and pay owner twice the rental to which he is otherwise entitled. If Railroad is unowned, you may buy it from the Bank. Get out of Jail, free. Advance token to nearest Utility. If unowned, you may buy it from Bank. If owned, throw dice and pay owner a total ten times the amount thrown. You are assessed for street repairs: $40 per house, $115 per hotel. Pay poor tax of $15. Go to Jail. Go directly to Jail. Do not pass Go. Do not collect $200."

The turnkey opens the blue door. The turnkey is known to the inmates as Sidney K. Above his desk are ten closed-circuit-TV screens —assorted viewpoints of the jail. There are three cellblocks—men, women, juvenile boys. Six days is the average stay. Showers twice a week. The steel doors and the equipment that operates them were made in San Antonio. The prisoners sleep on bunks of butcher block. There are no mattresses. There are three prisoners to a cell. In winter, it is cold in here. Prisoners burn newspapers to keep warm. Cell corners are black with smudge. The jail is three years old. The men's block echoes with chatter. The man in the cell nearest Sidney K. is pacing. His shirt is covered with broad stains of blood. The block for juvenile boys is, by contrast, utterly silent—empty corridor, empty cells. There is only one prisoner. He is small and black and appears to be thirteen. He says he is sixteen and that he has been alone in here for three days.
"Why are you here? What did you do?"
"I hit a jitney driver."

The series stands at three all. We have split the fifth and sixth games. We are scrambling for property. Around the board we fairly fly. We move so fast because we do our own banking and search our own deeds. My opponent grows tense.

Ventnor Avenue, a street of delicatessens and doctors' offices, is leafy with plane trees and hydrangeas, the city flower. Water Works is on the mainland. The water comes over in submarine pipes. Electric Company gets power from across the state, on the Delaware River, in Deepwater. States Avenue, now a wasteland like St. Charles, once had gardens running down the middle of the street, a horse-drawn trolley, private homes. States Avenue was as exclusive as the Brighton. Only an apartment house, a small motel, and the All Wars Memorial Building —monadnocks spaced widely apart—stand along States Avenue now. Pawnshops, convalescent homes, and the Paradise Soul Saving Station are on Virginia Avenue. The soul-saving station is pink, orange, and yellow. In the windows flanking the door of the Virginia Money Loan Office are Nikons, Polaroids, Yashicas, Sony TVs, Underwood typewriters, Singer sewing machines, and pictures of Christ. On the far side of town, beside a single track and locked up most of the time, is the new railroad station, a small hut made of glazed firebrick, all that is left of the lines that built the city. An authentic phrenologist works on New York Avenue close to Frank's Extra Dry Bar and a church where the sermon today is "Death in the Pot." The church is of pink brick, has blue and amber windows and two red doors. St. James Place, narrow and twisting, is lined with boarding houses that have wooden porches on each of three stories, suggesting a New Orleans made of salt-bleached pine. In a vacant lot on Tennessee is a white Ford station wagon stripped to the chassis. The windows are smashed. A plastic Clorox bottle sits on the driver's seat. The wind has pressed newspaper against the chain-link fence around the lot. Atlantic Avenue, the city's principal thoroughfare, could be seventeen American Main Streets placed end to end—discount vitamins and Vienna Corset shops, movie theatres, shoe stores, and funeral homes. The Boardwalk is made of yellow pine and Douglas fir, soaked in pentachlorophenol. Downbeach, it reaches far beyond the city. Signs everywhere—on windows, lampposts, trash baskets—proclaim "Bienvenue Canadiens!" The salt air is full of Canadian French. In the

Claridge Hotel, on Park Place, I ask a clerk if she knows where Marvin Gardens is. She says, "Is it a floral shop?" I ask a cabdriver, parked outside. He says, "Never heard of it." Park Place is one block long, Pacific to Boardwalk. On the roof of the Claridge is the Solarium, the highest point in town—panoramic view of the ocean, the bay, the salt-water ghetto. I look down at the rooftops of the side-avenue motels and into swimming pools. There are hundreds of people around the rooftop pools, sunbathing, reading—many more people than are on the beach. Walls, windows, and a block of sky are all that is visible from these pools —no sand, no sea. The pools are craters, and with the people around them they are countersunk into the motels.

The seventh, and final, game is ten minutes old and I have hotels on Oriental, Vermont, and Connecticut. I have Tennessee and St. James. I have North Carolina and Pacific. I have Boardwalk, Atlantic, Ventnor, Illinois, Indiana. My fingers are forming a "V." I have mortgaged most of these properties in order to pay for others, and I have mortgaged the others to pay for the hotels. I have seven dollars. I will pay off the mortgages and build my reserves with income from the three hotels. My cash position may be low, but I feel like a rocket in an underground silo. Meanwhile, if I could just go to jail for a time I could pause there, wait there, until my opponent, in his inescapable rounds, pays the rates of my hotels. Jail, at times, is the strategic place to be. I roll boxcars from the Reading and move the flatiron to Community Chest. "Go to Jail. Go directly to Jail."

The prisoners, of course, have no pens and no pencils. They take paper napkins, roll them tight as crayons, char the ends with matches, and write on the walls. The things they write are not entirely idiomatic; for example, "In God We Trust." All is in carbon. Time is required in the writing. "Only humanity could know of such pain." "God So Loved the World." "There is no greater pain than life itself." In the women's block now, there are six blacks, giggling, and a white asleep in red shoes. She is drunk. The others are pushers, prostitutes, an auto thief, a burglar caught with pistol in purse. A sixteen-year-old accused of murder was in here last week. These words are written on the wall of a now empty cell: "Laying here I see two bunks about six inches thick, not counting the one I'm laying on, which is hard as brick. No cushion for my back. No pillow for my head. Just a couple scratchy blankets which is best to use it's said. I wake up in the morning so shivery and cold, waiting and waiting till I am told the food is coming. It's on its way. It's not worth waiting for, but I eat it anyway. I know one thing when they set me free I'm gonna be good if it kills me."

How many years must a game be played to produce an Anthony J. Drexel Biddle and chestnut geldings on the beach? About half a century was the original answer, from the first railroad to Biddle at his peak. Biddle, at his peak, hit an Atlantic City streetcar conductor with his fist, laid him out with one punch. This increased Biddle's legend. He did not go to jail. While John Philip Sousa led his band along the Boardwalk playing "The Stars and Stripes Forever" and Jack Dempsey ran up and down in training for his fight with Gene Tunney, the city crossed the high curve of its parabola. Al Capone held conventions here—upstairs with his sleeves rolled, apportioning among his lieutenant governors the states of the Eastern seaboard. The natural history of an American resort proceeds from Indians to French Canadians via Biddles and Capones. French Canadians, whatever they may be at home, are Visigoths here. Bienvenue Visigoths!

My opponent plods along incredibly well. He has got his fourth railroad, and patiently, unbelievably, he has picked up my potential winners until he has blocked me everywhere but Marvin Gardens. He has avoided, in the fifty-dollar zoning, my increasingly petty hotels. His cash flow swells. His railroads are costing me two hundred dollars a minute. He is building hotels on States, Virginia, and St. Charles. He has temporarily reversed the current. With the yellow monopolies and my blue monopolies, I could probably defeat his lavenders and his railroads. I have Atlantic and Ventnor. I need Marvin Gardens. My only hope is Marvin Gardens.

There is a plaque at Boardwalk and Park Place, and on it in relief is the leonine profile of a man who looks like an officer in a metropolitan bank—"Charles B. Darrow, 1889–1967, inventor of the game of Monopoly." "Darrow," I address him, aloud. "Where is Marvin Gardens?" There is, of course, no answer. Bronze, impassive, Darrow looks south down the Boardwalk. "Mr. Darrow, please, where is Marvin Gardens?" Nothing. Not a sign. He just looks south down the Boardwalk.

My opponent accepts the trophy with his natural ease, and I make, from notes, remarks that are even less graceful than his.

Marvin Gardens is the one color-block Monopoly property that is not in Atlantic City. It is a suburb within a suburb, secluded. It is a planned compound of seventy-two handsome houses set on curvilinear private streets under yews and cedars, poplars and willows. The compound was built around 1920, in Margate, New Jersey, and consists of solid buildings of stucco, brick, and wood, with slate roofs, tile roofs, multimullioned porches, Giraldic towers, and Spanish grilles. Marvin Gardens, the ultimate outwash of Monopoly, is a citadel and sanctuary of the middle class. "We're heavily patrolled by police here. We don't take no chances. Me? I'm living here nine years. I paid seventeen thousand dollars and I've been offered thirty. Number one, I don't want to move. Number two, I don't need the money. I have four bedrooms, two and a half baths, front den, back den. No basement. The Atlantic is down there. Six feet down and you float. A lot of people have a hard time finding this place. People that lived in Atlantic City all their life don't know how to find it. They don't know where the hell they're going. They just know it's south, down the Boardwalk."

# The Curve of
# Binding Energy

Next to Helen Boyden, instructor of chemistry at Deerfield, McPhee's greatest science teacher has undoubtedly been Theodore B. Taylor. The two first met when McPhee undertook to write about nuclear energy. Before long, he encountered Taylor, a theoretical physicist who had designed many of America's atomic bombs. In recent years, Taylor had become alarmed at the proliferation of privately owned, casually guarded "weapons grade" nuclear materials—the inadvertent by-product of making electrical power with nuclear fission. Taylor insisted that a zealot with minimal training could easily steal the materials and fashion a crude bomb—a possibility that most officials vigorously denied.

The alarming elements in Taylor's story interested McPhee, but even more attractive was the scientist's ability to explain difficult matters in imagistic terms. He had rarely taught, yet seemed born to the art, for he could describe scientific procedures with a generous fund of vivid analogies. Like many physicists, Taylor was also a man of multiple interests, a devotee of music and billiards—the latter a useful skill for a student of atomic reactions.

*The Curve of Binding Energy* is dense and yet topical; its subject may seem alien to some of McPhee's usual readers, especially those allergic to science. Even some of his literate friends have scrambled the title, shredded the plot line, or lost the argument altogether. Even so, the volume was McPhee's second nominee for a National Book Award (1975). It passed instantly into paperback sales, was cited at congressional hearings, and became the basis for a television documentary on the making of home-style bombs.

In plan, the book begins with two parallel story lines, one describing special nuclear materials and the other depicting Ted Taylor's growth as a physicist and bomb designer. Those lines finally converge when McPhee and Taylor retreat to a Maryland cabin and there pursue, "in its many possible forms, the unclassified atomic bomb."

The present selections begin near that point in the story, proceed to a flashback describing Taylor's work on the "Orion Project," a fantastic spaceship powered by atomic explosions, and conclude with a scene of grim historical irony: the World Trade Center, a prime target for nuclear terrorists in New York, is heavily populated with Japanese businessmen, reminders of the world's first and only atomic victims.— WLH

---

I once asked Ted Taylor if he was at all worried about people making hydrogen bombs in their basements and, if so, how they might go about it.

He said, "I can't tell you anything at all about that except that my opinion is that a homemade H-bomb is essentially an impossibility. One can't even hint at the principles involved, beyond saying that it requires heating some material up to a terribly high temperature, which is why it is called a thermonuclear bomb. There are by now several thousand people who know how this is done, so the secret of the H-bomb will out somewhere along the line, but, even when it does, the fact remains: to make an H-bomb is not a basement operation. The project would take a large, well-organized group of people a great deal of time. The secret, incidentally, is not a matter of materials. It is a matter of design."

The design was hit upon by Stanislaw Ulam and Edward Teller in 1951. In the pages of a patent application they were described as the bomb's "inventors." After a long period of getting nowhere—an effort by many scientists, under considerable pressure from Washington— Ulam one day asked Teller to sit down in private with him and listen to an idea. They closed the door of Teller's office at Los Alamos and talked. Teller was much impressed with Ulam's idea and at once thought of a better way to do the kind of thing Ulam had in mind. The two men came out of the room with the answer to the problem of the hydrogen bomb. The rest was detail, albeit on a major scale—computer calculations, design, fabrication. The better part of two years went by before a task force was ready to go—in the fall of 1952—to Eniwetok to test the theory.

Not all Los Alamos theories could be tested. Long popular within the Theoretical Division was, for example, a theory that the people of Hungary are Martians. The reasoning went like this: The Martians left their own planet several aeons ago and came to Earth; they landed in what is now Hungary; the tribes of Europe were so primitive and barbarian that it was necessary for the Martians to conceal their evolutionary difference or be hacked to pieces. Through the years, the concealment had on the whole been successful, but the Martians had three characteristics too strong to hide: their wanderlust, which found its outlet in the Hungarian gypsy; their language (Hungarian is not related to any of the languages spoken in surrounding countries); and their unearthly intelligence. One had only to look around to see the evidence: Teller, Wigner, Szilard, von Neumann—Hungarians all. Wigner had designed the first plutonium-production reactors. Szilard had been among the first to suggest that fission could be used to make a bomb. Von Neumann had developed the digital computer. Teller—moody, tireless, and given to fits of laughter, bursts of anger—worked long hours and was impatient with what he felt to be the excessively slow advancement of Project Panda, as the hydrogen-bomb development was known. Kindly to juniors, he had done much to encourage Ted Taylor in his work. His impatience with his peers, however, eventually caused him to leave Los Alamos and establish a rival laboratory at Livermore, in California. Teller had a thick Martian accent. He also had a sense of humor that could penetrate bone. Dark-haired, heavy-browed, he limped pronouncedly. In Europe, one of his feet had been mangled by a streetcar.

Ulam was a Pole and had no inclination to feel thunderstruck in the presence of Hungarians, whatever their origins. His wife was vivacious and French. He worked short hours. He was heroically lazy. He was considered lazy by all of his colleagues, and he did not disagree. The pressures of the Cold War were almost as intense at Los Alamos as the pressures of the war that preceded it, but these pressures were resisted by Ulam. Mornings, he never appeared for work before ten, and in the afternoons he was gone at four. When Enrico Fermi organized hikes on Sundays, Ulam went along to the foot of the trail. Fermi, Hans Bethe, George Bell, Ted Taylor—up the talus slopes they went while Ulam sat below and watched them through binoculars. Many years after the first thermonuclear bomb had been successfully tested, Ulam's secretary cut out and tacked to a bulletin board a cartoon in which two cavemen were talking about a third caveman, who was standing off by himself. The caption was "He's been unbearable since he invented fire."

The object that had been sent out to Eniwetok was distinguished by its plainness and its size. It was a cylinder with somewhat convex ends. It was twenty-two feet long and five and a half feet in diameter. It was the result of Project Panda, and it was called Mike. It looked something like the tank on a railway tank car, and it weighed twenty-one tons. Inside it was at least one fission bomb, and a great deal of heavy hydrogen. Mike was placed in a building with metal siding which had been constructed for the purpose on an island called Elugelab, in the northern sector of the atoll. After Mike had exploded, nothing whatever remained where the island had been but seawater. The island had disappeared from the earth. The yield of the Hiroshima bomb had been thirteen kilotons. The theoretical expectation for Mike was a few thousand kilotons—a few megatons. The fireball spread so far and fast that it terrified observers who had seen many tests before. The explosion, in the words of Ted Taylor, who was not there, "was so huge, so brutal—as if things had gone too far. When the heat reached the observers, it stayed and stayed and stayed, not for seconds but for minutes." The yield of the bomb was ten megatons. It so unnerved Norris Bradbury, the Los Alamos director, that for a brief time he wondered if the people at Eniwetok should somehow try to conceal from their colleagues back in New Mexico the magnitude of what had happened. Few hydrogen bombs subsequently exploded by the United States have been allowed to approach that one in yield. The Russians, however, in their own pursuit of grandeur, eventually detonated one that reached just under sixty megatons—more than four thousand times the explosive yield of the Hiroshima bomb. Taylor guessed that if the Russians had wrapped a uranium blanket around it they could have got a hundred megatons, but he imagined they were afraid to go that far. Whatever the size of the big bombs—ten, sixty, or a hundred megatons—they had begun to dismay him long before they were tested. (In seven years at Los Alamos, he would work on the design of only one hydrogen bomb.) He was even sorry that he had designed the Super Oralloy Bomb, for the belief he had once held in the "deterrent posture" of such huge explosions had eventually dissolved in the thought that if they ever were used they would be "too all-killing"—that the destruction they would effect across hundreds of square miles would be so indiscriminate that the existence of such a weapon could not be justified on any moral ground. He reached the conclusion that an acceptable deterrent posture could only be achieved by making small bombs with a capacity for eradicating specific small targets. The laboratory's almost total emphasis in the other direction—toward the H-bomb—bothered him deeply. He began wondering just how small and light a nuclear explosive could be—how much yield could be got out of something with the over-all size of a softball. With George Gamow, he wrote a scientific paper called "What the World Needs Is a Good Two-Kiloton Bomb."

In 1953, Taylor was sent by Los Alamos at full pay to Cornell, to spend a year and a half getting his Ph.D. His mentor there was Bethe, who had long since become a close friend and counsellor—a relationship that continues. When Taylor returned to Los Alamos, he resumed the conception of a number of bombs whose names unmistakably indicate the direction of his effort: Bee, Hornet, Viper, the Puny Plutonium Bomb. The test of that last one was called "the P.P. shot," and it was the first known complete failure in the history of nuclear testing. "Now you're making progress," Fermi said. "You've finally fired a dud." The bomb had plenty of high explosive around an amount of plutonium so small that it remains secret, for the figure is somewhere near the answer to the root question: How small can a nuclear bomb be? In the absence of precise numbers, the answer would have to be: Pretty small. Fiddling around on this lightweight frontier, Taylor once designed an implosion bomb that weighed twenty pounds, but it was never tested.

Studying ordinary artillery shells, he replicated their external dimensions in conceiving fission bombs that could be fired out of guns. Being longitudinal in shape, these were not implosion bombs, of the Nagasaki type, but gun-type bombs—the kind that had been dropped over Hiroshima. The basic idea was to fire one piece of metallic uranium down a shaft and into another piece of metallic uranium, turning what had been two subcritical masses into one supercritical mass that would explode. Taylor called this exercise "whacking away at Hiroshima," and he performed it successfully, but he was not much interested in gun-type bombs. The Hiroshima bomb, which had been designed by a committee, was overloaded with uranium, and Taylor's summary description of it was that it was "a stupid bomb." Possibilities were so much greater in implosion systems. The Nagasaki bomb's nuclear core had been designed by Robert Christy, who taught physics and astrophysics at the California Institute of Technology, and returned frequently to Los Alamos as a consultant. Taylor, in his own words, would "light up" when he found that Christy had come to town. Christy showed great interest in what Taylor was trying to do, and gave him much encouragement.

As the bombs grew smaller, the yield did, too. So the obvious next step was to try to get the yield back up while retaining the diminutions of size and weight. Taylor incorporated an essentially new feature that might do just that. It was put into Bee and Hornet. At the sound and the sight of each of them—the big fireball, the loud bang—he knew at once that the feature had worked.

"What feature?" I asked him once.

"I can't say," he answered. "So far as that part of the discussion goes, we have come to a dead end."

Freeman Dyson, one of the preeminent theoretical physicists in the world, has not worked at Los Alamos but has had occasion in his career to review closely the work Ted Taylor did there. "His trade, basically, was the miniaturizing of weapons," Dyson has said. "He was the first man in the world to understand what you can do with three or four kilograms of plutonium, that making bombs is an easy thing to do, that you can, so to speak, design them freehand." Taylor's colleagues at the laboratory came to regard him as being "halfway between an inventor and a scientist." This is how Marshall Rosenbluth remembers him. Rosenbluth, who, like Dyson, is now at the Institute for Advanced Study, in Princeton, was at Los Alamos through the same years Taylor was. Rosenbluth worked principally on the thermonuclear bomb. "Ted was not a typical physicist working out little mathematical problems," Rosenbluth has said. "He thought more qualitatively. He made many inventions, and did a pulling together of the physics necessary for them. He did not spend his time working on the most esoteric of physics points." Once, on a visit to Los Alamos, I asked Carson Mark, director of the Theoretical Division, if he would tell me what Taylor's particular thumbprint had been, as a designer and as a physicist. Mark said, "There was a need for different kinds of physics. There was a need for different kinds of contributions. Many did long computations that took weeks. Ted did not. New ideas don't come this way. There were problems in physics which took months and months to solve, resulting in benchmark papers in the *Physical Review,* such as a study of neutron scattering from some particular material. Such things require a great deal of careful work. You need it. You value people who can do it right. Ted did not do much of this. Ted's papers were shorter, more qualitative—physics sketched out but not extensively explored. Figures were needed. Ted would guess. For exact figures, a man-year's work might be involved. Ted would not be doing that work. His style was a flair for qualitative sketching of a complicated process. He was conceptual. His numbers were reasonable but were not exact. With intensity, he thought outside the prescribed context. Others could answer questions if you asked them, but they did not keep thinking of so many unlikely things. Marshall

Rosenbluth and Conrad Longmire, for example, were strong physicists of a breadth and depth greater than Ted's. Ted's curiosity, his prying, his imagination—a combination equally valuable—exceeded theirs." Mark looked pensive for a while, and found an afterthought. "Ted may even have not been the most imaginative," he said. "We've had some real nuts around here."

While Ted's bombs grew smaller, some of his other ideas grew to epic proportions. He spent a lot of time walking aimlessly from corridor to corridor thinking about the slow production of plutonium. The A.E.C.'s plants at Hanford and Savannah River were literally dripping it out, and Ted thought he saw a way to make a truly enormous amount of plutonium in a short time. He wanted to wrap up an H-bomb in a thick coat of uranium and place it deep in arctic ice. When it was detonated, the explosion would make plutonium-239 by capturing neutrons in uranium-238—exactly what happened in a reactor. The explosion would also turn a considerable amount of ice into a reservoir of water, which could easily be pumped out to a chemical plant on the surface, where the plutonium would be separated out. Why not? Why not make tritium in the same way? Tritium, the heaviest isotope of hydrogen (one proton, two neutrons), is the best fuel for a thermonuclear explosion, and the most expensive (eight hundred thousand dollars a kilogram). Tritium is everywhere—in the seven seas, in the human body—but in such small proportions to ordinary hydrogen that collecting tritium in quantity from the natural world is completely impractical. So it is made, slowly, in production reactors. Ted wanted to do it a short way. Put a considerable amount of lithium around a thermonuclear bomb and emplace it under ten thousand feet of ice. Boom. An underground lake full of heavy isotopes. "That idea did not fly," said Carson Mark, in summary. "It properly received a lot of exploratory thought. It was a good idea. It would work, but it was too hard to do." These arctic ideas of Ted's became known as MICE—megaton ice-contained explosions. He found a serious supporter in John von Neumann, who was by then an A.E.C. commissioner. Von Neumann died two years later, in 1957, and the support died with him. Alternatively, Ted wanted to spread out on the ground somewhere a uranium blanket four hundred feet square. Then he would detonate a thermonuclear bomb in the air above it. Instantly on the ground there would be tons of plutonium. That idea did not even crawl.

Ted's imagination was given limited assignments as well as unlimited freedom. He was, after all, working for the government, and, as Marshall Rosenbluth remembers those days, "admirals and generals were forever calling up begging for appointments." One time, for example, Ted was asked to see how well he could do "in a certain yield range" in terms of "high efficiency, high compressions, high criticality"—no fancy innovations, just the best implosion bomb he could make within the parameters given. The result was Hamlet, the most efficient pure-fission bomb ever exploded in the kiloton range.

Driving around Los Alamos with him once, when I went along on a visit he made there in 1972, I asked him what he had done to occupy himself during the flat periods between projects, the lulls that would come in any pattern of conceptual work. He said, "Between bombs, we messed around, in one way or another. We bowled snowballs the size of volleyballs down the E Building corridor to see what would happen. We played shuffleboard with icicles." He supposed it helped relieve the tension, of which there was a fair amount from time to time. During the strain of preparation for the Mike shot, for example, a well-known theoretical physicist picked up an inkwell, threw it at a colleague, and hit him in the chest. He could be excused. His job was to make sure that the hydrogen bomb did not ignite the atmosphere. After the Livermore laboratory began making bombs in competition with Los Alamos, a rivalry developed that was at least as intense as the football rivalry between, say, Michigan and Michigan State. Each laboratory had its stars. Johnny Foster was the fission-bomb star of Livermore. Groups of scientists from the one laboratory would attend the other's bomb tests, and there was a distant sense of locomotive cheering in the air, of chrysanthemums and hidden flasks. If a Livermore bomb succeeded only in knocking off the top of its own tower, or a Los Alamos bomb was a dud, no one actually cheered, but some people felt better. Once, at Eniwetok, somebody decided to steal Livermore's flag, which was pinned to a wall in Livermore's barracks and included in its heraldry a California golden bear. From the central flagpole, Headquarters, Joint Task Force Seven, Eniwetok Atoll, the flag of Rear Admiral B. Hall Hanlon, commander of the task force, was removed in the dead of night. Hoisted in its place was the Livermore bear. The Admiral's flag was then pinned to the wall in the Livermore barracks. In the morning, Admiral Hanlon reacted as expected, personally yielding four kilotons, one from each nostril and one from each ear. What is that bear doing on my flagpole? Where is my flag? Where? God damn it, where? Captains, colonels were running around like rabbits under hawk shadow—and, of course, they found the Admiral's flag. Los Alamos had triumphed without a shot being fired.

An explosion, however large, was a "shot." The word "bomb" was almost never used. A bomb was a "device" or a "gadget." Language could hide what the sky could not. The Los Alamos Scientific Laboratory was "the Ranch." Often, it was simply called "the Hill." An implosion bomb was made with "ploot." A hundred-millionth of a second was a "shake"—a shake of a lamb's tail. A "jerk" was ten quadrillion ergs —a unit of energy equivalent to a quarter of a ton of high explosive. A "kilojerk" was a quarter of a kiloton. A "megajerk" was a quarter of a megaton. A cross-section for neutron capture was expressed in terms of the extremely small area a neutron had to hit in order to enter a nucleus —say, one septillionth of a square centimetre—and this was known as a "barn." Two new elements—numbers 99 and 100—were discovered in the debris resulting from Project Panda, the Mike shot. Some wanted to call element 99 pandamonium. The name it got was einsteinium.

Conversations were more likely to be in an idiom of numbers, though. Numbers, volumes, densities were the stuff of working thought, and of daydreams as well. Ulam announced one day that the entire population of Los Alamos could be crammed into the town water tower. Taylor figured out that the Valle Grande, a huge caldera in the mountains above Los Alamos, had been created by a thousand megatons of volcanic explosion. His conversation to this day is laced with phrases such as "of the order of" and "by a factor of," and around the top of his mind runs a frieze of bizarre numbers. He will say out of nowhere that his wife has baked a hundred and eighteen birthday cakes in the past twenty-five years, or that the mean free path of a neutron through a human being is eight inches. "The mean free path of a neutrino is greater than the diameter of the earth. They go right through the world." He says there are some numbers that are so large or so small that they are never seen, because they refer to nothing. "You never see a number larger than ten to the hundred and twenty-fourth, for example."

"Why not?"

"Because there is nothing bigger than that. That is the volume of the known universe in cubic fermis. A fermi is the smallest dimension that makes any sense to talk about—ten to the minus thirteen centimetres. That's about the diameter of an electron. Nothing we know of is smaller than that."

When I asked him how many atoms there were in his own body, he said, right back, "Eight times ten to the twenty-sixth."

We had lunch in the Los Alamos cafeteria one day with, among others, Ulam, who was now teaching mathematics at the University of Colorado but kept a house in Santa Fe and worked as a consultant at Los Alamos several months each year. Ulam began wondering aloud about the surface of a billiard ball and what it would look like if the billiard ball were magnified until its diameter were equal to the earth's. Would the irregularities of the surface be as high as the Himalayas? He decided they would. He asked Ted to come home for dinner with him and his wife, Françoise, and to bring me along. He drew a map of his neighborhood in Santa Fe and said he could not wait to lead the way because he had to leave the laboratory at four.

Ulam's house, behind a high wrought-iron gate in a warren of adobe, might have been the retreat of a minor grandee in the old quarter of Seville. It was on several levels, the lowest of which was the living room—down a few steps and into an outreaching white space that was at once expansive, under a fourteen-foot ceiling, and compact, with a tear-shaped white fireplace built into one corner. Logs were burning. They had been stood on end, and were leaning against the back of the fireplace. Cottonwood smoke was in the air. Stretched out on a large daybed during much of the evening—looking into the fire, or, with quick glances of interest or amusement, into the eyes of his wife and his visitors—was Ulam, inventor of the hydrogen bomb. A great variety of books in French and English lined the room. A grand piano stood in one corner, and on a tripod near it was a white telescope about five feet long. Ulam, always interested in the stars, had been connected with Los Alamos since 1943, and one of the earliest potentialities that occurred to him when he began to work on the Manhattan Project was that nuclear-explosive force could be used to drive vehicles from Earth into distant parts of space—an external-combustion engine, fuelled with bombs. Trim, tan across his bald head, obviously well rested, Ulam was sixty-two at the time. He looked no older than Taylor, who was forty-eight. He asked about the independent research Ted had been doing for many years in the field of nuclear-materials safeguards and was much absorbed by a story Ted told him about the attempted blackmailing in 1970 of a city in Florida. The blackmailer promised not to bomb the city out of existence in return for a million dollars and safe custody out of the United States. A day later, the threat was repeated, and with it came

a diagram of a hydrogen bomb. Taylor described the diagram to Ulam
—a cylinder filled with lithium hydride wrapped in cobalt, an implosion
system at one end of it—and nothing in Ulam's face or Taylor's manner
indicated that such a diagram might not be credible. The threat, though,
had been a hoax, perpetrated by a fourteen-year-old boy. The police
chose not to reveal to the public that the bomb in the threat was nuclear.
A judge, after sentencing the boy, suspended the sentence and put him
under the guidance of two scientists in the area, saying that talent such
as the boy had should be channelled in a positive direction, and not a
negative one, as might happen in a prison.

Taylor asked Ulam what was new in mathematics, and Ulam said
that the properties of infinity were of much philosophical interest, that
there was a lot of work being done on combinatorial mathematics as it
applies to biology, and that it was now possible to prove that there are
some theorems that can be neither proved nor disproved. Ulam's mind
wandered on to Shakespeare, to Gaudí, to Joseph Conrad—who, like
Ulam, was a Pole, and first learned English when he was about twenty
years old. Ulam wondered if it was possible to discern Conrad's origins
in an unlabelled quantity of Conrad's prose. "I never actually read
sentences," he said. "I have a good memory. I look at a page and see what
is there. But I think I miss a lot." He recalled his first arrival, many years
ago, at Cambridge University, and his first visit to Trinity Great Court
and the college room of Isaac Newton. He said, "I almost fainted."

Before we left, Ulam found a moment to say, out of Taylor's earshot, "I have known hundreds of people in science, and he is one of the
very few most impressive and inventive. I as a boy was always reading
Jules Verne. It was where I got my ideas of Americans. When I met Ted,
he fitted the ideas I formed as a boy of Americans, as represented by Jules
Verne. The trait I noticed immediately was inventiveness. Scientists are
of different types. Some follow rules and techniques that exist. Some have
imagination, larger perspectives. Often, Ted had the attitude of 'Ours not
to reason why.' He was intense, high-strung, introspective. 'If something
is possible, let's do it' was Ted's attitude. He did things without seeing
all the consequences. So much of science is like that."

Driving away from the lights of Santa Fe and up into the mountains
toward Los Alamos, Taylor fell into a ruminative mood, and eventually
said, "The theorist's world is a world of the best people and the worst
of possible results." He said he now saw all his work on light weapons
as nothing but an implementation of "pseudo-rational military pur-

poses." He said his belief in deterrent postures had eroded to zero. "I thought I was doing my part for my country. I thought I was contributing to a permanent state of peace. I no longer feel that way. I wish I hadn't done it. The whole thing was wrong. Rationalize how you will, the bombs were designed to kill many, many people. I sometimes can't blame people if they wish all scientists were lined up and shot. If it were possible to wave a wand and make fission impossible—fission of any kind —I would quickly wave the wand. I have a total conviction—now—that nuclear weapons should not be used under any circumstances. At any time. Anywhere. Period. If I were king. If the Russians bombed New York. I would not bomb Moscow."

Sometimes at the family dinner table, Ted Taylor will leave a conversation. He simply goes away, in every sense but the physical presence of his body in a chair. He stays away for varying lengths of time. When his thoughts have made their journey and come back, he will resume a conversation at the exact place he left it, as if all animation in the world had been suspended while he was gone. There was an entire weekend in 1957 during which he didn't come back at all. Not long before, he had moved with his family from Los Alamos to San Diego, and he was now working at a civilian laboratory that had been set up to make creative use of nuclear energy. Russia had just sent the world's first satellite into orbit, and Taylor had become occupied with the contemplation of ways to put big payloads into space cheaply—very heavy things, adequate for space exploration, not little capsules that might go into orbit for tens of millions of dollars. He concluded that the only way to do that was with nuclear energy. One of his wife's aunts was coming to visit for the weekend, and although he remained very much in and around the house, he made his metaphysical disappearance some hours before she arrived. He thought about Rover, a nuclear rocket under development at Los Alamos, but that was simply a reactor through which you pumped hydrogen. It could place on the moon a greater payload, by a factor of two or three, than a chemical rocket of the same weight at launch. But that was not enough—not for a ship of the size that he was beginning to conceive. He sought factors of at least a hundred. Eventually, he remembered Stan Ulam's idea that space payloads might be propelled with nuclear explosions. Ulam and Cornelius Everett had worked out calculations of the momentum transfer between a series of nuclear explosions and a mass. Taylor walked around and around his house, on an interior circuit through several rooms, and also around the outside. Once during the weekend, his wife had a chore to do that involved her carrying heavy buckets of sand. Her aunt said to her, "Caro, where is your husband? Why can't Ted be doing that?"

"He's thinking," Caro explained.

At first, one might imagine the idea—nuclear explosions driving spaceships—to be ridiculous. Surely an atomic bomb exploding close to a spacecraft would vaporize it then and there. Taylor remembered that on Eniwetok one time a fission bomb had been exploded from a tower and had knocked the four steel legs of the tower outward in four directions. The heat around the steel had been many times more than enough to vaporize it, but after the explosion the four struts were lying pretty much undamaged on the ground. Before the heat could destroy them, the shock wave had shoved the fireball up into the air.

This sort of phenomenon had to do with a field of study—weapons effects—in which Taylor had long taken a special interest. Two laboratories were busy making bombs, and no one, in his view, had been paying enough attention to various things the bombs might do. He thought there should be a third laboratory—a national weapons-effects laboratory—set up to discover new potentialities for the use of nuclear explosives, military and otherwise. Suppose you wanted to get rid of a city's port facility with a tidal wave and not get rid of the whole city. How would you do that? How could you dig a tunnel from New York to San Francisco? How might you destroy an enemy missile in flight without doing any damage to anything else? It was all in the special arrangement of the explosive, the enhancement of certain characteristics to obtain certain effects. How could you shove something that weighed a thousand tons into space? A fission bomb expands at an extremely high speed—about two and a half million miles an hour—and since the velocity required for escaping the earth's gravity is only twenty-five thousand miles an hour, a fission bomb might do. Clearly, it should be a shaped charge. The explosion should go in only one direction, as from a nozzle. What would it strike against? Once at Eniwetok, a physicist named Lew Allen had actually conducted a test to see what would happen if spheres of steel covered with graphite, the size of big pumpkins, were dangled from wires thirty feet from a twenty-kiloton bomb. If the struts of a tower had come through undamaged, how about the graphite-covered balls? The bomb was one that Ted Taylor had designed, and it was called Viper. Its shock wave took the balls with it. When the explosion was over, the balls were integral. Their steel interiors were undamaged. A few thousandths of an inch of graphite was gone from their surfaces. Why not set a nuclear bomb under a plate of steel and graphite on the bottom of a big ogival spacecraft, detonate it, and start for Mars? A short way up, lob another bomb out of the ship's interior. Detonate it. About a second later, lob out another bomb, and so forth. The ship would go straight to Mars, cutting across gravitational fields, violating all the rules for saving energy. There would be no sneaking in the back door, going the long way, as you would have to do with a chemical rocket, to save fuel. This ship would go essentially in a straight line, with a superabundance of energy, and it would be large enough for a crew of a hundred and fifty. During the opposition of Earth and Mars, which occurs every couple of years, the distance between them can be as little as thirty-five million miles or as much as sixty-three million miles. The round trip would take from three to six months. Long after Caro's aunt had gone, Ted asked why she had never arrived.

In 1956, Frederic de Hoffmann, once of the Theoretical Division at Los Alamos, had attracted physicists, chemists, and engineers to a schoolhouse in San Diego for a series of conferences on atomic energy. The building was the temporary headquarters of General Atomic, a division of General Dynamics headed by de Hoffmann. De Hoffmann was only thirty-two, but there was a mixture in him of sound physics and entrepreneurial verve that drew people of the highest level to the schoolhouse: Hans Bethe, Glenn Seaborg, Edward Teller, Freeman Dyson. Alvin Weinberg, of Oak Ridge, was there, and so was Manson Benedict, of M.I.T. Ted Taylor was there, and Marshall Rosenbluth. Mornings, they heard lectures in nuclear technology. Afternoons, they discussed things that might be built. At one such conference, Teller made a keynote talk. He said that what the world needed was "an inherently safe reactor"—something that you could, in effect, give to schoolchildren without fear of hurting them. Three teams were formed—a safe-reactor team, a ship-reactor team, and a team that would explore theoretical possibilities for a high-temperature gas-cooled reactor. The schoolyard was equipped with picnic tables that had blackboards for tops and chalk in recessed pockets. The tables were surrounded by bougainvillea and cups of gold. Mayonnaise got all over the blackboards, and calculations tended to skid. The blackboards were not used much. Taylor, Dyson, and Andrew McReynolds, an employee of General Dynamics, were on the safe-reactor team. Taking advantage of something called "the warm-neutron effect," they invented a reactor that would go subcritical if it got too hot —and thus, in an emergency, would shut itself off. It was called TRIGA. Taylor went to work for General Atomic. Dyson went back home, to the Institute for Advanced Study, in Princeton. There are fifty-three TRIGAs now—research reactors—in fifteen countries around the world. They are absolutely free of ordinary reactor-safety problems—no meltdowns could ever occur, or poisonous clouds break out from their containment. TRIGAs could be built, in much larger form, as commercial power reactors, but they gobble up neutrons and might be too expensive to be competitive in the business world.

Taylor's spaceship required federal support, and it got nowhere coldly until April, 1958, when it was presented to Roy Johnson, chief of the Advanced Research Projects Agency, in Washington. Having looked at all sorts of paper payloads sitting on paper rockets, Johnson was suddenly confronted with a plan for a trip to Saturn, among other places, in something the size of a sixteen-story building. He said, "Everyone seems to be making plans to pile fuel on fuel on fuel to put a pea into orbit, but you seem to mean business." The agency checked out the project—Marshall Rosenbluth had pulled together what he called "the first rough crack at the feasibility physics"; de Hoffmann's General Atomic would be in over-all administrative charge; and Ted Taylor, the ship's inventor, would serve as project manager. The agency decided that it was a crazy idea from some very good people, and offered a million dollars to support it in its first year. The project was named Orion.

General Atomic assembled, eventually, about forty people to work on Orion—under maximum-security conditions. Among them was Dyson, who, when he heard about Orion, had taken a leave of absence from the Institute for Advanced Study. He moved to California and went to work full time with Taylor. The presence of Dyson was in itself an antidote to skepticism. That he would give up everything else he was doing to assist in one endeavor could not help but signify much about that endeavor. To Dyson himself, Orion suggested not only a scientific instrument but an imperative for the future of the world. He saw the human race running out of frontiers, and he considered frontiers essential to the human psyche, for without them pressures would build that would implode upon the race and destroy it. The planets were unpromising, because of their apparent inability to support life. Dyson speculated instead about comets. Comets had abundant water and, among other things, nitrogen and carbon. They seemed to be logical places to colonize.

Extrapolating from the frequency with which comets come into the solar system, it could be concluded that comets by the thousands of millions must be out there in space awaiting colonists. To provide warmth and air, trees would be grown on comets. The leaves would be genetically reprogrammed to adapt to conditions of space. Nothing would inhibit growth on a comet, so the trees would reach heights as great as a hundred miles. Returning in a sense to an earlier *modus vivendi*, people would live among the roots of these great trees, whirling through space with the basic requirements for life ready to hand.

Dyson reasoned that going through a series of energy crises would be a common experience to all civilizations in the universe. After running through the resources on its own planet, a given civilization would then logically turn to the nearest sun. The minuscule fraction of total sunlight that actually strikes a planet could not be of extensive use, so a resource-impoverished civilization, in order to assure almost indefinite survival, would send giant plates of materials into orbit around its sun, forming a great discontinuous shell, a titanic nonrigid sphere, conserving almost all the heat and light and photosynthetic sustenance the sun would give. To this end, Dyson imagined, an advanced civilization could dismantle a neighboring planet—one comparable to Jupiter in our system—whose mass would supply enough material for a shell around the sun.

No chemical rocket making slow ferries to the nearby moon was ever going to hint at the vehicular capabilities necessary for enterprises on such a scale. Ted Taylor's Orion was something quite different, though. Large enough to carry machine shops and laboratories, it could move through space at about a hundred thousand miles an hour, top speed. Whenever the day might come that people would earnestly wish to get about in the solar system, this would be the way to do it.

Dyson, a professor at the institute that had been the working milieu of Einstein, had already taken a singular place on the highest level of theoretical physics in the twentieth century, so the impressions he formed of Ted Taylor in San Diego are illuminating not only of Taylor but of Dyson: "As a mathematician and physicist, Ted was slow. It took him a long time to understand things on the technical level. He is a splendid example of the man who ripens late. Ted was not able to learn a great deal from books. He is a special kind of physicist, with a feeling for something as a concrete object rather than for equations you write down about it. In a European system, after an experience such as the one he had at Berkeley, he would never have had a chance. I have a low opinion of higher education. Ted had no time for such nonsense, and in that respect he was like Einstein. He was like Einstein, too, in his style of thinking. Both were theoretical. Neither did physics experiments in the conventional sense. Both of them were extraordinarily unmathematical. Ted thinks of real things. He does not think in equations. Einstein, in his young days, was the same way. His thought processes were extremely concrete. Ted taught me everything I know about bombs. He was the man who had made bombs small and cheap. For Orion, having them small and cheap was the point. We worked together on the problem of designing the bomb units. The problem was to blow out the debris in one direction as far as you could, with a controlled-velocity distribution. Very few people have Ted's imagination. Very few people have his courage. He was ten or twenty years ahead of the rest of us. There is something tragic about his life. He was the Columbus who never got to go and discover America. I felt that he—much more than von Braun or anyone else—was the real Columbus of our days. I think he is perhaps the greatest man that I ever knew well. And he is completely unknown."

Essentially flat on the bottom, Orion was going to look like the nose of a bullet, the head of a rocket, the hat of a bishop. The diameter would be a hundred and thirty-five feet. The intended launching site was Jackass Flats, Nevada, where Orion would rest on a set of eight towers, each two hundred and fifty feet high. At the end of the countdown, it would rise into the sky on a columnar fission explosion. In Taylor's words, "It would have been the most sensational thing anyone ever saw." Inside Orion would be two thousand nuclear bombs. Stored in cans, they would be dispensed one at a time down a shaft and through a hole in the bottom of the ship. For insight into the engineering of this mechanical operation, the Coca-Cola Company was consulted with reference to the technology of its coin-operated Coke machines. Apparatus of the Coke-machine type would move the bombs out of storage bays and set them up at the head of the shaft. Then they would be blown out of the ship by compressed nitrogen and detonated about a hundred feet below. The initial launching bomb would yield only a tenth of a kiloton. The next bomb, a second later, would yield two-tenths of a kiloton. Two hundred kilotons in all would be needed for the ship to get out of the atmosphere, and this thrust would be delivered by fifty bombs of graduated range, the fiftieth of which, at twenty kilotons, would be of the force that destroyed Nagasaki. Each bomb would need something stuck to it that would become debris and go up against the ship, pushing more emphatically than would the shock wave alone. Hydrogen was best for the purpose, but water would do, and so would polyethylene. The successive explosions would fling plastic at the spaceship to make it go. The National Aeronautics and Space Administration called Orion's nuclear explosives "pulse units." The Air Force called them "charge propellant systems." Taylor called them bombs.

The pusher plate—the bottom of the ship—was its most important component, what with twenty-kiloton bombs going off a hundred feet away. Intense effort went into the consideration of substances of which the pusher plate might be made. Substances tried in experiments included steel, copper, aluminum, and wood. Ironwood might do, because wood is a poor conductor of heat. In one experiment, a couple of pounds of high explosive were detonated a foot from an aluminum plate that was backed by heavy springs. The plate shattered. It had been a uniformly thick (quarter-inch) disc. A thinner aluminum plate was made. Its thickness tapered toward its edges. Boom. It did not shatter. Uneven stresses had broken the other one. These stresses disappeared in the taper of the thinner one. A lesson learned—you taper your pusher plate. Each explosion could remove a few thousandths of a centimetre of the plate's surface but no more, since the pusher plate was the one thing in Orion that could not be replaced during a voyage. Someone left a thumbprint on an aluminum pusher plate before a test explosion. The grease of the thumbprint prevented explosive erosion altogether. A lesson learned—grease would be sprayed onto Orion's bottom between shots.

Above the pusher plate would be a set of huge pneumatic "tires" connected through a chassis to gas-filled piston shock absorbers fifty feet high. A person riding in the chambers above would experience what Taylor describes as "a pulsating effect, a bouncy ride—but not too much so." In all, there would be seventy-five tons of shielding between the passengers and the explosions. Weight was no problem. Orion could carry tractors, big telescopes, two hundred tons of water, a complete kitchen, refrigeration, washing machines, toilets. "We had an aversion to weight-minimizing. We did not need to recycle urine, for example. We would have just thrown it over the side. We could have taken barber chairs, if we wanted them. Anything could be carried that might be necessary for a big-scale manned expedition anywhere in the solar system."

Taylor lived in a one-story clapboard house on a hillside in La Jolla, with orange and tangerine trees in his yard and a view of the blue Pacific.

Orion began in the schoolhouse, but de Hoffmann in time moved General Atomic to three hundred acres of country land, where he built his nuclear Xanadu of circular and curvilinear buildings surrounded with tennis courts, pools, eucalyptus, hibiscus, ground cedar, bougainvillea, and secluded stone benches for classified discussions. Ted barely noticed. He was on his way to Pluto. He meant to go himself. It never crossed his mind that he would not. He told his children that he was taking tail medicine every night, and that he would grow a tail that would help him keep his balance during stopovers on the moon. The children never saw the medicine, but they believed him, and occasionally they felt his lower spine to see how the tail was coming along. At night, he would lie down with his children on a canvas tarpaulin in the back yard and show them Orion and Mars. He described conditions on all the planets. All over the kitchen walls he put up diagrams of pusher plates, each nuance of which was explained at length to Caro.

"I don't think it ever mattered if I understood what he said or not. The farther he got into space, the more earthbound I became. There are so many things to do, and someone had to do them. We had a lot of children, for goodness' sake."

"I never imagined myself sitting at the throttle. I dreamed of looking out a porthole at the rings of Saturn, sometimes the moons of Jupiter. We would not have landed on Jupiter itself. The mass and gravity are so great that if you put something down on it it would probably sink into a soup of methane, or whatever it is. It doesn't sound like much of a place to go. The remotest place I expected to see was Pluto, where the sun is a pale disc and there is deep twilight at noon. Cold, cold, cold. But still a world."

"What he really wanted was a rock of Mars on the mantelpiece."

"People have worked out what it would take to graze the sun—to get inside a flare, so that the flare goes over your head. Imagine looking out a window and seeing that! To think of the sun filling up half your field of view is almost unbearably exciting. I had a recurrent dream that began with Orion. I was alone in the ship, and outside it I saw many stars. I busied myself within the ship and, a little later, looked out again. There was nothing. Nothing at all. I was beyond the stars, beyond the universe. I woke with a feeling of total terror. For that matter, whenever I saw myself looking through a porthole at Jupiter filling half the sky I would get the scared feeling I have had since childhood, and which I have never understood. In La Jolla, I had a three-and-a-half-inch second-hand telescope I'd bought for fifteen dollars. I used to sit in the back yard with Freeman Dyson and look at the planets and the stars. I would see my own moon of Jupiter. Dyson knew in far greater detail what was there."

Years later, Dyson gave a lecture titled "Mankind in the Universe" before the German and Austrian Physical Societies in Salzburg. He said, in part:

The beginning of the space age can be dated rather precisely to June 5, 1927, when nine men meeting in a restaurant in Breslau founded the Verein für Raumschiffahrt. The V.F.R. existed for six years before Hitler put an end to it, and in those six years it carried through the basic engineering development of liquid-fuelled rockets, without any help from the government. This was the first romantic age in the history of space flight. The V.F.R. was an organization without any organization. It depended entirely upon the initiative and devotion of individual members. . . . In a strange way, these last desperate years of the Weimar Republic produced at the same time the splendid flowering of pure physics in Germany and the legendary achievements of the V.F.R.—as if the young Germans of that time were driven to make their highest creative efforts by the economic and social disintegration which surrounded them. . . .

I now pass on to the year 1958. . . . I was one of a small group of scientists in America who were passionately interested in going into space but were repelled by the billion-dollar style of the big government organizations. We wanted to recapture the style and spirit of the V.F.R. And for a short time I believe we succeeded.

Our leader was a young physicist called Ted Taylor, who had spent his formative years at Los Alamos designing nuclear weapons. We started out with three basic beliefs. (1) The conventional von Braun approach to space travel using chemical rockets would soon run into a dead end, since manned flights going farther than the moon would become absurdly expensive. (2) The key to interplanetary flight must be to use nuclear fuel, which carries in each kilogram a million times as much energy as chemical fuel. (3) A small group of people with daring and imagination could design a nuclear spaceship which would be both cheaper and enormously more capable than the best chemical rocket. So we set to work in the spring of 1958 to create our own V.F.R. We called it Project Orion.

We intended to build a spaceship which would be simple, rugged, and capable of carrying large payloads cheaply around the solar system. We felt from the beginning that space travel must become cheap before it can have a liberating influence on human affairs. So long as it costs hundreds of millions of dollars to send three men to the moon, space travel will be a luxury which only governments can afford. . . .

It is in the long run essential to the growth of any new and high civilization

that small groups of men can escape from their neighbors and from their governments, to go and live as they please in the wilderness. A truly isolated, small,
and creative society will never again be possible on this planet. . . .

We have for the first time imagined a way to use the huge stockpiles of our
bombs for better purpose than for murdering people. My purpose, and my belief,
is that the bombs which killed and maimed at Hiroshima and Nagasaki shall one
day open the skies to man. . . .

It should be clear to everybody that Apollo is an international sporting
event, in which science has only a subsidiary role. . . . Apollo will take men
beautifully for short trips to the moon. But as soon as we are tired of this
particular spectacle and wish to go farther than the moon, we shall find that we
need ships of a different kind.

I once asked Dyson to describe Ted Taylor during the days of
Orion, and he said, "I think of him mostly in La Jolla sitting under the
stars and dreaming how we would go there. He loved the beauty of the
stars. We sat there watching the planets go by. He didn't know much
about them from a scientific point of view. He just loved to look at them.
Did I intend to go, too? Oh, yes. Oh, very much so. Mars was 1965, if
all had gone well, but I was more interested in Saturn, really. I said
Saturn by 1970. One knows that Saturn has a lot of water available. You
could refuel there. And the puzzles about Saturn are extremely interesting. For example, its satellite Iapetus is white on one side and black on
the other. Why? That's what we'd like to know. Saturn would have been
a two-and-a-half-year trip. Ted was fortunate in his marriage to Caro.
She has great inner resources and would have made a perfect Penelope
to his Odysseus. What was interesting was the amount of people and stuff
we could have taken along in a payload of hundreds of tons. We could
have stopped on the moon for a couple of months and really done some
exploring. We always thought of the moon as being essentially a rather
useless piece of real estate, though. Everything depended on whether we
could find hydrogen there. It might have been a refuelling base. Ted,
incidentally, was extremely good as a boss. He had time for everybody.
He never got in a hurry. He had the gift of getting people to perform at
their best."

Inevitably, a Super Orion occurred to Dyson—a ship immensely
larger than the sixteen-story building under contemplation. So Taylor
spent an afternoon figuring out how heavy Chicago was. What would it
take to propel downtown Chicago through space at a few million miles
an hour? Dyson had the answer. He imagined something a mile in

diameter—using H-bomb propellants. The idea was to absorb all energy, then reradiate it at lower temperatures. Therefore, the pusher plate would be made of copper, which has high heat conductivity and would take the heat inside and then radiate it to space. This was a star ship, not a planet ship. Parts would be put into earth orbit by rocket, and the ship would be assembled up there. It would go out of the solar system and off to a nearby star in a voyage of a few hundred years. Its fuel would be a million hydrogen bombs. Taylor reports that Dyson would never smile when he talked about these things. "Dyson is a thousand years ahead of his time. He would disagree with that. He would say, 'Maybe a hundred.' "

Out to Point Loma, across the bay from downtown San Diego, Taylor and the others would take model Orions to test them in flight. Point Loma was a spectacular loaf of high cliffs and chaparral-covered hills reaching out into the Pacific. With shrieking seabirds overhead, small Orions would rise on clouds of flame and, generally, break to smithereens. The art became refined, though, and one day in 1959 a one-metre model blasted off and kept on going. Five movie cameras, operating at different speeds, followed the flight. The one-metre model —size of, say, a doghouse—had bombs inside that were made of high explosive. They were packed in cans strung together with Primacord, so the explosions could proceed from can to can. Each can had a metal plate on its bottom for "slight directivity"—to shape, somewhat, the charge. Boom. Rise. Boom. Rise. Boom. As the explosions came, they were orange and red and white and black, and they spread out hugely to all sides, with the small Orion sitting on them and climbing into the air. Boom. Orion went higher. Boom. Billows of smoke and fire. The thing was now a hundred feet in the air. Boom. If the ship happened to tilt on one blast, the next blast corrected the tilt. The flight was stable. Errors in timing or position were self-correcting. On up it went until the bombs were gone. A parachute opened, and the model slowly came down.

Orion attracted an impressive list of earnest supporters, among them Niels Bohr, Harold Urey, Curtis LeMay, Hans Bethe, Theodore von Karman, Arthur Kantrowitz, and Trevor Gardner. In 1961, Ted Taylor went alone to Huntsville, Alabama, to explain Orion to Wernher von Braun. Von Braun had no initial interest; he was just performing a courtesy. The Air Force had asked him to listen. While Ted talked with him—about temperatures, pressures, and other data—von Braun closed his eyes in apparent concentration, but Ted soon realized that von Braun was sound asleep. After a time, when von Braun's eyes opened, Ted turned on a movie projector and showed him, in slow motion as well as standard speed, flights of the one-metre model. Von Braun sat bolt upright. His face spread out in a big toothy grin. He asked for details. Could Ted give him certain data? Temperatures? Pressures? Von Braun was a vocal advocate of Orion thereafter.

Taylor worked on Orion seven years, the last of which were worrisome times, as the Air Force, which had taken charge of the project and had to present it as a military enterprise in order to get funds, moved to subvert Orion's purposes. "Whoever builds Orion will control the earth!" said General Thomas Power, of the Strategic Air Command. Power and a few others in the Air Force had in mind a space battleship with full-blown guidance systems and directional A-bomb explosives for bringing down missiles. It could run away from an enemy or it could turn around and take whatever might come—presenting its pusher plate to anything that came near it. Go ahead. Hit me. Orion could resist a megaton explosion five hundred feet away.

The limited-test-ban treaty of 1963 forbade nuclear explosions in space and in the atmosphere, and thus led to the indefinite suspension of Orion. "Just a few little twists of events and everything we were trying to do with Orion would have come through," Taylor has lamented. "It was, as Dyson put it, 'something more than looking through the keyhole of the universe.' It was opening the door wide."

Little Boy, of Hiroshima, was a thirteen-kiloton bomb. It killed nearly a hundred thousand people—a fact later filed under weapons effects. The most densely populated sector of the world is the part of Manhattan Island synecdochically known as Wall Street, where, in a third of a square mile, the workaday population is half a million people. If all the people were to try to go outdoors at the same time, they could not do so, because they are too many for the streets. A crude bomb with a yield of only one kiloton could kill a couple of hundred thousand people there. Weapons effects. Because the tall buildings would create something known as "shadow effect," more than twenty-five kilotons would be the yield necessary to kill almost everybody in the financial district. High dams taper, are thinner at the top. One kiloton would destroy at least the upper half of any dam in the world. Hoover Dam has the biggest head of water in the United States. A bomb dropped behind it into Lake Mead and set to go off at a depth of fifty feet would pretty much empty the lake. Weapons effects. The yield necessary to kill everyone in the Rose Bowl is a fizzle yield, something on the scale of one-fiftieth of a kiloton—so little that it would be not shock or fire but gamma rays that did the killing. A tenth of a kiloton detonated outside an electric-power reactor could breach the containment shell, disable the controls, and eliminate the emergency core-cooling system. There is more long-lived radioactivity in a reactor that has been running for a year than there would be in a bomb of a hundred megatons. A bomb with a yield of a fiftieth of a kiloton exploded just outside the spent-fuel pools at a reactor or a reprocessing plant could send downwind enough strontium-90 alone to kill tens of thousands of people. The placement of an explosion—where it happens—is what matters most, and that depends on purpose. The Hiroshima and Nagasaki bombs were exploded eighteen hundred and fifty feet in the air, because the guess was that from that height the bombs would accomplish the most damage through shock, fire, and radiation effects. A low-yield bomb exploded inside one of the World Trade Center towers could bring it down. The same bomb, if exploded outside, would perform erratically. The Pentagon is a hard target, because it is so spread out. A low-yield bomb exploded in the building's central courtyard would not be particularly effective. To crater the place and leave nothing but a hole in the ground, a full megaton—set off in the concourse, several levels under the courtyard—would be needed. Weapons effects.

A one-fiftieth-kiloton yield coming out of a car on Pennsylvania Avenue would include enough radiation to kill anyone above the basement level in the White House. A one-kiloton bomb exploded just outside the exclusion area during a State of the Union Message would kill everyone inside the Capitol. "It's hard for me to think of a higher-leverage target, at least in the United States," Ted Taylor said one day. "The bomb would destroy the heads of all branches of the United States government—all Supreme Court justices, the entire Cabinet, all legislators, and, for what it's worth, the Joint Chiefs of Staff. With the exception of anyone who happened to be sick in bed, it would kill the line of succession to the Presidency—all the way to the bottom of the list. A fizzle-yield, low-efficiency, basically lousy fission bomb could do this."

The Massachusetts Turnpike, as it bisects Boston, passes directly underneath, right through the basement of, the Prudential Center, a building complex that includes a fifty-two-story skyscraper. "All you'd have to do is stop, lift the hood, and beat it," Taylor noted as we drove through there one day. We went up to the top of the building to view the city. After a long look and a long pause, he said he could not imagine why anyone who went to the trouble to make a nuclear bomb would want to use it to knock over much of anything in Boston.

Driving down from Peekskill, another time, we found ourselves on Manhattan's West Side Highway just at sunset and the beginning of dusk. There ahead of us several miles, and seeming to rise right out of the road, were the two towers of the World Trade Center, windows blazing with interior light and with red reflected streaks from the sunset over New Jersey. We had been heading for midtown but impulsively kept going, drawn irresistibly toward two of the tallest buildings in the world. We went down the Chambers Street ramp and parked, in a devastation of rubble, beside the Hudson River. Across the water, in New Jersey, the Colgate sign, a huge neon clock as red as the sky, said 6:15. We looked up the west wall of the nearer tower. From so close, so narrow an angle, there was nothing at the top to arrest the eye, and the building seemed to be some sort of probe touching the earth from the darkness of space. "What an artifact that is!" Taylor said, and he walked to the base and paced it off. We went inside, into a wide, uncolumned lobby. The building was standing on its glass-and-steel walls and on its elevator core. Neither of us had been there before. We got into an elevator. He pressed, at random, 40. We rode upward in a silence broken only by the muffled whoosh of air and machinery and by Taylor's describing where the most effective place for a nuclear bomb would be. The car stopped, the door sprang back, and we stepped off into the reception lounge of Toyomenka America, Inc., a Japanese conglomerate of industries. No one was behind the reception desk. The area was furnished with inviting white couches and glass coffee tables. On the walls hung Japanese watercolors. We sat down on one of the couches. "The rule of thumb for a nuclear explosion is that it can vaporize its yield in mass," he said. "This building is about thirteen hundred feet high by two hundred by two hundred. That's about fifty million cubic feet. Its average density is probably two pounds per cubic foot. That's a hundred million pounds, or fifty kilotons—give or take a factor of two. Any explosion inside with a yield of, let's say, a kiloton would vaporize everything for a few tens of feet. Everything would be destroyed out to and including the wall. If the building were solid rock and the bomb were buried in it, the crater radius would be a hundred and fifty feet. The building's radius is a hundred feet, and it is only a core and a shell. It would fall, I guess, in the direction in which the bomb was off-centered. It's a little bit like cutting a big tree."

In dark-blue suits, in twos and threes, Japanese businessmen came out of the warrens of Toyomenka. They collected at the elevator shaft. In voluble streams of Japanese, they seemed to be summarizing their commercial day. More came, and more. None of them seemed to notice or, certainly, to care that we were there. "Thermal radiation tends to flow in directions where it is unimpeded," Taylor was saying. "It actually flows. It goes around corners. It could go the length of the building before being converted into shock. It doesn't get converted into shock before it picks up mass."

We went down a stairway a flight or two and out onto an unfinished floor. Piles of construction materials were here and there, but otherwise the space was empty, from the elevator core to the glass façade. "I can't think in detail about this subject, considering what would happen to people, without getting very upset and not wanting to consider it at all," Taylor said. "And there is a level of simplicity that we have not talked about, because it goes over my threshold to do so. A way to make a bomb. It is so simple that I just don't want to describe it. I will tell you this: Just to make a crude bomb with an unpredictable yield—but with a better than even chance of knocking this building down—all that is needed is about a dozen kilos of plutonium-oxide powder, high explosives (I don't want to say how much), and a few things that anyone could buy in a hardware store. An explosion in this building would not be completely effective unless it were placed in the core. Something exploded out here in the office area would be just like a giant shrapnel bomb. You'd get a real sheet of radiation pouring out the windows. You'd have half a fireball, and it would crater down. What would remain would probably be a stump. It's hard to say which way the building would fall. It would be caving one way, but it would be pushed the other way by the explosion." Walking to a window of the eastern wall, he looked across a space of about six hundred feet, past the other Trade Center tower, to a neighboring building, at 1 Liberty Plaza. "Through free air, a kiloton bomb will send a lethal dose of immediate radiation up to half a mile," he went on. "Or, up to a thousand feet, you'd be killed by projectiles. Anyone in an office facing the Trade Center would die. People in that building over there would get it in every conceivable way. Gamma rays would get them first. Next comes visible light. Next the neutrons. Then the air shock. Then missiles. Unvaporized concrete would go out of here at the speed of a rifle shot. A steel-and-concrete missile flux would go out one mile and would include in all maybe a tenth the weight of the building, about five thousand tons." He pressed up against the glass and looked far down to the plaza between the towers. "If you exploded a bomb down there, you could conceivably wind up with the World Trade Center's two buildings leaning against each other and still standing," he said. "There's no question at all that if someone were to place a half-kiloton bomb on the front steps where we came in, the building would fall into the river."

We went back to the elevator, and when the car stopped for us it was half filled with Japanese, who apparently quit work later than everyone else in world trade. Thirty-eight floors we fell toward the earth in a cloud of Japanese chatter, words coming off the Otis walls like neutrons off a reflector. In the middle of it all, I distinctly heard one man say a single short sentence in English. He said, "So what happened then?"

# The Survival of the Bark Canoe

For many of his early summers, McPhee went to a canoe-tripping camp in Vermont called Keewaydin. In the camp's dining hall was a venerable bark canoe, suspended from the rafters, grown dusty and brittle from its long years of dry dock. At mealtimes McPhee studied that canoe diligently, and one year he finally determined to rebaptize it afloat. The task required a dark night, fellow conspirators, and liquid fortification. But the old canoe sank dismally, and the party struggled for several pre-dawn hours to return it to the rafters. All went undetected until breakfast, when water dripped from the boat onto the plates of diners below.

McPhee still loves to canoe, or to write about canoe trips and white-water races. When he learned that a young man in New Hampshire was making bark canoes by hand, in the Indian fashion, he looked him up, observed the building process, and asked to voyage with the artisan into Maine's wilderness. Later, McPhee intended to write a glorious tribute to atavism and its survival. He might well have hung the trip on Keewaydin's rafters. Henri Vaillancourt had proved a superb craftsman, but he was a perfect "bummer" (his favorite expression) of a voyageur; inexperienced in the use of canoes yet a master of their repair. McPhee's story of this misadventure moves with the assurance of a writer who has mastered his craft, his reflector oven, and his polished, reflective prose. Like Henri's canoes, the narrative is tight and seamless, lashed together with precise descriptions and fluctuating moods, then decorated with ingenious motifs, "set pieces" on loons, voyageurs, Indians, and Thoreau.

Thoreau's presence in the narrative is hardly accidental. McPhee claims to know Thoreau only slightly, yet the description of his methods —notes, journal, a transparency of narrative time and persona—could be a self-portrait as well: "With the advantage of retrospect, he reconstructed the story to reveal a kind of significance that the notes do not reveal. Something new in journalism."—*WLH*

———————————

In the middle of one morning, Vaillancourt left the shop, got into his car, drove two or three miles down the road, and went into woods to cut a birch. The weather was sharp, and he was wearing a heavy red Hudson's Bay coat. His sandy-brown hair, curling out in back, rested on the collar. He carried a sheathed Hudson's Bay axe and a long wooden wedge and a wooden club (he called it a mallet) of the type seen in cartoons about cave societies. His eyes—they were pale blue, around an aquiline nose over a trapper's mustache—searched the woodlot for a proper tree. It need not be a giant. There were no giants around Greenville anyway. He wanted it for its sapwood, not its bark—for thwarts (also called crosspieces and crossbars) in a future canoe. After walking several hundred feet in from the road, he found a birch about eight inches in diameter, and with the axe he notched it in the direction of a free fall. He removed his coat and carefully set it aside. Beneath it was a blue oxford-cloth button-down shirt, tucked into his blue-jeans. He chopped the tree, and it fell into a young beech. "Jesus Christ!" he said. "It is so frustrating when Nature has you beat." The birch was hung up in the beech. He heaved at it and hauled it until it at last came free.

What he wanted of the tree was about six feet of its trunk, which he cut away from the rest. Then he sank the axe into one end of the piece, removed the axe, placed the wedge in the cut, and tapped the wedge with the mallet. He tapped twice more, and the entire log fell apart in two even halves. He said, "You get some birch, it's a bastard to split out, I'll tell you. But, Christ, this is nice. That's good and straight grain. Very often you get them twisted." Satisfied, he shouldered the tools and the wood, went back to the road, and drove home.

In the yard, he split the birch again, and he now had four pieces, quarter-round. One of these he cut off to a length of about forty inches. He took that into the shed. He built a fire, and in minutes the room was warm. He sat in his rocking chair and addressed the axe to the quarter-round log—the dark heartwood, the white sapwood. Holding the piece vertically, one end resting on the floor, he cut the heartwood away. He removed the bark and then went rapidly down the sapwood making angled indentations that caused the wood to curve out like petals. He cut them off, and they fell as big chips to the floor. A pile began to grow there as the axe head moved up and down, and what had been by appearance firewood was in a short time converted to lumber—a two-by-three, knot-less board that might almost have been sawn in a mill.

He then picked up his crooked knife and held its grip in his up-turned right hand, the blade poking out to the left. The blade was bent near its outer end (enabling it to move in grooves and hollows where the straight part could not). Both blade and grip were shaped like nothing I had ever seen. The grip, fashioned for the convenience of a hand closing over it, was bulbous. The blade had no hinge and protruded rigidly—but not straight out. It formed a shallow V with the grip.

Vaillancourt held the piece of birch like a violin, sighting along it from his shoulder, and began to carve, bringing the knife upward, toward his chest. Of all the pieces of a canoe, the center thwart is the most complicated in the carving. Looked at from above, it should be broad at the midway point, then taper gradually as it reaches toward the sides of the canoe. Near its ends, it flares out in shoulders that are penetrated by holes, for lashings that will help secure it to the gunwales. The long taper, moreover, is interrupted by two grooved protrusions, where a tumpline can be tied before a portage. The whole upper surface should be flat, but the underside of the thwart rises slightly from the middle outward, then drops again at the ends, the result being that the thwart is thickest in the middle, gradually thinning as it extends outward and thickening again at the gunwales. All of this comes, in the end, to an adroit ratio between strength and weight, not to mention the incidental grace of the thing, each of its features being a mirror image of another. The canoe's central structural element, it is among the first parts set in place. Its long dimension establishes the canoe's width, and therefore many of the essentials of the canoe's design. In portage, nearly all of the weight of the canoe bears upon it.

So to me the making of a center thwart seemed a job for a jigsaw, a band saw, a set of chisels, a hammer, a block plane, a grooving plane, calipers, templates, and—most of all—mechanical drawings. One would have thought that anyone assertive enough to try it with a knife alone would at least begin slowly, moving into the wood with caution. Vaillan-court, to the contrary, tore his way in. He brought the knife toward him with such strong, fast, heavy strokes that long splinters flew off the board. "Birch is good stuff to work with," he said. "It's almost as easy to work as cedar. This feels like a hot knife going through butter. I used to use a drawknife. That God-damned thing. You've got to use a vise to hold the work. With the crooked knife, I can work in the woods if I want.

I saw an Indian on TV in Canada using one. I got one, and I worked and worked with it to get the knack. Now it almost feels as if it's part of me. If anybody ever comes out with a tool that will rival a crooked knife, I'd like to hear about it." He sighted along the wood, turned it over, and began whipping splinters off the other side. He said that steel tools had come with the white man, of course, and that most people seemed to imagine that Indian workmanship had improved with steel tools. "But I doubt it," he continued. "With bone and stone tools, it just took longer. The early Indians relied more on abrasion. With the exception of the center thwart, there is no fancy carving in a canoe. It's all flatwork. In fact, I'm doing experiments with bone tools." He stopped carving, reached to a shelf, and picked up a bone awl. "Make two holes with a bone awl in a piece of cedar, take out the wood between the holes with a bone chisel, and you have a mortise for a thwart to fit into." He reached for a piece of cedar (wood debris was all over the shop), made two holes, picked up a wooden mallet and a bone chisel, and made a mortise in the cedar. Then he picked up the long, curving incisor of a beaver. "I made a knife last winter out of a beaver's tooth," he said. "The original crooked knife was made out of a beaver's tooth." He sat down and continued to carve. The strokes were lighter now as he studied the wood, carved a bit, studied the wood, and carved some more. The piece was beginning to look roughly like a thwart, and the gentler motions of the knife were yielding thin, curling shavings that settled down on the bed of chips and splinters around his feet.

"Where the crooked knife was, the bark canoe was," he said. "People from Maine recognize the crooked knife. People from New Hampshire do not. All they knew was the drawknife. The God-damned drawknife—what a bummer."

The bark canoe was also where the big white birches were, and that excluded a good part of New Hampshire, including Greenville. Vaillancourt goes north to find his bark. The range of the tree—*Betula papyrifera,* variously called the white birch, the silver birch, the paper birch, the canoe birch—forms a swath more than a thousand miles wide (more or less from New York City to Hudson Bay) and reaches westward and northwestward to the Pacific. Far in from the boundaries of this enormous area, though, the trees are unlikely and always have been unlikely to grow large enough for the building of good canoes, and this exclusion includes most of the West, and even the Middle West. The biggest trees and the best of Indian canoes were in what are now New Brunswick, Nova Scotia, Maine, Quebec, and parts of Ontario. Even within this region, the most accomplished craftsmen were concentrated in the east. Of these, the best were the Malecites. So Henri Vaillancourt builds Malecite canoes. Before all other design factors, he cares most about the artistic appearance of the canoes he builds, and he thinks the best-looking were the canoes of the Malecites. The Malecites lived in New Brunswick and parts of Maine. Vaillancourt builds the Malecite St. John River Canoe and the Malecite St. Lawrence River Canoe. He builds them with modifications, though. Toward the end of the nineteenth century, tribes started copying one another and gave up some of the distinctiveness of their tribal styles, and to varying extents, he said, he has done the same.

His carving became even slower now, and he studied the piece carefully before making his moves, but he measured nothing. "There's really no need for feet and inches," he said. "I know more or less what's strong and what isn't. If I want to find the middle of this crosspiece, I can put a piece of bark across it from end to end, and then fold it in half to find the center." He had measured the length—thirty-five inches—and had cut to it exactly. In the spring, when the time came to make the gunwales, he would measure them as well. But that is all he would measure in the entire canoe. According to the prescript passed on by Adney and Chapelle, the center thwart he was working on should taper

slightly in thickness each way from its center to within 5 inches of the shoulders, which are 30 inches apart. The thickness at a point 5 inches from the shoulder is ¾ inch; from there the taper is quick to the shoulder, which is 5/16 inch thick, with a drop to ¼ inch in the tenon. The width, 3 inches at the center, decreases in a graceful curve to within 5 inches of the shoulder, where it is 2 inches, then increases to about 3 inches at the shoulder. The width of the tenon is, of course, 2 inches, to fit the mortise hole in the gunwale.

Yet the only instruments Vaillancourt was using to meet these specifications were his eyes.

He finished off the tumpline grooves. The thwart appeared to be perfect, but he picked up a piece of broken glass and scraped it gently all over. Fine excelsior came away, and the surface became shiningly smooth. It was noon. He had cut the birch in the woods at half past nine. Now he held the thwart in his hand, turning it this way and that. It was a lovely thing in itself, I thought, for it had so many blendings of symmetry. He said he could have done it in an hour if he had not been talking so much. And he was glad the tree in the woods had turned into this thwart instead of "all the chintzy two-bit things they make out of birch—clothespins, dowels, toothpicks, Popsicle sticks." As he worked, he had from time to time scooped up handfuls of chips and shavings and fed them into the stove. Even so, the pile was still high around him, and he appeared to be sitting in a cone of snow.

He soon added more to the pile. From the rafters he took down a piece of cedar and, with the knife, sent great strips of it flying to the floor. He was now making a stempiece, the canoe part that establishes the profile of the bow or the stern. "Sometimes, when there are, you know, contortions in the grain, you can get into a real rat's nest," he said. "Around a knot, there will be waves in the grain. You cut to the knot from one side, then the other, to get a straight edge. At times like that, I'm tempted just to throw the thing out."

The wood he was working now, though, was clear and without complications, and after a short while, in which most of it went to the floor, he had made something that looked very much like a yardstick—albeit a heavy one—a half inch thick. Its corners were all sharp, and it seemed to have been machine-planed. Then he pressed the blade of the crooked knife into one end of the stick and kept pressing just hard enough to split the stick down fifty per cent of its length. He pressed the knife into the end again, near the first cut, and made another split, also stopping halfway. Again and again he split the wood, going far beyond the moment when I, watching him, thought that further splitting would be impossible, would ruin the whole. He split the board thirty-one times —into laminations each a half inch wide and a sixteenth of an inch thick. And all the laminations stopped in the middle, still attached there; from there on, the wood remained solid. "You split cedar parallel to the bark," he commented. "Hickory you can split both ways. There are very few woods you can do that with."

He plunged the laminated end of the piece into a bucket of water and left it there for a while, and then he built up the fire with scraps from the floor. In a coffee can he brought water to a boil. He poured it slowly over the laminations, bathing them, bathing them again. Then he lifted the steaming cedar in two hands and bent it. The laminations slid upon one another and formed a curve. He pondered the curve. It was not enough of a curve, he decided. So he bent the piece a little more. "There's an awful lot of it that's just whim," he said. "You vary the stempiece by whim." He liked what he saw now, so he reached for a strip of basswood bark, tightly wound it around the curve in the cedar, and tied it off. The basswood bark was not temporary. It would stay there, and go into the canoe. Bow or stern, the straight and solid part of the stempiece would run downward from the tip, then the laminated curve would sweep inward, establishing the character of the end—and thus, in large part, of the canoe itself.

The canoe-end profile was the principal feature that distinguished the styles of the tribes. The Ojibway Long-Nose Canoe, for example, had in its bow (and stern) an outreaching curve of considerable tumblehome (an arc—like a parenthesis—that turns more than ninety degrees and begins to come back on itself). The end profiles of the Algonquin Hunter's Canoe were straight and almost vertical, with a small-radius ninety-degree curve at the waterline. The departure from the vertical was inward, toward the paddler. The end profiles of certain Malecite canoes were similar, but the departure from vertical was outward. Other Malecite canoes had long-radius, "compass sweep" bows and sterns.

I mentioned to Vaillancourt that, before and during college years, I had spent a lot of time around a place in Vermont that still specializes in sending out canoe trips, and a birch-bark canoe hangs in the dining hall there.

"Near Salisbury," he said. "Lake Dunmore—am I right?" He took down a worn, filled notebook and began to whip the pages. "Let's see. Yeah. Here. Keewaydin. Is that it?"

That was it. He had not been there, but he would stop by someday. He hoped to see every bark canoe in existence. There were, for example, sixteen bark canoes in Haliburton, Ontario; one in Upper Canada Village, near Morrisburg, Ontario; a couple at Old Jesuit House, in Sillery, Quebec. In his notebook he had the names and addresses of museums, historical societies, and individuals from Maine to Minnesota, Nova Scotia to Alberta, and as far south as Virginia. Peter Paul, a Malecite in Woodstock, New Brunswick, had one. Vaillancourt had been to see him. The most skillfully built birch-bark canoe he had ever seen was made in Old Town, Maine, and was signed "Louis P. Sock." "I've seen only two or three canoes that were near perfect," he said. "But I've never seen a bark canoe that wasn't graceful. I've never seen an Eastern Cree canoe or a Montagnais. Most of the canoes I've seen did not have a definite tribal style. There's a bark canoe on Prince Edward Island. A sign says it's a Micmac canoe. It isn't."

I told him I'd long ago been told that the bark canoe at Keewaydin was an Iroquois.

He said he doubted that very much, because the Iroquois, except in early times, had had limited access to good birch, and had made their canoes—when they made canoes at all—out of elm or hickory bark. Various tribes had also used the bark of the spruce, the basswood, the chestnut. But all were crude compared to birch. If they wanted to get across a river, they might—in one day—build an elm-bark canoe, and then forget it, leave it in the woods. "You couldn't, by any stretch of the imagination, compare an elm-bark or a hickory-bark canoe to a birch canoe," he said. "Barks other than birch bark will absorb water the way wood will. Canoes made from them—even well made—got waterlogged and heavy. Most were just, you know, rough shells. Good for nothing, like automobiles. Automobiles last, you know, five or six years. A birch-bark canoe lasted the Indians ten."

I asked him how much experience he had had by now in more modern canoes. He said he had been in an aluminum canoe twice and in wood-and-canvas canoes only a few times in his life. Otherwise, he had never paddled anything but a birch-bark canoe. He did not paddle much around home, he said, because when he went canoeing he wanted to go to Maine.

"Where in Maine?"

"Oh, up north of Moosehead Lake. The Penobscot River. Chesuncook Lake. Caucomgomoc Lake. It's not just to get out in the canoe—it's to get out and see wildlife. A moose, you know, thirty feet away. Next time I go, I'm going down the Penobscot and on to the Allagash lakes."

I said, "Next time you go, I'd like to go with you."

He said, "Bring your own food."

I had been yearning to make a trip into that region for what was now most of my life. Keewaydin had run trips there, but one circumstance or another had always prevented me from going. Just the thought of making a journey there in a birchbark canoe was enough to make me sway like a drunk. I thought of little else through the winter and the spring.

The days are hot, and we often dip our cups in the river. Henri prefers Tang. He has the powder in his pack and a plastic jug by his feet as he paddles. He also has a supply of white bread—several loaves of it —and when he is hungry he pours honey onto the bread. In five minutes, he can prepare and finish a meal. Then he is ready to move on. We are in no hurry, like the shooting stars.

The river has many riffles, too minor to be labelled rapids. Nonetheless, they are stuffed with rock. The angle of the light is not always favorable. The rocks are hidden, and—smash—full tilt we hit them. The rocks make indentations that move along the bottom of the canoe, pressing in several inches and tracing a path toward the stern. It is as if the canoe were a pliant film sliding over the boulders. Still, I feel sorry and guilty when we hit one. I have been in white water and Rick has not, so he has asked me to paddle in the stern—to steer, to pick the route, to read the river—and I reward his confidence by smashing into another rock. Nothing cracks. If this were an aluminum canoe, it would be dented now, and, I must confess, I would not really care. Of all the differences between this canoe and others I have travelled in, the first difference is a matter of care about them. The canoes can take a lot more abuse than we give them, but we all care. Landing, we are out of the canoes and in the water ourselves long before the bark can touch bottom. We load and launch in a foot of water. The Indians did just that, and the inclination to copy them is automatic—is not consciously remembered—with these Indian canoes.

Once, on the upper Delaware, in a fifteen-foot rented Grumman canoe, I ran through a pitch of white water called Skinner's Falls. On a big shelf of rock at the bottom of the rapid, a crowd of people watched. When the canoe came through dry, they gathered around and asked how that was done. They said they were novices—a ski club on a summer outing—and none of them had been able to run the rapid without taking in quantities of water. "Well," said my wife, getting out of our canoe, "if you think you've seen anything yet, just wait until you see what is going to happen now. My husband spent his whole childhood doing this sort of thing—and so did that man up there in the other canoe. The two of them are now going to run the rapid together."

I walked up the riverbank. When I joined my friend and got into his canoe (also a fifteen-foot aluminum), I saw that one of the skiers had set up a tripod on which was mounted a sixteen-millimetre movie camera. My wife later told me she had said to them that it was good that they had the camera, because they would be able to study the film and learn a great deal. Skinner's Falls is easiest on the right. It gets worse and worse the farther to the left you go. So, for the rash hell of it, we dug in hard, got up to high speed, and went into the extreme left side of the rapid. The canoe bucked twice before the bow caught a rock that swung us broadside to the current and into a protruding boulder with a crash that threw us into the white river and bent the canoe into the shape of the letter C.

I have chosen not to tell that story to Rick Blanchette, for no one has ever cared more for a fifteen-thousand-dollar sports car (or, for that matter, for a work of sculpture) than he cares for his birch canoe.

Henri hits a rock; slides right; hits another. "I'd venture to say it would be easier to rip a wood-and-canvas canoe than a birch-bark," he says. "Anyhow, I've never, you know, ripped one." Henri paddles like an Indian. His stroke is a short, light, rapid chop. White people tend to take longer, harder strokes, which use a great deal more energy, he says. He appears relaxed in the stern of his canoe—leaning back, looking for wildlife, his paddle in motion like a wire whisk. Warren, in the bow, digs a large hole in the river with every stroke, contributing to the over-all effort the higher part of the ratio of power. We kneel, of course, and lean against the thwarts. There are no seats in these canoes. Kneeling is the natural paddling position anyway. It lowers the center of gravity, adds to the canoe's stability, brings more of the body into the stroke. Arms don't ache. You don't get tired.

We are seeing only ducks and muskrats on the big river, so we go into small streams in search of moose. These tributaries, tortuous and boggy, have all the appearance of moose country—Pine Stream, Moose-horn Stream. Moose tracks are everywhere—great cloven depressions in the mudbanks. Paddling silently, we move upstream—half, three-quarters of a mile. No moose. Henri is good at the silent paddle—the blade feathered on the recovery from each stroke and never coming out of the water. However, he is having difficulty travelling in the channel. The stream is only a few yards wide and has many bends. The canoes keep hitting the banks and sticking in the mud. With some trepidation, I suggest that there are bow strokes—draw, cross-draw, draw-stroke, pry, cross-pry—intended to help the canoe avoid the banks of the river. Trepidation because it is astonishing how people sometimes resent being told how to paddle a canoe. I have paddled on narrow, twisting rivers in New Jersey with good friends—easygoing, even-tempered people— who got royally incensed when I suggested that if they would only learn to draw and cross-draw they would not continue to plow the riverbanks. The look in their eyes showed a sense of insult, resting on the implication that every human being is born knowing how to use a canoe. The canoe itself apparently inspires such attitudes, because in form it is the most beautifully simple of all vehicles. And the born paddlers keep hitting the banks of the rivers. Mike Blanchette, though, in the bow of our canoe, to my relief, is not offended. Nor is Warren. They quickly pick up the knack of the pry and the draw—ways of moving the bow suddenly to left or right. Henri shows interest, too, inadvertently revealing that he knows almost nothing about paddling in the bow. His interest is genuine but academic. The bow is the subordinate position in a canoe. The person in the stern sets the course, is the pilot, the captain. The Blanchettes and I regularly change positions in our canoe, but Henri never leaves the stern.

Eventually, we give up the mooselook and go back to the main stream. Henri says it is all but impossible to go down the West Branch of the Penobscot River from North East Carry to Chesuncook Lake without seeing a number of—not to mention one—moose. Deriding us, a screaming seagull flies high above the river. We are two hundred river miles from the sea. Some substitute. In lieu of a moose, a seagull.

The Abnakis lived here. And the first whites to come into this lake-and-river country were hunters. They went back with stories of white pines so big that four men, grasping hands, could not reach around them. The next whites who came were timber cruisers. They made trips not unlike the one we are making—wandering at will in bark canoes—noting, and marking on inexact maps, the stands of pine. The big trees were there for the taking. They tended to cluster on the shores of the lakes. Loggers and log drivers followed, of course. Indian, hunter, cruiser, lumberer—this progression, in such beautiful country, could not help but lead to the tourist, the canoe-tripping tourist, and among the first of these (in all likelihood, *the* first tourist in the Maine woods) was Henry David Thoreau. He made two bark-canoe trips here, in 1853 and 1857, each time with an Indian guide. He went down this river. He went to the lake where Henri Vaillancourt—a hundred and twenty years later—would hide the felled cedar. Looking for moose in the night, he went up Moosehorn Stream. No moose. He had in his pack some pencils and an oilskin pouch full of scratch paper—actually letters that customers had written to his family's business, ordering plumbago and other printing supplies. On the backs of these discarded letters he made condensed, fragmentary, scarcely legible notes, and weeks later, when he had returned home to Concord, he composed his journal of the trip, slyly using the diary form, and writing at times in the present tense, to gain immediacy, to create the illusion of paragraphs written—as it is generally supposed they were written—virtually in the moments described. With the advantage of retrospect, he reconstructed the story to reveal a kind of significance that the notes do not reveal. Something new in journalism. With the journal as his principal source, he later crafted still another manuscript, in which he further shaped and rearranged the story, all the while adhering to a structure built on calendar dates. The result, published posthumously in hardcover form, was the book he called *The Maine Woods*.

Henri Vaillancourt's familiarity with books appears to be narrow, but he has read Thoreau—from *Walden* to *Cape Cod*, and most notably *The Maine Woods*. Rick Blanchette is saturated in Thoreau. In every segment of the river, they remember things Thoreau did there—places where he camped, where he collected flora, where he searched for moose. "I'm into Thoreau, too," Mike has said. "He writes about pickerel fishing, turtle hunting—the things I know and do."

Vaillancourt is transfixed by the knowledge that Thoreau, at North East Carry, actually watched a group of Indians making bark canoes. "All of them sitting there whittling with crooked knives! What a life! I'd give anything to have been there."

Back and forth between our two canoes, bits of Thoreau fly all day.

"Thoreau said the nose of the moose was the greatest delicacy, and after that the tongue."

"Thoreau said it is a common accident for men camping in the woods to be killed by a falling tree."

"Do you remember during the Allagash and East Branch trip when he said that all heroes and discoverers were insane?"

"No, that was in *Cape Cod*."

"Some people think he was humorless, you know. I disagree."

"Thoreau said . . ."

"Thoreau believed . . ."

"Do you remember the passage where . . ."

When it is not my turn to paddle and I am riding in the center of the canoe, I read to catch up. Thoreau's trips were provisioned with smoked beef, coffee, sugar, tea, plum cake, salt, pepper, and lemons for flavoring the water. His tent was made from cut poles and cotton cloth. He had one blanket. He carried his gear in India-rubber bags, and it included an extra shirt, extra socks, two waistcoats, six dickies, a thick nightcap, a four-quart tin pail, a jackknife, a fishline, hooks, pins, needles, thread, matches, an umbrella, a towel, and soap. For foul weather, he had an India-rubber coat, in which he sweated uncomfortably and got wetter than he would have in the rain. He ate his meals from birch-bark plates, using forks whittled from alder. For relief from mosquitoes, he wore a veil; he also threw damp leaves onto the fire and sat in the smoke. He slept in smoke, too—burning wet rotting logs all night.

Thoreau's guide on the first canoe trip was Joe Aitteon, and, on the second, Joe Polis—both Penobscots from Indian Island in Old Town, Maine. Henri Vaillancourt is at least as interested in these Indians as he is in Thoreau—particularly in Polis, who made his own canoes. Polis and Aitteon travelled light—no changes of clothing. Aitteon was a log driver. Polis was the better woodsman. Polis had represented his tribe in Washington. He had visited New York. He said, "I suppose, I live in New York, I be poorest hunter, I expect." Thoreau hired him for eleven dollars a week, which included the use of his canoe. Some eighteen feet in length, thirty inches wide, and a foot deep in the center, it was a longer, narrower canoe than the Vaillancourt canoes we are using. Thoreau's first canoe—on the 1853 trip with Aitteon—was more than nineteen feet long, and the bark was painted green. Our paddles are made from birch. Thoreau's were made from sugar maple. Thoreau was discomforted by the confinement of the paddling position, and he used the word "torture" to describe it. Sometimes he stood up in the canoe to stretch his legs. He appreciated nonetheless the genius of canoe technology. "The canoe implies a long antiquity in which its manufacture has been gradually perfected," he wrote in his journal. "It will ere long, perhaps, be ranked among the lost arts."

When Thoreau, from Mt. Katahdin, saw neither clearings nor cabins across huge domains of forest, lake, and river, he said, "It did not look as if a solitary traveller had cut so much as a walking-stick there." On closer view, though, from water level, he saw the stumps of timber a great deal larger than walking sticks. He saw dry-ki, too. The first dams (small dams, built to raise the lakes a few feet to serve, in various ways, the convenience of logging companies) had been built in 1841, and now, after a dozen years and more, "great trunks of trees stood dead and bare far out in the lake, making the impression of ruined piers of a city that had been—while behind, the timber lay criss-a-cross for half a dozen rods or more over the water." Dry-ki (the syllables rhyme) apparently derives from "dry kill": wood killed as a result of the dams and now, as dry as bone—gray, resins gone—crudely fencing the shores of open water. Thoreau always hoped to see some caribou but saw none. Of the caribou, Polis said, "No likum stump. When he sees that he scared."

The stumps that scared Thoreau were the stumps of the giant pines. To cut and take those trees was "as if individual speculators were to be allowed to export the clouds out of the sky, or the stars out of the firmament, one by one." If the attitudes behind such rapine were to go on unchecked, he said (a century and a quarter before the great ecological uprising), "we shall be reduced to gnaw the very crust of the earth for nutriment." And what of the remaining "stately pines"? Twenty years before the first national park, and more than a century before the Wilderness Act, he asked, "Why should not we . . . have our national preserves, where . . . the bear and panther . . . may still exist, and not be 'civilized off the face of the earth'?" The Maine of his bark-canoe trips was the deepest wilderness Thoreau would see in his lifetime. Today, astonishingly, it looks much the same as it did when he saw it. Lake and river, many thousands of miles of shoreline are unbroken by human structures and are horizoned only with the tips of spruce. The lakes are still necklaced with dry-ki, some of it more than a century old. Dry-ki has come to be regarded as charming. It certainly makes good firewood, a smokeless fire.

After forty-odd miles of Penobscot River, we are impatient for a change. For all its big bends and deadwaters—larger dimensions the farther we go—the river is now hemming us in, and we anticipate Chesuncook Lake, a burst of space. The skyline is opening up some. The lake must be around the next, or the next, bend. Thoreau said that in this same reach of the river he found himself approaching the big lake "with as much expectation as if it had been a university." The river debouches. The lake breaks open. We move out onto it and look to the right down miles of water and far beyond to the high Katahdin massif. Katahdin is a mile high. The lake's elevation is less than a thousand feet. Katahdin stands alone. The vast terrain around it is the next thing to a peneplain. Wherever you paddle through this country, when you move out onto the big lakes you can look to the southeast and see Katahdin.

A steady wind is blowing from the direction of the mountain, and since we are heading north we hold the canoes together and put up an improvised sail. Supported by two paddles as masts, the sail is the largest plastic bag I have ever seen—five by five feet. It is something called a Gaylord liner and comes from the small plastics factory in Greenville, where both Blanchettes work. The canoes move smartly before the wind. Indians used great sheets of bark as sails, and moose hide as well. According to *The Bark Canoes and Skin Boats of North America,* Indians of prehistory "may have set up a leafy bush in the bow of their canoes to act as a sail with favorable winds." At any rate, "the old Nova Scotia expression 'carrying too much bush,' meaning over-canvassing a boat, is thought by some to have originated from an Indian practice observed there by the first settlers." Thoreau sailed using a blanket. Our plastic sail sets Henri Vaillancourt off on a long, surprising tirade against the mills and factories of Greenville, which he says are sweatshops, exploiters of immigrant labor. "I'm glad I don't have to work in one of those places," he says. "Particularly that plastics shop. What a rip-off!" For Mike, the plastics shop is a summer job. He is a student at the University of New Hampshire. His brother, Rick, who is already a college graduate, wants to be a librarian in a New England college. He works full time in the plastics shop and also takes graduate courses in library science at Fitchburg State. Water rushes by and between the canoes. Holding the polyethylene sail, Rick quotes one of his favorite lines from Thoreau, which was occasioned by Thoreau's first night here on Chesuncook. He had moose meat for dinner and afterward went for a walk. "For my dessert," he said, and Rick is now quoting him, "I helped myself to a large slice of the Chesuncook woods, and took a hearty draught of its waters with all my senses."

Vaillancourt sneers. "Some dessert," he says. "Thoreau was a great guy, but a little far-flung there at times. What a crackpot—a real feather-brain, a very impractical person."

Blanchette is annoyed. Vaillancourt is amused. Blanchette says, "Yes? Well, the most influential man of this century will turn out to be Thoreau, who lived in the century before."

"He was extreme," Vaillancourt goes on. "He would not cut down a live tree. You can use nature without destroying it. I have an aunt in Concord. I asked her what people there thought of Thoreau, and she said, 'He was a real bum.' "

"Thoreau actually started a couple of forest fires in his time," Blanchette admits. "One in Concord. The other on Mt. Washington. When the fires went out of control, Thoreau just walked away."

"He said he thought he could make a bark canoe," Vaillancourt adds. "I doubt very much if he could have. That Aitteon, for an Indian, didn't know much, either. Thoreau asked him about the canoe, how the ribs were attached to the gunwales, and he said, 'I don't know. I never noticed.' Aitteon saw a porcupine once and thought it was a bear."

The Gaylord liner is pulling us up the west side of Gero, a big island.

Near the island shore, Vaillancourt sees two, three, four tall specimen birches, paper birches—perfection trees. He decides in an instant to camp below them tonight.

Henri Vaillancourt once had a dead bear in his room at college. This emerges as we move north on the northernmost arm of Chesuncook Lake. Between the canoes, idle conversation is for us what the *chansons* were for the *voyageurs*. Up at six, we have been on the water since seven-forty-five. The wind has not yet come up for the day. The canoes tend to separate. One or the other moves wide or falls behind. The gap extends until it reaches a kind of psychological apogee, at which moment binding forces begin to apply, and the two canoes—alone on hundreds of acres of water—draw slowly together until they all but touch.

Rick Blanchette says to Henri, when the gap is narrow, "So. How are you?"

"Fine. How are you? Still working down at the plastics shop?"

"Yes. Still building canoes?"

"Yes."

"How are the wife and kids?" Henri has no wife and kids.

"Fine. How are *your* wife and kids?"

Rick has none, either, but this ritual occurs at least twice a day.

I have told them they sound like Kordofan Arabs, who say to one another:

"God bless you."

"How is your health?"

"Thanks be to God, well."

"God bless you."

"How are your camels?"

"Thanks be to God, well. How are your camels?"

"Thanks be to God, well. How are your cattle?"

"Thanks be to God, well." And so on through any living thing in sight or mind.

And now Henri says to Rick, "How are your camels?"

And Rick says, "Thanks be to God, well. How are your cattle?"

And—to put a stop to it—I say, "God bless you. How is your dead bear?"

Henri explains that it was a cub and did not take up much space in the room.

"A *cub!*" Warren Elmer says, and his paddle stops.

"Someone had shot it, and my roommate got it from a butcher. I wanted to have the skin."

"I'd like to have the skin of the person who shot it," Warren says, and with his paddle rips a hole in the lake.

"If someone shot it, you know, someone might as well make use of it," Henri says, with a dismissive shrug. The gap begins to widen again. He takes the lead. He likes to be in the lead. He crosses our bow—so close that we have to stop to let him pass.

There has been an inordinate amount of talk this morning about Mud Pond Carry, which is only a mile or so ahead of us, and which comes back into the conversation now as we make the first portage of the trip—although "portage" is hardly the word for it. A scant fifty feet separates Chesuncook Lake from Umbazooksus Stream, across the low remains of an earth-fill logging dam. The topographic map indicates that Mud Pond Carry, two miles long, is a straight walk with a gentle rise of seventy feet followed by a gentle drop of sixty. There is tension, though, in Henri's voice when he talks about it, and in Rick's as well— a lot of verbal flexing and dancing around, with tremors at the mention of the name. I don't understand why. Perhaps it is because Thoreau got lost there—wandered right off into the woods, and was found, by his guide, many miles away.

We move on up Umbazooksus Stream, which is almost a deadwater —a current so light it can scarcely bend grass. We have come into a quiet, somewhat eerie chamber in the woods. Inaccurately, it puts forth a sense of lurking harm, and someone mentions *Deliverance*. We have all read the book or seen the movie—about four men on a canoe trip, one of whom is sexually abused at gunpoint by a stubbly-bearded mountain man—and among us *Deliverance* has become a sort of standing joke, like the plastics shop and the camels. *Deliverance* may have been set at the far end of the Appalachian chain, but its thought-wave effects seem to have reached to wherever canoes may float, and in one way or another we have all been warned not to go on canoe trips. Were we crazy? Did we realize what could *happen* out there? Had we seen *Deliverance?*

James Dickey, author of the novel and of the script of the film, lives on an artificial lake in Columbia, South Carolina. He teaches creative writing at the university there. He owns an aluminum canoe, and, by the report of colleagues, has logged in it journeys of impressively short distance. Students gather around him, and he says, "We need white water!," and they address the canoe to the shore of the flat brown lake.

Dickey goes into the house and comes back with a half-gallon bottle of bourbon, glasses, and ice. He goes in again, and comes out with his bow and arrow, his Martin guitar, and more duffel and cargo, until the canoe, loaded and launched, is low in the freeboard with students, writer, and gear. The canoe goes over the water. Then the water goes over the canoe. The canoe rolls, spills everyone. The guitar floats away. Dickey struggles to his feet. The lake comes up to his knees.

Such germinal scenes, transmuted in the treasuries of the author's imagination, have led to the impression that this mildest, gentlest, safest of outdoor activities—pursued for generations by summering teachers and Explorer Scouts—is a fear-shot thing to do. We decide that Umbazooksus Stream is James Dickey country, and around the next bend we will encounter the Umbazooksus Stationary Rapist, who, truth be told, is flown in each day from Boston. With thumbless hands, he strums a banjo while he waits.

From time to time, we encounter on the rivers and lakes other people in canoes. Warren and I, on a long walk in the woods one day in the hope of seeing wildlife, see instead two travelling canoemen in yellow slickers drinking canned beer by their beached canoe. As we emerge from the woods and walk toward them, incredible fear comes into their eyes. We are hairy—I with a stubble, Warren with a Visigoth's beard. We have no apparent canoe. We look "native" enough to rape a stone. One of the men has cherubic cheeks and fair hair and a fat tummy and small eyes, and he seems to be aware of his unfortunate resemblance to the victim in *Deliverance*. The closer we move, the beadier the eyes become. The beer can is up like plasma. We are now on top of these men, and there is nothing warm in their regard, which seems to say, "One more step and we'll scream."

"Hello," Warren says.

"Hi," I insert.

Warren speaks to them of routes and the weather. It is at once apparent that he has been miscast. His voice is all wrong to bear freight of danger, ignoble tones of any kind. The beer descends. The eyes debead. The scene uncreates itself.

Facts fulfill fiction sometimes, though. The river in the South that is most often identified as *Deliverance* country has attracted many hundreds of people who might otherwise have never in their lives stepped into a canoe. With some apparent sense of secondhand macho and shared novelistic experience, they have set out in canoes on the river; and, like boys from Hotchkiss and Groton being gored in the streets of Pamplona, a few of them have been killed—the ultimate adventure—but not by the gun of a strange aggressor. They have been killed by fast-moving water, with which their experience was limited to having seen it on film.

Dickey is not responsible, of course. He did not create foolhardiness. All he created was an imaginative book full of wildly impossible canoeing scenes—canoes diving at steep angles down breathtaking cataracts, and shooting like javelins through white torrents among blockading monoliths—and a film that was faithful to the book. A canoe trip is a society so small and isolated that its frictions—and everything else about it— can magnify to stunning size. When trouble comes on a canoe trip, it comes from the inside, from fast-growing hatreds among the friends who started. Perhaps Dickey delivered less than he might have when he brought trouble in from the outside.

Henri says that his reaction to *Deliverance,* while seeing the movie, was that he couldn't care less who was doing what to whom but he was shocked and alarmed by what was happening to the canoes.

Dingbat Prouty, a hundred years ago, was a logger who worked in this region of the woods, and one noted day he nearly drowned in a multiple tragedy in fast water, at a pitch on the Penobscot that took the lives of three of his companions. Prouty, swimming to safety, pulled himself up on a huge log that was floating in an eddy, and there he searched his soaked clothing, found his pipe and some tobacco that was dry, and had himself a quiet, contemplative smoke while the corpses went on downriver. "Ain't he a James Dickey bird!" said another logger, who watched him sitting there. The year was 1870. "Now, ain't he a James Dickey bird!" The expression was used to describe any person whose words or actions were filled with striking incongruities; and here, north of the Moosehead, it was universally understood.

We take a clearer look at the stream. If ever there was moose country, it is Umbazooksus Stream—with its broad meanders through fields of sedge, its occasional dead standing trees. The stream is quiet and protected, surrounded by forest. We decide that we are going to see a moose here. We will stop paddling, stop talking, and stay until a moose shows up or the stream freezes. We settle down to wait. Stillness envelops us. It is the stillness of a moose intending to appear.

Thoreau was here on the twenty-seventh of July. Polis, his guide, told him that "Umbazooksus" meant "Much Meadow River." Thoreau described it in his journal as "a very meadowy stream, and deadwater.

... The space between the woods, chiefly bare meadow . . . is a rare place for moose." He described the sedges, the wool grass, the abundant colonies of common blue flag. The year was 1857, and nothing has discernibly changed since then. "It was unusual for the woods to be so distant from the shore," he continued. "There was quite an echo from them, but when I was shouting in order to awake it, the Indian reminded me that I should scare the moose, which he was looking out for, and which we all wanted to see. The word for echo was Pockadunkquaywayle."

It is, of course, possible that a long brown snout will appear, a rack of antlers—unfortunately, a buck. We have seen no deer, but there are enough around—five per square mile of the Maine forest. Deer are so suburban, however, that for me they would frankly disturb the atmosphere of this remote northern stream. Deer intensely suggest New Jersey. One of the densest concentrations of wild deer in the United States—fifty per square mile—inhabits the part of New Jersey that, as it happens, I inhabit, too. Deer like people. They like to be near people, and New Jersey has more people per acre than any other state. People move out of the city to a New Jersey town and turn rhapsodic at the sight of deer. They write letters, songs, poems implying that they now live on the edge of wilderness. ("There were *deer* outside the window this morning.") Thoreau mentions a "deer that went a-shopping" in the streets of Bangor, explaining that deer "are more common about the settlements." Deer use the sidewalks in the heart of Princeton. A year or so ago, I saw a buck with a big eight-point rocking-chair rack looking magnificent as he stood between two tractor-trailers in the Frito-Lay parking lot in New Brunswick, New Jersey. When the buckshot season comes, New Jersey's deer know it, and at the sound of the first blast they get up on people's porches or stand around on lawns, waiting it out. The season lasts a week, in December. If the deer are patient, they die of old age. Meanwhile, they love apples. They like alfalfa, soybeans, clover, and lettuce. They like much of the truck in the gardens of man. In long files, they move through woodlots from orchards to gardens to the edges of fields. When the squirrels stop playing on the ground and run up into the trees, the herd is coming, travelling into the wind. A doe appears. Another. Another. Sometimes twenty go by, and then there is a skip in time. Now the main buck, the king of the herd, steps out of the woods. Hunters—watching from cover or from tree stands—will choose a buck in summer and take movies of him through the fall, waiting for December. Deer particularly gravitate to semi-rural research centers, of which there are many around Princeton, spaced like moons through the wooded countryside. The hunters know the size and special characteristics of each herd: the Squibb herd, the Dow Jones herd, the Western Electric herd, the Mobil Oil herd. The Institute for Advanced Study has extensive woodlots, and the smartest deer on earth are in the Institute herd.

If a deer would degrade this place slightly, a moose, on the other hand, would stir the morning. Our patience endures, though, no more than an hour. Like Thoreau before us, we fail to see a moose on Much Meadow River. Above us, a loon flies, laughing. We move on up the stream to its source—Umbazooksus Lake. A strong north wind has come up, and we have to fight it across the lake to the beginning of the carry.

Henri is edgy before the start. With considerable meticulousness, he slowly ties his tumpline to the center thwart and adjusts his carry board, which is tied to the thwart with a rawhide thong. The tump will fit across his forehead and pick up some of the canoe's weight. The carry board, a flat piece of cedar, a modified shingle, will place weight on the back of his head and the middle of his shoulders. Thoreau described such a carry board in *The Maine Woods,* and Henri has made this one from Thoreau's description. I ask him if the carry board generally helps a lot, and he says he will soon find out.

"You've always done without one?"

"I've never made a portage before."

With the exception of the fifty-foot carry we made into Umbazooksus Stream, he says, this is the first portage of his life.

In astonishment, I ask him, then, how many canoe trips he has made, and he says four—all short ones, and all without portages. I remember the little thirteen-foot canoe he was determined to bring on this trip, and I now understand why. He is well prepared, though, with his tump and carry board, and with two paddles tied to the thwarts so the flat of the blades will rest on his shoulders. He flips the canoe and holds it by the gunwales above him, the bow tip resting on the ground. He lowers the canoe into place on his shoulders. The bow swings upward to a point of balance. He adjusts the tump on his forehead. The over-all rig rides lightly. He starts off fast, almost at a trot, and disappears up the trail. His manual is in his head. "The Indian started off first with the canoe and was soon out of sight, going much faster than an ordinary walk," wrote Thoreau in his journal, describing the start of this portage.

Mud Pond Carry is the way of traffic north, and has been, apparently, since a time soon after the invention of the canoe. So many feet have scuffed across these two miles that the trail is a worn trench, lying well below the surrounding terrain, just as roads in Somerset, many centuries old, run in deep grooves between the fields around them. It is impossible to imagine how Thoreau could have got lost here, how he got out of the long ditch and wandered away, for in his time it was already deep. He called it "a loosely paved gutter" and a "very wet and rocky path through the universal dense evergreen forest . . . where we went leaping from rock to rock and from side to side, in the vain attempt to keep out of the water and mud." If Mud Pond Carry were more ample, we could paddle across it in the canoes, for it is a trail full of water. From one end to the other, bullfrogs live in the portage.

Rick, lighter than Henri and with the heavier canoe, has no tump-line or carry board, and the paddles, almost from the start, cut into his shoulders. With a pack basket and other gear, I walk in front of him and test the footing, so he can avoid following where I sink in deep. The water in the portage is not just standing there in pools. It actually runs—a man-made (foot-made) stream. As we cover the first mile, the current is coming toward us. I keep calling back to Rick, telling him when to step up on "the bank," because the mud is too deep, and when to step back into the trail, because the canoe would otherwise strike the encroaching trees. Now and again, the strain of the canoe's bulk and the knee-wrenching slipperiness underfoot cause him to stop and rest, but he declines all offers of assistance. It is clearly quite important to him that he carry the canoe to the far end by himself. It is his first portage, too.

In the second mile, we notice that the current in the carry is now moving away from us. We have crossed the height of land. The water that ran toward us was on its way to the Penobscot River and Penobscot Bay. The water now running away from us is by nature Allagash flow, headed north to Canada, to go down the St. John to the Bay of Fundy. For some sixty years after Yorktown, Great Britain was under the impression that this height of land was the boundary between the United States and Canada—a viewpoint that contained within it an excuse for war, but the king of Holland was called upon as mediator and the opportunity passed. The king saw the Mud Pond Carry only on a map, and Thoreau thought this a pity, because "the king of Holland would have been in his element" here.

At the Mud Pond end of the carry, Henri combs and recombs his hair. He shows no inclination to go back and get his packs. By conventional procedure, the person not carrying the canoe takes some of the

duffel halfway and then goes back for the rest; meanwhile, the canoe
carrier goes to the far end, then returns for the gear that has been left
at the halfway point. Henri, who has worked out so many of his skills
empirically, obviously means to do the same with portaging, and the
precedent he sets now is that carrying the canoe is all he will do. Someone
else will have to go back for his packs. Warren does so, with a cheerful
shrug.

For thirty miles up the Allagash lakes—Chamberlain, Eagle,
Churchill Lake—we fight the north wind. Much of the time, we lose. For
hours it stops us—blows so hard that we can't move. It brings frustration
and fans dissension. It's a real muzzler, a nose-ender. Henri's advertised
philosophy—"Take it easy, see some wildlife"—has long since shriv-
elled, and now blows completely away. Nothing can distract him—
neither a mink nor a marten nor a buff-colored hawk clinging to a
swaying fir—from his apparent need not to take it easy. When the wind
defeats us and we have to wait, he prowls, fidgets, and swears. At home,
he can carve for ten straight hours, but here he cannot sit still.

Even Mud Pond, which is only one mile by two, is a brownish froth,
uncrossable, and to get to the other side we have to make a high circle
in the lee of the northern shore. Henri, whose talents do not include map
reading, wanders up the inlet stream. The Blanchettes call him back. The
outlet stream is too shallow for riding, so we walk down it with our hands
on the floating canoes. We enter a bay of Chamberlain Lake. The bay
is small—only two or three hundred acres—and almost completely landlocked. At the far end is a gap in the trees, beyond which is open water.
It is fairly hard work just to traverse this little bay, for the oncoming
waves are high enough to wash into the canoes—into Henri's in particular. Finally, we near the gap, and through it can more clearly see the
main body of the lake—storied, wind-ridden Chamberlain. For thirty-
odd years, I have been hearing tales of this lake and how it is a whistling
groove whose waves stand up like the teeth of a saw. The lake surface
out there now is as white as a fast rapid. The waves are two feet high.
We pause in the narrows, watch the big rollers, and take out on the shore
beside them. The sun is falling. We will wait for morning and hope for
calm.

Warren and I jump into the water and—to get the grit of travel out
of our hair—shampoo with Lava soap. Henri unloads his canoe and
takes Mike Blanchette in his bow, and they go out to play with the big

waves. The canoe nearly broncos them into the water, and they run for shore. Clean, feeling good, Warren and I build a bonfire of dry-ki in the lee of the forest and beside a big rock on the beach. Henri and the Blanchettes make their fire back in the woods. I go down in my pack for my pharmaceutical bottles, which are white and plastic and contain bourbon and gin. Henri makes himself a gin-and-Tang. There are worse things in life than stopping early for the day, surveying whitecapped water across the rim of a tin cup, standing in a wind where no-see-um no fly. Warren and I cook dried hamburgers in a bucket of noodles. Henri eats his green jerky and gray oatmeal. Facing the big dry-ki fire, a trayful of gingerbread rises to unprecedented heights in my reflector oven. Henri wolfs it when the tray is passed to him. He announces that he has decided to buy a reflector oven.

Well beyond noon, we are still held fast by the wind. It has subsided a little, but the lake remains a whitecapped sea. One senses that we will be on it soon. Henri is using the word "bummer" at about double the rate he was using it an hour or two ago. The wind and Henri's patience are drawing lines across the day, and when the lines converge we will load up and go.

Just a few feet inside the treeline on the shore, the wind is filtered and calmed. Looking out on the lake from between two trees is like looking through a window at a storm. It is pleasant here, and warm. I could stay here for a week, not to mention the hours that are left in this day. I would very much like to sleep and read and—no matter how much time it takes—outlast the wind. But that would be the Indians' way, and Henri is not an Indian. Restless, impatient to move forward and cover ground, he paws the beach. He throws a rock in the water. He curses the wind. He says, "Christ, it's quiet enough. Let's go." It would take a meteorologist to tell us whether the wind is stronger or weaker than it was when we put in to shore. The waves are rolling hard, but the waiting, apparently, has built the case for going. We load the canoes and shove off.

We dig into the lake. We paddle and bail, bail and paddle—draining the bilge with drinking cups. We are struggling to get to the north end, about three miles away, and gambling that the wind will not rise to an even higher level before we are in the lee of the north-end woods. Why do we need these miles now? Why does Henri have this compulsion to move? Is he Patton? Sherman? Hannibal? How *could* he be, when the only regimentation he can tolerate is the kind he creates as he goes along? These are thoughts not composed in tranquillity but driven into the mind by the frontal wind. Why do we defer to him? Why do we look to his decisions? Is it only because he made the canoes, because the assumption is that he knows what is best for them and knows what they can do and ought not to do? His judgment draws attention to itself, right enough. On the Penobscot River, he went "out for a spin" in heavy, gray dusk and was gone long after dark—much longer than he wished or intended. What was he doing? He was struggling to pick his way through boulders and up a set of minor rapids he could not see. A camper on the riverbank, that same day, asked him if his canoe was not too low in the freeboard for paddling on open lakes, and he said, "Not really. They don't really ride low. You can design a canoe to do anything." But here he is on Chamberlain Lake, bailing six inches of water from between his knees and whisking with his paddle, while Warren, like a tractor, pulls the canoe. A suspicion that has been growing comes out in the wind: Henri's expertise stops in "the yard"; out here he is as green as his jerky.

After two hours of paddling, we have gone a mile and three-quarters, but we are at least not going backward. We begin to feel the protection of the land ahead of us, and Rick and I point off the wind and head more directly for the carry at the northeast corner of the lake. Mike, though, does not like rolling in the troughs of the waves. He says to his older brother, "Do you think we'll have trouble taking these waves broadside, Rick?"

"We'll head out a little," Rick answers.

"No. Follow Henri, Rick. Follow Henri."

Mike is a pessimistic soul, and he is convinced that—as he puts it —"if the canoe turns over, you're a goner." All the more touching is his belief that Henri will see him through.

Rick defers to Henri, too, but less so. Rick is Henri's lifelong friend. The differences between them must attract the one to the other. Rick is self-effacing and thoughtful, and he is less impressed than he might be with his own intelligence. He has no apparent special talent, and he admires greatly Henri's single-minded dedication, his artistry, and his adroitness with his tools. Rick introduced Henri to Beethoven and, in all likelihood, to Thoreau. Subtly, in one way or another, he seems to have been helping Henri along for years. Rick seems to sense frailty and unsureness under Henri's carapace of bluntness, and is always ready to give him the benefit of the doubt. Rick is sensitive to Henri's insensitivities—to his opinionated arrogance, to his inconsiderate manner, to his platoon-leading orders. In Rick's long, contemplative glances, Warren and I can see him weighing the effect of Henri's directives.

Warren, who has the misfortune to be paddling in Henri's bow, is by now suffering from acute propinquity, and, being a silent man, takes it out on the lake. His strokes are delivered with killing strength, and in their canoe it is Warren who is defeating the wind. The more Henri orders him around, the harder Warren must work to work off his anger. It is an asset to have such an engine in the bow. Warren and I are more or less guests on this trip, so we defer to Henri. We have, however, tried to make suggestions—where to stay, when to go, what to head for—but the results have been dismal, and we have learned that suggestions are challenges to the tacit commander. We go when he is ready. We stop when he wants to stop. We stay where he wants to stay. He does not seek out the consensus of the group, and when it comes his way he almost automatically rejects it.

Some of these thoughts subside with the wind as we move in among the sedges in the corner of the lake. We are finished at least with the winds of Chamberlain, having climbed ten miles through them an inch at a time.

An isthmus half a mile wide separates Chamberlain from Eagle, and a steam-powered continuous cable once ran across it, hauling logs from one lake to the other on little steel trucks. All the thousands of bolts, steel clamps, steel saddle, steel tracks, and fourteen tons of cable were brought into the woods over winter ice or in canoes and other boats, following the route we have followed. The conveyor lasted about six years—at the beginning of the twentieth century. Beside what is left of it we portage now. The track is still there, upgrown with trees. The portage trail is firm and open, and easy going all the way. Just before the shore of Eagle, we drop our packs, set down the canoes, and stare in disbelief at what may be the most incongruous sight any of us has ever seen: two full-scale steam locomotives, alone in the woods, abandoned. They, too, were brought in here in fragments and assembled in the woods. Standard-gauge track—seventy-five miles from the nearest railroad—was laid so that logs could be moved a few miles over the height of land. The trains began running in 1927 and were used for only a season or two. The track they ran on has been all but closed over by the woods.

We go down to the shore and look at Eagle Lake. It is a big one, and four miles of it stretch north in front of us before it bends to the west and out of sight. The wind and the whitecaps are worse than they were on Chamberlain—a forbidding gale. Henri sucks on a blade of grass and paces around saying, "Christ, what a bummer." It is as clear to him as to the rest of us that there will be no moving into such a wind. We eat lunch. It is four-thirty in the afternoon. The wind will drop soon, Henri tells us. Meanwhile, Henri's packs are still at the other end of the carry. The Blanchettes go back to fetch them for him.

After two more hours, big gray waves are still coming down the lake, rolling before the wind. Unfortunately, this is a bad place to spend a night, because the mechanized loggers gave it a century's fouling and the century isn't over yet. Rust is everywhere—rusty spikes, rusty hunks of the conveyor. To accommodate incoming logs, landfill was shoved into the lake, so the shore is artificial and swampy and strewn with boulders and still jagged with the corpses of water-killed trees. Mike wants to stay here, in this oxidized hole of commerce. He is so tired that it looks good to his eyes. He says it is as good as any campsite we've seen. Rick watches Henri and says nothing. Warren and I move our packs up the portage trail, planning to sleep there and avoid the junk yard. When we return to the lakeshore, Henri says the wind is declining. It is seven-thirty now, and the lake is indeed calming down. We will paddle at night, Henri says, and take advantage of the absence of the wind. Warren looks around with incredulity, and even apprehension, in his eyes. He appears to be wondering how to make a straitjacket. We got up at five today. We have paddled ten miles into blistering wind and followed that with a portage. Now we are told that we are going to set out on another big lake for God knows where in the dark of night. Under the influence of the wind, our affection for our leader has been waning all day, and it now levels out at zero. We turn without comment and walk away.

Warren, who was recently discharged from the Marine Corps, says, "I feel as if I were back in uniform." We go up the trail to our packs and our tent, and pick them up, and carry them back to the lake. It is Henri's trip. We will paddle tonight.

There is a cut, a sluiceway, a small canal, that penetrates the shore. It was used to float logs to the conveyor. Henri and Warren load their canoe in the sluiceway and push off toward the open lake. Rick and Mike and I fill our canoe, and while we are handling the packs a six-inch leech excitedly swims among us, trying to get in on the fun. With everything aboard, the three of us prepare to step in. We do not know that two iron spikes, set in timber, stand upright underwater, the tip of each less than an inch from the underside of the floating canoe. We step in, one at a time, and we give the canoe a shove. It does not move. Water spurts upward in fountains, fast enough to swamp us instantly.

Jumping out, we shout for Henri. We unload the canoe, lift it ashore, and roll it over. Rick is struggling to control his distress. His canoe, a treasure to him, has two ugly holes in it, large enough and ragged enough to make one wonder how it can continue the trip. Henri, examining the wounds, curses Rick for negligence, for irresponsibility, for failure as custodian of a bark canoe. Rick does not try to demur.

Now, all at once, Henri stops his harangue and changes utterly. The man who has been pouting, sucking grass, and cursing the wind all afternoon is suddenly someone else—is now, in a sense, back in his yard, his hands on a torn canoe. The lacerations are broad, and the bark around them is in flaps with separating layers. "Make a fire," he says, and Warren and I move off for wood. "Rick, Mike, get bark. Get strips of bark. And cut a green stick."

Henri goes down into his pack for the small paper bag in which he keeps his pot of pitch. He has been touching up the canoes from time to time since we started, and now has about six ounces left.

The fire is going. He sets the pot on two burning sticks. It seems so vulnerable. What if the pitch spills or blazes up? Where are we then, with one canoe?

Thirty minutes ago, we were standing apart in groups, tense to the edges of rage, some of us committing verbal mutiny. Now we are all bustling in service to Henri—his surgical nurses, offering instruments to his hand. First—with his crooked knife—he cuts away what appears to me to be a considerable amount of bark, trimming the split and flapping laminations. He does not cut all the way through, for with the exception of the actual punctures most of the damage is in the outer layers. He cuts a wide, shallow crater around each wound—four to five inches in diameter—taking away about half the bark's layers.

He asks for the green stick and the fresh bark, and with them he makes a torch. He lights it, and moves it close to the bottom of the canoe. He takes a deep breath and steadily blows flame into and around one of the punctures. Gradually, the bark there lightens in tone and becomes bone-dry. Henri says it is not impatience but necessity that causes him to use the torch. Even if he were to wait many hours, the rent bark would not completely dry; and "if bark is not absolutely dry the pitch won't stick."

It is now too dark for him to see. He calls for the flashlight, and I get it from my pack and shine it on the canoe as he works. He removes the pot from the fire and—with a flat stick—paints the entire damaged area with pitch while the Blanchettes, one at each end, hold the canoe level. Henri pulls out the tail of his shirt and cuts it off. It is broadcloth, and he cuts out of it a circular piece, which he presses down onto the pitch. Calling for the pot again, he paints on more pitch, until the cloth is completely covered. Then, as the pitch cools, he presses it repeatedly with his thumb, licking his thumb as he goes along to keep it from sticking. The finished patch is a black circle, about six inches in diameter. It is in the center of the bottom of the canoe. "At home I'll cut an eye of bark and put a rim around it," Henri says. "Then the patch, you know, will look better."

It is too late to move now. We sleep beside the canoes and get up at five-thirty to continue the repair. The pitch, heating up in the morning fire, bursts into flame. Henri runs to it and smothers it with a coffeepot lid, but some is lost. Minutes later, the pitch catches fire again.

"Our pitch after this is going to be nil," Henri says. "That's no problem, though. I should have brought more pitch, but we can always get spruce gum. There's plenty of it around here."

Applying what is left to the other rip in the canoe, he says casually, "I've never had this happen before. I've never had to patch a canoe before." He pauses, and licks his thumb. "You could break a whole end off in the woods and still fix the canoe—that is, if you'd built a canoe before," he says. "If you hadn't, I think you'd be in trouble."

Mike says, "I wonder what will happen if those patches let go in the middle of the lake."

And Henri says, "I don't think they will."

There is a time of change in a wilderness trip when patterns that have been left behind fade beneath the immediacies of wind, sun, rain, and fire, and a different sense of distance, of shelter, of food. We made that change when we were still in the Penobscot valley, and by now I, for one, would like to keep going indefinitely; the change back will bring a feeling of loss, an absence of space, a nostalgia for the woods. The end has come, though. Henri has run out of Tang. Tang is his halazone, his palate's defense, his agent conversional for pure lakes and streams. Without Tang, he is without water.

The Caucomgomoc roadhead is about twenty miles away—prospectively a long day's journey, since three of the twenty miles are forest portage trail. We are up in the morning at half past four.

On the water, in the post-dawn light, the canoes slide across a mirror so nearly perfect that the image could be inverted without loss of detail. The lake is absolutely still, and mist thickens its distances and subdues in gray its islands and circumvallate hills. Warren and Henri are perhaps a hundred feet farther out than we are, and appear to be gliding through the sky: Henri's back straight, his hand moving forward on the grip of his paddle, his dark knitted cap on his head, his profile French and aquiline; Warren under the bright tumble of hair, his back bending. Their canoe was alive in the forest only months ago, and now on the lake it is a miracle of beauty, of form and symmetry, of dark interstitial seams in mottled abstractions of bark. The time is the present, of course—effectively, and importantly, now—yet without changing a grain of the picture this could be the century before, or the century before that, or the century when the whites first came here in Indians' bark canoes. Two straight wakes trace the way in silence toward the southern end of the lake.

The silence, after a time, is torn apart by a congress of loons: ten loons, racing in circles on the surface of the water, screaming, splashing, squealing like dogs, taxiing in long half-flying runs. For a full ten minutes they keep it up—a ritual insanity, a rampant dance of madness, a convincing demonstration that every one of them is as crazy as a loon.

The long carry has about every obstacle a carry can have, short of German shepherds trained to kill. It has quagmires, slicks of rock, small hills, down trees, low branches, and, primarily, distance. Three miles, even on flat ground, is a long way. In sheer ooze and muck, this portage is as wretched as the Mud Pond Carry. Warren departs first, with a large pack and the tent, to cross, return, and cross again—nine miles. Moving alone, he escapes the compass of tension. Mike follows soon after. Henri tells me not to go on my own but to stay back with Rick and guide and help him. "Stay close to Rick. . . . Stay with Rick. . . . Help Rick," he keeps saying as the three of us go up the trail. The implication is that Rick may collapse, and this is not lost on Rick, who is tight in the throat but seems all the more determined to carry the canoe the whole distance alone. Henri's canoe weighs sixty pounds, Rick's seventy. It is not the weight but the bulk that brings difficulty. Light branches of balsam springily push the hulls, staggering the walker beneath. With the slightest stumble, the canoes lurch forward, straining the muscles of the legs, neck, and back.

"Help Rick!"

Henri shows no inclination to move ahead by himself. To them both I call out the story of the terrain: "Watch a hole here! . . . The mud is a foot deep here! . . . Low branches here! . . . Step to the left of this little swamp!"

After a mile, Rick's resolve declines. He doubts if he can make it. He rests his canoe on an overhanging branch and asks me if at the halfway point I will give him my pack basket and other gear and take the canoe from there. With that to look forward to, he moves on.

Henri now steps into mud up to his knee and, with a cry, falls. On the way down, he twists his body and spreads his elbows to cushion—as far as is possible—the canoe. He does not seem to care if he cracks every bone in his body as long as he cracks not a rib of the canoe, which lands on top of him and squashes him into the mud.

He gets up cursing me. The fault is mine. I did not tell him where not to step.

I stay closer to him, the better to guide him. He lifts the canoe, moves on a short distance, then puts the canoe down. His Indian carrying board is hurting his head. "Give me your jacket," he says. I give him my jacket. "Get me some string." From my pocket I give him some cord. Terse, angry, he fashions a pad for his head. At this point, Henri seems frightened and shaken with doubt.

Rick, for his part, seems to be, if anything, stronger. Much of the strain has left his face. His vitality, his endurance seem to rise a bit with each part of Henri that comes unstuck.

Warren passes us, going the other way. It is Warren, really, who is defeating the portage—outwalking, outcarrying everyone else. He tells us we are more than halfway. The news is surprising and tonic. I look to Rick. My turn now? He has no thought of giving up his canoe.

After another half mile of narrating the trail, I have become both restless and guilty. I tell Henri I feel pinned down, leading him through the woods, slowly, while Warren is doing so much of the work.

"Well, I'm carrying my share," Henri answers emphatically. Apparently, he wants to believe it. "Anyways," he adds, "Warren is a backpacker. He likes what he is doing."

Not far from the portage end—two hours after the start—Henri calls a halt at a stream for a drink. I am about to go back to help Warren, but Henri insists that I stay—that it is more important to guide the canoes safely to the end of the carry. Raspberry bushes are in fruit around the stream. At leisure, he eats from them. Now and again, he combs his hair. Rick notices moose tracks, large and fresh. We look around. No moose. Henri finds pin cherries and eats them, too. Twenty minutes go by. Warren by now is in his seventh mile. On his back is one of Henri's packs. The other is clutched in his arms.

Henri is a hero of the portage ends, for at such places we encounter other travellers passing through, and they are generally awestruck by the bark canoes. Henri overcomes his constitutional shyness. He moves in close. He fixes his eyes on one of his elbows and answers questions, quaffs the commentary, until the supply is gone.

"Your canoes look Indian, but you don't."

"Did you make them from a kit?"

"Is that real birch bark?"

"Where do you buy them?"

"They looked too fakey to be fake, so I figured they had to be the real thing."

"I've always thought it was painted on."

"Those are old ones, aren't they? All patched up like that?"

"They don't make them like that anymore."

"Congratulations. That's the best imitation of a birch-bark canoe I've ever seen."

("Our little canoe, so neat and strong, drew a favorable criticism from all the wiseacres among the tavern loungers along the road," wrote Thoreau as he approached the woods.)

Henri seems disappointed at portage ends if no one is there. He is not disappointed now. Six men in plastic canoes arrive to begin the carry.

"Are they real?" one of them asks.

"Do you mind if we look them over?"

"You *made* them?"

"*Really?*"

They, in turn, have something to tell us. In Ciss Stream, which lies between the long portage and Caucomgomoc Lake, they saw, thirty minutes ago, a cow moose. Warren arrives with the packs. We load and go.

Ciss Stream, from the portage to the lake, does not drop one inch, and is a deadwater with meanders so curving that they almost form oxbows. In near silence, we steal around its unending bendings through the sedge. Everything is right. The breeze is toward us. The bends conceal us. And the so-called stream is a bog of dry-ki and water-standing grasses—a phreatophytic meadowland, a magnification of Umbazooksus Stream. Our chances thus seem one in one. Another bend. Another scene. No moose. No moose—just the craggy spars of the dry-ki pointing lifeless into the sky. Thousands of trees, dead a century, fill the swamps here, and they are eerily beautiful, silver gray. The logging dams on Caucomgomoc destroyed them so long ago that they are now thought picturesque, their root structures webbing upward thirty feet above the sedge-meadow plain. People came here and killed these trees, and created this unearthly beauty. Another bend. No moose.

A mother merganser races squawking out of the sedge and starts down the stream before the two canoes. Screaming, feigning injury, displaying an awkward wing, she leads us around another bend. She will not give up. She will not shut up. She keeps her position, about a hundred feet in front of the canoes, for fully half a mile, raucous all the way. She wrecks the mooselook for good and all. At last, she rises flippantly into the air and flies back to her chicks where she left them.

We round the last bend, and swing into Caucomgomoc. It is two miles wide, and we have about six miles to go—to its far, northwestern corner. Coming directly at us across the lake are the highest waves we have seen yet, driven by a western wind. Henri, in his own drive for the finish, moves straight out onto the water and begins to plow headlong for the farther shore. His caution—what there was of it on Eagle and Chamberlain—is gone. To me, it seems a certainty that we are going to swamp, that we will complete the day with a long, slow swim, dragging the canoes to shore. I check my boots, my pack, to make sure they are firmly tied. I am ready to shrug and see what happens. Warren, however, is not. Having absorbed Henri in silence for something like a hundred and fifty miles, he now turns suddenly and shouts at the top of his lungs, "You God-damned lunatic, head for the shore!" The canoes turn, and head for the shore.

We are pinned down for the rest of the afternoon, squatting among boulders, eating chocolate in the wind—watching the whitecaps, the rolling, breaking, spraying waves. Then, with amazing suddenness after the fall of the sun, the wind subsides and dies. The lake becomes still, smooth, a corridor of glass. We venture out, timid, remembering the wind, then forget it and go straight down the middle the last six miles, mirrored as in the early morning, and under cumulus mountains, in alpenglow, scarlet.

As we touch shore, a young couple with a Grumman canoe are preparing to leave, to paddle into the evening to camp who knows where.

She grips her paddle as if it were a baseball bat. He instructs her to separate her hands. Practicing paddling, she strokes the air, pulling the blade past her the narrow way. Stepping into the canoe, she sits in the bow seat, ready to go. But the canoe is beached, fifteen feet from the water. She gets out. He shoves it over the gravel. They get in and paddle off. They go down the lake half a mile, then turn around and come back. They have left standing open all the doors of their car, which is covered with fresh white letters: "JUST MARRIED. BUZZ ON."

Henri cuts poles to support both canoes on the rooftop of his car. Fifteen miles down the dirt-and-gravel road, in what is now the black of night, we are blinded by the oncoming headlights of a many-ton truck, a logging truck—the immense, roaring descendant of the West Branch Drive. The lights are so bright that Henri pulls to the side. On and on the truck approaches, an omnivorous machine, swallowing earth and sky. In the blackness, it dominates all—all light, all sound. Suddenly, though, there is another sound, distinct from the engine's churning. The truck is forcing something up the road, something moving in flight before it, that now, within inches of our windows, pounds by. A hoofbeat clatter, a shape as well, a stir of dust, a glimpse of a form, a terrored eye, a spreading rack—a moose. A bull moose.

It is many hours to the end of Maine. The last glimpse of Henri must wait until then. He has—in Greenville, New Hampshire—one final thing to say to Warren, one farewell remark. He says, "Thanks for taking care of the canoe."

# A John McPhee Checklist
## (1960–1976)

BOOKS (all New York: Farrar, Straus and Giroux)
*A Sense of Where You Are* (1965)
*The Headmaster* (1966)
*Oranges* (1967)
*The Pine Barrens* (1968)
*A Roomful of Hovings and Other Profiles* (1968; has items marked\*)
*Levels of the Game* (1969)
*The Crofter and the Laird* (1970)
*Encounters with the Archdruid* (1971)
*The Deltoid Pumpkin Seed* (1973)
*The Curve of Binding Energy* (1974)
*Pieces of the Frame* (1975; has items marked †)
*The Survival of the Bark Canoe* (1975)

THE NEW YORKER
†"Basketball and Beefeaters" (March 16, 1963), 186–94
"A Sense of Where You Are" (January 23, 1965), 40–91
\*"Fifty-Two People on a Continent" (March 5, 1966), 101–50
"The Headmaster" (March 19, 1966), 57–159
"Oranges" (May 7, 1966), 142–181; (May 14, 1966), 144–99
\*"A Roomful of Hovings" (May 20, 1967), 47–137
"The Pine Barrens" (November 25, 1967), 67–147; (December 2, 1967), 66–144
\*"Templex" (January 6, 1968), 32–67
\*"A Forager" (April 6, 1968), 45–104
\*"The Lawns of Wimbledon" (June 22, 1968), 32–57
"Levels of the Game" (June 7, 1969), 45–111; (June 14, 1969), 44–81
"The Island of the Crofter and the Laird" (December 6, 1969), 69–105; (December 13, 1969), 61–112
†"Reading the River" (March 21, 1970), 126–133
†"From Birnam Wood to Dunsinane" (October 10, 1970), 141–7
"Encounters with the Archdruid" (March 20, 1971), 42–91; (March 27, 1971), 42–80; (April 3, 1971), 41–93

†"Ranger" (September 11, 1971), 45–89

†"The Search for Marvin Gardens" (September 9, 1972), 45–62

"The Deltoid Pumpkin Seed" (February 10, 1973), 40–73; (February 17, 1973), 42–77; (February 24, 1973), 48–79

†"Travels in Georgia" (April 28, 1973), 44–104

"The Curve of Binding Energy" (December 3, 1973), 54–145; (December 10, 1973), 50–108; (December 17, 1973), 60–91

†"Firewood" (March 25, 1974), 81–105

†"Ruidoso" (April 29, 1974), 83–114

"The Survival of the Bark Canoe" (February 24, 1975), 49–94; (March 3, 1975), 41–69

"The Atlantic Generating Station" (May 12, 1975), 51–100

"The Pinball Philosophy" (June 30, 1975), 81–3

"The Keel of Lake Dickey" (May 3, 1976), 43–73

"What They Were Hunting For" (September 27, 1976), 80–122; (October 4, 1976), 40–73

"THE TALK OF THE TOWN," THE NEW YORKER

"Big Plane" (February 19, 1966), 28–9

"Thomas Pearsall Field Hoving" (March 5, 1966), 35–7

"Coliseum Hour" (March 12, 1966), 44–5

"Beauty and Horror" (May 28, 1966), 28–31

"Girl in a Paper Dress" (June 25, 1966), 20–1

"Ms and FeMs at the Biltmore" (July 2, 1966), 17–18

"On the Way to Gladstone" (July 9, 1966), 18

"The License Plates of Burning Tree" (January 30, 1971), 20–2

"Americans" (December 25, 1971), 25–7

"The Conching Rooms" (May 13, 1972), 32–3

"Sullen Gold" (March 25, 1974), 32–3

"Flavors & Fragrances" (April 8, 1974), 35–6

"Police Story" (July 15, 1974), 27

"The P–1800" (February 10, 1975), 30–2

ARTICLES IN OTHER MAGAZINES *(selected)*

*Time* cover stories on Mort Sahl (August 15, 1960); Jean Kerr (April 14, 1961); Jackie Gleason (December 29, 1961); Sophia Loren (April 6, 1962); Joan Baez (November 23, 1962); Richard Burton (April 26, 1963); Barbra Streisand

(April 10, 1964); the New York World's Fair (June 5, 1964)

†"... Josie's Well," *Holiday* (January, 1970), 66+

†"Pieces of the Frame," *The Atlantic* (January, 1970), 42–7

†"Centre Court," *Playboy* (June, 1971), 102+

"Tennis," *The New York Times Book Review* (June 10, 1973), 1+

"The People of New Jersey's Pine Barrens," *National Geographic* Vol. 145 (January, 1974), 52–77. Pictures by W. R. Curtsinger

FICTION

"The Fair of San Gennaro," *The TransAtlantic Review,* No. 8 (Winter, 1961), 117–28

"Eucalyptus Trees," *The Reporter* (October 19, 1967), 36+

"Ruth, the Sun Is Shining," *Playboy* (April 1968), 114+

JOHN McPHEE is a staff writer for *The New Yorker.* He lives and works in Princeton, New Jersey. He has written twelve previous books published by Farrar, Straus and Giroux.


WILLIAM L. HOWARTH teaches English at Princeton University. He is editor in chief of *The Writings of Henry D. Thoreau,* published by Princeton University Press.